American Trails Series
XXIV

The Great Medicine Road

Narratives *of the* Oregon, California, *and* Mormon Trails

PART I: 1840–1848

Edited by
Michael L. Tate

With the Assistance of
Will Bagley and Richard L. Rieck

THE ARTHUR H. CLARK COMPANY
An imprint of the University of Oklahoma Press
Norman, Oklahoma
2014

This book is published with the generous assistance of The Kerr Foundation, Inc.

Library of Congress Cataloging-in-Publication Data

The great medicine road : narratives of the Oregon, California, and Mormon Trails / edited by Michael L. Tate, with the assistance of Will Bagley and Richard Rieck.

volumes cm. — (American trails series ; v. 24)

Contents: pt. 1. 1840–1848 — pt. 2. 1849 — pt. 3. 1850–1855 — pt. 4. 1856–1869.

Includes bibliographical references and index.

ISBN 978-0-87062-428-5 (pt. 1 : hardcover : alk. paper) — ISBN 978-0-87062-433-9 (pt. 2 : hardcover : alk. paper) — ISBN 978-0-87062-434-6 (pt. 3 : hardcover : alk. paper) — ISBN 978-0-87062-435-3 (pt. 4 : hardcover : alk. paper) 1. Oregon National Historic Trail—History—Sources. 2. California National Historic Trail—History—Sources. 3. Overland journeys to the Pacific—History—Sources. 4. Frontier and pioneer life—West (U.S.)—Sources. 5. West (U.S.)—History—19th century—Sources. I. Tate, Michael L., editor.

F597.G77 2014
978'.02—dc23

2014009341

The Great Medicine Road: Narratives of the Oregon, California, and Mormon Trails is Volume 24 in the American Trails Series.

The paper in this book meets the guidelines for permanence and durability of the Committee on Production Guidelines for Book Longevity of the Council on Library Resources, Inc. ∞

1 2 3 4 5 6 7 8 9 10

Contents

Illustrations

Maps

Acknowledgments

When Merrill J. Mattes published *Platte River Road Narratives: A Descriptive Bibliography of Travel Over the Great Central Overland Route to Oregon, California, Utah, Colorado, Montana, and Other Western States and Territories, 1812–1866* in 1988, he provided the essential guide to stimulate a new generation of scholarship about western migration and the people who faced its challenges. This masterful bibliographer identified 2,082 diaries, journals, reminiscences, memoirs, and correspondence collections spread across the entirety of the nation—many located in prestigious archives, others serialized in forgotten nineteenth-century newspapers, and a smaller number privately published by obscure presses. Two qualities typified virtually all these sources. First, they were the products of men, women, and children who wrote authentically about their own trail experiences. The overwhelming majority had no intention of describing these events for the broad public or relating them to later generations of readers for profit. Rather, they hoped merely to maintain a private record of the sojourn or, at best, to relate practical knowledge to family members and friends who might someday join them in the Far West. Second, because these record keepers were traveling across an unfamiliar landscape and under difficult circumstances, their writings sometimes contained erroneous information about geographic features, about the great varieties of Natives whom they encountered, and about the larger historical events transpiring around them.

This new multivolume series, *The Great Medicine Road*, now attempts to allow a select group of those unheralded overlanders to speak to a new generation of readers who have little direct understanding of earlier events. The words that fill these pages are their words, but my editorial remarks help correct their errors, elucidate matters with additional information, and facilitate an easier reading of each original text without modifying words or meanings.

While Mattes's massive bibliographical guide made it possible for me to identify, locate, and select the best primary sources to include in this multivolume series, two other people deserve special acknowledgment for uncovering additional collections not discovered by Mattes. Will Bagley, renowned trails historian and author of the ongoing Overland West series for the University of Oklahoma Press, teamed with Richard L. Rieck, professor of geography and frequent author of trail literature, to pinpoint scores of new sources. They worked to devise an updated list of what seemed to be the most important items that appeared in Mattes's *Platte River Road Narratives*, as well as their own extended list.

Rieck also did yeoman's service in transcribing some of the more important handwritten diaries and correspondence collections that have remained largely unused by modern historians. Both men, armed with a fascinating assemblage of pioneer records, next approached Robert Clark, editor-in-chief of Arthur H. Clark Company, to test the marketplace for possible publication of the most informative of these primary accounts. Having previously published the heralded *Covered Wagon Women* series (editor, Kenneth L. Holmes) and *News of the Plains and Rockies, 1803–1865* series (editor, David A. White), Clark welcomed the project. Unfortunately, Bagley and Rieck subsequently became involved in other trails research and were unable to pursue the envisioned series any further.

Fortunately for me, Clark asked if I would be interested in undertaking the project following consultation with the two cocreators of the concept. Having just completed *Indians and Emigrants: Encounters on the Overland Trails* (2006) and other trails writings, I jumped at the chance to guide the massive undertaking to its logical conclusion—a representative coverage of the Oregon, California, and Mormon Trails from 1840 to 1869. Over the next two years, I visited many of the far-flung archives, secured copies of rare sources through interlibrary loan services, and made the final selection of items for publication in the first volume of the series. I included many of the citations from the extended Bagley-Rieck list, but also deleted some citations and added others that I felt worked best in the anthology format.

Throughout the following two years, I slowly edited these sometimes illegible pioneer annals. Mark Walters, interlibrary loan director at the University of Nebraska at Omaha, aided the process immeasurably by securing even the most obscure of sources to double check original texts and to find corroborating evidence for some of the claims within those texts. Research funds supplied by the Charles W. Martin and Mary C. Martin Fund at the University of Nebraska at Omaha facilitated travel for archival research, as well as some library service costs. Appropriately, the Martin Fund was created to recognize the memories of a husband and wife team who had devoted much of their attention to trails history and to the formation and maintenance of the celebrated Oregon-California Trails Association (OCTA). As fellow Omaha residents who attended many of the same regional events that I did, they helped turn my scholarly interests toward westward migration, and their frequent loan of photocopied manuscript diaries made my early research endeavors much easier.

Three other persons who have long been recognized for their academic contributions to trails history also deserve my thanks. Robert Munkres, now retired from college teaching and currently living in Estes Park, Colorado, is an expert on the Platte River section of trails history, and his numerous publications over the years have helped guide me through the geographic and human dimensions of the story. Essential to correcting my errors and offering thoughtful commentary about the overall content of this first volume in the series were David Bigler and Susan Badger Doyle, both of whom read the completed manuscript. They are scholars whose names are instantly recognizable among western historians, and their collective reputation for thoroughness was certainly reflected in the close readings they gave to this work. I also wish to thank Karlene Santibanez, Don Porter, and Bev Gilson (all descendants of William Porter) for making available their massive *A Family History*, edited by Mary E. Porter (2001 reprint), as well as family photographs. Equally important was Stephenie Flora, who transcribed several original sources and placed them on her website. Absolutely essential to the project's completion was Editor-in-Chief Chuck Rankin and his staff at the University of Oklahoma Press, who helped better focus the study and reduced it to a more manageable size. My special appreciation goes to copy editor Melanie Mallon, who provided a far more thorough reading of the manuscript than I could have ever expected. Her meticulous attention to detail eliminated errors and improved the readability of the book.

Gaining rights and permissions to reproduce these primary sources and the accompanying illustrations was an extensive undertaking in its own right, since so many institutions had to be contacted. Especially helpful in this regard were Superintendent Ken Mabery and resource management specialist Robert Manasek at the Scotts Bluff National Monument in Gering, Nebraska, who provided the watercolor paintings by William Henry Jackson; Geoff Wexler, library director at the Oregon Historical Society in Portland; David Aamodt, curator of the National Frontier Trails Museum in Independence, Missouri; Phil Smoley, president of the Lake County Historical Society in Lakeport, California; Susan Snyder at the Bancroft Library, University of California, Berkeley; David Kingma, archivist at the Foley Library of Gonzaga University in Spokane, Washington; Jon Maxedon at Amador County Archives in Jackson, California; Denise Jones, senior archivist at Hudson's Bay Company Archives in Archives of Manitoba, Winnipeg; Bernie Rhoades in Edgewood, Washington; Henry Strobel at St. Boniface Archives and Museum in Sublimity, Oregon; Hailey Walker at the Church History Library of the Church of Jesus Christ of Latter-day Saints in Salt Lake City, Utah; Karin Morey at Clackamas County Historical Society in Oregon City; Scott Rook at the Oregon Historical Society in Portland; Anne E. Cox at the State Historical Society of Missouri in Columbia; Lisa Marine, image reproduction and licensing manager at the Wisconsin Historical Society in Madison; George H. Thompson at the Meriam Library at California State University, Chico; and Michael Roux, rights and permissions officer at University of Illinois Press.

Amid all the people who helped see this volume through to printed form, none is more important than my daughter Kerin Tate. She was a masterful editor for the multiple drafts of this manuscript, correcting not only stylistic errors and syntax problems, but also pointing out my historical miscues. She typed all the drafts, checked original documents against my transcriptions, prepared the exhaustive index, secured the rights and permissions, and probed scattered archival materials to find out additional information about some of the otherwise obscure lives of these "common people." Without her endless efforts, this volume could not have been completed.

Editorial Procedures

AMID ALL THE scholarly syntheses readily available today to an inquisitive reading audience, a fundamental task still remains for both professional and avocational historians. It is our responsibility to allow the pioneer generation to speak directly to modern audiences through the publication of their original diaries, journals, memoirs, and correspondence. It is also our duty to further research the people and events, and provide detailed editorial content so that their accounts can assume a larger context than the writers originally intended.

Several models already exist for this concept, but two published series merit special attention for comparison's sake. Kenneth L. Holmes's eleven-volume collection, *Covered Wagon Women: Diaries and Letters from the Western Trails, 1840–1903*, helped rebut the long-held myth of the transcontinental migrations as largely a male story. Holmes purposely limited the number of explanatory footnotes throughout the series and allowed the original authors to speak for themselves without overwhelming their words with extraneous minutiae. He did, however, provide an overview essay for each volume to briefly describe trail conditions during the years covered by that particular volume. He also provided fairly lengthy introductory remarks at the head of each primary document to identify some of the more important people mentioned in the source, and to further explain important events found therein. The entire series, plus a final cumulative index volume, was published in hardback by the Arthur H. Clark Company, and it received laudatory reviews from scholars across the nation. The popularity of the collection led the University of Nebraska Press to republish paperback editions of all the volumes between 1995 and 2000, under its heralded Bison Books imprint.[1]

A second series of vital firsthand accounts appeared in 1996, also under the direction of Arthur H. Clark Company. David A. White expertly edited eight volumes of primary materials, which he entitled *News of the Plains and Rockies, 1803–1865: Original Narratives of Overland Travel and Adventure Selected from the Wagner-Camp and Becker Bibliography of Western Americana.* White took a larger view than Holmes in his selection of documents for inclusion in the anthology. He chose primary accounts not only from overlanders, but also from explorers, fur traders, Santa Fe Trail entrepreneurs, settlers, missionaries, miners, railroad builders, Indian agents, and mail service executives. He provided more detailed introductions to each of the documents, thereby placing each of them within a larger national context. Unlike Holmes's series, White chose not to include editorial endnotes for each document. Each primary text is therefore printed as it originally appeared, except for the addition of a fairly lengthy bibliographical reference list germane to each document.

The structure of this new trail series entitled *The Great Medicine Road: Narratives of the Oregon, California, and Mormon Trails, 1840 to 1869*, does not rigidly conform to the approach either Holmes or White used, but it does borrow from the successful elements that each employed. My editorial work focuses on four types of contributions. First, I constructed a fairly lengthy introduction for each document to relate additional information about the author, his or her background and reasons for undertaking the trip, and highlights of the author's subsequent life. Second, I provided new, bracketed [ ] information throughout the full text of each document. This allowed me to provide full names of people who were mentioned only by a first or last name, and it provided a means to correct significant misspellings in the original version. Third, I created footnotes for each original diary, journal, memoir, interview, and set of letters. These editorial notes are extensive for most items, and they provide essential corrections and elucidations on matters falsely or inadequately explained in the original manuscript. Such a

[1]Clark, "Kenneth L. Holmes," 548–54.

comprehensive editorial process makes the entire collection far more valuable to researchers and casual readers alike. Finally, I have prepared an extensive bibliography to fully identify all sources used in the editorial process and to suggest further reading matter for researchers.

When Merrill J. Mattes assembled his masterful descriptive bibliography *Platte River Road Narratives* in 1988, he was able to identify 2,082 eyewitness accounts of travel on the Oregon, California, and Mormon trails, beginning with Robert Stuart's famous 1812 sojourn and ending with Sarah A. Wisner's obscure 1866 journey. Some of the items were published in the twentieth century, but usually without editorial notes or corrections. Other of the firsthand sources had never been printed or transcribed; they existed only in the original diary format, complete with worm holes and the occasional indecipherable handwriting of their original chroniclers. These became the collective "documentary gold mine" from which so many excellent secondary accounts have been written over recent decades.

Since the appearance of Mattes's bibliography, scholars such as Will Bagley and Richard L. Rieck have identified more than one hundred additional primary accounts. Likewise, Kate B. Carter's three multivolume series, *Our Pioneer Heritage*, *Treasures of Pioneer History*, and *Heart Throbs of the West* have been rediscovered by a new generation of researchers, who have gleaned vital information from the once-overlooked interviews and memoirs. Equally important institutions in the recovery of new material are the Church History Department of the Church of Jesus Christ of Latter-day Saints (Salt Lake City, Utah), the National Frontier Trails Center (Independence, Missouri), and the Oregon Historical Society (Portland).

The many documents that compose this first volume in the series focus on overland migrations occurring between 1840 and 1848. They therefore represent merely the initial phases of the Oregon, California, and Mormon trails history because each route continued to be used even beyond the 1869 completion of the first transcontinental railroad. Several future volumes will be published in the series to carry the story through 1869. They will follow the same editorial format established in this initial venture. Throughout publication of the entire series, the editorial additions will strengthen the utility and credibility of the original primary sources, but the original authors will continue to speak in their own words to a new generation of Americans.

When I first prepared volume 1 of this series for publication, I adopted a pragmatic selection process. Most important, I wanted to choose primary accounts that were truly representative of the great migrations to Oregon, California, and Salt Lake City during the formative years extending from 1840 through 1848, and via the central Great Plains routes along the Platte and Sweetwater rivers. Furthermore, these selections had to be rich in details and diverse in the experiences of their individual authors. I also wanted to capture both men's and women's voices in the chosen documents, as well as a wide spectrum of ages, home state residences, reasons for undertaking the westward journey, and personal adjustments to trail life.

In pursuit of these goals, I found many documents that rightfully deserved inclusion in this anthology. Thus, my original manuscript for this first volume totaled almost a thousand pages and included the diaries, journals, memoirs, and letters of forty-one people. The painful process of subsequently reducing this rich collection to a mere fifteen choices yielded a tighter and more easily marketable book, but the deleted items cried out for some recognition of their own. Editor-in-Chief Chuck Rankin then suggested that I use this space to list citations for the omitted documents so that readers could make use of them in their own reading and research. Some of these documents are available online, and I have included website locations for these, as well as the more traditional citations. Unfortunately, the websites include only the full text of each document and do not contain my introductions or endnotes. The list of additional valuable primary materials is printed here in chronological order for the reader's convenience.

1840

Abigail Smith to Brother and Sister Kirby, Walla Walla, September 18, 1840. Typescript of holograph letter in Merrill J. Mattes Library Collection, National Frontier Trails Museum, Independence, Missouri. Transcription by John Mark Lambertson.

1841

Martha Williams Reed. "Old California Pioneer Passes Away At Fallbrook. Martha Williams Reed, Age 87, Crosses the Plaines by Ox-Team in the Early Gold Excitement of California." *Fallbrook Enterprise* (California), January 12, 1917. Unedited digital copy at www.oregonpioneers.com/williams.htm (accessed October 15, 2013).

1842

Francois Xavier Matthieu. "Reminiscences of F. X. Matthieu." Edited by Horace Sumner Lyman. *Oregon Historical Quarterly* 1 (March 1900): 73–104.

Elwood Evans. "Thomas J. Shadden." Biographical profile in *History of the Pacific Northwest, Oregon and Washington*, vol. 2, 552–53. Portland, Ore.: North Pacific History Company, 1889.

1843

Alexander Blevins. "Reminiscence of 1843 Emigration to Oregon." Published as "An Interesting Interview with An Aged Couple, Who Were With the First Train which Crossed the Rocky Mountains From The East." *The Valley Review* (Lodi, California), March 29, 1879. Digital copy at www.oregonpioneers.com/Blevins_Interview.htm (accessed October 15, 2013).

Sarah Jane Hill. "Our Trip to Oregon." Handwritten reminiscences. MSS 1508. Oregon Historical Society, Portland.

1844

Samuel B. Crockett to Dear Friends, February 16, 1845. As Copied from the Original by Alfred B. Loop, July 6, 1931. Typescript MSS 1500, Oregon Historical Society Library, Portland.

Martha Ann Morrison [Minto]. "Female Pioneering in Oregon [1844]." 1878 interview. Typescript, MSS P-A 51. Hubert Howe Bancroft Collection, Bancroft Library, University of California, Berkeley.

Thomas C. Shaw. "Reminiscences of 1844." *Oregon Statesman*, May 22 and June 12, 1885. Digital copy at www.oregonpioneers.com/tcshaw.htm (accessed October 15, 2013).

"Oregon and California." *New York Tribune*, June 11, 1844, and June 24, 1844.

1845

Arthur H. Thompson. "From The Oregon Emigrants." *Chicago Democrat*, August 27, 1845, October 21, 1845, and December 2, 1845.

Maria King and Stephen King to Dear Mother, Brother, and Sisters, April 1, 1846. MSS 1508, Oregon State Historical Society, Portland.

William B. Ide. "From our Oregon Correspondent." 2 Letters. *Sangamo Journal* (Springfield, Illinois).

Letter dated May 13, 1845, printed June 5, 1845.

Letter dated June 25, 1845, printed September 4, 1845.

"Oregon and California." Correspondence of the *Pittsburgh Gazette*. Reprinted in *Ohio Repository*, May 29, 1845.

1846

Joseph Hardin Cornwall. "Coming to the Oregon Country of the Cornwall Family." *Oregon Statesman*, July 12, 1941–August 13, 1941.

Mary Elizabeth Munkers Estes. "Crossing the Plains in 1846: As Told by Mrs. Mary Elizabeth Munkers Estes While Sitting by Her Fireside Christmas Eve 1916." Digital copy at http://freepages.history.rootsweb.ancestry.com/~cchouk/oregon_trail/crossing/munkers.htm (accessed October 15, 2013).

Selim E. Woodworth, "Three Letters from Oregon and California."

"Letter from an Officer of the Navy." Written May 14, 1846, and published in *New York Home Journal*, June 13, 1846.

"Letter from Oregon." Written June 15, 1846, and published in *New York Home Journal*, August 8, 1846.

"Letter from California by an Officer in the Navy." Written February 6, 1847, and published in *New York Home Journal*, July 31, 1847.

John Lose to Mr. Editor, undated letter, early 1847. Printed in *Defiance* (Ohio) *Democrat*, November 4, 1847.

Benjamin S. Lippincott Letters, 1847–1851. MSS 95/15 c, Bancroft Library, University of California, Berkeley.

Benjamin S. Lippincott to John L. Stephens, February 6, 1847.

Benjamin S. Lippincott to Bub [Robert Lippincott?] March 22, 1847.

1847

Joseph Henry Brown. "Recollection of 1847 Trip to Oregon." Typescript. Special Collections, Knight Library, University of Oregon. Copy in Oregon-California Trails Manuscripts, Merrill Mattes Library, National Frontier Trails Museum, Independence, Missouri.

James Madison Coon and Nancy Coon. "The Diary of James Madison Coon and Nancy Iness (Miller) Coon on the Oregon Trail From Mercer County, Illinois to Clackamas County, Oregon in 1847." Edited by Robert Lewis. Digital Copy at www.rootsweb.ancestry.com/~orbenton/COONDIAR.htm (accessed October 15, 2013).

Loren B. Hastings. "Diary of Loren B. Hastings: A Pioneer of 1847." In *Transactions of the Fifty-First Annual Reunion of the Oregon Pioneer Association for 1923*, 12–26. Portland, Ore.: F. W. Baltes, 1926.

"Late From California." *Telegraph and Democratic Review* (Alton, Illinois), August 27, 1847.

John S. Snook to Mr. Editor. *Defiance* (Ohio) *Democrat*, August 19, 1847.

1848

Benjamin Cleaver. "Letters from the West—1848–1850." Eight letters to the *Alton* (Illinois) *Telegraph and Democratic Review.*

Letter of February 4, 1847, printed February 11, 1848.
Letter of June 30, 1848, printed November 17, 1848.
Letter of July 8, 1848, printed November 17, 1848.
Letter of March 5, 1849, printed August 31, 1849.
Letter of March 16, 1849, printed August 31, 1849.

Letter of April 19, 1849, printed August 31, 1849.
Letter of March 4, 1850, printed July 26, 1850.
Letter of March 6, 1850, printed July 26, 1850.

James F. Reed. "From California, a Letter from James F. Reed," August 14, 1848. *Illinois Journal* (Springfield), July 4, 1849. Transcribed by Kristin Johnson.

Introduction

IN 1840, THE vast area stretching from the state of Missouri to the Pacific coastline represented an exotic but alien landscape to most Americans. Although explorers and fur traders had visited many of the remote corners of the Trans-Mississippi West by that time, the general public lacked precise knowledge of what was yet to be discovered there. Even a decade later, maps and sketchy information published in the valued trail guidebooks offered only descriptions of landmarks and camping conditions along the well-traveled trails to Oregon, California, and the Salt Lake Valley. To most Americans (and Europeans, for that matter) the greater West was therefore synonymous with the concept of terra incognita, an unknown and threatening expanse of wilderness, or an unredeemable "Great American Desert," as extrapolated from the writings of Lieutenant Zebulon Pike and Major Stephen Long.

Yet, between 1841 and 1866, more than five hundred thousand people migrated to these faraway places, and the majority remained in the West after their initial domicile there.[1] Social historian Daniel J. Boorstin paid homage to these nameless migrants in his prize-winning volume *The Americans: The National Experience* (1965), in which he stressed their creation of "transient communities," as opposed to the long-standing Turnerian emphasis on their pattern of "rugged individualism." Boorstin further argued that the overland pioneers were not interested in rejecting the traditional institutions and folkways that had defined their lives in the East. Nor did they wish to fragment society by creating an extreme version of individual rights to supersede the collective needs of the broader commonwealth of people.

---

[1]Mattes, *Platte River Road Narratives*, 5.

Before or soon after they departed the jumping-off towns in western Missouri and Iowa, most overlanders organized themselves into migrating companies, complete with democratically elected officers and a constitution or legal code drafted by the company's adult members. Although these partnerships formed, separated, and re-formed during the ebb and flow of the two-thousand-mile trip, their constituents never viewed this process as a rejection of the broader community concept. Likewise, upon reaching their intended destinations, the members of these transient bodies seamlessly separated themselves again from the larger group to more easily achieve their original family goals. The separations were completely amicable, and each family attached itself to an existing community of greater permanence in the new environment of the West.[2]

In describing his "rebirth concept" of transient communities, Boorstin quoted the advice provided in Captain Randolph B. Marcy's *Prairie Traveler, a Hand-Book for Overland Expeditions* (1859): "An obligation should then be drawn up and signed by all the members of the association, wherein each one should bind himself to abide in all cases by the orders and decisions of the captain, and to aid him by every means in his power in the execution of his duties; and they should also obligate themselves to aid each other, so as to make the individual interest of each member the common concern of the whole company."[3] In this light, the migrating caravans that traversed the Oregon, California, and Mormon trails between 1840 and 1869 should be regarded as mobile institutions of shared interests, rather than as chaotic bands of fierce rivals.

The desire for mutual aid and harmony did not, however, imply that every individual was driven by the same motivations to undertake the migration, nor should we infer that they all experienced the trip in the same way, or shared the same perceptions of their sojourn. The rich literature provided by their letters, diaries, journals, and memoirs strongly testifies to the great diversity of experiences and perceptions rather than a uniformity of remembered events.

[2]Boorstin, *The Americans*, 65–72.

[3]Marcy quoted in Boorstin, *The Americans*, 68–69.

Some fretted about leaving friends and family members forever; others worried about reestablishing their lives in distant and alien lands. Many also voiced a fear that dangers along the trail were so overwhelming that they or their loved ones might not survive the perilous journey. A small portion of these, including Benjamin Franklin Bonney, received not an encouraging farewell from their friends and neighbors but rather ominous warnings that they would certainly perish in the foolhardy venture.[4] In keeping with that fatalistic outlook, the men of Sarah Sutton's 1854 wagon train prepared special boards and laid them across the floor of one wagon so that they could be used for constructing a coffin in the likely event that a member of the party should die while on the trail.[5] Even more pessimistic was the mother of nine-year-old Barnet Simpson, who grew so distraught about warnings of impending doom that, prior to undertaking an 1849 Oregon trip, she wove burial shrouds for members of her family.[6]

Yet, for all the pessimism related in these three examples, most overlanders undertook the journey with ample conviction that their efforts would secure them a better life. A mid-century collapse of the agricultural economy in the Mississippi River Valley, frequent sicknesses, unpredictable weather, a longing to get away from the vexatious slavery issue, a desire to escape religious persecution, a passion to Christianize and "civilize" Indians, the promise of virtually free land in the verdant Willamette Valley of Oregon, and the allure of California gold made up a partial list of push-and-pull factors that had awakened public interest in the West.[7]

By the 1830s, the Mississippi River Valley had passed beyond its initial frontier stage of development and now truly shared in the national economy. Unfortunately, many of these newly created states plunged recklessly into land speculation and expensive programs for internal improvements. Easy money became available because U.S. and British banks issued bonds backed by an unreliable credit structure that was

[4]Bonney, "Recollections of Benjamin Franklin Bonney," 37.

[5]Kenneth L. Holmes, in Sutton, "A Travel Diary in 1854," 15.

[6]"Barnet Simpson," 31.

[7]Historian Walter Nugent suggests "five motivators for migration into the West" in Nugent, *Into the West*, 4–6.

poorly regulated. At the beginning of the decade, prosperity seemed widespread, but many agriculturalists were hopelessly in debt and terrified of losing equity in their farms. British banks tightened credit in 1837, and many of America's weaker banks collapsed under the pressure of debt reduction. In the Panic of 1837, agricultural prices dropped below the cost of production, and many overextended farmers were driven from their homes by mortgage lenders and tax collectors.[8]

During the same depression era, many residents of the Ohio and Mississippi River valleys suffered from a combination of fever and chills commonly referred to as ague. Diarists attributed this to the extreme heat and cold of the region and believed that it would spread as population increased and more land was cultivated. Some were only too happy to leave the malarial areas of Ohio, Michigan, Illinois, Kentucky, and Missouri. In 1843, Daniel Waldo's wife told her husband, "If you want to stay here another summer and shake your liver out with fever and ague, you can do it; but in the spring I am going to take the children and go to Oregon, Indians or no Indians. They can't be any worse than the chills and fever!"[9] Craven Hester, a successful lawyer in Indiana, also made the decision to uproot his family and travel to California for health reasons. "My father is going in search of health, not gold," wrote fourteen-year-old Sallie Hester in 1849.[10]

In his authoritative trail study, *The Plains Across* (1979), historian John D. Unruh, Jr., emphasized the difficulty that families faced in making such life-altering decisions. One article published in the influential St. Louis *Daily Missouri Republican* in 1847 contended that any man subjecting his family to a journey over the mountains and deserts in search of "worthless territory" was obviously deranged, and that only those who were young, male, and single should be allowed to indulge in the insanity.[11] Yet, warnings such as this never seemed to slow the pace of national migration, noted Unruh.

Less than a decade after American missionaries began their pros-

[8]Robbins, *Our Landed Heritage*, 59–71.

[9]Geer, *Fifty Years in Oregon*, 218.

[10]Hester, "The Diary of a Pioneer Girl," 1, 235.

[11]Unruh, *Plains Across*, 42.

elytizing among the Indian tribes of the Pacific Northwest, "Oregon fever" gripped the republic. Regional and national newspapers set the tone as boosters of the faraway land by emphasizing the salubrious climate, fertile soil, plentiful timber, and abundant wildlife in the Willamette River Valley. Responding to the rising level of interest, President James K. Polk pressured a treaty with Great Britain in 1846 that gave the United States sole title to the Oregon country south of the forty-ninth parallel.[12] Then came the added incentive of the Donation Land Claim Act of 1850, which stated that each single white male citizen eighteen years or older was entitled to 320 acres of land. His wife could hold an additional 320 acres in her own right, making it one of the most liberal land laws in U.S. history. During the five years the Donation Act existed, more than 8,450 claimants acquired more than 2.8 million acres of land in the Pacific Northwest.[13]

Unlike the Oregon case, California did not initially receive extensive publicity or national boosterism. Even though the Bidwell-Bartleson party pioneered the way to California as early as 1841, most Americans were reluctant to cross the seemingly endless desert lands of the Great Basin and then confront the mighty granite face of the Sierra Nevadas. These early images were strongly reinforced by the experiences of the Donner party, whose members became trapped in the snow-bound Sierras in 1846 and resorted to cannibalism to survive the winter ordeal.[14]

American acquisition of California from Mexico under terms of the 1848 Treaty of Guadalupe Hidalgo, followed by the writings of prominent western travelers such as Captain John C. Frémont, finally helped popularize the economic potential of the territory. But it was the accidental discovery of gold along California's American River on January 24, 1848, that ultimately awakened the dreams of young men in the United States, Europe, and the wider world. Motivated by rumors that gold lay scattered on the ground's surface—plentiful, free, and unclaimed—naïve young men rushed to the gold fields in hopes

---

[12]Billington, *Far Western Frontier*, 69–72, 79–87, and 154–59.

[13]Johansen and Gates, *Empire of the Columbia*, 290–92.

[14]Billington, *Far Western Frontier*, 73–78, 92–95, and 112–14.

of assembling a sizable fortune in record time. Unlike the Oregon-bound emigrants, who generally migrated as family units and with the intention of remaining in the Pacific Northwest, many California miners hoped to return to their eastern homes and resume their lives, albeit with a higher standard of living.[15]

Somewhat atypical of the male-dominated pattern of early migration to California was the family of Josiah and Mary Variel. Together with their three-month-old son and three-year-old daughter, they departed New Harmony, Indiana, in April 1852. Mary later recalled, "My husband and I were greatly interested in the inducements that a trip to California offered, and while we frequently discussed the possibilities of such a venture, we were thoroughly alive to and considered fully the toil, danger and uncertainty that would attend it, but countless stories of boundless gold fields, where we could go out with a basket and pick up a supply of gold nuggets at any time overcame any fears we had entertained, and we concluded to join the first expedition that was organized in our neighborhood." The spirited couple expected to be gone only two years, certainly enough time for them to collect all the wealth they needed, or so they mistakenly thought, for they ultimately elected to remain in Comptonville, California, but not as prospectors.[16]

At the other extreme were the experiences of Missouri prospector James B. Evans, who wrote to his brother from Frenchman's Bar on California's Yuba River in October 1850. The extensive letter described just about every possible trail calamity that could occur, and his unfortunate company apparently experienced all of them. Among other things, disease, starvation, exhaustion, fetid water, loss of livestock, incessantly bad weather, and troublesome Indians had transformed the journey into a nightmare. To his brother, and all other family members and friends who needed to hear his sad tale, Evans drafted a strong warning: "Be it known throughout the world, to remotest nations, from the shivering Laplanders to the rude Hottentots, that if any man hereafter should take a notion to come to California—not

[15]Billington, *Far Western Frontier*, 218–31.

[16]Variel and Variel, "A Romance of the Plains," 30.

to cross the Plains for Lord sake!!!! Come by water—or stay home . . . $2500000000000000000000000000000 and no sense would not induce me to cross the long plains again."[17]

The pioneering efforts of overlanders bound for Oregon and California contributed to the saga of another group who looked west for solutions to their unique problems. Members of the Church of Jesus Christ of Latter-day Saints, or Mormons, founded in New York state in 1830 by the prophet Joseph Smith, composed the most unified and innovative of pioneer groups to migrate west in the mid-nineteenth century. The Saints attempted to establish their religious center first in New York, then Ohio, and finally in the present-day Kansas City area of Missouri. In 1839, after these attempts collapsed under the weight of verbal and physical attacks by their detractors, they created the city of Nauvoo, Illinois, on the banks of the Mississippi River. But their commitment to the controversial issue of plural marriage, as well as growing economic and political jealousies among their Gentile neighbors, inevitably created an atmosphere of tension and instability wherever they settled. Within five years of their pioneering the prosperous Nauvoo community, LDS members again became the targets of intimidation and overt violence.

In 1844, Joseph Smith and his brother Hyrum were arrested on questionable charges of riot and destruction of private property. Despite a promise of protection from civil officials in the nearby town of Carthage, a mob descended on the lightly guarded jail and killed the two religious leaders. The Mormon governing body, the Quorum of Twelve Apostles, under the leadership of Brigham Young, realized the need to move their community to a distant place where its members could practice their faith in semi-isolation, a place that would not attract other settlers during the coming decades.[18]

Following a directive by the state of Illinois that revoked the Mormon charter rights to Nauvoo, Young ordered the first company across the frozen Mississippi River into southeastern Iowa on February 4,

---

[17]Evans, "A Missouri Forty-Niner's Trip Across the Plains," 39.

[18]Stegner, *Gathering of Zion*, 17–34.

1846. Traveling westward through the southern counties of Iowa, they migrated in parties of hundreds, fifties, and tens, all organized around an elaborate plan established by the Quorum. Unlike the overlanders who set out along the Oregon and California trails, the Mormon faithful eventually established Iowa camps, such as Garden Grove and Mount Pisgah, complete with shelters, grist mills, carpentry shops, blacksmith forges, and farm lands. These communities and others like them, which were subsequently built along western segments of the Mormon Trail, assured continuity and predictability for the thousands who would soon follow in this incremental method of travel. By June 14, 1846, the advance guard of the migrants, including Brigham Young, had reached the Missouri River, where they soon created Kanesville on the Iowa side of the Missouri River and Winter Quarters on the Nebraska side.[19]

Young's Pioneer Band of 143 individuals pushed westward along the north bank of the Platte River during the following spring and summer, finally arriving at the future site of Salt Lake City in July 1847. They began immediately to plow crop land, build homes, and construct irrigation networks, all in preparation for the thousands who would soon follow. By 1856, nearly 40,000 LDS members had immigrated to the State of Deseret, carved from the arid lands of the Great Basin. During that same decade, many new converts from western Europe began arriving, first by ship passage across the Atlantic Ocean, then by rail to the Midwest, and finally completing the overland adventure by wagons or handcarts along the well-defined Mormon Trail. Although the California gold rush precluded their hopes for at least a decade of semi-isolationism in the desert, their overwhelming numbers and physical control of the vast region assured that they would not be driven out of their lands as had been the earlier pattern in the East.[20]

Despite Mormon efforts to provide a safe and predictable overland journey through their tightly knit communal experience, some of the Saints were forced by circumstance to assume an unconventional means of travel. Edwin Alfred Pettit was only thirteen years old at

[19]Stegner, *Gathering of Zion*, 43–55.
[20]Anderson, *Desert Saints*, 83–107.

the time of the exodus from Nauvoo. Having lost both his parents five years earlier, he and his siblings had fallen under the legal control of a court-appointed guardian. His older sister and her husband decided to go west with the initial 1846 migration groups that were leaving Nauvoo. Edwin was determined to go with them, despite opposition from the rest of his siblings and guardian. In an effort to catch up with his sister, Edwin and a friend secretly slipped out of the house and tramped all day without food. Search parties failed to find the boys, who stayed out on the Iowa prairie rather than going into a Mormon camp where they might be discovered. Then, disguised as a girl, wearing false curls and a sunbonnet, Edwin successfully crossed the Des Moines River on a flatboat in the company of several other girls, the boatman none the wiser. Cautiously, he rode side-saddle, thus avoiding any further chance of being recognized before reaching his sister's camp at Indian Creek. Together, the company continued on to Winter Quarters in the spring of 1847, joining the main body of Saints who had been camped there all winter.[21]

As suggested by the specific human experiences provided in this general introduction, the history of the Oregon, California, and Mormon trails was defined not by a single story, but rather a collage of thousands of stories, each unique in its own ways. Some people welcomed the great adventure that lay ahead, and they remained optimistic even amid adversity on the trail. Others feared the prospect of a move that not only would separate them from family and friends, but also might lead to the forfeiture of their lives. Some proved more adept at adjusting to the rigors and opportunities of trail life than did other fellow travelers, who complained incessantly, avoided hard work, and found ways to blame everyone else for their failures. Gender differences sometimes provided alternate vantage points for judging the experience, as did the generational differences that separated children from octogenarians.

Changes over time also affected the perceptions of emigrants. For instance, persons who traveled west in the early 1840s found little more than primitive trails. In contrast, migrants of the late 1860s

[21]Madsen, *I Walked to Zion*, 71–73.

faced a greater chance for Indian problems than the pioneers of the early 1840s, but the later arrivals also found more physical improvements along the three routes. Likewise, international events changed the history of the trails. Not until 1846 did the United States acquire sole rights to the Oregon country from the British, and not until the Mexican War of 1846–1848 did the nation bring California and the vast Mexican Cession lands into its fold. Although both acquisitions evidenced an imperialistic side, their outcomes ended all equivocation about American sovereign rights in the Far West.

Finally, the long-term life choices made by overlanders reflected the same diversity pattern that the original migration had. Many became permanent settlers in the evolving communities where they first laid down their roots. Others returned to their eastern homes, either in fulfillment of their original plan or because of the ill luck they had encountered in the West. Still others became part of an ever-mobile population in the western territories and states by relocating time and again, forever seeking new opportunities in unfamiliar places.

Today's remembrances of the Oregon, California, and Mormon trails encompass some of the most iconic images in American history. Dime novels, romanticized artwork, Hollywood movies, and historical reenactments keep the spirit alive for generations far removed from the actual events. Twentieth-century historians have devoted their efforts to separating fact from fiction, and they have successfully interpreted the larger importance of these events. This series of volumes, *The Great Medicine Road*, now attempts to blend the original pioneer spirit that was voiced through the memories of the original overlanders with the rich scholarship that has been produced during the past century and a half. Only with this blending of both can today's generation fully appreciate one of the greatest mass migrations in American history.

Maps

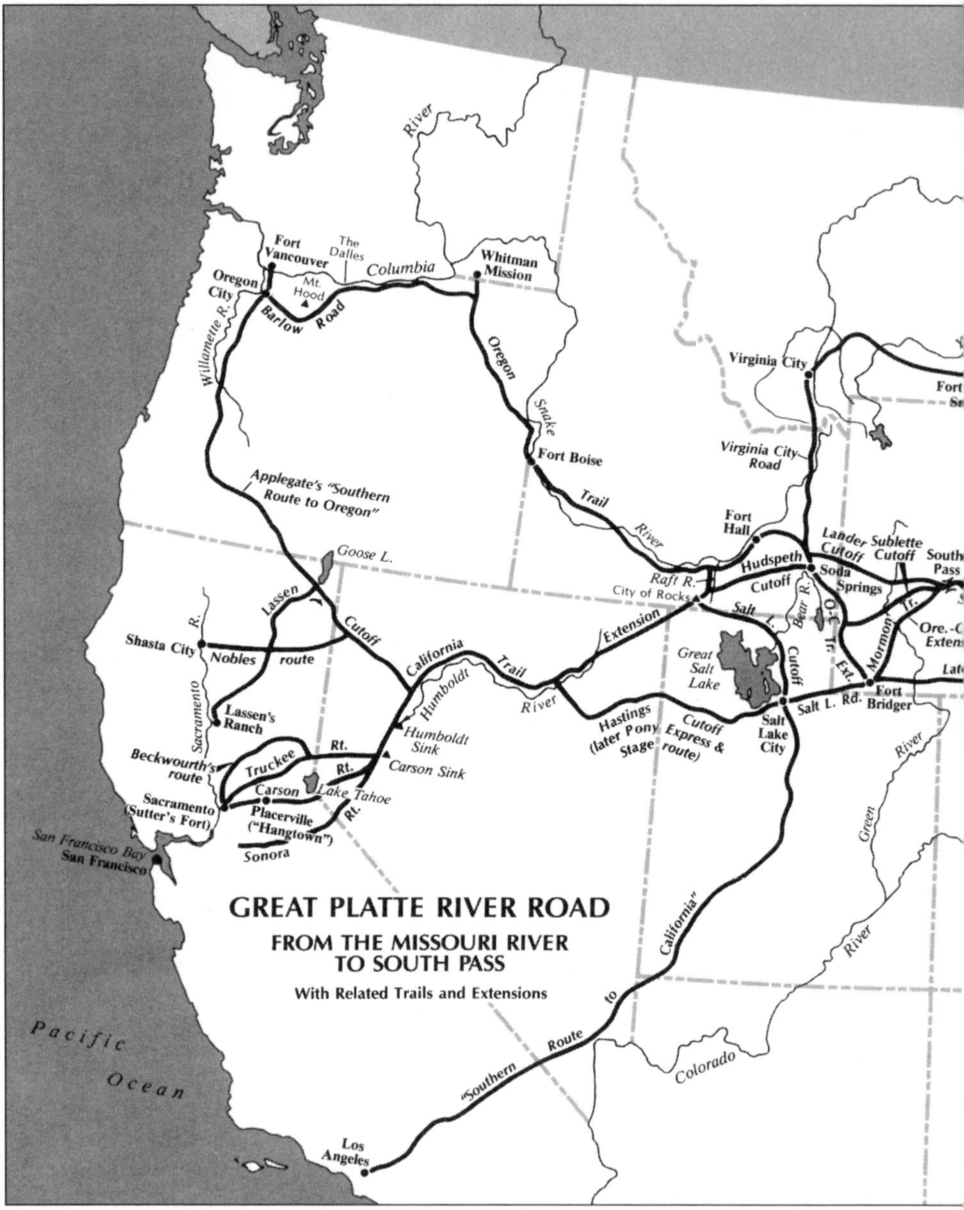
GREAT PLATTE RIVER ROAD
FROM THE MISSOURI RIVER
TO SOUTH PASS
With Related Trails and Extensions
Fort Vancouver
The Dalles
Columbia
Whitman Mission
Oregon City
Mt. Hood
Barlow Road
Willamette R.
Oregon
Snake
Fort Boise
Trail
River
Virginia City
Virginia City Road
Fort Hall
Lander Cutoff
Sublette Cutoff
Hudspeth Cutoff
Soda Springs
Raft R.
City of Rocks
Salt L. Cutoff
Bear R.
O. S. Tr. Ext.
Mormon Tr.
Fort Bridger
Salt L. Rd.
Applegate's "Southern Route to Oregon"
Goose L.
Lassen Cutoff
Shasta City
Nobles route
Sacramento R.
Lassen's Ranch
California Trail
Humboldt River
Humboldt Sink
Carson Sink
Extension
Great Salt Lake
Hastings Cutoff
(later Pony Express & Stage route)
Salt Lake City
Beckwourth's route
Truckee Rt.
Carson Rt.
Lake Tahoe
Sacramento (Sutter's Fort)
Placerville ("Hangtown")
Rt.
Sonora
San Francisco Bay
San Francisco
Green River
Colorado
"Southern Route to California"
Pacific Ocean
Los Angeles

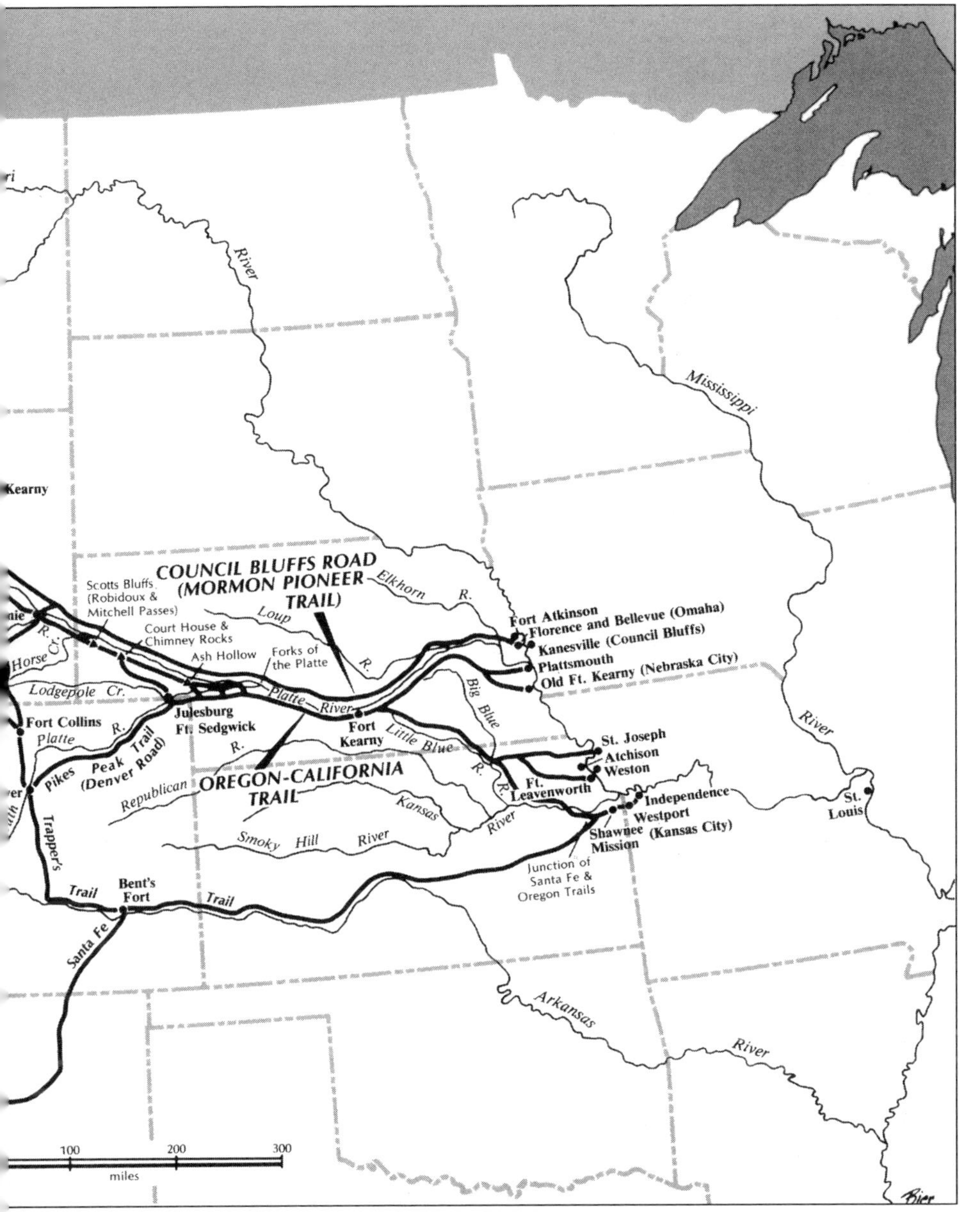

Map 1. From Merrill Mattes, *Platte River Road Narratives*. Copyright 1988 by the Board of Trustees of the University of Illinois. *Used with the permission of the University of Illinois Press.*

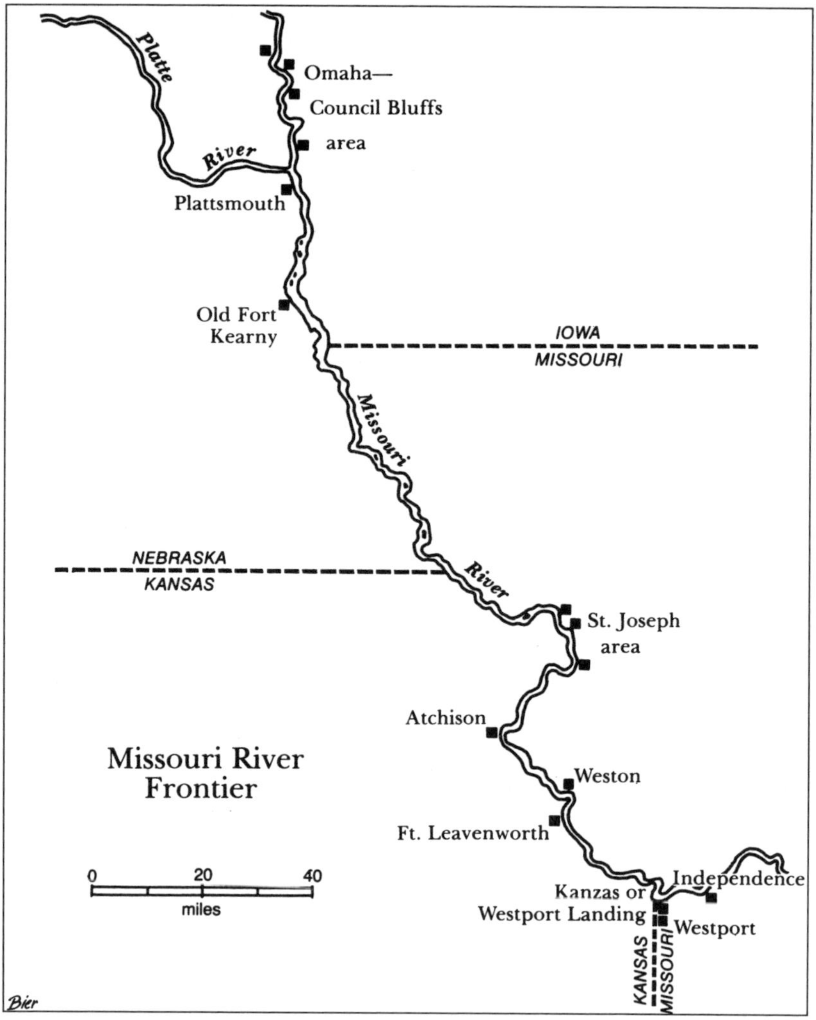

MAP 2. From John D. Unruh, *The Plains Across: The Overland Emigrants and the Trans-Mississippi West, 1840–60*. Copyright 1979 Board of Trustees of the University of Illinois. *Used with the permission of the University of Illinois Press.*

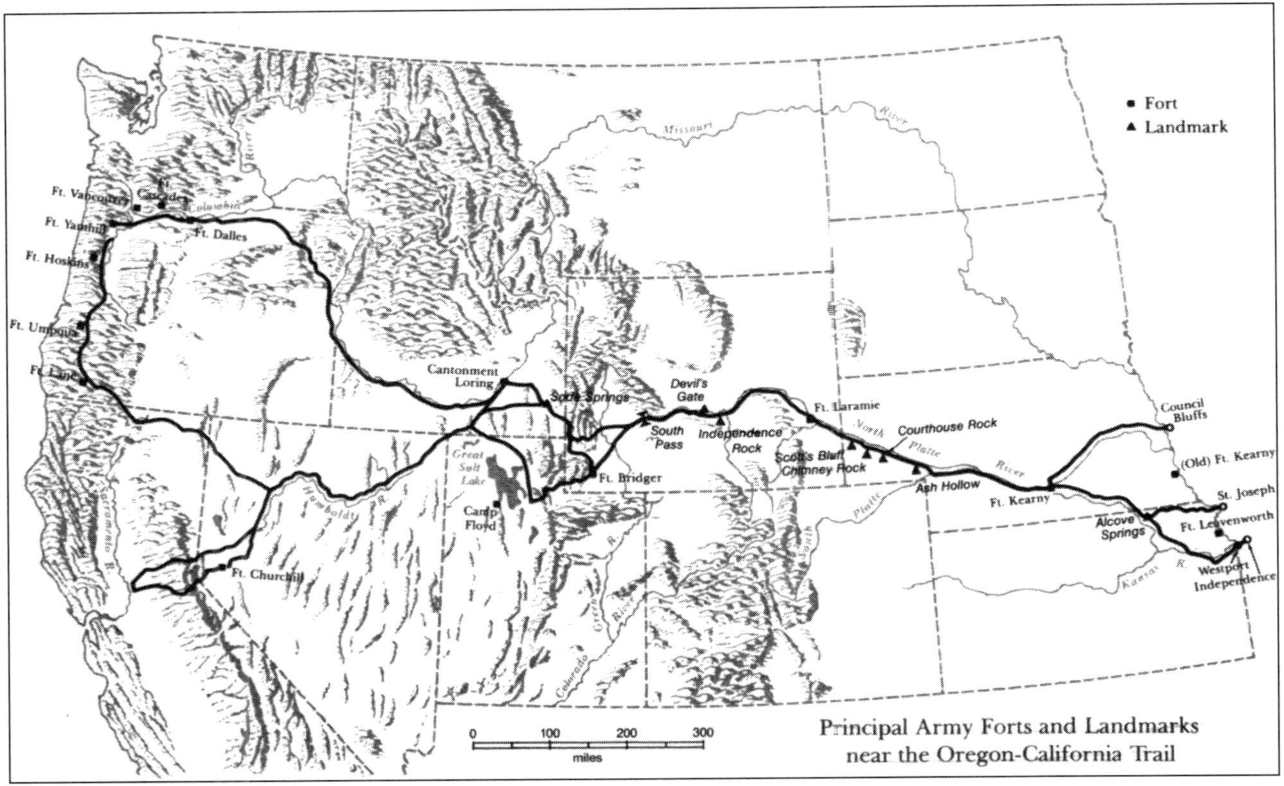

MAP 3. From John D. Unruh, *The Plains Across: The Overland Emigrants and the Trans-Mississippi West, 1840–60*. Copyright 1979 Board of Trustees of the University of Illinois. *Used with the permission of the University of Illinois Press.*

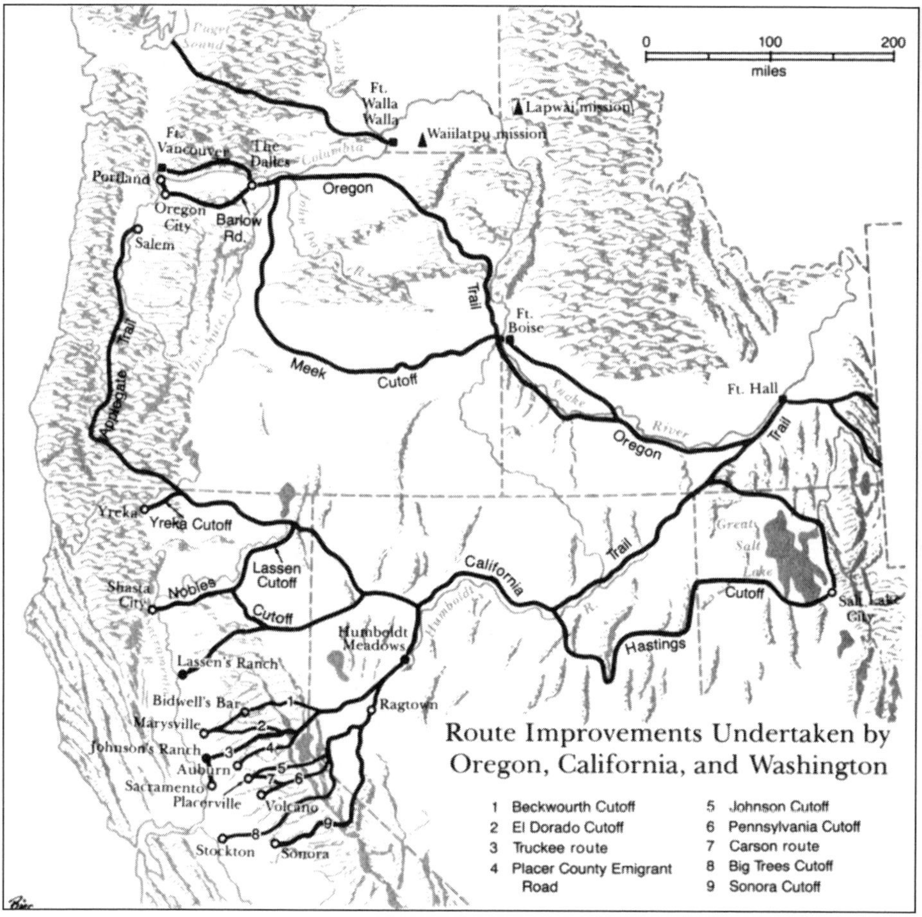

Map 4. From John D. Unruh, *The Plains Across: The Overland Emigrants and the Trans-Mississippi West, 1840–60*. Copyright 1979 Board of Trustees of the University of Illinois. *Used with the permission of the University of Illinois Press.*

1840

Pierre-Jean De Smet on the Indian Missions

Father Pierre-Jean De Smet is one of the most recognized figures among those who directed Catholic missionary activities for the Indian tribes of the Pacific Northwest. During the 1840s, he repeatedly traveled across the northern plains and Rockies between St. Louis, Missouri, and Oregon country, often alongside celebrated fur traders and among well-known emigrant wagon trains. Although it was not part of his original plan to promote the American political advance into this remote corner of North America, his writings were widely circulated among Catholics and Protestants alike. These publications, mostly compiled from lengthy letters, such as the one printed below, exclaimed over the bounties of the Pacific Northwest and popularized the economic potential of the region to families who were contemplating a relocation there. The rich details of his letters helped eloquently capture the multifaceted accomplishments of his long and fruitful life.

De Smet was born on January 30, 1801, in Dendermonde (Termonde), Belgium, to a devoutly religious family. He migrated to Baltimore, Maryland, in 1821, immediately entered a novitiate of the Jesuit order, and two years later transferred to the newly opened novitiate in Florissant, Missouri. There he completed his religious instruction while listening to the adventurous stories of trappers, river boatmen, and travelers returning from the Indian country to the west. Ordained as a priest in 1827, he taught at the University of St. Louis and made several trips to Europe between 1833 and 1837.

The young man's ambition to become a missionary to the indigenous tribes was finally realized in 1838 when he ascended the Missouri River

Pierre-Jean De Smet.
Courtesy of the Library of Congress, Prints and Photographs Division, LC-DIG-cwpbh-03561.

to present-day Council Bluffs, Iowa, where he ministered to a band of Potawatomi Indians. While at that station, he met an even more exotic delegation of Natives, representatives of the Flathead Nation from western Montana who were on their way to St. Louis seeking American missionaries, trade, and technology. De Smet interpreted the chance meeting as God's personal call to him, and he succeeded in gaining Jesuit approval to proceed to the far-distant land. During the spring of 1840, he accompanied a caravan of fur traders to the last official rendezvous at Green River, and from there he made his way to the Flathead heartland. His two wonderful months spent among these receptive people convinced the young priest to return via the Missouri River to St. Louis, where he could recruit other priests to return with him to the mountain paradise. This 1840 trip is fully described in De Smet's February 4, 1841, letter, which is reproduced and edited in this selection.

De Smet's second trip to the Northwest began from Westport, Missouri, in May 1841, in the company of fellow priests, fathers Nicholas

Point and Gregori Mengarini, as well as three lay brothers—William Claessens, Charles Huet, and Joseph Specht. Guiding the party was celebrated mountain man and explorer Thomas Fitzpatrick, who possessed firsthand knowledge of much of the vast area through which they would travel. To ensure greater protection and more efficient use of manpower along the line of march, De Smet's party traveled with the equally famous Bidwell-Bartleson party, most of whose members would eventually separate from the priests at Soda Springs and turn southwestward toward Mexican California. From that juncture in the trails, De Smet and his small party of priests, lay brothers, trappers, teamsters, and pleasure seekers pushed northwestward. Eventually the Jesuits established St. Mary's Mission in the Bitterroot Valley, near present-day Missoula, Montana. Sister missions were later established among the Kalispel Indians at St. Ignatius, the Yakamas at Fort Colville, and the Coeur d'Alenes at Sacred Heart Mission.

The relative success of the northwestern missions proved that De Smet's "soft-glove" approach to Christianizing Indian nations could bear fruit if Indian spiritual traditions were also respected. Throughout the 1840s and 1850s, he made several trips to Europe and the eastern United States to recruit personnel and financial resources for the expansion of these missions. In 1844, he helped the Sisters of Notre Dame establish a convent in the fertile agricultural environment offered by Oregon's Willamette Valley. Simultaneously, he led four priests into Idaho to establish a mission among the Kalispel tribe and further explored the vast hunting grounds of the Blackfoot Indians. The Blackfoot were noted for their friendship for the British-owned Hudson's Bay Company and for their enmity toward Americans ever since their first confrontation with the Lewis and Clark expedition.

Although Father De Smet completed the last of his missionary trips to the Far West in 1851, he did not disappear from the western scene. In that same year, he was an active participant in bringing together enemy and allied tribes for a great council held at Horse Creek near Fort Laramie. During the 1857–58 Mormon War, he played a visible role in trying to mediate differences between the federal government and the Mormon leadership. In the same vein, he served as an intermediary during the

Yakima Indian War in northeastern Washington, when, in 1858–1859, gold miners poured over tribal lands. Finally, in 1868, De Smet was able to gain an audience with the Hunkpapa Sioux leader Sitting Bull in the aftermath of bloody fighting along the Bozeman Trail. Though he was not able to establish universal trust and peace among the northern Plains tribes, he was recognized by many Indians as an honest broker, who could fairly convey their viewpoints to white authorities. Father Pierre-Jean De Smet died in St. Louis from Bright's disease on May 23, 1873.

Because De Smet was so prolific with his correspondence, information abounds on his travels, relationships with various Indian nations, descriptions of the diverse landscapes, and personal contacts with British and American fur traders. To understand the vast extent of his experiences and his keen insights into human motivations, readers should therefore sample his *Life, Letters and Travels of Father Pierre-Jean De Smet, S. J., 1801–1873*, 4 vols., edited by Hiram M. Chittenden and Alfred Talbot Richardson (1905); and *Letters and Sketches: With a Narrative of a Year's Residence among the Indian Tribes of the Rocky Mountains* (1843). This second book was edited by Reuben Gold Thwaites and republished as volume 27 of the renowned Early Western Travels, 1748–1846, series (1906). Despite the richness of De Smet's writings, the quality of biographies about his life range broadly. The popularly conceived *Black Robe: The Life of Pierre-Jean De Smet* (1964), by John Upton Terrell, is readily available but superficial and error prone. Far stronger in depth of research and understanding of Jesuit-Indian relations is John J. Killoren, *"Come, Blackrobe": De Smet and the Indian Tragedy* (1994).

Persons interested in De Smet's association with the 1841 Bidwell-Bartleson wagon train will find considerable coverage in Doyce B. Nunis, Jr., ed., *The Bidwell-Bartleson Party: 1841 California Emigrant Adventure* (1991); and Michael J. Gillis and Michael F. Magliari, *John Bidwell and California: The Life and Writings of a Pioneer, 1841–1900* (2004).

The larger story of Catholic missionary activities in Oregon country is ably interpreted in Robert Ignatius Burns, *The Jesuits and the Indian Wars of the Northwest* (1966); and Robert H. Ruby and John A. Brown, *Indians of the Pacific Northwest* (1981). De Smet's relationships with Thomas Fitzpatrick and other fur traders during his numerous overland crossings is presented in LeRoy R. Hafen, *Broken Hand: The*

Life of Thomas Fitzpatrick, Mountain Man, Guide and Indian Agent (1931). This includes De Smet's role in the important 1851 Horse Creek Council. Also helpful in understanding his later role as a peace negotiator among the Lakota Sioux is Robert M. Utley's *The Lance and the Shield: The Life and Times of Sitting Bull* (1993).

The following De Smet letter describes his 1840 journey with a group of frontiersmen to the last fur-trading rendezvous on the Green River, his warm reception among the Flatheads, and his subsequent trip down the Missouri River to St. Louis. From this first, and arguably most important, of his excursions to the Pacific Northwest, he conceived the grand plan for future Jesuit missionizing efforts throughout that region. This letter originally appeared in the Reuben Gold Thwaites edited version, which was printed in volume 27 of the Early Western Travels series. Although De Smet's original text is retained without changes in both Thwaites's and my copy, I have added new editorial notes and parenthetical commentary to the original text to better identify the people and explain the events.

PIERRE-JEAN DE SMET, "REPORT ON HIS 1840 WESTERN TRIP," FROM *LETTERS AND SKETCHES: WITH A NARRATIVE OF A YEAR'S RESIDENCE AMONG THE INDIAN TRIBES OF THE ROCKY MOUNTAINS*, VOL. 27 OF EARLY WESTERN TRAVELS, 1748–1846, SERIES, EDITED BY REUBEN GOLD THWAITES, WITH UPDATED INTRODUCTION AND EDITORIAL NOTES FOR THIS NEW ANTHOLOGY (CLEVELAND, OHIO: ARTHUR H. CLARK, 1906).

St. Louis University, Feb 4, 1841.
To The Rev. F. J. B.

Rev. and Dear Sir:

I presume you are aware, that in the beginning of last Spring, I was sent by the Right Rev. Bishop of St. Louis,[1] and my Provincial, on an exploring expedition to the Rocky Mountains, in order to ascertain

[1]De Smet received his authority and instructions for the 1840 journey to the Flathead country from Father Joseph Rosati. See De Smet, *Letters and Sketches*, 136n.

the dispositions of the Indians, and the prospects of success we might have if we were to establish a mission among them. It is truly gratifying to me to have so favorable a report to make.—My occupations do not allow me to enter into all the details; I shall therefore be satisfied at present with giving you a brief sketch of my journey and its result.

I started from Westport [Missouri] on the 30th of April, in company with the Annual Expedition of the American Fur Company, which for this year had appointed the rendezvous on Green River, a tributary of the Rio Colorado of the West.[2] Captain [Andrew] Dripps, who commanded the caravan, treated me on all occasions with the most polite attention.[3] On the 6th day of our journey I was seized with the fever and ague, and have been subject to it for nearly five months.[4] Nothing particularly worth noticing, occurred during the journey, except, when we halted in the village of the Sheyennes [Cheyennes].[5]

[2]In his later recollections, Joel P. Walker, older brother of celebrated mountain man Joseph Reddeford Walker, remarked that the trading expedition that left Westport, Missouri, on April 30, 1840, consisted of forty men of the American Fur Company, heading thirty mule-drawn carts and sixty pack mules. Also included was Walker's wife, children, and his sister-in-law, as well as three Oregon-bound Congregationalist missionaries and their wives, who drove two wagons. The latter party included Reverend Harvey Clark and laymen Philo B. Littlejohn and Alvin T. Smith, along with their wives. See Barry, *Beginning of the West*, 392.

[3]Andrew Drips (c. 1789–1860) joined the Missouri Fur Company in 1820 and became a partner in the fur-trading enterprise two years later. In that capacity he relocated up the Missouri River to present-day Bellevue, Nebraska, where he operated a company trading post. After the demise of the Missouri Fur Company, and following several years of other partnerships, Drips joined the American Fur Company. Government officials recognized his experience among Plains and Rocky Mountain Indian tribes, and he held the coveted appointment of special Indian agent for the Upper Missouri from 1842 until 1846. See Harvey L. Carter's profile of Drips's life in Hafen, *Mountain Men and the Fur Trade*, 8:143–56.

[4]Elsewhere De Smet wrote that the alternating chills and fevers did not dissipate until he reached the Yellowstone River area on his return trip down the Missouri River to St. Louis. The attacks became so severe that his friends encouraged him to return directly to Westport. Declining their worthwhile advice, De Smet wrote, "My desire of seeing the nations of the mountains prevailed over all their good reasons." See De Smet, *Life, Letters and Travels*, vol. 1, 202–203.

[5]Despite his affirmation in this letter that not much happened during the westward crossing of the Great Plains, De Smet left a wonderfully detailed account of that part of his journey in another of his writings. The pages are filled with information about tribes settled in northeastern Kansas and east-central Nebraska; animal life along the Platte River; and notable landmarks such as Chimney Rock, Fort Laramie, Laramie Peak, Red Butte, and South Pass. Most notable were his frequent descriptions about how the desertlike qualities of the plains would greatly restrict future settlement. Yet, he also believed that farms and settlements would spring up along the rivers. He likewise predicted the future conflicts between "savagery and civilization" along these arteries of travel. See De Smet, *Life, Letters and Travels*, vol. 1, 201–15.

I was introduced to the Chiefs as a minister of the Great Spirit: they showed me great deference, and I was invited to a feast. I had to pass at first through all the ceremonies of the calumet; the great chief approached me to shake hands, and gave me a heartfelt "How do you do."—"Blackgown," said he, "my heart was filled with joy when I learned who you were. My lodge never received a visitor for whom I feel a greater esteem.[6] As soon as I was apprised of your coming, I ordered my great kettle to be filled, and in your honor, I commanded that my three fattest dogs should be served up." The bravest warriors of the nation partook of the repast, and I availed myself of the opportunity to explain to them the most important tenets of Christianity. I told them the object of my visit, and enquired whether they would not be satisfied to have also Black-gowns among them, who would teach them to love and serve the Great Spirit, as he wished. "Oh yes," they eagerly answered, "we will gladly provide for every thing that they stand in need of; they will not die of hunger amongst us." I have no doubt but a zealous missionary would do a great deal of good among them. They are about two thousand in number. Their language, it is said, is very difficult. On the 30th of June we arrived at the rendezvous.[7] An escort of warriors had been provided for me by the Flat-heads.[8] Our

---

[6]De Smet's visit among the Cheyennes came at a time when the northern and southern bands of the tribe were relatively friendly toward Americans. Their major combats lay in the future—during the Civil War and post–Civil War years—and, in 1840, American fur traders were still vital to a fast-changing Indian technology and economy. This meeting place was on the Laramie River near the fur-trading post popularly known as Fort Laramie. For additional discussion of the meeting, see De Smet, *Life, Letters and Travels*, vol. 1, 210–12.

[7]The 1840 rendezvous was held in the upper valley of the Green River in western Wyoming. It marked the last official rendezvous, an event that had been held annually since 1825. Despite attendance by illustrious traders such as Andrew Drips, Jim Bridger, and Henry Fraeb, this final "Rocky Mountain trade fair" attracted only a few hundred individuals. A general decline in the availability of furs and the construction of permanent trading posts such as Fort Laramie, Fort Hall, and Bent's Fort in the heart of trapping country rendered William Ashley's rendezvous system virtually obsolete. See Gowans, *Rocky Mountain Rendezvous*, 194–98; and Billington, *Far Western Frontier*, 64–66.

[8]The fact that the Flathead delegation had traveled to the rendezvous site to guide De Smet's party back to their distant villages indicates that a sizable portion of the Flatheads did want Catholic missionaries in their country. Their presence at the rendezvous also demonstrated their desire for greater trade with the American fur companies. Among the Flatheads were Peter Left Hand, who went on to the villages to announce the approach of the Jesuits, and Young Ignace, who remained with De Smet's party as its chief guide. See De Smet, *Life, Letters and Travels*, vol. 1, 216n.; and Killoren, *"Come, Blackrobe,"* 58–61.

meeting was that of children who come to meet their parent, and in the effusion of their heart, they bestowed upon me the fondest names with a simplicity truly patriarchal. They told me of all the interesting particulars of their nation, and of the wonderful preservation of sixty of their men, in a battle against two hundred Black-feet, which lasted five whole days, and in which they killed fifty of their enemies, without losing a single man of their number. "The Great Spirit watched over them;" they said, "he knew that we were to guide you to our camp, and he wanted to clear the road of all the obstacles that you might have found on your way. We trust we will not be annoyed any more by the Black-feet; they went off weeping like women." We thanked heaven for the signal preservation, and implored its assistance for the new and perilous journey we were on the point of undertaking. The Indians of different nations and the trappers, had assembled at the rendezvous in great numbers, for the sake of the trade. On Sunday, the fifth of July, I had the consolation of celebrating the holy sacrifice of Mass *sub dio*. The altar was placed on an elevation, and surrounded with boughs and garlands of flowers; I addressed the congregation in French and in English, and spoke also by an interpreter to the Flat-head and Snake Indians.[9] It was a spectacle truly moving for the heart of a Missionary, to behold an assembly composed of so many different nations, who all assisted at our holy mysteries with great satisfaction.—The Canadians sung hymns in French and Latin, and the Indians in their native tongue. It was truly a Catholic worship. . . . This place has been called since that time, by the French Canadians, *la prairie de la Messe*.

About thirty of the principal chiefs of the Snake Indians invited me to a council. I explained to them the christian doctrine in a compendious manner—they were all very attentive—they then deliberated among themselves for about half an hour, and one of the chiefs, addressing me in the name of the others, said: "Black-gown, the words of thy mouth have found their way to our hearts; they never will be

[9]De Smet used the term Snakes to refer to several bands of Northern Shoshones who attended the 1840 rendezvous. Although Snake was a term widely used by fur trappers to refer to these diverse bands, the word had a pejorative connotation and was soon to be used by many other overland travelers of the mid-nineteenth century. See Gowans, *Rocky Mountain Rendezvous*, 195–97; and Murphy and Murphy, "Northern Shoshone and Bannock," 284–307.

forgotten. Our country is open for thee; come to teach us what we have to do, to please the Great Spirit, and we will do according to thy words." I advised them to select among themselves a wise and prudent man, who, every morning and evening, should assemble them to offer to Almighty God their prayers and supplications; that there the good chiefs should have an opportunity of exhorting their warriors to behave as they ought. The meeting was held the very same evening, and the great chief promulgated a law, that for the future, the one who would be guilty of theft, or of any other disorderly act, should receive a public castigation. On Monday, 6th, we proceeded on our journey. A dozen Canadians wished to accompany me, to have an opportunity, as they said, to practise their religion. Eight days afterwards we arrived safely in the camp of the Flat-heads, and Ponderas, or Pends d'oreilles.[10]

Immediately the whole village was in commotion; men, women and children, all came to meet me, and shake hands, and I was conducted in triumph to the lodge of the great chief Tjolizhitzay, (the Big face.) He has the appearance of an old patriarch. Surrounded by the principal chiefs of the two tribes, and the most renowned warriors, he thus addressed me: "This day Kaikolinzosten (the Great Spirit) has accomplished our wishes, and our hearts are swelled with joy. Our desire to be instructed was so great, that three times had we deputed our people to the Great Black-gown[11] in St. Louis, to obtain a father. Now, Father, speak, and we will comply with all you will tell us. Show us the road we have to follow, to come to the place where the Great Spirit resides." Then he resigned his authority to me; but I replied that he mistook the object of my coming among them; that I had no other object in view, but their spiritual welfare; that with respect to temporal affairs, they should remain as they were, till circumstances should

[10] De Smet's reference to the Pend d'Oreille tribe refers to the present-day Kalispel people, who were closely affiliated with the Flatheads. The chief phonetically referred to in De Smet's following paragraph as Tjolizhitzay (the Big Face) was more appropriately called Bear Looking Up, or Standing Grizzly Bear. He was referred to as a Flathead chief, but his ancestry was largely Kalispel. He accepted baptism from De Smet and the new name Paul, but the hasty conversion in no way implies that he rejected traditional ways to become a Christian. See Ruby and Brown, *Indians of the Pacific Northwest*, 83.

[11] Tjolizhitzay's reference to the "Great Black-gown" is to the bishop of St. Louis, Father Joseph Rosati, who oversaw all Catholic missionizing activities in the northern Rockies.

allow them to settle in a permanent spot.—Afterwards we deliberated on the hours proper for their spiritual exercises and instructions. One of the chiefs brought me a bell, with which I might give the signal.

The same evening about 2,000 persons were assembled before my lodge to recite night prayers in common. I told them the result of my conference with the chiefs; of the plan of instructions which I intended to pursue; and with what disposition they ought to assist at them, etc. Night prayers having been said, a solemn canticle of praise of their own composition, was sung by these children of the mountains, to the Author of their being. It would be impossible for me to describe the emotions I felt at this moment; I wept for joy, and admired the marvellous ways of that kind Providence, who, in his people, to announce to them the glad tidings of salvation. The next day I assembled the council, and with the assistance of an intelligent interpreter, I translated into their language the Lord's Prayer, the Hail Mary, the Apostle's Creed, the ten Commandments, and four Acts. As I was in the habit of reciting these prayers, morning and evening, and before instructions, about a fortnight after, I promised a beautiful silver medal to the one who would recite them first. One of the chiefs rising immediately, "Father," said he, smiling, "that medal is mine," and he recited all the prayers without missing a word. I embraced him, praised the eagerness which he had evinced of being instructed, and appointed him my Cathecist. This good Indian set to work with so much zeal and perseverance, that in less than a fortnight all knew their prayers.

Every morning, at the break of day, the old chief is the first on horseback, and goes round the camp from lodge to lodge. "Now my children," he exclaims, "it is time to rise; let the first thoughts of your hearts be for the Great Spirit; say that you love him, and beg of him to be merciful unto you. Make haste, our Father will soon ring the bell, open your ears to listen, and your hearts to receive the words of his mouth." Then, if he has perceived any disorderly act on the preceding day, or if he has received unfavorable reports from the other chiefs, he gives them a fatherly admonition. Who would not think, that this could only be found in a well ordered and religious community, and yet it is among Indians in the defiles and vallies of the Rocky Mountains!!! You have no idea of the eagerness they showed to receive religious instruction. I explained the christian doctrine four times a day, and nevertheless my lodge was filled, the whole day, with people eager to hear more. At night I related those histories of the Holy Scriptures that were best calculated to promote their piety and edification, and as I happened to observe, that I was afraid of tiring them, "oh no," they replied, "if we were not afraid of tiring you, we would gladly spend here the whole night."[12]

I conferred the holy sacrament of Baptism on six hundred of them, and if I thought it prudent to postpone the baptism of others till my return, it was not for want of desire on their part, but chiefly to impress upon their minds a greater idea of the holiness of the sacrament, and of the dispositions that are required to receive it worthily. Among those baptised, were the two great chiefs of the Flat-heads and of the Ponderas. As I recited the catechumens to a heartfelt contrition of their sins, the Walking Bear, chief of the Ponderas, answered: "Father, I have been plunged for a number of years in profound ignorance of good and evil, and no doubt, during that time, I have often greatly displeased the Great Spirit, and therefore I must humbly beseech his pardon. But when I afterwards conceived that a thing was bad, I banished it from my heart, and I do not recollect to have since deliberately offended the Great Spirit." Truly, where such dispositions are found, we may well conclude that a rich harvest is to be gathered.

I remained two months among these good people, and every day they were adding to my consolations, by their fervor in prayer, by their assiduity in coming to my instructions, and by their docility in putting into practice what they had been taught.

The season being far advanced, and as I had waited in vain for a safe opportunity to return to St. Louis, I resolved to commit myself entirely to Providence, and on the 7th of August,[13] I took leave of my

[12]De Smet's discussion of the mass conversion of Indians upon his first meeting with them is somewhat misleading. The Shoshone and Kalispel "converts" were embracing not all features of Catholicism, but rather those activities which were already in tune with their traditional spiritual views. They were eclectic in matters of religion, always choosing the elements that made sense to them within their own cultural framework. Catholicism, with its rich ceremonialism, provided another layer of religious instruction, but not at the price of relinquishing older traditions and spiritual meanings. See Murphy and Murphy, "Northern Shoshone and Bannock," 296–302.

[13]He actually departed for St. Louis on August 27, 1840, rather than August 7, with over 1,600 baptisms having been performed by him and his fellow priests among a number of tribes. See Killoren, *"Come, Blackrobe,"* 78; and De Smet, *Life, Letters and Travels*, vol. 1, 233.

dear Neophytes. I appointed one of the chiefs to replace me during my absence, who should preside in their evening and morning devotions, and on the Sabbath exhort them to virtue, baptize the little children, and those who were dangerously ill. Grief was depicted on the features of all, and tears were glistening in every eye. The old chief addressed me, saying, "Father, the Great Spirit accompany thee in thy long and dangerous voyage; every day, morning and evening, we will address to him our humble supplications, that thou mayest arrive safely among thy brethren. And we will continue to do so, till thou be again among thy children of the mountains. We are now like the trees that have been spoiled of their verdure by winter's blast. When the snow will have disappeared from these vallies, and the grass begins to grow, our hearts will begin to rejoice; when the plants will spring forth our joy will increase; when they blossom, it will still be greater, and then we will set out to meet you. Farewell, Father, farewell."

The Chiefs would not suffer me to depart by myself—thirty of the bravest warriors were deputed as a safeguard to traverse the country of the Black-feet, who are very hostile to the whites, and they were instructed to accompany me, as far as need would be of their assistance. I resolved to take on my return a different route from the one I had taken in coming. I was induced to do so, in order to visit the Forts of the American Fur Company on the Missouri, and on the Yellow Stone, to baptize the children. After five or six days travelling, we fell in with a war party of the Crow Indians, who received us very kindly, and we travelled together for two days. Then we directed our course to the Big Horn [River], the most considerable of the tributary streams of the Yellow Stone [Yellowstone River]. There we met another party of the same nation, who were also amicably disposed towards us. As there was question about religion, I availed myself of the opportunity to express to them the main articles of the Christian faith, and as I was depicting in lively colors the torments of hell, and had told them that the Great Spirit had kindled this fire of his wrath, for those who did not keep the commandments I had explained to them, one of the Chiefs uttered a horrid shriek. "If this be the case," said he, "then I believe there are but two in the whole nation who will not go to that place; it is the Beaver and the Mink; they are the only Crows who never stole, who never killed, nor committed all the excesses which your law prohibits. Perhaps I am deceived, and then we must all go together." When I left them on the next day, the Chief put a fine bell on my horse's neck, and invited me to take a turn round the village. Next, he accompanied me for six miles.

After several days of a painful journey over rocks and cliffs, we arrived at last at the fort of the Crows.[14] It is the first the American Fur Company possessed in that country. My dear Flat-heads edified all the inhabitants by their fervor and their piety. As well in the fort, as on the road, we never missed performing in common, our evening and morning devotions, and singing canticles in honor of the Almighty. Frequently, during my stay with them, they had given me abundant proofs of their trust in Providence. I cannot forbear mentioning one instance that occurred during my travels in this place. One day as dinner was preparing and provisions scarce, a countryman of mine, who accompanied me, suggested the propriety of keeping something in reserve for supper. "Be not uneasy," said the chief, called Ensyla,[15] "I never missed my supper in my life. I trust in the mercy of the Great Spirit, he will provide for all our wants." We had just camped at night, when the chief killed two stags. "Did I not tell you right?" he remarked, smilingly, to my companion. "You see the Great Spirit does not only provide for our wants of this evening, but he gives us also a supply for to-morrow."

Now began the most difficult and most perilous part of our journey. I had to pass through a country supposed to be overrun by war parties, of the Black-feet, Assineboins [Assiniboins], Gros Ventres, Arikaras, and Scioux [Sioux]. All these nations entertained the most hostile dispositions toward the Flat-heads. I therefore dispensed with their

[14]This fur-trading post was either Fort Cass, at the mouth of the Bighorn River, or Fort Van Buren, on the south bank of the Yellowstone River at the mouth of Rosebud Creek. They were built by A. J. Tulloch for the American Fur Company in 1832 and 1835 respectively. See De Smet, *Letters and Sketches* 146n, and Killoren, *"Come, Blackrobe,"* 62.

[15]Ensyla, more often spelled Insula (Red Feather), proved to be one of the earliest and most enduring friends of De Smet and the other Catholic priests. De Smet baptized him and gave him the name Michael, though his reputation as a Flathead leader was won more on the battlefield against other tribes than it was as a peace maker. Insula's wartime exploits are briefly summarized in Ruby and Brown, *Indians of the Pacific Northwest*, 84.

services any farther. I again excited them to continue the good work they had begun; to be steadfast in their faith; regular in their devotions; charitable towards one another. I embraced them all and took my leave. Mr. John de Velder,[16] a native of Ghent in Belgium, had volunteered his services to me at the Rendezvous. In consideration of the bad state of my health, I deemed myself very happy to accept of them; he has never left me since. He was now to be my only travelling companion. As there is no road, we followed the direction of the river; at intervals we were obliged to make immense circuits to avoid the steep and craggy hills that defied our passage. For two hundred miles, we had continually death before our eyes. On the second day, I discovered before daylight a large smoke at a distance of about a quarter of a mile. We hastily saddled our horses and following up a ravine we gained a high bluff unperceived. At night we did not dare to make fire for fear of attracting notice. Again about dinner time, we found on the road the carcase of a Buffalo, killed only two hours before; the tongue and the marrow bones with some other dainty pieces had been taken away. Thus the kind providence of our God took care to supply our wants.

We took a direction contrary to the tracks of the Indians, and spent a safe night in the cliffs of the rocks. The next day we struck upon a spot where forty lodges had been encamped, the fires were yet in full blaze. Finally, we crossed the Missouri [River] at the same place where, only an hour before, a hundred lodges of ill-minded Assineboins had passed, and we arrived safe and unmolested at Fort Union, situated a few miles above the mouth of the Yellow Stone. In all these Forts great harmony and union prevail; Mr. Kipps,[17] the present administrator of them, is a gentleman well worthy of his station. Every where I was

[16]John de Velder, the Anglicized version of Jean-Baptiste de Velder, had served as an unofficial translator and intermediary for De Smet ever since the two had first met at the 1840 fur trade rendezvous. The two friends traveled together on the return trip all the way to Westport, Missouri. See Killoren, *"Come, Blackrobe,"* 61–63.

[17]James Kipp (not Kipps), was born in Montréal in 1788 and became a trapper in the Red River country by age twenty. In 1822, he joined the Columbia Fur Company and built the first trading post among the Blackfeet in 1831. After the merger of the Columbia Fur Company with the American Fur Company, Kipp built Fort Union at the juncture of the Yellowstone and Missouri rivers. There, and later at Fort Clark, he entertained many frontier travelers, including De Smet and artists George Catlin, Karl Bodmer, and Rudolph Friederich Kurz. See Mattison, "James Kipp," 201–205.

treated by these gentlemen with the greatest politeness and kindness, and all my wants were liberally supplied. As I was relating the particulars of this dangerous trip to an Indian Chief, he answered: "The Great Spirit has his Manitoos; he has sent them to take care of your steps and to trouble the enemies that would have been a nuisance to you." A Christian would have said: Angelis suis mandavit de te, ut custodiant te in omnibus viis tuis. On 23rd of September we set out for the village of the Mandans, in company with three men of the fort, who had the same destination. We met on the road a party of 19 Assineboins, who were returning to their country from an unsuccessful expedition against the Gros Ventres. Their looks indicated their bad intentions: although we were but five in number, we showed a determined countenance, and we passed unmolested. Next day we crossed a forest, the winter quarters of the Gros Ventres, and Arikaras, in 1835. It was there that those unfortunate tribes were nearly exterminated by the small pox.[18] We saw their bodies wrapped up in Buffalo robes, tied to the branches of the largest trees. It was truly a sad and mournful spectacle. Two days later we met the miserable survivors of these unhappy tribes. Only ten families of the Mandans, once such a powerful nation, now remain. They have united with the Gros Ventres and Arikaras. They received me with great demonstrations of friendship; I spent that night in their camp, and the next day crossed the Missouri in their canoe, made of a buffalo skin. The next day we came to the first village of the Arikaras, and on the following day to their great village, consisting of about a hundred earthen wigwams. This tribe also received me very kindly. On the 6th of October, we started from the Mandan village, for Fort Pierre, on the little Missouri;[19] a

---

[18]The 1837 smallpox scourge along the Missouri River was especially destructive for the Mandans, Hidatsas (Gros Ventres), and Arikaras, who caught the disease from fur traders heading upriver from St. Louis. The Mandans suffered the most, and they deserted their primary village to erect new earth lodges three miles upriver. Meanwhile, Arikaras had moved into the abandoned Mandan village, and here they were contacted by De Smet. See De Smet, *Letters and Sketches*, 150n; and Cash and Wolff, *Three Affiliated Tribes*, 39–44.

[19]In 1831, Bernard Pratte and Company established Fort Pierre on the Missouri River, about three miles north of the present-day South Dakota capital at Pierre. Because of its location as a supply center on the Missouri River, it served several fur trade companies operating farther north on the river and by overland routes west to Fort Laramie. The U.S. Army purchased the post in 1855, but it was abandoned on May 16, 1857. See Frazer, *Forts of the West*, 136.

Canadian, whose destination lay in the same direction, accompanied us. The Commandant of the Fort had recommended to us in a special manner to be on our guard against the Jantonnois, the Santees, Jantous, Ankepatines, Ampapas, Ogallallas, and Black-feet Scioux, who have often proved very troublesome to white strangers.[20] On the third day of our journey we fell in with an ambuscade of the Jantonnois and Santees; they did not do us any harm, but on the contrary treated us very kindly, and at our departure loaded us with provisions. The next day we fell in with several other parties, who showed us much kindness. On the ninth day we were on the lands of the Black-feet Scioux; this country is undulating and intersected with numberless little streams. For greater caution we travelled in ravines. Towards dinner time, a fine landscape, near a delicious spring, seemed to invite us to take some repose. We had scarcely alighted, when all on a sudden a tremendous yell alarmed us, and from the top of the hill under which we were, the Black-feet darted upon us like lightning. "Why do you hide yourselves?" asked the Chief, in a stern voice. "Are you afraid of us?" Dressed in my cassock with a crucifix on my breast,—a costume I always wear in the Indian country,—it appeared to me that I was the subject of his particular enquiry. He asked the Canadian what kind of a man I was. The Frenchman said I was a Chief, a Black-gown, the man who spoke to the Great Spirit. He assumed immediately a milder countenance, ordered his men to lay down their arms, and we performed the ceremonies of shaking hands and smoking the calumet of peace. He then invited me to accompany them to the village, situated only at a short distance. It consisted of about a thousand souls. I pitched my tent at some distance, in a beautiful pasture, on the margin of a fine stream, and invited the great chief to partake of a supper with me. As I said grace before meal, he enquired of the Canadian what I was about. He is addressing the Great Spirit, was the reply, in gratitude for the food he has granted us. The chief nodded a sign of

[20]De Smet's unconventional spellings of the various Sioux divisions are properly identified as Jantonnois (Yanktonais); Jantous (Yanktons); and Ampapas (Hunkpapas). The remaining groups are readily identifiable—Santees, Oglalas, and Blackfeet (not to be confused with the Blackfoot of western Montana).

approbation. Shortly after, twelve warriors, in full costume, stretched a large buffalo robe before the place where I sat. The chief, taking me by the arm, invited me to sit down. I was under the impression that there was question again of smoking the calumet. Judge of my astonishment, when the twelve warriors, seizing each a piece of the robe, took me up, and headed by their chief, carried me in triumph to their village. In the lodge of the great chief, the most conspicuous place was assigned me, and he addressed me thus: "This day is the happiest of my life. For the first time do we behold among us a man who is so closely united with the Great Spirit. Black-gown, you see before you the chief warriors of my tribe; I have invited them to this feast, in order that they may keep the remembrance of your coming among us as long as they shall live." Then he invited me to speak again of the Great Spirit, (to say grace), I began in the name of the Father and of the Son, etc., and immediately all present lifted up their hands towards heaven; when I had concluded they all struck the ground. I asked the chief what they meant by this ceremony. "When we lift our hands," said he, "we signify that all our dependence is on the Great Spirit, and that he in his fatherly care provides for all our wants: we strike the ground to signify that we are only worms and miserable creeping beings in his sight." He asked me in his turn, what I had told to the Great Spirit. Unhappily, the Canadian was a poor interpreter, still I endeavored to make them understand, as well as I could, the Lord's Prayer. The chief showed great eagerness to know what I said.—He ordered his son and two other very intelligent young men to accompany me to the fort, in order to learn the principles of the Christian doctrine, and to be at the same time a safeguard against the Indians who might be inimically disposed towards us. Two days afterwards we met an Indian, whose horse was bending under a load of buffalo meat. Seeing us without provisions, he requested us to accept what we might stand in need of, advising us to take the whole, for, said he, in the vicinity of the fort, game is very scarce. Five days afterwards we arrived at Fort Pierre. Thence I travelled through prairies for nineteen days successively. We were often obliged to cook our victuals with dried herbs—not a stick was to be found. When I arrived at Fort

Vermillion,[21] I was apprised that the Santees had been on a warlike expedition against the Pottawatomies, of the Council Bluffs, among whom I had labored the two preceding years.[22]

I invited them to a council, and gave them a severe reprimand for violating the solemn promise they had made me the preceding year, of living with their neighbors on amicable terms. I showed them the injustice of attacking a peaceable nation without being provoked; the dreadful consequences of the Pottawatomies' revenge, that might end in the extinction of their tribe. I was requested to be once more the mediator, and they told me that they had resolved to bury the tomahawk forever.[23]

I have lost two horses on the road; the one I was riding could hardly support me any longer, and I was yet three hundred miles distance from the Council Bluffs. I resolved of course to embark on the Missouri, and engaged a native Iroquois to be my pilot. At first we were favored with fine weather, but this lasted only a few days. Very soon inclement weather set in with frost and snow; and several times as we drifted down the rapid stream, our frail canoe was on the point of being dashed to pieces against the numberless snags that obstruct its navigation. This dangerous trip lasted ten days. We generally spent the night on a sand bar. We had only a few frozen potatoes left when we perceived a beautiful deer gazing at us, and apparently waiting to receive its mortal blow. We shot at it. At last we arrived safe at the bluffs, and on the same night the river was closed by ice.

---

[21]Vermillion Post, located near where the Vermillion and Missouri rivers intersect in present-day southeastern South Dakota, played a significant role in American Fur Company trade with the Yanktons and Brulé Sioux. See Phillips, *Fur Trade*, 2:412.

[22]In 1838, De Smet had been assigned as a missionary to the Potawatomi people, who had been resettled at present-day Council Bluffs, Iowa, on the Missouri River. His successful work with the Potawatomis at St. Joseph's Mission and his chance meeting with a delegation of Flatheads there were the elements that compelled him to make the 1840 journey to the Flathead country. The Potawatomis were relocated to eastern Kansas in 1846, and another Catholic mission was quickly established for them. See De Smet, *Life, Letters and Travels*, vol. 1, 157–59; and Mullin, "Father De Smet and the Pottawattamie Indian Mission," 192–216.

[23]De Smet provided further information about his 1839 travels from the St. Joseph's Mission to southern South Dakota, where he had urged the Yanktons to end their raids against the peaceful Potawatomis. During this trip, he also spent time among the Omahas, whose destruction by smallpox he witnessed firsthand. See De Smet, *Life, Letters and Travels*, vol. 1, 179–92.

So many escapes from the midst of so many dangers thoroughly convinced me that this undertaking is the work of God—omnia disponens fortiter et ad finem suam conducens suaviter. (Who reacheth from end to end mightily, and ordereth all things sweetly.)[24] I am now preparing for my return, and will start early in Spring, accompanied by three Fathers and as many Brothers.[25] You are aware such expeditions cannot be undertaken without the necessary means, and the fact is, I have no other reliance than Providence and the kindness of my friends. I hope they will not be wanting. I know that you must feel deeply interested in this meritorious good work, I therefore take the liberty of recommending it to your generosity, and that of your friends—every little contribution will help. I will be very grateful to you, if you have the kindness to forward to my address at St. Louis University, Mo., before the end of March, or middle of April, the amount you have collected.

I recommend myself and my dear Neophytes to your good prayers and holy sacrifices, and rest assured that we shall not forget our benefactors.

P. J. De Smet, S. J.

---

[24]De Smet made the difficult trip down the Missouri River from Fort Pierre to Council Bluffs using both boat and horseback as dual means of travel. He left Council Bluffs on December 14, reached Westport on December 22, and disembarked at St. Louis on December 31, 1840. See Barry, *Beginning of the West*, 409.

[25]De Smet refers here to his preparations for his spring 1841 return to the Northern Rockies with Fathers Nicholas Point and Gregori Mengarini, as well as the three lay brothers. See Barry, *Beginning of the West*, 428–29.

1841

Nancy Roberts Kelsey, "Own Story of Her Life"

Nancy Roberts Kelsey accompanied one of the most celebrated wagon trains bound for the Far West, and in doing so she gained recognition as the first white woman to cross the Sierra Nevadas into California. As the only adult female in the famed Bidwell-Bartleson party of 1841, she joined what many historians have regarded as the first sizable wagon train to follow the main routes of what later became known as the Oregon and California trails. Among the group of sixty to seventy overlanders was Father Pierre-Jean De Smet and several other Jesuit missionaries headed to the land of the Flathead Indians, guided by experienced mountain man Thomas Fitzpatrick. Although the missionaries had a relatively specific destination in mind when they set out, the other members of the train possessed only the haziest notions of where they would settle and the route they would follow. Furthermore, with the exception of Fitzpatrick and four trappers, none of these argonauts had previously experienced the unique hardships of the Great Plains, Rocky Mountains, or Great Basin, and none had ever participated in this type of protracted journey with strangers.

When the disparate groups finally assembled near the Kansas River, they decided to cast their lots together as a single body, and they elected officers in democratic fashion. Unfortunately, the first of their democratic decisions hampered the success of the migration. Instead of selecting the more reliable but youthful John Bidwell as the expedition's leader, the members chose the hot-tempered John Bartleson as their captain, partly because of his advanced age of fifty-four. Within

Nancy Kelsey.
From the Grizzly Bear, *February 1915.*

a week, the party was overtaken by Reverend Joseph Williams who took his Methodism quite seriously and was quick to make moral judgments about his fellow travelers, including Bartleson, whom he harshly termed a "backslider," and Fitzpatrick, whom he denounced as a "wicked worldly man." Personality conflicts and dissension dominated the journey until they reached Soda Springs and decided to split up. Fewer than half of the members turned northward, heading up the Snake River toward the Columbia River and ultimately the Willamette Valley of Oregon. Among their number were the Jesuits, who soon expanded their religious activities among tribes of the Bitterroot Valley. Also in this Oregon-bound group were the families of Isaac and Samuel Kelsey.

The larger number of the caravan followed Bidwell's dream of a new agricultural paradise in Mexican California. Among those who crossed the Great Basin and set out toward the Sierra Nevadas was Benjamin Kelsey, his wife, Nancy, and their one-and-a-half-year-old child, Martha Ann, who supposedly were the first white woman and infant to traverse the rugged Sierras. Armed only with imprecise knowledge about the landscape that lay before them, the group departed the

Great Salt Lake in September 1841 and struck toward the Humboldt River. This desert transit created enormous hardships for humans and livestock alike, so much so that they abandoned their wagons at the foot of the Pequop Mountains in northeastern Nevada and packed whatever items they could on the remaining horses. By the time they finally reached the reliable waters of the Walker River, the party was facing great privation, and some even argued for turning back rather than facing the great granite fortress of the Sierras. Guided by a local Indian named Kis-Kis, they began their ascent through canyons and along ledges so narrow that some of the pack animals toppled over the cliffs. When their guide abandoned them, they had no choice but to keep moving westward, ever aware that the early snows could possibly strand them in the high elevations with few supplies.

Despite the odds against them, they finally reached the relative safety of the San Joaquin Valley, but a summer drought limited the availability of grasses for their livestock and game to hunt. On November 4, 1841, they reached their destination—the ranch of John Marsh—which was little more than a collection of dilapidated adobe buildings. Marsh, the man whose letters had encouraged the Missourians to migrate to California, treated the overlanders to a fine party, but he also caused great resentment when he charged a five-dollar "emigration fee" and an exorbitant "boarding fee" to the settlers. Members of the Bidwell-Bartleson wagon train subsequently dispersed to find work and begin new lives, probably never fully realizing how important their pioneering effort would be in the annals of the overland trails. John Bidwell went on to prominence as a land baron and politician, but most of the party was like the Kelsey family. They were practical people who sought neither fame nor fortune from their part in the epic transcontinental journey.

When Nancy Kelsey agreed to the following interview in 1893, she talked less about the arduous trip to California and more about her family's life *after* they settled there. Among other things, she discussed California life in the years leading up to the Bear Flag Revolt, including her family's friendly association with the powerful Vallejo clan. Events concerning the American uprising of 1846 received some attention in the narrative, notably the reasons for her husband's enmity toward John C. Frémont. Also detailed are the events associated with their brief venture in Oregon, Indian problems, their relocations between several California settlements during the 1850s, and their tragic 1861 move to Texas, where an Indian attack upon the family led to the scalping of their teenaged daughter Mary Ellen and her death five years later. Benjamin Kelsey died in 1888, while the family was living in Los Angeles, and Nancy remained active in community affairs until her death from cancer in 1896. Known as the "Cuyama Angel" because of her care for ill and destitute people in the community, her funeral attracted numerous mourners, but few knew the full details of her adventurous life.

The story of Nancy Kelsey is still plagued by gaps in information that never will be completely filled. Complicating this issue is the fact that her 1893 interview was eventually published in several versions, and these variations have confused researchers on important matters. It also still remains unclear as to who recorded the notes from the interview, and how literal was the transcript in capturing her exact words. Historian Doyce B. Nunis, Jr., suggests that the transcriptionist was admiring neighbor Addison Powell; Roy M. Sylar contends that Nancy's daughter Nancy Rose (Kelsey) Clanton recorded the interview. Text of the memoir was first published in the *San Francisco Examiner* on February 5, 1893, and versions were reprinted in the February 1915 issue of *Grizzly Bear*, under the title "A California Heroine," and again repeated in the February 1937 issue of the same publication. In his masterful bibliography of the overland trails, Merrill Mattes awarded a high rating of four stars to the *Grizzly Bear* version. A final version appeared in the *Oakland Tribune* on September 27, 1925.

The copy that was chosen for inclusion in this book is "Nancy (Roberts) Kelsey's Own Story of Her Life," which was originally published in the February and May 1983 issues of the *Pomo Bulletin*. This periodical of the Lake County Historical Society in Lakeport, California, is the most complete copy of the original interview, and its intrinsic value is strengthened by the useful editorial notes added by Roy M. Sylar. In this new reprint, I have chosen to retain Nancy Kelsey's original words in capital letters throughout. The smaller printed (uncapitalized passages) are prefaced at each appropriate juncture by the word "Note," and they represent the detailed editorial comments of Sylar. Likewise, the uncapitalized words and phrases that appear *within parentheses* beside Kelsey's words represent Sylar's editorial additions to correct spellings, names, dates, and other information that were erroneous or missing from the original transcript. To avoid confusion with Sylar's editorial supplements, I have restricted my own editorial remarks and informational changes to the footnotes and to *bracketed* words inside the Kelsey text and inside Sylar's editorial notes.

Researchers who wish to know more about the Bidwell-Bartleson wagon train and the role of the Kelsey family in its overland crossing will be rewarded with a rich literature that has survived from other members of the same party. Among the most important primary sources are Pierre-Jean De Smet, *Life, Letters and Travels of Father Pierre-Jean De Smet, S. J., 1801–1873*, vol. 1 (1905); Nicholas Point, *Wilderness Kingdom* (1967); John Bidwell, *Echoes of the Past* (1900); Nicholas "Cheyenne" Dawson, *Narrative of Nicholas "Cheyenne" Dawson* (1933); and Joseph Williams, *Narrative of a Tour from the State of Indiana to the Oregon Territory in the Years 1841–2* (1977). A useful overview of the wagon train members who turned north toward Oregon is found in H. E. Tobie, "From the Missouri to the Columbia, 1841" (1937).

For the California-bound party, see the details offered in Doyce B. Nunis, Jr., *The Bidwell-Bartleson Party* (1991). This excellent anthology reprints the surviving letters, diaries, and reminiscences of other people who were traveling in the Bidwell-Bartleson party. It also provides introductions and editorial notes for each source. Researchers who wish further biographical information on specific people mentioned by Nancy Kelsey should especially consult pages 256–68. Also see John Bidwell, *A Journey to California* (1964). Helpful in sorting out how the diverse groups came together to form a single wagon train in eastern Kansas is Louise Barry, *The Beginning of the West* (1972), 428–30; and the more definitive editorial work of historian Doyce B. Nunis, Jr., in Josiah Belden, *Josiah Belden: 1841 California Overland Pioneer* (1962), 126–36. The best biography of Bidwell's fascinating life is Michael J. Gillis and Michael F. Magliari, *John Bidwell and California* (2003). Information on the later lives of family members appears in Mrs. Eugene Fountain, "The Four Kelsey Brothers" (1964–1965); and William R. Benson, "The Stone and Kelsey 'Massacre' on the Shores of Clear Lake in 1849: The Indian Viewpoint" (1932). Brief coverage of the scalping of daughter Mary Ellen by Comanches in Texas is reported in A. J. Sowell, *Early Settlers and Indian Fighters of Southwest Texas* (1900), 787. The most complete secondary account of the family appears in Philip H. Ault, "Pioneer Nancy Kelsey: 'Where My Husband Goes, I Go'" (1992).

NANCY KELSEY,
"NANCY (ROBERTS) KELSEY'S OWN STORY OF HER LIFE,"
POMO BULLETIN (FEBRUARY 1983),
LAKE COUNTY HISTORICAL SOCIETY, LAKEPORT, CALIFORNIA.
NOTES BY ROY M. SYLAR.

As printed in the February 1983 issue of the Pomo Bulletin *(As told to her daughter, Nancy Rose (Kelsey) Clanton, and recorded in a little leather-bound book only shortly before her death in 1896. Notes have been added to confirm her story and to supply additional information of other related events omitted by Nancy.)*

(Compiled and copied by Roy M. Sylar.)

"SO IT IS MY HISTORY YOU WANT? WELL IT WOULD MAKE A BOOK. THE REMARKABLE ADVENTURES OF MY LIFE ARE AS CLEAR AS IF THEY HAPPENED YESTERDAY. I SUPPOSE THE REASON FOR THIS IS BECAUSE MY MIND IS NOT STUFFED SO FULL OF EDUCATION AS MOST OF THE MINDS ARE AT THIS DAY AND AGE.

"I WAS BORN IN BARREN COUNTY, KENTUCKY, IN 1823 (1 August, 1823), AND MY PARENTS TOOK ME TO JACKSON COUNTY, [Independence] MISSOURI, IN 1826. I WAS MARRIED TO BENJAMIN KELSEY WHEN I WAS VERY YOUNG (14th of October 1839) AND STARTED OVERLAND WITH HIM TO CALIFORNIA IN 1841 (10th of May 1841). WHY DID WE COME SO LONG BEFORE GOLD WAS

DISCOVERED? WELL IT IS BECAUSE OF MR. KELSEY'S HEALTH AND ADVENTUROUS DISPOSITION.

"IN 1837, DR. JOHN MARSH[1] LEFT JACKSON COUNTY, MISSOURI, WITH SOME TRADERS FOR MEXICO. HE MANAGED TO GET THROUGH SONORA (Desert) TO GUAYMAS, AND THERE TOOK A SCHOONER TO MONTEREY, CALIFORNIA. HE MANAGED TO GO UP SAN FRANCISCO BAY AND LOCATE A RANCH NEAR THE MOUTH OF THE SAN JOAQUIN RIVER. HE SENT A LETTER AROUND THE HORN TO MISSOURI, AND HIS WONDERFUL DESCRIPTION OF THIS COUNTRY STARTED US ON OUR ADVENTURES. WE RECEIVED HIS LETTER IN DECEMBER 1840. THE DOCTOR INFORMED MY HUSBAND THAT HE MUST EITHER GO (by way of) THE MOUNTAINS, OR BY SEA. (The mountain route was chosen.) IT WAS A GREAT UNDERTAKING TO COME HERE, AS WE HAD NO ROADS AND NO PILOT, EXCEPT THE SETTING SUN.

Note: Marsh had also sent [John] Bartleson, or [John] Bidwell, an unconfirmed map showing a route across the Rocky Mountains to the headwaters of the so called "Mary's River," thence along that river to San Francisco Bay and Marsh's rancho. Apparently he thought the Sacramento River was a continuation of the Mary's [Humboldt River] and had little, or no, knowledge of the desert and mountain barriers in between. It was on the basis of this map that the Bartleson-Bidwell Party planned their route to California.

"IN MAY 1841, MY HUSBAND SOLD OUT HIS POSSESSIONS, RAISED A COMPANY OF 40 MEN AND WAS READY TO START.

[1]John Marsh, a graduate of Harvard University, lived for six years in New Mexico and Sonora before arriving in California in January 1837. Although licensed as a medical doctor, his interests soon gravitated toward land ownership, and he acquired from local Mexican authorities the right to establish a ranch at the foot of Mount Diablo. Active in his association with Swiss land baron John Sutter, he began writing letters to Missouri to encourage immigration to California. John Bidwell later acknowledged that one of these letters had motivated him to set out for California in 1841. Marsh was murdered in 1856 by a group of robbers. As the Bidwell-Bartleson party discovered, Marsh was a "generally disagreeable man," more interested in profiting from a beleaguered wagon train than in helping its members. See Bancroft, *Works of Hubert Howe Bancroft*, vol. 21, *History of California* 4:730–31; and Bidwell, *Echoes of the Past*, 15. Bidwell described the nature of Marsh and his particular offenses and called him "the meanest man in California." See Bidwell, *A Journey to California*, 54–55.

Captain Fitzpatrick (Thomas "Brokenhand" Fitzpatrick) and thirty more men joined us. They were on their way to establish a mission among the Flathead Indians near the Columbia River. The third day the Indians (friendly Pawnees) towed us across the Call River (Kansas River) in rawhide boats made of buffalo skins. Our oxen swam the river with our wagons.

Note: Nancy's story is interrupted here to fill in a few details regarding the party making this initial adventurous trek in the west in 1841.

John Bidwell, a twenty-year old schoolteacher, had organized the Western Emigration Society which aroused considerable interest among pioneers seeking new lands. In April and May 1841 there were approximately 500 persons assembled at Sapling Grove, near Independence, Missouri, in answer to his call for those wishing to start the trip to California and Oregon Territory, but adverse reports of the hardships and dangers to be encountered along the little known and unblazed trails, plus the apparent youth of the man who was supposed to lead them, discouraged a great number so that when it came time to leave there were only sixty souls willing to take the chance, with four Kelsey brothers and families among them. Also among this group was John Bartleson who threatened to withdraw the support of his eight well armed and well equipped men if he was not named Wagonmaster. Needing this support for the trip into the unknown, Bidwell condescended [consented] and Bartleson had his way. Thus the group became known as the "Bartleson Party."[2] They left Sapling Grove on the 10th of May and three days later, as they were preparing to cross the Kansa[s] River in Indian Territory, they were joined by a party of sixteen missionaries and mountain men led by Thomas "Brokenhand" Fitzpatrick, who were making their way to Flathead Indian country.[3] Soon thereafter they were joined by Reverend Joseph

[2]John Bidwell's negative impressions of John Bartleson at the inception of the trip are stated in Bidwell's *Echoes of the Past*, 22, but Bidwell noted that Bartleson's men were needed to bolster the company's numbers at the beginning of the trip. A list of people who joined the Bidwell-Bartleson party is found in Bidwell, *A Journey to California*, 22–23. Bartleson returned to Missouri in 1842 and died in Jackson County on October 7, 1848. See Nunis, *Bidwell-Bartleson Party*, 257.

[3]The three Roman Catholic priests were Fathers Pierre-Jean De Smet, Nicholas Point, and Gregori Mengarini. They were joined by ten or eleven Canadians, trapper John Gray, and a young English adventurer named W. G. Romaine. See Bidwell, *Echoes of the Past*, 24–25.

Williams and James "Jimmy" John, two lone travelers who caught up with them and swelled the party to seventy-eight persons. By the time this party had reached Green River Valley on the west side of the Rocky Mountains, their number had dwindled to sixty-eight. Upon reaching Soda Springs (now in Idaho) the party split into three groups to go their separate ways, although two of the groups were to travel together as far as Fort Hall. The Missionary party was now down to eight persons including Father Pierre-Jean DeSmet and guided by Fitzpatrick. Twenty-six persons including Samuel and Isaiah [Isaac] Kelsey, and Richard Williams, and their families, headed on to the Willamette Valley of Oregon, and the other thirty-four cast their lot in blazing the California Trail. The California bound group included: Elias Barnett, John Bartleson, Josiah Beldon [Belden], William Belty, John Bidwell, Henry Broloski [Brolaski], David W. Chandler (alias J. M. Jones), Joseph B. Chiles, Grover [Grove] C. Cook (later married Rebecca Josephine Kelsey), V. M. Dawson, Nicholas "Bear" or "Cheyenne" Dawson, Talbot Green (alias Paul Geddes), George Henshaw, Charles Hooper, Henry Huber, James "Jimmy" John, Thomas Jones, Andrew Kelsey, Benjamin Kelsey and his wife and daughter, Nancy (Roberts) Kelsey and Martha Ann Kelsey (14 years [months] old), John McDowell, Green (Samuel) McMahon [Samuel Green McMahan], Nelson McMahan, Michael C. Nye, A. Gwinn Patton, Robert Richman [Rickman], John Roland, John L. Schwarts [Schwartz] (alias John DeSmart), James P. Springer, Robert H. Thomas, Ambrose Walton, Major Walton, and Charles Weber (alias Carlos Waver).

Nancy's story continues:

"MY, THE TURKEYS AND DEER WE DID KILL BEFORE WE STRUCK THE PLATTE! THE EVENING WE STRUCK THE PLATTE (River) WE HAD A WEDDING. IT WAS MISS WILLIAMS TO "ZED" KELSEY, ONE OF MY HUSBAND'S FOUR (three) BROTHERS, WHO BELONGED TO THE COMPANY.

Note: Isaiah [Isaac] "Zed" Kelsey married Winnifred Williams at the banks of the Platte River, in Indian Territory [Nebraska], on 1 June 1841, while enroute to Oregon. The ceremony was performed by Reverend Joseph Williams (no relation to the bride). Isaiah [Isaac] and Winnifred were to make their home at Hillsboro, Washington County, Oregon, where they spent the rest of their lives. Reverend Williams was an ordained Methodist minister, 63 years old and father of sixteen children, when he decided to go West and preach the Gospel among the Indians. In a book he was to write later, he condemned the party as a "wicked band of back-sliders" because only a few would attend his services held along the trail.[4]

"Here I witnessed my first cyclone.[5] It came within a mile of us and I will never forget the awful sight. I saw trees going through the air with their roots and all, just as they were pulled from the ground. If it had struck us our friends left behind would never have known what happened to us. Here on the Platte was where we killed our first buffalo.

There was a fellow we called "Bear" Dawson. He was so named because he told a rather big bear story. How you would have laughed if you had seen him come into camp one day. He was entirely naked. The Indians had found him and stripped him of all his clothes and then started him out to find camp. We corralled ourselves with our wagons and sent three men out to council with them. Fortunately the chief knew Fitzpatrick, and Fitz knew him. The chief and three warriors remained with us over the night, while the rest camped nearby. The next day they all went north, as they said, to fight the Blackfeet.[6]

[4]For his account of the trip, see Williams, *Narrative of a Tour*, which was originally published in 1843. It also contains considerable information about his relationship with the other Protestant missionaries after he settled in Oregon, as well as his contentious relationship with John McLoughlin of the Hudson's Bay Company.

[5]Bidwell's recollection of this tornado and fierce hailstorm on the South Platte River describes the funnel as only a quarter mile away, and the people were braced against their wagons to prevent them from overturning. See *Echoes of the Past*, 32.

[6]For Dawson's own account of this unnerving episode with Cheyennes, see Dawson, *Narrative of Nicholas "Cheyenne" Dawson*, 11–12. For other eyewitness details, see Bidwell, *Echoes of the Past*, 28–30. These very same Cheyennes followed along with the wagon train for two days of trading and socializing before they departed to raid the Blackfeet. Also see Belden, *Josiah Belden*, 38–39.

Note: As reported by Bidwell, there were about forty Cheyennes in this war party that caught and stripped Dawson while he was out hunting. They then followed him back to camp where Fitzpatrick spent most of the night bartering with them to get most of Dawson's clothes back, but finally gave up on his other possessions. As Fitz told the others, Dawson was lucky to escape with his life and should be satisfied.

Only parts of the next few lines of Nancy's story are legible, as recorded in the little leather-bound book. Missing words have been assumed to add continuity.

"IT WAS DANGEROUS FOR US FOR A WEEK AS WE TRAVELED THROUGH A SURGING (herd of buffalo.) WE WERE AFRAID THAT (they would run) OVER US IN THEIR STAMPEDE. (When we) arrived in BLACK-(foot territory we) STOPPED FOR A FEW DAYS AT A LARGE ROCK (Independence Rock) AND DRIED MEAT (from the buffalo we had killed.)

Note: While camped here the party started the tradition of leaving their names on Independence Rock. Bidwell reports great herds of buffalo passing the camp and causing much concernation [consternation] among the party. At night they would have to post men who kept up a steady fire with their guns so the herds would split around the camp. A number of oxen from their stock joined the herds. Jimmy John enjoyed killing buffalo bulls, but Bidwell did not care much for the slaughter, and reported it so.[7]

"AT STEAMBOAT (Soda) SPRINGS (we rested) OUR STOCK, WHILE MR. [Charles] (Hooper hunted for game for our camp.) HE AND TWO OTHER MEN WHO WENT WITH HIM (came upon a band) OF PIUTES [Paiutes]. THE CHIEF (was peaceable and) RETURNED WITH THEM AS HE (had never seen) A WHITE WOMAN.

"HERE THE MISSION PARTY LEFT US. ALL OF THE WOMEN BUT MYSELF WENT WITH THE MISSION PARTY FOR THE COLUMBIA

[7]Many in the party delighted in killing large number of bison along the North Platte River, but Bidwell condemned their waste and contrasted their behavior with the Cheyennes, who killed only what they needed for food. See Bidwell, *Echoes of the Past*, 30.

[River], while I went with my husband and 32 men westward toward the land of California. I say 32 men, but one was only a boy and his name was John Bidwell [21 years old] and he now owns the Chico Ranch. (Location of Chico, California.)

Note: The missionaries and the Willemette [Willamette] Valley bound group remained together only as far as Fort Hall on the Snake River, then went their separate ways. Two of the California bound party also went to Fort Hall to see if they could employ a guide to lead them to California. Finding none, they returned the way they came and caught up with the others for the trek across the desert and mountains to Marsh's rancho.[8] *As for Nancy's comment about the age of John Bidwell, he was born at Chautauqua County, New York, in 1831, this making him between 20 and 21 years of age by the time the party reached Soda Springs, the parting place of the parties. It was in early August 1841, when the parting took place.*

"Let's see, there was Captain Webber (Charles Weber, alias Carlos Waver) who founded Stockton [California], Colonel Richmond (Robert Richman) [Rickman], Captain Joe Childs (Joseph B. Chiles), Josiah Beldon [Belden], and Charley Hooper who were with the crowd. Also Colonel Barlson (John Bartleson). Oh, what a time we did have on the Humboldt (Humboldt River of Nevada) where we had to leave our wagons and proceed on horseback. I had a young babe (Martha Ann Kelsey) to take care of too. At one place the Indians surrounded us but my husband, Ben, leveled his gun on the Chief and made him order his Indians out of arrow range.

[8]Bidwell mentioned in *Echoes of the Past* (pp. 37–39) that during the division of the wagon train at Soda Springs, George Simpson headed back to Fort Laramie, and three others—Henry Peyton, Elisha Stone, and Amos E. Frye—turned back at Green River, hoping to reach the eastern settlements. Bidwell was particularly happy that Benjamin and Nancy Kelsey "remained firm, refusing to be diverted from our original purpose of going direct to California" (p. 38).

Note: Nancy's "Oh, what a time we had on the Humboldt", covers much adventure and hardship. The party became completely lost on the salt flat desert of Great Salt Lake as they searched for the "Mary's River" [Humboldt River] shown on Marsh's map. They finally picked up the Humboldt River, and assuming this to be the "Mary's", followed it to Carson Sink in Nevada. They were surprised to find this river dwindling in flow as they proceeded downstream. By the time they reached the Sink [Humboldt Sink] they had already abandoned their wagons and taken to horseback, but continued to drive their oxen as a food supply on hoof. It was only upon reaching the Sink that they realized there were still greater mountain barriers to cross if they were to reach their destination. Ben Kelsey insisted on keeping the oxen, but they were too slow for Bartleson who, with his small group of followers, would often abandon the main party only to return a while later and beg for food. After passing Carson Sink the party followed up the Walker River, only to come up against the Sierra Nevada Mountains where they took a short rest, but one cold morning when ice started to form it urged them on.

"On my birthday, which was the first day of August, 1841, we camped on the summit of the Sierra Nevadas at the headwaters of the San Joaquin River.

Note: Nancy was a bit confused when recalling at what point her birthday occurred some 55 years later. This event took place as they crossed the summit of the Rocky Mountains, not the Sierra Nevadas, since the party reached Soda Springs, where the original party split into three groups, on 11 August, 1841. It was mid-October when this California-bound group reached the summit of the Sierras. They had made their crossing by way of Sonora Pass and it was by way of the Stanislaus River, a tributary of the San Joaquin, that they made their way down into the San Joaquin Valley.

"Of course we did not know where we were. The party scattered here to find the best way to descend the mountains. I was left with my babe alone, and as I sat there on my horse and listened to the sighing and moaning of the winds through the pines, it seemed the loneliest spot in the world. The descent was so abrupt that an Indian, who had come to us on the mountain, was allowed to lead my horse for part of the way. At one place an old man of the party (George Hanshaw) [Henshaw] became so exhausted, or nearly so, that they had to threaten to shoot him before he would proceed.

"At another place four pack animals fell over a bluff and we never tried to recover them. They had gone so far that it was no use to think of it. We were then out of provisions as we had eaten all of our cattle. I walked bare-foot until my feet were blistered. For two days I had nothing to eat but acorns, my husband came near dying of cramps and it was suggested we leave him out, but I protested and declared I would never leave him as long as there was life. We killed a horse and stayed over until the next day when he was able to go on.

"My husband's brother (Andrew Kelsey) and a man named Jones (Thomas Jones) had strayed from our party while in the mountains (they had been sent out to scout for a route) and we thought them dead, but found their tracks and concluded that they were still alive. This later proved correct. One time I became so weak that I lay down on the ground while Ben went out and killed a deer.

"The San Joaquin Valley was a very dry plain with hardly any grass for our stock (horses and mules), as they had no rain in California for eighteen months, as we afterwards found out. After we had traveled for two days on the plain, Charley Hooper succeeded in killing two coyotes and they were cooked and shared among us.

"As we neared Doctor Marsh's ranch, which is near what is now Martinez, who should come to us but Mr. Jones (Thomas Jones), who was one of the supposed dead men, and one of Dr. Marsh's Indians. They had some farina for me and led us to the ranch, where we arrived on 4 October [November 4] 1841,—55 years ago.

Note: To cross the 9626 feet high Sonora Pass of the Sierra Nevada Mountains, even by modern roads in this day and age, is a chore unto itself, let alone for what it must have been to those weary travelers who had nothing to guide them and who had expended all their energies and resources getting this far on their more than 3000 mile journey across the unknown to reach California. Nancy's story hardly begins to tell of the hardship and trials encountered during the crossing. However, it is remarkable how accurately she could recall the events of her life in 1893, at the age 70 years, when she was then suffering from cancer. Records kept by others, including John Bidwell, bear out her story in almost every detail, except the dates of when the party crossed the Sierra Nevada Mountains and their arrival at Marsh's rancho.

"In December we went up with Sutter (John Sutter) to his fort on the Sacramento River. We were fifteen days making the trip in a rowboat rowed by Indians. Sutter instructed them to swim to the shore with me and child (Martha Ann) in case the boat should capsize. We arrived at the fort on Christmas Day, where I met Joel Walker, who had just arrived with his wife and children.

"So, you see, I was the first American woman in California. I preceeded Mrs. [Mary] Walker by some five months. This winter was a very wet one and in the spring of '42, in April, we left the kitchen door of Sutter's Fort and landed near Cash Creek [Cache Creek, the outlet for Clear Lake] where we camped all summer, killed deer and elk, made Spanish boots out of their hides and saved the tallow.

Note: It was not until the last half of October, 1841, that the Party reached the summit of the Sierra Nevadas, and on 22 October when they killed the last of their oxen for food. It was on 4 November, not 4 October as stated by Nancy, that they arrived at Dr. Marsh's rancho. There are those who say that Mrs. Joel [Mary] Walker was the first white woman to enter California by the overland route, which is probably so, having come down from the Willamette Valley of Oregon where she and her husband were the first white settlers. But it was Nancy (Roberts) Kelsey who was first to cross the Sierra

Nevada Mountains into California by the shorter route, later known as the "California Trail". Their arrival within the state was only a few days apart.

"One day Salvador Vallejo (brother of General Mariana Guadalupe Vallejo) and his men chased a runaway negro nearly into our camp and shot him four times and then ran their swords through him. They said they ran their swords through his body to bring them good luck.

"Salvador then unarmed us and ordered us to be taken to the mission (at Sonoma), but our men stole into their camp that night and quietly recaptured their weapons and we returned to Sutter's Fort. With the profits we made on this hunt, we bought one hundred cattle and took them to Oregon in the spring and summer of 1843. When we started to Oregon we had some trouble to get the cattle to cross the river (Sacramento River) and while the men were working with them the Indians came into camp, took all the guns, and put them in a heap. They were entirely nude and I beckoned to the men for help. "Bear" Dawson came and shot one of the Indians within a few feet of me. They then compelled the rest of them to help (with the cattle crossing). One Indian was forced to swim the river and tow me and the child across in a canoe. The men held guns on him while he did so. It was not a very pleasant situation, I assure you. As the least turn would have upset the boat. Dawson was not to blame for shooting the Indian, as he drew his bow first.[9]

Note: Nicholas Dawson started as a schoolteacher, but that was too tame for him. He left home in Arkansas and wandered the West for six years before returning home to marry a former pupil and bring her to California. He died at the age of 83 years.

[9]In his later reminiscences, Nicholas Dawson omitted mention of this violent event, but he did describe important trade with California Indians that provided necessary food to the hungry overlanders. See Dawson, *Narrative of Nicholas "Cheyenne" Dawson*, 21–22.

"We waited on the west bank of the river for ten days until Joe Gale and (Joel) [Joseph] Walker came up with us. This was the last time I saw John Bidwell. He was on his way to his Chico ranch. He had some trinkets to trade to the Indians.

Note: Bidwell was founder of Chico, California, which was located on his original ranch. He was first to discover gold on the Feather River. He later went into politics, was a California Congressman, five times candidate for governor of the state, and ran for President of the United States on the Prohibition ticket in 1892. He died at Chico on 5 April 1900.

"Near Mount Shasta the Indians bothered us very much by stealing our stock. I crossed the headwaters of the Sacramento (River) fifteen times in one day, and all the time carrying my child on the same horse that I rode. In these mountains one night, the Indians shot several of our horses. The next morning we broke camp with some men remaining to guard the carcasses. We had not gone far when the Indians rushed in for the meat and our men killed several of them.

"We had only proceeded a mile further when Indians assembled in front of us and opened fire. We had a pitched battle in which we had several horses killed and those Indians who were not killed managed to escape. During the fight I sat on my horse and saw it all. One night we had twenty-five horses stolen and a nice mare shot through with an arrow within forty feet of where I was sleeping. The next morning we had another fight with the Indians and I counted twelve of them as they went down before our guns.

"Going down the Siskiyou Mountains[10] we had several

[10]The Siskiyou Trail served as a natural passageway between California and Oregon and had been used by the Hudson's Bay Company intermittently since the 1830s to transport furs from northern California to Fort Vancouver. See Carey, *General History of Oregon*, 243–44; and Gudde, *California Place Names*, 311.

OF OUR CATTLE SHOT FROM AMBUSH AS WE TRAVELED ALONG. AT ELKHORN WE SAW THE BONES OF MEMBERS OF THE HUDSON BAY COMPANY WHO WERE KILLED AT THIS PLACE: EXCEPT TOM KYE, WHO WAS A HALF-BREED HIMSELF. I HAVE SEEN TOM SEVERAL TIMES. HE DID NOT CARE FOR MUCH BUT TO KILL INDIANS AFTER THAT, AND PROVED HIMSELF AT THE BUSINESS.

Note: Northern California and southern Oregon had many bloody Indian wars in those and following years. With the Spanish Missions stopping at Sonoma, the Indians resisting Spanish and Mexican rule for nearly a century had assembled in the area and tried to stop all persons daring to venture into their territory. Overton Johnson and William Winters [Winter], writers and historians, had this to say about the area after visiting there in 1843.[11] *"These southern vallies of oregon, though their present state of nature so lonely, so wild and so secluded; though they now threaten the travelers who pass, at intervals of years, with dangers from rugged mountain path, the swollen torrents and savage arrow; though many a gloomy glen, and rocky gorge, and dark and tangled wood which have been stained with conflict, or storied by some savage ambuscade, still stands to awaken terror in the passerby; yet these vallies, not withstanding their wildness and danger, offer inducements (deadly to the fate of the natives) for which, ere long, the stronger hand of the white man will beat back the present and implaceable inhabitants and make them homes for civilization."*[12]

"WE SOLD OUR STOCK AT FORT VAN COOVER (Fort Vancouver of the Hudson Bay Company on the banks of the Columbia River), BOUGHT DRYGOODS AND MERCHANDISE AND RETURNED TO CALIFORNIA IN 1844. ON OUR RETURN WE HAD BUT FIVE MEN AND AGAIN OUR STOCK WAS STAMPEDED BY INDIANS AT SHASTA. BY THIS TIME I HAD TWO CHILDREN. WHILE THE ARROWS WERE FLYING INTO CAMP I TOOK ONE BABE AND HID

[11] Johnson and Winter, *Route Across the Rocky Mountains*, quote on p. 47.

[12] For the bloody events associated with the Oregon-California border area in the late 1840s and 1850s, see Beckham, *Requiem for a People*, which helps explain the origins of conflict from both Indian and white points of view.

IT IN THE BRUSH AND RETURNED AND TOOK THE OTHER CHILD AND HID IT ALSO. THE MOON WAS SHINING BRIGHTLY AND IT SEEMED TO ME THAT EVERY TIME A GUN WOULD FIRE, THAT I COULD HEAR AN INDIAN FALL INTO THE RIVER. AS I HID THE LITTLE ONES IN THE BRUSH, I WONDERED IF I WOULD EVER SEE DAYLIGHT AGAIN. JUST THINK OF IT. THERE WE WERE WITH ONLY FIVE MEN AND IN ALL, POSSIBLY FIVE HUNDRED INDIANS. (Probably less). WE WERE GLAD TO GET BACK TO SUTTERS FORT AGAIN.

Note: Nancy only briefly passed over this period in her life, but there were certain occurances taking place that are important to her story. Ben and Nancy took up a cabin at Hillsboro [Washington County, Oregon], near his brother Isaiah, where they spent the winter and their third child, Sarah, was born. In the meantime, Ben's father and mother, David and Susan (Cazort) Kelsey, and the rest of their ten children, had arrived in the Willamette Valley from Missouri.

This was Ben and Nancy's third child. Samuel Kelsey (I) died at Sutter's Fort in early 1842, soon after they first arrived there. Baby Samuel lived only 8 days.

The newly arrived brother and sisters were: Elizabeth (Kelsey) East and family; Margaret Frances (later Bussell); Loretta (later Willaims) [Williams]; Rebecca Josephine (later Fowler/Cook/Grattan); David Crockett [Kelsey]; and America (later Hyman) Kelsey. All except Elizabeth and Isaiah were to become early California settlers. As stated before, Isaiah settled at Hillsboro, and the East family settled at Dallas,[13] *Polk County, Oregon, where Elizabeth spent the rest of her life. It was at Ben and Nancy's winter cabin in Hillsboro that Rebecca Josephine married her first husband, Willaim [William] Fowler, on 12 December 1843, and Margaret Frances married*

[13]Dallas was originally settled in the 1840s as the community of Cynthia Ann. Later the name was changed to honor George Mifflin Dallas, who had served as James K. Polk's vice president during the acquisition of Oregon. Although the community's founding fathers failed to win designation as county seat of Polk County, they later raised $17,000 and secured the important branch line of a narrow gauge railroad. See McArthur and McArthur, *Oregon Geographic Names*, 204.

Willaim [William] Bussell on 10 May 1844. The five men making the return trip to California, as mentioned by Nancy, were: Ben, Andy, Sam, and David Kelsey (their father), and their various families, plus either William Fowler, or William Bussell, David and Susan's new Sons-in-law. When David reached California he settled his family at Stockton, where he died of smallpox contacted while befriending an Indian, in 1845. He is buried near the intersection of Fremont and Eldorado Streets in the Civic Center of Stockton. His wife, Susan, and daughter, America, also caught the smallpox. Susan was blinded by the disease and spent her remaining years with her son, Isaiah, at Hillsboro, Oregon, where she died in 1856. America recovered, married George F. Wyman at Sutter's Fort on 7 August 1846, and died at Halfmoon Bay, California on 8 May 1916. It is not known what became of David Crockett Kelsey, the youngest of the Kelsey boys, but he was also on this return trip to California.

Nancy (Roberts) Kelsey's Own Story of Her Life
Continued in the May 1983 issue of the Pomo Bulletin

Part II

"In 1845, we built log cabins in Napa Valley. There was a man named Tilburn lived there then. We were in Napa Valley when the Mexican War, or the Revolution as we called it then, broke out. (1846). My husband offered his services to Fremont (John Fremont). Fremont ordered my husband to kill poor old Don Bersesse (Don Francisco or Nazario Berryessa) whom they had taken from his home on the pretense of capturing him. Good old Don was a neighbor of ours, and a better man never lived, so my husband thought. And of course he refused to do it and expressed his opinion of anyone who would do such a thing. My husband said he would even die himself before he would kill his old friend. Another man obeyed the order and shot the old man down.[14] Mr. Kelsey from that day forth had a personal enmity of the general (Fremont). Years later, Mr. Kelsey applied for a pension, and as he was not regularly mustered in (the U.S. Army) it was necessary for him to get Fremont's recognition, and when the application was made, Fremont refused to sign it.

Note: A part of Nancy's statement about the senseless killing of old Don Berryessa (and a companion) [two companions, the De Haro twins] needs clarification. After the capture of Sonoma by the "Bear Flag Party" on 14 June 1846, John Fremont and his soldiers were called in to put down any resistance to the takeover of Northern California by the Americans. Captain Joaquin de la Torre did organize a resistance group and Fremont and a contingent of the Americans went looking for them to do battle. At the old San Rafael Mission it was found that the Mexicans had circled to the north and were awaiting assistance from south of San Francisco Bay, so it was decided to wait and intercept the men from the south. After a time Don Berryessa and a companion were seen approaching the mission and Fremont ordered Ben Kelsey to go out and shoot them down, as he, Fremont, 'didn't want any live prisoners in his camp." Ben refused, in no uncertain terms, to carry out the order because Berryessa was a good friend of his, and besides, the approaching Mexicans were unarmed. Fremont then gave the order to Kit Carson and Granville Swift, who carried it out without hesitation. Fremont was never to forgive Ben for refusing his order, nor Ben to forgive Fremont for having the order carried out.

"I was sent to Fort Sonoma and rode the distance horseback and carried a one month old babe in my arms (Andrew, Ben & Nancy's fourth child, born 7 April 1846). I was so weak when I arrived at my destination that I could hardly stand up.

---

[14]John C. Frémont later claimed that he ordered the deaths of José de los Reyes Berryessa, the father of Sonomá's alcalde, and two other Hispanic men in retaliation for the murders of two members of the Bear Flag Revolt. Frémont's action produced anger not only among the native California population, but also among Anglo members of the Bear Flag Revolt who liked and respected the Berryessa family. One of the witnesses, Jasper O'Farrell, sent a letter to the *Los Angeles Star* condemning Frémont and referring to him as a man "I must always look upon with contempt and consider as a murderer and a coward." See Rosenus, *General M. G. Vallejo*, 150–51.

"I found Mrs. [Francisca Benicia Carrillo] Vallejo at Sonoma. Her husband had been captured and sent to Sutters Fort. One day an Indian came to Sonoma and the Americans stopped him outside and searched him. On his person, wrapped in bark, they found a letter addressed to Mrs. Vallejo from the Mexicanos requesting her to give a supper in the back yard and at that time they would rush in and kill their enemies. Mrs. Vallejo wrote a reply that the American cannon would kill them all off if they attempted it. Lieutenant [Archibald] Gillespie sent a letter to my husband to overtake Fremont, who had started for Oregon, and tell him to return and help protect Sonoma from the expected attack.[15] My husband did so and when Fremont arrived, his men had not changed their clothes for a month. A hired woman and myself sewed on shirts every day until all of his men had a change. I also baked bread for Fremont during that time.

"The Mexicanos had a man locked up in the Petaluma ranch house[16] (belonging to Gen. Vallejo) and word came that they intended to kill him. Captain (Ezekial) Merritt took several men there and released Todd (this was a man named Cox) their prisoner, who was in a nude condition. They had a fight doing it in which several Mexicanos were killed, but no Americans.

Note: William L. Todd was a nephew to Mrs. Abraham Lincoln and designer of the California Bear Flag raised at Sonoma on 14 July 1846, thus initiating the winning of the state from Mexico. The women furnishing the cloth and sewing the flag were: Nancy Kelsey, Mrs. Benjamin Dewell

[15]Nancy Kelsey's chronology and facts seem confused here since Lieutenant Archibald Gillespie's attempt to reach John C. Frémont along the California-Oregon border occurred prior to the killing of José de los Reyes Berryessa. Also Gillespie traveled directly to Frémont's camp rather than relying on the latter to receive a message from him and return to the Monterey area. See Billington, *Far Western Frontier, 1830–1860*, 163–64.

[16]A photograph of Mariano Guadalupe Vallejo's Rancho Petaluma, as seen in its dilapidated state in the 1870s, appears in Rosenus, *General M. G. Vallejo*, 131.

and Mrs. Mathews. Many of our present day writers leave Nancy out of the making of the "Bear Flag" because some historian said she must have been a very rough person and not deserving of such honors, all because of her devotion to her husband.

"I seldom saw Kit Carson as he was generally away scouting. My goodness, he was wild as a deer. Lindsay [Lindsey] Carson was there with his family, and he and his brother Moses had a ranch up on the Russian River.

Note: Lindsay [Lindsey] and Moses Carson were half-brothers to Kit. Lindsay [Lindsey] later acquired a ranch in Lake County. Other Carsons in Lake County included Andrew Jackson Carson and John M., who may have been cousins to the others. Nice, California, is located on property first taken up by Andrew Jackson Carson.

"After the war there seemed to be some immigration into the country and Mr. [Benjamin] Kelsey and General Vallejo built themselves a sawmill and the enterprise proved very profitable to them. They had from twenty-five to thirty men working for them in the mill and I did all the cooking for them. We had some burrs (grinding stones) in the mill which ground all our flour. Some of the log-rollers (lumberjacks) afterward became very wealthy.

"When gold was discovered (1848), my husband sold out his (interest in the mill) to General Vallejo and went to the mines. He (later) bought sheep in Sonoma at a dollar a head and sold them at the mines at sixteen dollers per head. I suppose that is what you call 16 to 1. When he returned he told me that if I could lift the saddle-bags in which was the gold that he received for his sheep, he would give it all to me, but I couldn't move them. At Kelsey Dry Diggings, 1848, Mr. Kelsey worked Indians and made as high as $100 per day to the Indian. Of course, this kind of digging did not last long.

Note: Kelsey Dry Diggings, or what is presently known as the small community of "Kelsey", is located about six miles north of Placerville, California. The first 36 Indians used to work these diggings were from Lake County, and all returned home well satisfied with their pay. Ben then took fifty more Indians to the diggings, but when he became ill and had to be carried back to Sonoma, these were left on their own at the site. In the wild activity and excitement of the "gold-fever" prevailing at the time, when the California goldrush was just getting underway, the leaderless Indians wandered off and only a few managed to return to their homes. Ben Kelsey has been much criticized for this event by those wishing to do him harm. The main abuse being precipitated by a native named Augustine who claimed to be a surviver, but who was not even there. At the time, Augustine had been taken to Napa to make adobe bricks, from where he had escaped and was in hiding.[17]

Ben did make a considerable fortune during this period. On one occasion he paid $75,000 ransom to save his brother, Samuel, from being shanghaied aboard a ship bound for China. In a speech delivered by Gen. Mariano G. Vallejo at Santa Rosa on 4 July 1876, he gives this account: "To give an idea of the speculative spirit aroused in those days I may state that I was present when Mr. Benjamin Kelsey lent to Mr. Griffith $25,000 at 25 percent, compound interest per month! Captain Frisbie was also present and declared the borrower must be insane: but in the end Griffith paid principal and interest according to the agreement." In this speech, Vallejo brought out the little known fact that he and Ben were appointed the first Indian Agents for California by the interim government set up before California became a state. This appointment was approved by General Stephen W. Kearney [Kearny], civil governor, after takeover from Mexico.[18]

---

[17]Roy Sylar's editorial remarks exonerate the Kelsey brothers from widespread charges that they mistreated Indian laborers. Other eyewitnesses, however, contended that the brothers were among the worst villains in abusing Indians and reducing them to debt peonage. Others charged them with starving their Indian workers. See Cook, *Conflict Between the California Indian and White Civilization*, 305, 311, 320, 475n; and Nunis, *Bidwell-Bartleson Party*, 262–63.

[18]Military governor Stephen Watts Kearny did appoint Mariano Guadalupe Vallejo as Indian subagent of the Sonoma district, but no such official status was extended to Benjamin Kelsey. Vallejo's jurisdiction included the important Clear Lake area, where the Kelsey brothers—Benjamin, Samuel, and Andrew—settled. Andrew was killed by Indians at the Clear Lake ranch in 1849. See Benson, "The Stone and Kelsey 'Massacre,'" 266–71.

"In 1849, we started a trading post way up on the Sacramento River where Mr. Kelsey took sick and we had to bring him down to be doctored. When he returned, his property had been abandoned to the Indians and they made use of the opportunity.

"We bought Salvador Vallejo's stock and applied for a grant of land consisting of nine square leagues bordering clear lake, but the grant was not completed when the Mexican War broke out and we finally lost out. Andy Kelsey and Charley Stone were killed on the ranch by Indians in 1849.

Note: Captain Salvador Vallejo had originally applied for a grant of 16 square leagues (92,000 acres) bordering Clear Lake, for military services to the Mexican government, but the grant was not yet approved when the Mexican War broke out. He had moved in cattle and horses, which had multiplied, and sold these to the partnership of Edward Shirland, Charles Stone, and the Kelsey brothers Benjamin, Samuel and Andrew. This was in country still occupied by Indians, to the north of Napa Valley. About 1846 Charles Stone and Andrew Kelsey moved in to occupy the land and oversee the herds, and to build themselves an adobe dwelling, at what is now Kelseyville, using forced Indian labor, as was the long established custom of the Spanish and Mexican missionaries before them. They were only two white men among approximately a thousand Indians, and used a select few to control the others. In the fall of 1849, two of the Indian overseers, Shuk and Xais by name, agreed to kill a steer on the sly for some natives living nearby. To accomplish this chore they secreted away Stone's and Kelsey's favorite horses to use for the job, which was to be carried out on a rainy night. In attempting to rope the steer one of the horses got away and the Indians returned home empty-handed, and minus one horse. Knowing they would be punished when the loss was discovered, they decided to kill the two white men, after an all night session with others in on the scheme. The next morning, as Stone ventured forth and was preparing to light a fire under a large kettle of grain used to feed the workers, he was shot through with an arrow but managed to fight his way back into the adobe house where he died in the attic. Andy Kelsey was caught at the door of the adobe and after a fierce struggle, made a run for the nearby creek with an arrow in his back. Upon swimming the creek he was captured on the other side and held while a spear was driven through his heart. This is the story told by Rag-Ga-Nal (Wampum Gatherer) Benson, a half-breed Indian who learned it from those participating in the affair. Since this incident brought on the Bloody Island Massacre of Indians by U.S. Army troops the following year, it is much publicized in Lake County history and has been used by some to damage the Kelsey image. A number of variations of the murders have been published, but since Benson obtained his version directly from the participants, it is believed to be the only true one. When the newly formed California government took over, the Salvador Vallejo grant was denied, so the partnership of Shirland, Stone and the Kelsey brothers lost out.

As for the forced labor treatment of Indians in California, Theodore H. Hittall had this to say, regarding Spanish rule, in his 1897 "History of California." [Theodore H. Hittell, History of California, *4 vols. San Francisco, 1885–1897.]*

"It depended on the individual character of the missionary priest on how the Indians were treated. Besides being priest, teacher, general provider and physician, the missionary was also taskmaster and despot over the liberty and even life of his subjects, and absolutely irresponsible. He assumed the right not only to impose regulations, but to judge what constituted offences; and was always attended by soldiers entirely dependent on his will to carry out sentences. The most usual punishments were whippings, imprisonment, or the stocks, though sometimes death was inflicted."

The History also tells us how monitors were assigned to each village, or rancheria, to spy on his neighbors and report their delinquencies. How all were required to labor in the fields under threat of lashings by the soldiers, who were always on the lookout for delinquents. It goes on to state: "It cannot justly be claimed their (the Indians) condition were bettered by being herded up, taught to repeat prayers and responses they could not understand and much less appreciate, and compelled to their unwilling tasks by the lash. Also it cannot be justly claimed that an occasional dish of pozoli (cooked grain or maize) and reception into the bosom of the church were fair equivalent for the loss of being masters of their own actions and pursuit of happiness in their own way. None of them so far as has been found, were ever cultivated into better men or women; nor were any of them, or their descendants, advanced in the path of genuine civilization." Stone and Kelsey patterned their treatment of Indians in a like manner. This is not to condone their actions, but to show they were not alone at the time, and do not deserve all the blame for their action.

"In the same year (1849) I was riding into Sonoma from a place we had bought, about a mile from town, when an ugly looking Indian tried to lasso me. He tried to get me to run my horse so he could drag me off, but I refused, and kept him from it only by threatening to shoot him if he raised his rope. I had left my pistol at home and was unarmed, but he concluded to let me go and not risk it. He cursed me and I went into the fort and told about it. The Indian was captured and sentenced to 100 lashes. I went home with the medicine I had bought for my sick husband, but instead of taking it, he rode into town and shot the Indian dead.[19]

"In 1850, we went to Humboldt (Bay) and shipped our things by water. The mountains, in what is now called Mendocino County, were very rough and we did not see a white person on the trip. Some Indians opened fire on us, but my husband killed the chief and the rest ran away. Our trip to Humboldt proved unprofitable.

Note: Nancy & Ben were among the first settlers at Eureka and Arcata on Humboldt Bay. The fight with Indians as they crossed through the wilds of Mendocino County is verified by an account appearing in the 13 September 1850 edition of the Daily Alta California newspaper of Sonoma. This article

[19]Members of the Kelsey family seemed to experience more "Indian problems" in California and Oregon than did most families, but they had a reputation for causing their own problems in some cases. The hundred lashes delivered on this Indian and his subsequent murder by Benjamin Kelsey were fairly typical of the actions taken by many settlers in the 1850s. See the numerous eyewitness examples presented in Heizer, *Destruction of California Indians.*

says in part: "There is a brotherhood of Kelseys living in Sonoma who are among the oldest settlers of the State. These brothers have been at open anmity with the Indians of the country. One of their number was killed some time since, by a party of Indians, for cruelty to one of their tribes—. The Kelsey brothers, we are told, started from Sonoma about six weeks since, taking with them their "household goods", with the intention of living their residence upon the broad lands that border Humboldt Bay. On their way across the mountains which separate the valley of Sacramento from the coast waters, they were attacked by a party of Indians, and quite a severe battle ensued. Some gentlemen who arrived in Sonoma, on Monday last, brought intelligence of the skirmish, which the Kelseys emerged unhurt. These gentlemen are from Trinity, and report having been robbed of everything enroute, by the Indians, who are infuriated against the whites, particularly against the Kelsey brothers." Samuel Kelsey was with Nancy & Ben on their crossing to Humboldt Bay.

"In 1851, I returned to our place at Sonoma. I came down by water on a little boat called the "Sea Gull"[20] and we came within two lengths of the boat of striking a rock. My husband and colonel Mc Gee (Col. Redik McKee, [Redick McKee][21] newly appointed U.S. Indian Agent for California) went through the Shasta and down the Sacramento River.

"We had sold our stock on the lake ranch, and receiving only $13,000 down. We never succeeded in getting the rest.

[20]The *Sea Gull* was a large ship captained by a Mr. Tichenor, who in March 1851 began the run between San Francisco and Portland for a charge of eighty dollars to each passenger. See Lockley, *Conversations with Pioneer Men*, 129–30.

[21]In 1850, President Millard Fillmore appointed three agents to oversee Indian affairs in adjoining districts of California—Oliver Wozencraft, George Barbour, and Redick McKee. They were directed to meet with tribal representatives, negotiate the formation of reservations, and pay compensation to tribes in cases where their rights had been violated. Although McKee took his responsibilities seriously, state militia forces attacked Indian encampments regardless of whether they were guilty of depredations. Unfortunately all three agents became wrapped up in financial scandals that destroyed their credibility. See Hurtado, *Indian Survival*, 118, 132, 137, 140–41.

Note: After the murders of Andy Kelsey and Charles Stone, in 1849, the Lupyomi Rancho in Lake County remained unattended for a time, and a Public Administrator took over when title to the ranch, purchased from Salvador Vallejo, was denied by the newly formed State government. The Public Administrator then sold all the cattle and horses left in the area, "as is, where is", to a group of men including Lindsay [Lindsey] & Moses Carson, J. Broome Smith, and Edwin A. Sherman, who formed a company to take over the stock belonging to the remaining partners of Shirland, Stone, and the Kelsey brothers. These men made three stock drives of 1200 to 1500 head of cattle and hundreds of horses each, (estimated total of 4200 cattle and about 1200 horses), from which the original partnership realized $13,000 as down payment, or $2.50 a head. Since sheep were selling at $16 at the goldfields, it is wondered what became of the rest of the profits from this sale).

"In 1859, we started for Mexico for my husband's health. In 1861, we drifted into Texas where we were attacked by Comanche Indians. The men were out hunting turkeys and a neighbor woman and myself were along with our children when I discovered the Indians approaching our camp, which was situated in a brushy place, and I loaded the guns we had, and suggested we hide ourselves. The oldest two girls (Margret [Margaret] and Mary Ellen) ran and hid in the brush and the sixteen year old boy (Andrew) looked out for himself by hiding alone. We and the smaller children hid ourselves in a cave in the side of a ravine. I could hear the Indians above, but they did not discover us. I had forgotten to hide the money which we brought along to buy cattle for the California market, which was all we did own on earth and amounted to $10,000. After they had taken the money, pillaged the camp and started off, they found the girls. They succeeded in catching one of the girls (Mary Ellen) and the other said she could hear the blows as they struck her down. Poor girl, she was only thirteen years old, and even now I can hear the screams that she made when they caught her.

"We returned to camp and heard the girl's (Margaret) story, but could not find the captured one. She had recovered sufficiently to wander around in search of help. Oh, the anxiety of that night! We found her the next day and my anguish was horrible when I discovered she had been scalped. My husband and seventeen men followed them (the Indians) for 200 miles, but failed to overtake them. The poor girl (Mary Ellen) died in Fresno when she was eighteen years old, from the injuries she had received six (five) years before. My girl (Margaret) always said one of the brutes was a white man painted as an Indian.

Note: Mary Ellen lived in a demented condition the rest of her short life, after being scalped by the Comanches.

"When we came back through to California we had but one Indian fight on the way, which was at Rock Springs, New Mexico.

Note: This one last fight with Indians is glossed over by Nancy with this one statement. She and Ben were driving sheep back to California and either Apaches or Navahos tried to steal them, but were driven off.

"I have lived in Owens Valley at the time of the big earthquake there. I have enjoyed riches and suffered the pangs of poverty. I saw General Grant (U. S. Grant) when he was little known. I baked bread for General Fremont and talked to Kit Carson. I have run from bear and killed most other kinds of wild game.

"My husband died in Los Angeles in 1888—. And thus ends Nancy (Roberts) Kelsey's own story of her life, as told by herself.

Note: Nancy was born 1 August 1823 at Barren County, Kentucky and died at her homestead in Cuyama Valley, Santa Barbara County, California, 9 August 1896, a victim of cancer. Her grave in lonely Cottonwood Canyon, is monumented by a full length bronze slab, provided by the Miocene Chapter of the Native Daughters of the Golden West, on which is depicted a covered wagon in raised relief and the inscription: "The Burial Place of Nancy Kelsey, Born 1823, the First White Woman to Cross the Plains and Over the Sierra Nevada Range into California. She Is Also Known as the Betsy Ross of California."

After their many adventures, Ben and Nancy took up residence in Cuyama Valley, but a drought drove them to Los Angeles where Ben took a job building roads, and where he died in 1888 and is buried in the old Rosedale Cemetery. After his death Nancy moved back to Cuyama Valley where she was known as the "Cuyama Angel" because of her care for the sick and those in need. Her last two wishes were to be buried beside her husband, and in a "Store-bought coffin". However, only the last was realized, because of the difficulty in transporting her body from the isolated place of her death. Her "store-coffin" was brought in by pack-mule and she was buried near her last place of residence by sympathisizing neighbors. Nancy died alone and unattended, as she would have it. A neighboring rancher had dropped by for a chat, and finding her stock unattended, entered her cabin to find her body lying on the floor. Thus died Nancy (Roberts) Kelsey, Western pioneer and the first American woman to brave the unknown dangers of the "California Trail", and make California history.

Ben and Nancy had ten children during their long period of marriage, which are skipped over in her narrative. These were: Martha Ann, born 1839, who made the crossing into California with her parents; Samuel (I), born 1842 at Sutter's Fort but lived only eight days; Sarah Jane, born 1843 at Hillsboro, Oregon; Margaret, born 1844 in Napa Valley; Andrew, born 1846 in Napa Valley, Mary Ellen, born 1848 and scalped by the Comanches in 1861; Nancy Rose, born 1852; Georgia, born 1857; William, born 1859; and Samuel (II), born about 1861.

1842

Medorem Crawford, "Trip Across the Plains"

Raised in central New York but ambitious about seeking new opportunities in the West, twenty-three-year-old Medorem Crawford decided to accompany family friend Elijah White to Oregon. White had first traveled to the Pacific Northwest as early as 1837, when dispatched there by the Methodist Board of Missions. Now, in 1842, he led the first substantial American migration to the rich agricultural lands of the Willamette Valley (second only after the Bidwell-Bartleson party of 1841). As Crawford's journal indicates, the transcontinental crossing did not go smoothly from the time they departed from Independence, Missouri. Members of the sixteen-wagon caravan bickered over whether to remain several days with a sick woman or continue the trip without delay. White's order to kill all the dogs of the party because of their constant yelping and frightening livestock, as well as to prevent rabies, outraged many people and brought doubt about his leadership abilities. Only after Lansford Hastings was elected to replace White did tensions subside, but even then the physical demands of the western passage proved challenging. Some members were even reduced to carrying personal possessions on their backs after departing Fort Hall. As the subagent for local Indian affairs, White represented federal interests in Oregon, but he also worked with local settlers to create a legislative framework that had not yet been approved in Washington, D.C.

Medorem Crawford's journal of the 1842 trip remains one of the most important accounts of the early migrations to the Pacific Northwest.

The wealth of detailed information about specific landmarks along the Oregon Trail represented a virtual guidebook even before any official guidebooks were published. He also reported candidly the daily concerns of overlanders who had little advance knowledge of what landscape lay over the next hill or what new dangers they might encounter each week. In short, this wagon train was like an untested experiment that had to invent its own rules for the great migration. Fortunately, Stephen H. L. Meek, experienced fur trapper and brother of Joe Meek, served as guide and general adviser to the caravan.

Medorem Crawford not only weathered the trials and tribulations of the 1842 transcontinental crossing, he went on to achieve success in his personal and public life in Oregon. He later married Adeline Brown, a member of the same wagon train, and he became a highly respected regional freighter, hauling goods around the Willamette Falls for later-arriving sojourners. Between 1847 and 1849, he served in Oregon's provisional legislature and in 1860 was elected to the Oregon State Legislature. During the Civil War, his expertise was sought out by federal officials in Washington, D.C., who assigned him to a military rank of captain in the U.S. Volunteers. He successfully led protective expeditions along the Oregon Trail during 1861–1863, a period that witnessed increased tensions with Indians and shortages of supplies in the West. In 1864, Crawford was appointed collector of internal revenue for Oregon, a position he held for five years. Following that stint as a federal officer, he served as appraiser of customs at Portland between 1871 and 1875. After putting public life behind, he assumed an active farmer's life in Yamhill County, Oregon, until his death in 1891. In its obituary column, the *Morning Oregonian* declared of Medorem Crawford: "As a pioneer he was among the most intelligent, far-seeing and energetic, and as a State-builder, he bore a very important part."

Crawford's journal of the 1842 overland trip was first published in *Sources of the History of Oregon*, vol. 1 (Eugene, Ore.: Star Job Office, 1897), with only brief biographical remarks by F. G. Young. This rather obscure version was reproduced as *Journal of Medorem Crawford* (Fairfield, Wash.: Ye Galleon Press, n.d.). Also useful for understanding

Medorem Crawford.
From Pioneers of 1842. *Courtesy of Clackamas County Historical Society, Oregon City, Oregon.*

Crawford's role in the 1862 Oregon Trail caravan is his official report to Brigadier General Lorenzo Thomas. This has been reprinted and edited in Medorem Crawford, "Report of Captain Medorem Crawford" (1984). Merrill Mattes awarded four stars of excellence to Crawford's 1842 journal. Now, with this new printing, emerges a copy of the journal that contains editorial notes and corrections of the original text.

The first entry of Crawford's journal began with March 17, 1842, in Havana, New York, and continued as he traveled by rail and boat to St. Louis, and eventually to Independence, Missouri. I have begun reprinting the journal with the entry of May 6 at Independence as twenty-three-year-old Crawford made preparations to head west into "Indian Country" with this important wagon train.

Medorem Crawford, "Journal of Medorem Crawford: An Account of His Trip Across the Plains with the Oregon Pioneers of 1842." In *Sources of the History of Oregon*, vol. 1, edited by F. G. Young, pp. 3–26. Eugene, Ore.: Star Job Office, 1897.

[May] 6. [1842] Rode to Independence from camp 18 M. [May] 7, Returned, 3 more waggons came to camp. May 8, Sunday went to Shawnee meeting, returned by way of Mission. 10 Uncommon dry an hot, no rain since we came to camp. 12, went to Independence, a fine shower. 14, Doctor [Elijah White] came to camp with 36 Cattle. 16 Left camp at 1 o'clock E. drove 15 mi. and camped at 7 o'c. E. on the Santafe rout,[1] found water pleanty, wood & pasture scarce.

In our company were 16 waggons & 105 persons including children & 51 men over 18 years of age 17. Started at 9 o'c. M. detained 1/2 hour by losing the trail. Left the Santa Fee trail at 2 o'c and camped at 1/2 past 3 evening, weather verry warm. Traviled about 12 miles. 1 more wagon and 3 men came on. 18. A violent rain this morning much excitement in camp about Dogs: 22 dogs shot, stoped raining 9 o'c.

May 18, Started at 1 o'clock E. without a track endeavoring to find the right trail. Camped on the right trail at 7 o'c. E. Traviled 10 miles.

19. A severe rain this morning; laid out and got verry wet. Started at 1/2 past 9 M. detained by crossing 2 creeks stoped at 2 E. traviled 5 miles.

20. Verry heavy rain last night & cloudy this morning. Moved camp about one mile. All gone ahead except 3 wagons who are detained with a sick child.

21. Another rainy night & cloudy cold & uncomfortable morning. Mrs. Lancaster's[2] only child a daughter 16 months old died 10 o'clock

[1]By 1842, the Santa Fe Trail was already well established, having been regularly traveled for the previous twenty-one years. Thus it was only logical that Crawford's group would head slightly southwest through modern Kansas City before turning north, where they intersected with the trail that came out of Westport. Within a few short years, this second route became more popular and made it unnecessary for travelers to initially dip south along the Santa Fe Trail. See Franzwa, *Maps of the Oregon Trail*, 17–37.

[2]Refers to Judge Columbia Lancaster, his wife, and their ailing infant daughter. Judge Lancaster did make a complete journey, in 1847, to Oregon country and had a successful career there. See Hastings, *Emigrants' Guide to Oregon and California*, 7.

M. the Doctor called the disease symptomatick fever accompanied with worms. Continues to rain moderately. May 21. After burying the child we started and drove 6 miles.

22d Sunday started at 7 o'clock M. and drove 25 miles over a beautiful country; camped in good season. 23d Some rain last night & cloudy cool morning. Started at 9 o'clock M. drove to the Kansas river and crossed with safty, Distance 10 miles. 24. Stoped today to repair waggons.

25. Started at 4 o'clock E. drove 6 miles camped at 7 o'clock E. part of the company still ahead. 26. Started at 7 o'clock M. considerable rain, overtook company at 2 o'clock, took dinner and all started together. Camped on Vermillion Creek at 7 o'clock E. traviled 18 miles.

May 27. Mrs. Lancaster verry sick & unable to travil. Part of the company unwilling to wait & went on, much dissatisfaction in the camp. Capt. [Elijah] White[3] rode on and found the company about 8 miles ahead they agreed to wait untill Sunday morning for Mr. Lancaster. The weather is verry fine and the country around delightful.

28. Rainy morning, Mrs. Lancaster some better. Started at 1/2 past 9 oc. M. Cleared off warm, arrived at camp 1/2 p. 4 o'clock E. traviled 8 miles, weather verry hot.

29. Sunday Mrs. Lancaster is verry low, much dissatisfaction in the camp, some want to go on and some want to stay. 3 wagons went on 2 miles, a very warm day. 30 All the wagons except Mr. Lancaster started at 1/2 past 6 o'clock M. cool wind. 30th May Mr. Lancaster concluded to take his wife back. Capt. White and others accompany him to the K.[ansas] river. Stoped to dinner 1 1/2 hours. Camped at 1/2 past 6 o'clock E. traviled 20 miles. 31. Started at 1/2 past 5 oc. M. Stoped 2 1/2 hours for dinner, camped on Blue River[4] at 4 o'clock E. traviled 15 miles; most splendid spring water there, met 4 waggons from the Mountains,[5] 3 o'clock.

June 1st Started at 1/2 5 M. commenced raining at 6 stoped 3 hours, went on after the rain ceased. Stoped 2 hours for dinner. Camped at

[3]Elijah White was elected leader of the expedition and was given the honorary title of captain. See Lovejoy, "Lovejoy's Pioneer Narrative," 241.

[4]This crossing is at the present-day Red Bridge, south of metropolitan Kansas City, and was used by wagons on both the Oregon and Santa Fe trails. See Franzwa, *Maps of the Oregon Trail*, 31.

[5]These four wagons were probably returning from fur trade activities in the Rocky Mountains.

5 o'clock E. traviled 10 miles. Doct. [Elijah] White overtook us at 4 o'clock E.

2d. Tremendous rain & wind last night. Commenced standing guard last night. Cold wind & disagreeable morning. Started at 1 o'clock E. Camped at 7. E. traviled 8 miles.

June 3d The company started at 5 oclock M. & left myself with 3 others to wait for Mr. [Hugh] Burns and others who were detained by Mr. Lancaster.

4. Started at 6 o'clock M. intending to go back to the Blue River & there stay for Mr. Burns. Met Mr. Burns & his company together with O'Fallen [William O. Fallon] 2 miles back, turned & came on with them. Stoped 2 hours for dinner. Camped at 6 o'clock, E. traviled 22 miles. Cold wind. 5. Sunday, Started at 6 o'clock M. Stoped 1 1/2 hours for dinner, overtook the company. Camped on the Blue [River] at 1/2 past 4 o'clock E. traviled 21 miles.

6. All started together at 7 o'clock M. commenced raining at 9, camped at 10, rain ceased, took dinner and started at 1 o'clock. Camped at 6 o'clock E. traviled 16 miles rainy night. 7. June, cold, damp, & disagreeable morning rained untill 10 o'clock M. Started at 1/2 past 1 o'clock, camped at 1/2 past 6 o'clock E. traviled 10 miles.

8. Cloudy morning started at 1/2 past 7 o'clock. Stoped for dinner at 1/2 p. 11: started at 1/2 p. 2. Camped at 7 o'clock E. on the head waters of the Blue R. which we have been following up for the last 3 days, good water & wood, traviled 16 miles.

9. Left Blue R. at 6 o'clock M. Crossed the Pawnee Trail at 8 o'clock. Stoped at 1/2 p. 12 for dinner without wood or water except what we carried with us. Started at 2 o'clock & traviled through a ridge of country destitute of wood & water. Camped at 7 o'clock E. on the Platte R. traviled 25 miles.

June 10. Started at 8 o'clock M. & followed up the Platte R. Stoped for dinner at 1/2 past 12, started at 2. Camped at 5 o'clock E. traviled 12 miles.

J. 11. Difficulty between Doct. White & John Force. Started at 8 o'clock M. stoped for dinner 2 hours, camped at 5 1/2 o'clock E. traviled 10 miles. 12. Sunday, Started at 7 o'clock M. Stoped at 12, found a band of Buffalo near the camp nearly 100 killed 3 very good Bulls. Started at 3, saw many Buffalo. Camped at 6 o'clock E. traviled 14 miles. Buffalo came close around the camp killed 6.

13. Large herds of Buffalo in plain sight around the camp. Started in good season. Saw thousands of Buffalo traviled 15 miles, little feed for horses.

June 14. Our animals alarmed last night by the Buffalo approaching the camp. 2 oxen shot by the Guard through mistake but neither of them killed. Started at 8 o'clock M. Commenced raining at 1/2 p. 11. Stoped for dinner at 12. Started 1/2 p. 2. Camped 18 miles.

15. Started at 7 o'clock M. Saw thousands of Buffalo near the trail stopped for dinner at 1/2 p. 11, good wood and pasture, but poor water, verry warm day.

The month for which Capt. White was elected being up the company elected Mr. [Lansford] Hastings by a majority of 12 over Mr. [Stephen] Meek.[6] Concluded not to move camp today, traviled 9 miles.

16. Remain in camp today to wash our clothes.

June 16. More difficulty and misunderstanding in the company. Doct. White with a few others concluded to leave.

17. Rain this morning. The majority of the company started at 8 o'clock under Capt. Hastings. Two waggons and 13 men remained [with] Capt. Fallen [Fallon]. Started at 11 o'clock passed the other party and camped at 6 o'clock. They passed us again and camped 3 miles ahead, we traveled 14 miles, quite cold.

18. Started at 7 o'clock. Cold wind & extremely uncomfortable. Commenced to rain at 10 o'clock stoped. Started at 2 camped at 7 on the South fork of Platte [River] traviled 18 miles. Capt. H.[astings] 2 miles ahead. For 2 days we have seen no Buffalo. Capt. Fallen [Fallon] brought us some meat.

June 19. Sunday, Started at 7, stopped for dinner 2 1/2 hours within 1

[6]By this point, Elijah White had been deemed unworthy of leadership by a majority of the party, and he was replaced by Lansford Hastings, who defeated Stephen Meek in a democratic election. Crawford was more than charitable toward his friend White on this issue because he implied that White merely stepped aside as "captain" because his month-long term had expired at that point. Indeed, on the next day, the caravan began to split up. See Hafen, *Broken Hand*, 180–81; and Hastings, *Emigrants' Guide to Oregon and California*, 8–9.

mile of Capt. Hastings. Camped on the Platte within 1/2 mile of the other company at 6, traviled 20 miles.

20. Capt. Hastings & comp. crossed over the river & we followed immediately.

The South Fork [of the Platte River] where we crossed is 1/2 mile wide but not deep the bottom is quick sand. Left the South Fork and took N. W. [direction] for the N[orth] Fork.[7] The other company went south of us. Camped on the North Fork. The other company 2 miles behind, traviled 15 M.

21. Started early and kept up the River good road in the forenoon. Stopped 3 hours for dinner, several hunters from the other company took dinner with us, some hills to cross Camped early traviled 20 miles.

22. Started early, good road. 3 men left the other Com. for Fort Laromie [Fort Laramie] took dinner with us.

22. Capt. Fallen [William O. Fallon] & Esq. [Nathaniel] Crocker went on to Fort L[aramie]. verry warm. Camped early traviled 20 miles. Mosketoes pleanty.

23. Started early, kept along the river, water good. Saw some boatmen from the Fort stoppod 3 hours for dinner. Camped early traviled 16 miles.

24. Started early drove verry fast stopped for dinner nearly oposite the Chimney a very remarkable mound rising like a pyramid some 100 feet and then a perpendicular column standing on the top probably 200 feet hign. Saw a Buffalo crossing the River, Chaised him back to the hills. The most remarkable thing I have seen is the deception in distances. Bluffs which appear within 1 mile are often 5 miles from us.[8] Camped early traviled 20 miles.

June 25. Started 7. Cattle's feet verry sore traviled slow. River bottom 3 to 5 miles wide, stopped for dinner 4 hours, verry hot, left the River

---

[7]Here the party had reached present-day North Platte, Nebraska, and they had moved up to the north branch of the Platte River. A detailed discussion of the various river crossings that developed over time in this area is found in Baresel and Baresel, "Trails and Fords," 13–24.

[8]Strangely enough the only landmark that Crawford mentioned in the Nebraska Panhandle is Chimney Rock. Unlike most travelers who recorded their impressions of nearly every bluff and unique rock formation along this leg of the trail, he merely described the Scotts Bluff area as "the most romantic scenery I ever saw." His remarks about the underestimation of distances between landmarks was a viewpoint shared by many overlanders.

[North Fork of the Platte River] traviled 12 miles. Camped without water or wood in a valley bordered on each side by high Bluffs presenting the most romantic scenery I ever saw.

26. Sunday, Started early without breakfast came to good wood and water at 8 o'clock. Camped on the side of a hill in a grove. Started 1 o'clock saw the other company coming on, drove to Horse Creek[9] camped traviled 14 miles. Horses verry much frightened about midnight nearly all broke lose.

27. Started at 4 o'clock without breakfast stopped on the River at 10 1/2 o'clock. Started at 1 o'clock verry sultry day. Cattle verry near giving out. Camped at sundown, traviled 18 miles.

28. Started late drove to the Forts by noon, traviled 10 miles. Found 2 Forts[10] with several men at each whose business it is to trade with the Indians. Capt. H. [Lansford W. Hastings] came up, 5 o'clock.

29. Preparing carts & disposing of our cattle in order to expedite our journey.

30. Verry buisy preparing to start tomorrow. July 1. Difficulty between Doct. White and Capt. Fallen [Fallon]. Fallen refused to go with us. Remained here all day. 2d joined the other company under Capt. Hastings. Started at 9 o'clock met a company from the mountains near the Fort. Camped at five, good wood and water poor grass, traviled 12 miles through a hilly and barren country.

July 3. Sunday Entered what is called the Black Hills.[11] Traviled 15 miles over bad road without seeing water. Mr. Fitch Patrick [Thomas Fitzpatrick] employed as guide came to camp.[12]

---

[9]Horse Creek, about halfway between Scotts Bluff and Fort Laramie, had been an important landmark since the early fur trade era and was the scene of an extraordinary Indian treaty council in 1851. See Hafen, *Broken Hand*, 284–300.

[10]One of these two fur-trading establishments is almost certainly Fort Platte (1841–1845), built by luckless trader Lancaster P. Lupton, and the other is possibly the early version of Fort William. See Hafen and Young, *Fort Laramie and the Pageant of the West*, 67–71; and Lupton, "Fort Platte, Wyoming," 83–108.

[11]Not to be confused with the more celebrated Black Hills of western South Dakota, this range of mountains lay directly west of Fort Laramie and includes the prominent feature known as Laramie Peak. See Franzwa, *Maps of the Oregon Trail*, 108–113.

[12]Elijah White hired experienced mountain man Thomas Fitzpatrick as a guide for $300 after the party split into two components. His task was to lead White's group to Fort Hall. See White, *Ten Years in Oregon*, 114.

4th. Waggon to repair. Wrote a few lines to my Parents. Started at noon had a verry rough road. Came to water 6 1/2 o'clock, traviled 11 miles. Cart broke down 2 miles from camp.

5. Repaired the cart. Started at noon found good water at three o'clock, had some heavy hills to rise. Buffalo very scarce. Camped early good wood, water and grass, traviled 9 miles.

6. Started at six drove on at a good pace until noon found a first rate camping place. Concluded to remain here today as there was no good chance ahead, traviled 12 miles.

July 7. Started early traveled over a rough mountainous & barren country found no good camping place until late afternoon traviled 16 miles, found a fine band of Buffalo cows.

8. Started at 8 o'clock had a verry hilly road stopped for dinner at 12 1/2 o'clock on creek started at 4 camped on the Platte, good wood and water but short grass, travlied 15 miles.

9. Started at 7 o'clock stopped at 9 1/2 on Deer Creek.[13] Second trial of Mr. [S. W.] Moss for not standing guard. Jury could not agree. Started at 2 camped at 7, traviled 15 miles. Saw several bands of fine Buffalo cows our hunter killed one I think decidedly the best meat I ever eat.

10. Sunday Started at 7 verry heavy west wind yesterday & today.

July 10. Sunday, Crossed over the Platte & camped traviled 11 miles.
11. Started at 8, left the Platte & Black Hills traviled 12 miles over hilly roads & camped in sight of the Red Butes[14] good water and grass but no wood. Cool wind.

12. Started in good season saw an abundance of Buffalo crossed some verry Rocky Hills said to be the commencement of the Mountains. Stopped for dinner 2 hours. Camped in a little valley surrounded with bushes grass good & first rate water and wood, traviled 16 miles.

---

[13]This landmark, in present-day Glenrock, Wyoming, later became a more famous spot along the Oregon and California trails when, in 1857, Joseph Bisonette established a trading post and blacksmith shop on the spot. It later served as a stage stop and Pony Express station but was burned down by the Sioux in 1866. See Haines, *Historic Sites along the Oregon Trail*, 173–76.

[14]Red Buttes is southwest of present-day Casper, Wyoming, and was an important location for several North Platte River crossing sites that developed in the 1840s and 1850s. See Haines, *Historic Sites along the Oregon Trail*, 188–89.

13. Verry cold, water in a pail froze ice like thick window glass.[15] Started early raized a long hill detained by wagons breaking down 1 hour.

July 13. Stopped for late dinner on verry warm road level and sandy not a particle of grass, passed bedds of white substance partaking of the nature of salt and magnetia &c. Camped at sunset on Sweet Water, traviled 20 m. Baily [Bailey] shot while walking through camp by accidental discharge of a gun from a waggon, he lived about one hour.[16]

14. Buried Baily near Independence Rock 1/2 mile from camp. My feelings on this occasion can hardly be described. A young man in the vigor of youth and health taken from our company wraped in a Buffalo Robe & buried in this dismal Prairie. What sad tidings for his Parents & friends who like my own are far from here. Went out hunting Buffalo.

July 15. Layed about 15 miles from camp last night in company with three others. Killed a Bull and as we had eaten nothing since we left camp we soon built a fire and roasted some meat, killed a cow about 11 o'clock, got into camp towards night found all the rest of the company had more meat than us. Today Capt. Hastings month being up himself and Lieu Lovejoy were re-elected.[17] 16. Concluded to move camp nearer to the Buffalo. Started at 8 o'clock followed up the Sweet Water [Sweetwater River] at the foot of a tremendous mountain composed of solid rock. Sweet water passes through a gap in this mountain, great curiosity.

July 16. Camped on Sweet water at 3 o'clock. Went with 2 others about 1 mile from camp and ascended the mountain after having

---

[15]Although this entry was dated July 13, and the daytime heat could produce intolerable temperatures, it was not unusual for overlanders to experience some nights on the High Plains of Wyoming when water would freeze. This is another reminder of the unpredictable nature of weather and other unpleasant realities of trail life. Entries to follow indicate how frequently members of the party traveled in cold and wet weather across Wyoming.

[16]Bailey's full name was not given, but death by accidental discharge of a firearm was a common event on the overland trail. It was not the last firearm accident for this party before they reached their Oregon destination. See Potter, "Firearms on the Overland Trails," 2–12; and Lovejoy, "Lovejoy's Pioneer Narrative," 244.

[17]Most of the party obviously approved the reelection of Lansford Hastings and Asa Lovejoy as leaders on the trail. No mention was made of whether Elijah White competed for a position in this election, or whether he was traveling with the second group.

viewed the rock we decended about half way when we discovered a party of 200 Indians approaching camp.

Made all possible haste to camp. Indians met us but let us pass. Found they had taken our Capt. & Lieu prisoners at the Independence Rock where they had been taking observations and brought them to camp. Showed no hostility. Presented them with tobaco.[18] Camped near us, traviled 12 miles. 17. Sunday After calling on us & receiving some ammunition they left & traviled up the River. We stay to make meat. Verry warm. Several men gone hunting. Verry difficult to get meat.

Mr. Bennitt's [Bennett] Daughter slightly wounded by an accidental discharge of a gun.

Monday July 18. We reluctantly remained here today. Several gone hunting slight shower of rain. Considerable of meat brought in today.

19. Started at 7 1/2 o'clock followed up the Sweet Water, tremendous Rocky Mountains on each side. Camped at 12 1/2 o'clock, good grass, water and wood, traviled 7 miles.

20. Stay here today to dry what meat we have and get more. Hunters driven into camp by the Indians who are scattered in small parties all around us. Indians take 2 horses from Binnit's [Bennett's] son & [David] Weston. They came to camp verry much frightened. Capt. & several others went out to see if they had any of our men several of whom were out yet. All came in safe. False alarm in the night.

Thursday, July 21. Stay here all this day. Brown lost a horse leg broke by a kick. Indians came back before noon a few came near camp & told many different stories. We observed they had more horses than when they went up. 280 were counted in their Party. They passed quietly by and said they were going home. Extremely warm.

22. Started at 7, traviled on at a good pace until 10 met a party of Shian [Cheyenne] Indians. Camped within two miles of their Village, about noon the Chiefs together with some hundreds of others came to camp. We made them presents of ammunition, tobaco &c. and

[18] This famous event at Independence Rock is described in detail in Lovejoy, "Lovejoy's Pioneer Narrative," 245–49; White, *Ten Years in Oregon*, 138–65; Hastings, *Emigrants' Guide to Oregon and California*, 11–16; and Matthieu, "Reminiscences of F. X. Matthieu," 80–83. Important details about the number of Indians involved and whether they were Shoshones or Sioux remain inconsistent in these primary sources.

smoked with them. Started after dinner passed their village which consisted of several hundred lodges.[19]

Friday 22d July. Several Indians accompanied us to camp. Mr. Fitch Patrick [Thomas Fitzpatrick] judged they were in the village of Crows, Shians [Cheyennes], & Sues [Sioux] between 4 & 5000. Many of our Company traded horses with them. Camped near sun set on Sweet Water, traviled 15 m.

23 Started at 7 1/2 o'clock, bad road. Crossed the Sweet Water a number of times, some verry narrow passes between the mountains. Camped on S. W. at noon, traviled 7 miles a small party of Indians came to camp, about 100 more Indians came to camp at 2 o'clock. They were a war party of Sues & Shians who had been to fight the Snakes [Shoshones]. They returned as usual in several parties another small party came up near night. A few came to camp to smoke.

Sunday 24. Started early left the creek & traviled over a hill of sand without a particle of grass ground covered with wild sage. Saw mountains with snowy sides far to the N. W. struck Sweet Water about noon stoped for dinner 2 1/2 hours crossed the creek several times afternoon.[20] Camped on the creek good wood and grass traviled 15 miles.

25 Started 6 1/2 o'clock rose a long hill came on the creek & camped at 11 for dinner drove two hours afternoon camped on the creek much the best grass we have seen since we left the Fort [Laramie] good spring water & pleanty of wood traviled 12 miles. Wild geese for several days have been frequently seen & fish are caught from Sweet Water creek.

Tuesday 26, July. The nights are astonishingly cold & the days are verry warm. Last night I lay under a thick Blanket & Buffalo Robe with my clothes on. Started early traviled over a long rocky hill camped at noon, got already to start after dinner and a waggon broke down stay here tonight, traviled 10 miles had a severe cold rain.

[19]Except for the "brief capture" of Lansford Hastings and Asa Lovejoy at Independence Rock, relations between this party and the different Indian groups encountered along the trail remained peaceful. Some of the encounters were spent in mutually beneficial trading transactions and in socially satisfying exchanges of information.

[20]The snow-covered peaks that Crawford saw to the northwest are the majestic Wind River Mountains of Wyoming.

27. Started early stopped a short time for dinner. Camped near sun set on Sweet Water, traviled 16 miles.

28. Started 7 o'clock left Sweet Water crossed the dividing ridge. Camped at 10 o'clock on a little stream running westward, traviled 6 miles. Left the cart here, one waggon left. Snowy mountains constantly in sight.

Friday 29. Started 7 o'clock traviled over a sandy barren country destitute of game & every thing but wild sage, high mountains north of us apparently 20 or 30 miles covered with snow. Camped after noon on Little Sandy Creek[21] which empties in Green River a verry pretty stream but much warmer than I expected traviled 14 miles.

30. Started early stopped on the creek for dinner 2 hours. Camped near sun set on Big Sandy Creek[22] traviled 20 miles.

31. Sunday. Rainy morning Started 7. Commenced raining verry cold & unpleasant. Considerable decending ground. Camped on the creek at 3 o'clock traviled 15 miles. Much talk about dividing the company at Green River.

August 1. Monday started at 7. Commenced raining soon rained moderately crossed Green River and camped 11 o'clock traviled 6 miles. Some of the company preparing to pack from here rainy afternoon and evening. 2d. Cold wet morning some making pack saddles and others repairing their waggons determined to take them through.

3. Capt. [Lansford] Hastings with 8 waggons started at 8 o'clock, Meek Pilot. The best wagons were taken on 2 were left standing the rest destroyed to repair others. In our camp there is 27 men, Mr. Fitchpatrick Captain and Pilot. Finished making packsaddles cashed goods and preparing to start tomorrow.

Thursday Aug. 4. All started with pack animals at 8 o'clock had verry little trouble on the way arrived at Ham's Fork of Green River at 4 1/2 o'clock. Camped good grass and wood traviled 20 miles in a

---

[21]Little Sandy Creek, approximately seven miles northeast of present-day Farson, Wyoming, was usually greeted with glee by overlanders because it provided the first dependable water since leaving Pacific Springs. See Haines, *Historic Sites along the Oregon Trail*, 244–45.

[22]Big Sandy Crossing was an important spot because it provided travelers with their last good quality water before they entered the 45-mile extent of the Little Colorado Desert, and before they reached the welcome water source of the Green River. See Haines, *Historic Sites along the Oregon Trail*, 245–47.

different direction from that which the waggons took. We saw high mountains covered with snow to the south west.

5. Started at 7, saw some of Capt. H. [Hastings] company the waggons camped 2 miles behind us last night. Said they had to leave one waggon the first day. Stopped early for dinner cashed liquor. Started & crossed a considerable hill cold and rainy afternoon got verry wet, rain ceased and we camped 5 o'clock on the same creek traviled 18 miles.

Saturday Aug. 6. Started early traviled 6 hours before dinner over a verry rough mountainous country in some places we were obliged to all follow one path. Camped near sunset on the same creek good grass little wood, Traviled 22 miles.

7. Started in good season followed up the creek some time crossed a hill to the north commenced raining crossed some verry bad water courses. Stopped for dinner at the side of a high mountain rain stopped started soon, rain and hail. Crossed two tremendous mountains and camped on Bear River near sunset traviled 25 miles. Saw a verry large Indian trail nearly fresh. The river runs nearly north here.

Monday Aug. 8. Started as usual followed down the River level road very high mountain on each side of the River Bottom which is better soil than we have seen for some time. Stopped on the River a short time for dinner. Two accidents this afternoon by falling from horses not serious. A few trout caught from the river Today. Traviled 20 miles and camped on Tommaux Fork [Thomas Fork].

9. Started early across the Fork and crossed over a tremendour mountain and stopped for dinner on the river, had level road this afternoon. Camped in good season on Tullock's Fork a Branch running from the Mountains into the River traviled 18 miles.

Wednesday Aug. 10. Saw fresh sines of Indians started early. Indians soon came to us. They were Ponarchs [Bannocks] and moving in the same direction with us many of them traviled with us until 3 o'clock when we struck the river and camped, traviled 16 miles. Several horses were procured from them on reasonable terms by our company. Their whole company soon came up and camped near us.

11. Some trading this morning started at 8 1/2 o'clock left the river before noon saw some of the finest springs of water which form a large creek. Saw the soda springs and Boiling springs the greatest Natural

Curiosity I ever saw.[23] Camped near soda springs good place traviled 15 miles. Some Indians came to camp.

Friday Aug. 12. Went to see the Boiling springs again this morning the hole through which the water spouts is about 1 foot in diameter the water which kept a continual Boiling rises frequently to the hight of 3 feet. It is said at times to rise much higher. It is Blood warm and has a sulphur and mineral taste there appears to be a species of Rock constantly forming around the hole which is already considerably elevated. There is a smaller hole near which appears to serve as a vent through which the air is constantly circulating. Started 7, a few Indians in camp 2 of our company started ahead for Fort Hall. Saw a singular spring partaking considerably of the quallities of soda.

Friday Aug. 12. Stopped for dinner about 2 o'clock. Started soon camped on Portnough [Portneuf River] traviled 23 miles.

13. Horses strayed off some distance from camp started in good season stopped early for dinner drove on again until near sunset and camped on Ross Fork in deep valley on a beautiful little stream traviled 25 miles. 14. Sunday. Started in good season and traviled verry fast in order to get to the Fort early as possible. Stopped for dinner on Ross Fork. Some Fort men came to camp started and crossed several spring Brooks camped on Snake or Lewis River near Fort Hall traviled 25 miles. 15. visited the Fort[24] found it much smaller than Laramie but verry well conducted. Commenced writing a letter.

---

[23]Soda Springs and Boiling Springs, located in today's Caribou County, Idaho, were as fascinating to other travelers as they were to Crawford. John C. Frémont (1843) designated the former as Beer Springs, "on account of the effervescing gas and acid taste," and because mountain men had already given it that name. William J. Scott (1846) dissolved sugar in the liquid and drank a gallon of it. Crawford's "Boiling Springs" appears to be the famous Steamboat Spring, which produced enough mineral water discharge that it sounded like a high-pressure steamboat boiler. See Haines, *Historic Sites along the Oregon Trail*, 285–88.

[24]Although the original stockade was only eighty feet square and the trading post buildings were primitive to say the least, Fort Hall was a welcome relief for overlanders who hoped to find blacksmithing services, healthy livestock, and some supplies for sale. Originally constructed in 1834 by Nathaniel Wyeth on the east bank of the Snake River, the post was purchased by the Hudson's Bay Company three years later. It was substantially rebuilt in 1838 and served emigrants until abandoned in 1856. The site is often confused with the like-named military post that was built some miles away. A full-scale replica stands today in nearby Pocatello. Dodds, "Fort Hall," 384. A lengthy but undocumented history appears in Robertson, *Fort Hall.*

Tuesday 16. Finished my letter to my Parents. Visited the Fort. Concluded not to start today. Wrote to W. C. Enos of St. Louis. Capt. H. [Lansford W. Hastings] with seven waggons came in. 18. Started about 9 o'clock kept down the River. Crossed several marshy places, verry warm day and much trouble with packs. Camped on the River, traviled 15 miles. 20. Started in good season saw the American falls.[25] It is not a perpendicular fall but more like rapids interspersed with large rocks. Met a large number of Indians. Doct. [Elijah White] went back and traded fish and horse from them stopped for dinner in a verry bad place. Doct. came up started camped on river traviled 12 miles.

Aug 21. Sunday. Concluded to wait for the Company as some are not satisfied to go without a Pilot. Company passed about 1 o'clock. We packed up and started found them Camped about three miles on the River. Mr. McDonald came up soon. 22d Started without breakfast and traviled verry fast until 8 o'clock stopped on a creek three hours. Started and drove on a trot nearly all day, verry rock hard for horses feet. The same Barren Country covered with sage continues. Camped on a Little Brook at 5 o'clock traviled 30 m good water and grass, little wood suffered very much with dust.

Tuesday 23d Aug. Started early drove fast. Came close to the river camped at 10 on Goose Creek. H. B. Company [Hudson's Bay Company] arrived 1 1/2 hours before us our cattle verry much fatigued concluded not to try to keep up with the H. B. Company with our cattle. Company started two hours before us we drove moderately camped early traviled 20 miles. Doct. White left us for the H. B. Company whom he intends to go with to Fort Vancouver. Only 8 men left in our Company without a Pilot. 24. Started in good season and traviled moderately , fine cool day camped about noon. Giger and others passed with many animals. Started at 2 1/2 o'clock. Camped on a verry pretty Brook traviled 18 miles. Tuesday Aug. 25. Started at 7 1/2 crossed two deep ravines, verry rocky, passed an old camping grd. at

[25]American Falls is an impressive geological feature denoting where the Snake River drops about fifty feet in stages and forms a cataract of foaming water. James A. Pritchard, who visited it in 1849, was struck by the fact that its roar could be heard miles away. Pritchard, *Overland Diary*, 109.

10 1/2 o'clock concluded not to stop drove on at a good pace decended into a tremendous valley with banks of perpendicular rock at least 200 feet high on the north side a large portion of water issues out of the rock nearly half way up. Camped at 3 2/3 o'clock on a large stream formed mostly by springs of the above description, traviled 21 miles.

26. Started at 7, kept down the Creek which is verry rapid left the Creek and decended a steep hill. Crossed a beautiful stream. Camped at 11. Started at 2 passed some Indian Lodges traded fish both fresh and dry left the river rose a tremendous hill travellid on till dark no appearance of water verry dark until 9 when the moon arose decended a tremendous hill found the river we left and camped at 10 o'clock night in a miserable sandy and rocky place traviled 30 M.

27. Saturday. Started at 8 kept down the river on the side of a steep bank where we were obliged to all follow one narrow path cross some steep ravines camped at 12 1/2 on an island in Snake river good grass concluded to stay here today and let our animals recruit, traviled 10 M.

28. Started early kept down the [Snake] river along a steep side-hill saw many Indians who live along the river and subsist principally on fish traded fresh fish from them. Sunday 28, Aug. Camped 11 1/2 for dinner several Indians in camp. Left the river for a short time after dinner saw large sandbanks drifted like snow. Camped on a slew of the river verry high grass, trav. 18 M. horses got frightened and ran some distance from camp, probably wolves.

29. Started at 7, cold morning followed down the [Snake] river awhile left the river verry barren country less sage than formerly. Crossed a large branch followed it through a tremenous gap in the mountain for at least two miles the rock standing up on each side probably 200 ft. Camped for dinner at the River many Lodges near several came into camp. 29. Followed down the river after dinner crossed onto an Island & camped near sunset, trav. 20 M.

30. Started at 7 kept down the River a short time took dinner on a small Branch verry poor grass. Find the country growing more barren not even producing sage. Camped near sunset on a beautiful little Branch in a valley surrounded on three sides by high hills traviled 18 miles.

31. Followed down the Branch to the river about 1 1/2 miles in search of the horses, found the River as well as the Branch flowing among high cliffs of rock with scarcely room for a path on its Banks. 31st Aug. Started at 7 1/2 rose a long hill astonishingly barren country decended to the river stopped for dinner tolerable good grass, found Indians pleanty towards evening. Camped near their village poor grass trav. 18. M.

Thursday Sept. 1st, 1842. Many Indians come to camp traded pleanty of fish started 8, crossed 2 small streams which are said to be hot water. It was discovered by some of our party attempting to drink they said the water burned their hands took dinner on the on the river verry warm day poor grass.[26] Camped on the river poor grass traviled 15 miles.

Friday Sept. 2d. Started at 8 1/2 no alteration in the general appearance of the country took dinner on the river verry poor grass Camped in the evening on Warior River a Branch of the Snake traviled 14 miles.

3d. Started 7 1/2 crossed W. R. arrived at Fort Boyzea [Fort Boise][27] at 9. Crossed over Snake River in a Canoe to the Fort which stands on the north side of the river procured some provisions. Crossed back traviled down the river a short distance & camped for dinner. Fort B. is a new Establishment. It has been a short time in operation but is not yet completed. We saw but one white man who was French. The company left the Fort on Thursday.

Sept. 3d. At the Fort we tasted musk mellon but of a very indifferent quallity. They raise corn & a few other vegetables in small quantities. From the fort we saw a large smoke at a distance supposed to proceed from a volcanick mountain. Left camp at 11 o'clock & traveled briskly over a sandy country suffered considerable for water as the day was exceedingly hot came to a creek about 6 oclock & never was water to me more exceptable though of a very indifferent quality, passed down

[26]These unnamed hot springs served as a good camp site for emigrant parties and are about nine miles east of present-day Mountain Home, Idaho. In 1843, John C. Frémont measured the temperature of the spring waters at 164 degrees. See Haines, *Historic Sites along the Oregon Trail*, 329–30.

[27]Fort Boise, built just below the junction of the Boise and Snake rivers in 1834, was a significant outlet for the fur trade operations of the Hudson's Bay Company. Much of the structure was badly damaged by floodwaters in 1853. This is not the same structure or location as the like-named military post that was built in 1863 to protect traffic on the Oregon Trail, and for miners who were headed to the Idaho goldfields. See Franzwa, *Oregon Trail Revisited*, 338–42.

the Creek a short distance at the foot of a mountain & found boiling water running out of the ground.[28] It made its appearance just above the age of the water in the River in a Boiling state for over a hundred yards it runs more or less. One of our company cooked a fish which he caught from the creek in about two minutes perfectly through. The water was so salt that the fish was sufficiently seasoned. Crossed the Creek & camped common grass traviled 15 m.

4. Concluded to stay here & let our cattle & horses rest today. Two of our company getting impatient left us this morning spent the day repairing, washing, &c.

Monday 5th Sept. Started at 7 1/2 oclock left the Creek our road led mostly through vallies we found more grass & and less sage than common came to a little water at 10 o'clock but concluded not to stop. Exceedingly warm came to a small stream at 2 oclock & camped. Cattle far behind & much fatigued traviled 16 m.

6. Started at 7 1/2 followed down the stream found Snake River close by followed it down about one mile & struck across a mountain. Came to a creek at 10 oclock. Stopped for dinner 3 hours our path wound along the sides of mountains & frightful precipices & in many places if our animals make one miss-step it would be certain death. The path continued up & down rocky hills until we came to a good camping ground about 5 oclock traviled 13 m.

7. Started at 7 1/2 rose a most tremendous hill the highest I have rose on the rout, got a fall from a horse hurt my foot some. The road is more precipitous than ever, up & down and constantly over rocks. Crossed several streams. Stoped for dinner at 10 oclock started at 1, and commenced climbing hills again crossed several small streams and found good grass most of the way came to the stream on which we camped last night. Camped at 4 oc traviled 10 miles.

Thursday 8, Sept. Horses strayed far from camp and instead of an early start as we intended we got off at 9 oclock we left the Branch and gradually a rose a long hill. Stopped for dinner on a small stream at 12 oclock started at 2 1/2 & continued to rise by degrees.

---

[28] These are the Malheur hot springs at the foot of Rhinehart Butte. See Haines, *Historic Sites along the Oregon Trail*, 346–47.

The country over which we have traviled to day is mostly covered with Bunch Grass which the Horses are very fond of. We at last found the top of the mountain at a distance we could see what we suppose to be the Blue mountains [Blue Mountains] and they struck us with terror their lofty peaks seemed a resting place for the clouds. Below us was a large plain and at some distance we could discover a tree which we at once recognized as "the lone tree" of which we had before heard. We made all possible speed and at 7 1/2 o'clock the advance party arrived at the Tree nearly an hour before the cattle. The Tree is a large Pine[29] stand[ing] in the midst of an immense plain intirely alone. It presented a truly singular appearance and I believe is respected by every traviler through this almost Treeless Country. Within a few yards we found pleanty of water and we soon made ourselves comfortable by a good fire. As soon as we arrived at the top of the hill in sight of the Blue mountains felt an uncommon chilly wind which increased so as to be uncomfortable befors we arrived. As soon as we reached the valley we found our old friend Sage flourishing in a most unwelcome manner. The grass about camp was not good, traviled 18 miles.

Friday 9, Sept. Horses far from camp this morning, found pleanty of frost on our beds and all about. Left camp at 8 oclock but was a long time finding the right trail. Cold wind from the B. [Blue] mountains on tops of which we soon discovered heaps of snow.

Came to a large Creek which we followed a while & stopped for dinner at 12 1/2 oclock. Started at 3 crossed the Creek. Crossed 2 more creeks soon and camped at 4 1/2 oclock. We should have traviled on but we was afraid of being in the night without water, this is the difficulty of traviling without a Pilot. Found good wood, water, and grass about at our camp traviled 11 miles. Cold wind.

Sept. 10. Saturday verry cold morning. Horses far from camp. Started at 8 oclock found good places for camping which we might have come to last night. Commenced rising gradually at 10 oclock continued to rise until 12 when we came to a tremendous hill to descend. The mountains on our left were close by they rose gradualy and were covered

[29]The Lone Pine stood at a point where many wagon trains made evening camp, but it was apparently cut down as early as 1843 by overlanders. See Haines, *Historic Sites along the Oregon Trail*, 351–52.

with Pine Trees. Our descent lasted for near an hour, about midway of the hill was a little water course crossing our path & afforded us a resting place around this place were several Pine Trees. I noticed the White Pine and the Spruce Pine. Some were verry tall & slim. From this little grove down the hill was more difficult all were obliged to dismount for safety. It was verry sidling and uncomfortable rocky. Below was a most beautiful valley as I ever saw [Grande Ronde]. We found good grass, a delightful road, & a fertile country in the valley, we crossed some small water courses and camp on a beautiful Creek at 3 o'clock good grass, & water & an abundance of wood traviled 20 miles found several well beaten trails leading from camp but none appeared fresh. After dark two Indians came to camp on horseback. They were of a different tribe from any which we had seen. They had traps and appeared to have been out but a short time. They told us that we could get to Wala Wala [Walla Walla] in 3 days.

Sept. 11. Sunday started at 7 1/2 o'clock with our Indians for Guide. They took us a northern direction & put us on the companies trail about 10 o'clock we then came to the Creek which we had left in the morning and followed it down. We discovered a band of Horses on the other side of the Creek. Our Indians left us about noon and crossed the Creek to these Horses which were being driven in the same direction we were going. We saw more Horses ahead. Came to an Indian village at 2 o'clock and camped near them, traviled 18 miles.[30]

The first thing to be attended to after we campd was to assertain whether we could get any provisions from the Indians. We found to our great joy they had pleanty and instead of starving as we expected we were able to trade enough fish to last us to Dr. Whitmans [Marcus Whitman].[31] There were several lodges & they were well clad & had

[30]As with so many other emigrants who traveled to Oregon in the 1840s and early 1850s, Medorem Crawford's party found the various Indian tribes of the Grande Ronde River–Blue Mountains–Umatilla River area to be not only friendly, but also very interested in trade with white travelers. Unfortunately, the entry of September 15 indicated some unexplained troubles.

[31]Marcus and Narcissa Whitman's Waiilatpu Mission was a welcome site for emigrants moving along the Oregon Trail in 1842–1844, but most later travelers bypassed it to save some distance along the trail. Crawford's comments about the friendly Cayuse Indians at the mission contrasts sharply with the realities of five years later, when the mission neophytes rose in rebellion and killed the Whitmans and other staff members.

hundreds of good horses and an abundance of provision. I have seen no Indians since I started which appear so happy & well provided for as these. The beneficial influence of the Missionary Society appears to have reached here. They attended morning and evening devotion in our camp.

12 Sept. Monday. Horses strayed far from camp and scattered among the Indians' Horses. The Indians showed moral honesty by bringing horses to us which had strayed by themselves to some distance. Started at 9 1/2 o'clock several Indians started with us one continued & said he would go to Dr. [Marcus] Whitmans. Commenced raising a Mountain by degrees. Came to trees, at first quite thin & without underbrush having fine grass. But as we arose we came to a densly timbered country, mostly pine & fir. The most beautiful tall straight trees. Our traviling through the timber was quite difficult as the path wound back and forth and many logs lay across it. We decended & arose a tremendous hill and about 3 o'clock our Indian Guide[32] beckoned us to take a by path to find water, we did so and after traveling a few hundred yards found a little opening of timber & pleanty of good water & some grass. Camped here for the night trav. 10 miles. Cool & cloudy considerable of rain after dark. Horses got frightened tied some up & the rest remained near.

Sept. 13 Tuesday. Started at 8 1/2 and followed back our path until we came to the main trail when we pusued our dismal rout, Our path today led through more dense places & driving our pack animals & cattle was almost impossible. Occasionally we found a clear spot frequently several acres together and in the forenoon several little springs of water, towards evening we left the timber and found ourselves on a rolling Prairie of good soil. Continued to decend until near sunset when to our great joy we found water and wood but poor grass. Camped traviled 20 miles.

Sept. 14. Our Indian Guide told us we would get to Dr. Whitman's today but we hardly expected it as our animals were verry much jaded. But it was nearer than we expected and we arrived at 3 o'clock and camped near his house traviled 8 m.

---

[32]The hiring of Indian guides along this stretch of the trail from the Grande Ronde to the Columbia River was common for overland expeditions during the 1840s and 1850s. See Tate, *Indians and Emigrants*, 68–72.

Dr. [Marcus] Whitman is a Missionary of the Presbyterian Order he has been in the Country six years. He has a verry comfortable house and is farming to a considerable extent. He has a Thrashing Machine & a grinding mill all under one roof driven by water power. Many Indians around him. I was never more pleased to see a house or white people in my life, we were treated by Dr. and Mrs. [Narcissa] Whitman with the utmost kindness. We got what provision we wanted on very reasonable terms. I have just heard of the Death of a young man who started from Independence with us. He was with the Hudson Bays Company and got drowned himself and horse crossing the Snake River soon after he left us. What is to me remarkable it was his gun and by an accident of his hand that put an end to poor Baily [Bailey] at Independence Rock. A small detachment, Forces' [John and James Force], from the hind company came up.

Sept. 15. Having recd verry bad treatment from the Indians we concluded to get away from here as soon as possible & try to find more grass, some of our company started before noon but we could not get ready until 3 1/2 oclock when we started down about 4 miles and found the rest of our company camped in an excellent spot. Forces came up also after dark. 16. Started at 8 oclock kept down the Walawala [Walla Walla] River and camped at 1 o'clock within 3 miles of the Fort [Walla Walla].[33] Traviled 12 miles. Visited the Fort saw Esqr [Nathaniel] Crocker, Doct. [Elijah] White had left before noon in the Companies Boat.

All the foremost company had gone by land except Esqr. & [S.W.] Moss who started this evening to overtake them. I had an introduction to Mr. McKenly [Archibald McKinlay] who is in charge at the fort. The Fort is rebuilding now having lately been burnt. It is situated on a miserable sandy barren place where the sand drifts with the wind like snow. The Walla Walla River emties in & forms the Columbia here.

[33]Fort Walla Walla, a Hudson's Bay Company trading post at the junction of the Walla Walla River and the Columbia River, was a place to purchase or barter for goods and livestock, as well as to secure passage down the Columbia River aboard company canoes and rafts. Archibald McKinlay (1811–1891), the chief trader there, retained the position until 1846, when failing eyesight forced him to take over Hudson's Bay Company operations in Oregon City. He continued private business operations in the Oregon City area, occupied a Donation Land Claim south of the community, and engaged in large-scale sheep ranching. McKinlay was the son-in-law of Peter Skene Ogden. See Sampson, *John McLoughlin's Business Correspondence*, 139–40.

17. Sept. Saturday started at 9 o'clock drove to the Fort found Mr. McKenly from home not to return until evening could not get the Doct's Things drove down the river and camped, traviled four miles. The rest of the company went on. The Banks of the River on each side present tremendous pinacles of rock mostly perpendicular. We find considerable of sage yet in places.

Sept. 18. Sunday. Went to the Fort before breakfast and got our things. Started at 9 1/2 o'clock lost two animals went back and found [them] and kept down the river, the most of time a steep bluff of rocks was on our left with occasional spots of grass sufficient for camping purposes stoped three hours for dinner, much sand and frequently in large drifts camped near sunset, traviled 12 m.[34]

Sept. 19. Started at 8 a'clock drove on at a good pace verry warm day camped in a good spot on the river traviled 15 m.

Sept. 20. Started at 8 o'clock kept down the river verry sandy barren country destitute of timber (crossed the Unadilla [Umatilla River]). Cold wind & little rain. Mr. Spaulding & Lady [Henry H. and Eliza Spalding][35] over took us at noon rain increased. Camped at 4 o'clock, traviled 18 miles. Considerable rain. Cleared off before bed time. Mr. Gray [William Gray][36] called at camp on his return from Vancouver.

21. Started at 10 o'clock and parted with Mr. & Mrs. Spalding who in consequence of some intelligence from Mr. Gray resolved to return. Cold wind. Camped at 5 o'clock, traviled 20 miles.

22. Started late, cold wind bad road, traviled 18 miles.

---

[34]Crawford took the land route that went down the south bank of the Columbia River rather than the river route most emigrants took.

[35]Henry H. Spalding and his wife, Eliza, accompanied Marcus and Narcissa Whitman to Oregon to begin mission work among the Indians. The more time the two families spent together on the trail, the more animosity that developed between them. The Spaldings set up a mission at Lapwai, near present-day Lewiston, Idaho, where they had remarkable success among the Nez Percés. They escaped the Whitman Massacre of 1847 but soon abandoned the Lapwai Mission and moved to the Willamette Valley, where Eliza died in 1851. Henry remarried and returned to the Nez Percés in 1871, representing the Presbyterian Board of Foreign Missions. He died at Lapwai in August 1874. See Thrapp, *Encyclopedia of Frontier Biography*, 1342–44, 1558–60.

[36]William H. Gray accompanied Marcus Whitman to Oregon and made another transcontinental trip in service of the American Board of Commissioners for Foreign Missions. He resigned in 1842 and moved to the Willamette Valley, where he became a prominent pioneer and published *History of Oregon* in 1864. He died in 1881. See Thrapp, *Encyclopedia of Frontier Biography*, 583–84.

23. Started late, tremendous west wind, lost my horse last night, Indians brought him into camp this morning, verry rock road over steep sidling places, crossed a large creek about noon. Camped at 4 o'clock. Traviled 11 miles.

24th Sept. Started verry late, tremendous west wind & sand drifting like snow in our faces, passed over some large drifts. Came to a tremendous rapid Creek, obliged to take all our effects over in a canoe which was dangerous. Passed tremendous rocky falls in the River. Large Indian town, traviled 6 m.

25 Sept. Sunday, I feel bad this morning in consequence of getting wet yesterday and my eyes are much affected by the flying sand. Started at 11 o'clock traviled over hills & sidling places, saw a high snowy peak which we understand to be Mt. Hood. Passed the Dalls [The Dalles] or rapids of the river which is a singular sight. Arrived at Mr. [H. K. W.] Perkins at 3 o'clock, found our old company there, traviled 8 miles. Mr. Perkins preached in camp this evening.

26. Visited Mr. Perkins at his house. Was verry kindly rec'd and hospitably treated, got potatoes &c. and started at 1 o'clock with an Indian Guide, rose a long hill and left the river, traviled over the most romantic country I have yet seen. The day is very pleasant indeed and the tall trees through which we are passing adds much to the beauty of the prospect. On our left arises Mt. Hood with its snowy peak glistening in the sunbeams, on the right & about the same distance Mt. Helena [Mt. St. Helens] which resembles Mt. Hood verry much. As we descended towards evening we saw far below us the river flowing as it were & dividing the two snowy peaks. We descended a considerable of a hill and found the pleasantest camp, the best wood, grass, and water we have had in a long time, travilled 12 miles.

27. Started early arose and decended several rocky hills. Camped in the woods verry little grass indeed, traviled 11 m.

28. Started at 8 1/2, got behind on account of a mule being lost. Our company left us. We started at 9 o'clock, missed one of our Indian horses but I thought he was with the other company. We came to a verry rapid river just as they were across, very difficult crossing on account of large rocks and deep water, almost impossible to get along

up the steep hills over the rocks & between the trees. Caught up with the company at 11 o'clock, found my horse not there started back to find him, found him at the camp we left had much difficulty to get him along. Two Indians overtook me at the river on my return with 5 good horses. I traviled with them until dark when we came to an Indian Camp where we concluded to sleep. I got a few berries and a little fish for my supper. I crossed several rapid streams flowing from those snowy mountains before I got to Camp where I slept. We found no grass for our horses at all, traviled 13 miles.

29. Arose early after a verry uncomfortable night's rest having only one blanket and a piece of Robe. My horses looked so bad I got one of the Indians horses to ride, started early without eating a particle, found the road horrible beyond description, met John Force soon who said he had lost 2 horses & was in search. The company had all tied up their horses to trees except the two that he had lost. He returned with us and gave up the search, overtook the rear of the company about 10 o'clock. One of our mules had been lost the day before while I was gone back for the horse. The horse I went back after gave out from hunger & fatigue, being verry poor, and I was obliged to leave him in the woods, traviled along all day over hills and precipices, rocks and mire holes, over logs and under trees and across rapid streams, until at sunset we found a verry little grass not worth mentioning & camped, traviled 20 miles. I found my apetite verry good having eat verry little in 36 hours.

30. Started early, found our animals verry hollow and weak, passed down and crossed the stream found considerable grass in 2 miles from camp, traviled on until 11 o'clock when we stopped to bait our animals which were starving, started at 1 and drove on over as bad and some worse roads than ever, having frequent mire holes with logs in them, traviled up and down long hills and stopped at dark with verry little grass and the most dismal & unpleasant camp I ever saw, traviled 13 miles.

Sunday, October 1st, 1842. My horse cannot be found this morning. 3 out of 5 of our riding animals give out so we have to start on foot. Starting at 8 1/2 found my horse on the way, horid road, logs & mud holes. Doct. [Elijah] Whites American mare verry near giving out, found some grass and stopped at noon, traviled 5 miles. Concluded to stay here tonight.

Oct. 2, Sunday. Started at 9 o'clock some bad road met 3 of the young men who went down first, arrived at their camp at 4 1/2 o'clock, good grass and water, traviled 16 miles.

3d. A few of us accompanied those who were here before us to the Falls of Willamut [Willamette Falls] where we found many people & considerable of buisness. Saw Dr. White & others who arrived before us, we were handsomely recd and kindly treated.

4. Packed up and started 9 oclock called at the Falls and took dinner, found some of the men who came over with us at work on a mill. Mr. Jones [Hardin Jones] & a man by name of Cooke much injured by blasting rocks, drove on and overtook our pack. Camped on a Creek. Traviled 10 miles.

5. Started at 9 1/2 crossed several streams, bad road. Camped in the settlements at the house of a Frenchman who treated us verry kindly, traviled 10 m.

October 6. Started late took a round about road arrive at the mission at 2 o'clock, traviled 10 miles. Oct. 7. Rode about to see the country like it much. This is among the first frosty nights.

8. Went to the mill with Mrs. & Miss Brown. Mr. Benitt [Bennett] and Pomeroy [Dwight or Walter Pomeroy] together with several young men arrived in the settlement.

9. Sunday. Attended church twice today. Oct. 10. Mr. Pomeroy returned to the Falls [Willamette Falls].[37] I crossed the River to see the country, stayed all night with Mr. O'Neil. 11. Rainy morning cleared off soon. Crossed the River & stayed all night at the Doct. House. 12. Clear fine weather. 13. Went with Mr. Shortess & Doct. Babcock to Youngs valley. Beautiful country, returned and wrote to my Father. 14. Commenced working a little. 18. Oct. Rainy morning cloudy day. 19. Oct. Rainy morning, cloudy & thick mist. 20. Rainy morning, cloudy day & some rain, rainy night. 21. Cloudy morning and day.

---

[37]The name Willamette Falls was later changed to Oregon City. See McArthur and McArthur, *Oregon Geographic Names*, 4th ed., 559.

1843

Jesse Looney, Letter from Oregon

This letter from Jesse Looney to his brother-in-law, Major James C. Bond, in Warren County, Illinois, was sent via John C. Frémont, who was returning from his exploration of the Far West. Almost a year transpired before it reached its destination.

Jesse Looney left his Illinois home in 1843, bound for the Willamette Valley, but because of his party's late arrival in Oregon and the difficult passage that still remained along the Columbia River route, he decided to winter at the Whitman Mission at Waiilatpu. As revealed in the following letter to his brother-in-law, the lengthy layover allowed him ample time to strengthen the health of his livestock and make repairs for the final push westward. The Indians were friendly, food was varied and plentiful, and the refinements of the mission provided some of "civilization's" comforts. The advice to his brother-in-law, and any other would-be emigrants, was wise and practical. Noteworthy was his admonition that calves should be left behind, not only because their physical weakness would lead to almost certain death, but also because their endless care would endanger the health of their mothers. Looney also noted how many yoke of cattle should be taken per wagon, how much flour and bacon should be packed, and what items should be minimized or left behind entirely. Finally, he added that leaving the Missouri River jumping-off towns should commence "as soon as the grass will admit." Having embarked from Independence, Missouri, on May 22, his group was somewhat disadvantaged, and he indicated that this departure was about one month too late.

Jesse Looney.
From Joseph Gaston, The Centennial History of Oregon, 1811–1912 *(1912).*

Looney had the reputation of being a meticulous planner, and this was evidenced in his preparation for the migration. A brief biographical article written years later affirmed that he had outfitted three wagons for the trip. The first, built with a leak-proof bed, was intended to ford streams and rivers while keeping dry the most important contents. The second one, called the "fiddle," was designed to carry special loads. He emphasized essentials—food, clothing, garden seeds, and agricultural tools—rather than furniture and other heavy items. The family never seemed to go hungry, and on several occasions, they shared food with less-fortunate companions.

Accompanying Jesse Looney, his wife, Ruby, and six children was a young man who performed some of the cooking, camp chores, and, presumably, wagon driving. This unnamed helper received board and "free" passage to Oregon. No doubt, he also helped with the maintenance of twenty head of cattle, four brood mares, and extra oxen that the family took along. The trip to the Pacific Northwest ended successfully for the Looneys, and they were regarded by later settlers as one of the true pioneer families. Jesse served in the provisional legislature in 1846, and the family laid down important roots in the future state of Washington.

Although this manuscript letter is housed in the Oregon State Historical Society Library, and copies have been deposited in other collections, it has also been published previously. Under the title "A Letter By One of the Immigrants of 1843," it appeared in an obscure collection of letters, interviews, and miscellany collected by the Works Progress Administration during the 1930s. The anthology was published in a two-volume edition entitled *Told by the Pioneers: Reminiscences of Pioneer Life in Washington* (1937–1938). In Merrill J. Mattes's bibliographical masterpiece, *Platte River Road Narratives*, he awarded the letter only two stars out of a possible five, largely because of its brevity rather than the quality of its contents. A slightly different version was made available electronically at www.oregonpioneers.com/JLooney_Letter.htm (accessed October 15, 2013), but the variations between the two are mainly in the paragraphing formats. The copy printed here is from *Told by the Pioneers*. Supplementary material added to this introduction is taken from Sarah H. Steeves, *Book of Remembrance of Marion County, Oregon, Pioneers, 1840–1860* (1927), and Louise Barry, *The Beginning of the West* (1972). The Steeves book (pp. 21–25) lists the names of other people in the wagon train, the full names and marriage partners of Looney's children, and the important events in family history after their settlement in Oregon. The biographical profile published in Steeves's book was assembled in 1927 by Frances Looney Cornell, a daughter of Jesse and Ruby Looney.

JESSE LOONEY TO JAMES C. BOND, OCTOBER 27, 1843, WAIILATPU, OREGON TERRITORY. MANUSCRIPT LETTER, MSS 2263, OREGON HISTORICAL SOCIETY, PORTLAND.

Waiilatpu, Oct. 27, 1843
Jesse Looney to James C. Bond,
Greenbush, Warren County, Ill.

Dear Sir: I embrace the opportunity of writing to you from this far western country, afforded me by the return of Lieutenant Frémont to the States this winter.[1] He thinks he will be at Independence, Missouri, by January next, which will be in time for those who intend coming next season to this country to get some information about the necessary preparations to be ready for the journey.

It is a long tiresome trip from the States to this country, but the company of emigrants came through safely this season to the number of a thousand persons with something over a hundred wagons to this place, which is two-hundred-and-fifty miles east of the Willamet[te] Valley, and, with the exception of myself and a few others, have all gone on down there, intending to go through this winter if possible. About half of them have traded off their stock at Walla Walla, twenty-five miles below here and are going by water. The balance went on by land to the Methodist Mission, one-hundred-and-seventy-five miles below this, intending to take the water there.[2]

---

[1]During 1843–1844, John C. Frémont conducted a fourteen-month congressionally funded exploration across Kansas and up the front range of the Rockies to South Pass. From there, the elite party of topographical engineers and soldiers moved northwestward up the Snake River to the Columbia River, where they completed a mapping of the Pacific Northwest region that was begun in 1841 by Commodore Charles N. Wilkes's naval reconnaissance. By October 1843, the forty-man expedition, guided by experienced mountain man Thomas Fitzpatrick, was at Marcus Whitman's Waiilatpu Mission. It was at this spot that Jesse Looney entrusted this letter to the Frémont column to deliver to the post office in Independence, Missouri. Delivery of the epistle was long delayed, however, because Frémont did not head immediately east from Oregon. He first explored parts of northern Nevada and California, where he camped at John Sutter's baronial fortress in the Sacramento Valley. Only after that brief interlude, and while under some pressure from Mexican officials in California, did he finally depart for the East. This extensive journey was the basis of Frémont's successful publication, *Report on the Exploring Expedition to the Rocky Mountains in the Year 1842, and to Oregon and North California in the Years 1843–44* (1845). See Goetzmann, *Army Exploration*, 85–101; and Carey, *General History of Oregon*, 381–89.

[2]The only choice for overlanders before 1847 was between taking boats and rafts down the Columbia River or following the south bank route, which was difficult for wagons. They could sell their

I have stopped here in the Walla Walla valley to spend the winter, in order to save my stock. This is a fine valley of land, excellent water, good climate and the finest kind of pine timber on the surrounding mountains, and above all, a good range for stock both summer and winter. The Indians are friendly and have plenty of grain and potatoes, and a good many hogs and cattle. The missionaries at this and other missions have raised fine crops of wheat, corn, potatoes, etc., so that provisions can be procured here upon as good or better terms than in the lower settlements at present. Cattle are valuable here, especially American cattle. Things induced me to stop here for the winter, save my stock and take them down in the spring.

In preparing for the journey of Rocky Mountains, you cannot be too particular in choice of a wagon. It should be strong in every part and yet it should not be very heavy. The large size, two-horse Yankee wagons are the most substantial wagons I have seen for this trip. You should haul nothing but your clothing, bedding and provisions. Goods are cheaper here than in the States. Let your main load be provisions—flour and bacon. Put in about as much loading as one yoke of cattle can draw handily, and then put on three good yoke of cattle and take an extra yoke for change in case of failure from lameness or sore necks, and you can come without any difficulty. The road is good, much better than we had expected, but is long. Bring all the loose cattle you can, especially milk cows and heifers. Do not attempt to bring calves. They will not come through, and by losing them you will be in danger of losing their mothers.

I cannot urge you too strongly to be sure to bring plenty of provisions; don't depend on the game you may get. You may get some and you may not. It is uncertain. We were about five months on the way to this place. I had plenty of flour, etc., to do me, but most of the company

---

livestock and load their families and provisions on rafts that would transport them to the confluence of the Columbia and Willamette rivers at present-day Portland. Before the Barlow Road opened in 1845, packing parties with livestock traveled down the south bank of the Columbia River from Fort Walla Walla to the Willamette River, but very few wagons attempted the difficult passage. After the Barlow Road opened, they could continue along the trail in their wagons and swing along the southern slopes of Mount Hood toward future Portland. Looney more specifically mentions that livestock could be sold at the Hudson's Bay Company trading post at Walla Walla or farther west at The Dalles, where the Methodist Mission operated under the auspices of Reverend H. K. W. Perkins.

were out long before they got here, and there is little or nothing in the way of provisions to be had at the forts on the way. I would advise you to lay in plenty for at least five months, for if you get out on the way, you will have trouble to get any till you get here.

I advise you to start as soon as the grass will admit. We might have started near a month sooner than we did, and then would have been here in time to have gone through with our cattle this winter. We left Independence, Missouri, the 22nd day of May and we are just about a month too late.

Myself and family were all sick when we left and continued till we left Blue River [Little Blue or Big Blue River], and the wind and rain, but when we reached the highlands along the Platte we began to mend. My health is better than for years, and so far as I have seen this country I think it is very healthy. There were five or six deaths on the road, some by sickness and some by accident, and there were some eight or ten births. Upon the whole we fared better than we expected. We had no interruptions from the Indians. Our greatest difficulty was in crossing rivers.

Mrs. L. [his wife, Ruby Bond Looney] says prepare with good strong clothing or sage-brush will strip you. This shrub is very plenty, and was hard on our teams, especially those that went before, but it will not be so bad on those that come next year for we have left a plain, well beaten path all the way.

I will have a better opportunity of giving you accounts of this country next spring, and I want you to write the first chance and to direct to the settlement of Willamet[te]. So no more, but remain,

Your brother till death,

Jesse Looney.

John M. Shively, "Route and Distances to Oregon and California"

John M. Shively was a prominent member of the 1843 Peter H. Burnett–Jesse Applegate wagon train, which departed Independence, Missouri, in mid-May 1843 and reached the Hudson's Bay Company post at Fort Vancouver on November 10. The combined company included at least 560 migrants, 120 wagons, and 2,000 head of livestock. Although the massive expedition soon divided into several smaller and more manageable companies, the members of each unit traveled close to each other and maintained an amiable relationship as they traversed most of the Great Plains segment of the Oregon Trail. After leaving Fort Laramie, however, they traveled at varying speeds and increasingly separated from each other as they tried to achieve a greater sense of maneuverability.

Three years after experiencing these realities, Shively advised other would-be emigrants to observe that "They will quarrel, and try to enforce non-essential duties, till the company will divide and subdivide, the whole way to Oregon. When you start over these wide plains, let no one leave dependent on his best friend for any thing; for if you do, you will certainly have a blow-out before you get far." Indeed, he was seeking only the most self-sufficient candidates for future migrations, not slothful or dependent souls who intended to rely on the good will and labors of others.

John M. Shively was born in Shelby County, Kentucky, on April 2, 1804, and, as a young man, achieved some measure of financial success. His early years as a teacher soon gave way to the dry goods business, a trade he learned at all levels. Following his marriage to Martha Ann Johnson in 1836, he opened several general merchandise stores in St. Louis, but these were forced to close in the wake of the great financial Panic of 1837.

After his wife died in childbirth in 1842, he gave up a surveying job and prepared to begin a new life in Oregon. He spent much of 1843 advertising across Missouri that he would personally lead a large wagon train across the Rockies to the Pacific Northwest. He apparently recruited almost three hundred expectant followers and even undertook a quick trip to the nation's capital to win government authorization for a military escort to accompany them to the Willamette Valley. Not only did the military escort fail to materialize, but of the three hundred promised recruits, only a handful joined him at the Independence, Missouri, rendezvous spot. Signing on with the Burnett-Applegate wagon train was his only alternative, and he did so without reluctance.

Some years after completing the 1843 migration, Shively wrote: "Six hundred and forty acres of land is what induced me to come to Oregon, and I got it." Despite the frequently voiced opinion that missionary Marcus Whitman had played a pivotal role in promoting the western migration of the Burnett-Applegate wagon train, Shively vehemently denied this, as did several other members of the company. Upon reaching the new land, his interests were clearly within the temporal, not the spiritual realm. He laid out a land claim and initiated the settlement of Astoria, near the original 1811 fur-trading post bearing John Jacob Astor's name. This enterprise had been purchased by the British-owned North West Company in 1813 and renamed Fort George. Shortly after marrying his second wife, Susan Elliott, on March 30, 1847, in Arlington, Virginia, Shively was chosen as the postmaster of Astoria. He held this position and the designation as justice of the peace for the small town until 1849. At that time, he traveled south to the California gold fields, found considerable quantities of the metal, but lost it all in a ship wreck as he returned to Astoria. Over the next several years, he worked as a surveyor and road commissioner in Astoria. He made another small fortune prospecting for gold in Shively's Gulch during southwest Oregon's gold rush, and in transporting supplies to other miners. He finally returned to Astoria, where he died on April 4, 1893, after spending his last five years as a bedridden patient at St. Mary's Hospital.

Despite all his accomplishments, Shively's name is not widely recognized today. Persons who are familiar with his role in promoting the Oregon Trail migration know him as the author of *Route and Distances*

John M. Shively.
Courtesy of the Oregon Historical Society, BB004572.

to Oregon and California, which is reprinted and edited here. This 21 × 12–centimeter, fifteen-page guidebook was intentionally designed to fit into the pocket of the average overland emigrant. Like other trail guides published during the 1840s and 1850s, it was filled with practical information about preparing for the trip and conditions that would be encountered at various locations. At the conclusion of the booklet, Shively indicated that he was preparing another guide to relate additional information about climates, soils, and "native productions" of Oregon and California, complete with a map of both regions, but it was never published.

Besides his guidebook, John Shively's most important record of personal events on the trail and in Oregon appeared in his 1883 "Memoir," which was edited by Howard M. and Edith M. List, and published in the *Oregon Historical Quarterly* (1980). An excellent assessment of his multifaceted life is profiled in David H. White, *News of the Plains and Rockies, 1803–1865*, vol. 2, *Santa Fe Adventurers and Settlers* (1996), 353–58, which also includes a copy of his 1846 trail guide. Another copy of the rare trail guide appears in Dale Morgan, ed., *Overland in 1846* (1963), 734–42, but neither reprinted edition contains any explanatory notes about precise passages within the text. Additional information on Shively's various contributions to the history of Astoria can be found in Charles H. Carey, *General History of Oregon Through Early Statehood* (1971), 369, 737.

JOHN M. SHIVELY, *ROUTE AND DISTANCES TO OREGON AND CALIFORNIA, WITH A DESCRIPTION OF WATERING PLACES, CROSSINGS, DANGEROUS INDIANS, ETC.*
(WASHINGTON, D.C.: WILLIAM GREER, 1846).

The Road to Oregon and California, Across the Rocky Mountains.

When the emigrants start to the sun-down diggings of Oregon, they should not fancy that they are doing some great thing, and that they need military array, officers, non-commissioned officers, &c: all this is folly. They will quarrel, and try to enforce non-essential duties, till the company will divide and subdivide, the whole way to Oregon. When you start over these wide plains, let no one leave dependent on his best friend for any thing; for if you do, you will certainly have a blow-out before you get far. I would advise all young men who have no families to have nothing to do with the wagons nor stock. Buy two horses and two good mules in your own neighborhood; for if you depend upon getting animals on the frontier, you will have to pay very high for them; make your way to Independence [Missouri] with your provisions—such as cannot be obtained at Independence: here get pair-fleshes[1] for your pack-mules, enough of flour and bacon to season it,

[1]He probably means parfleches, which were commonly used by Plains Indians to transport and store items, ranging from food to personal accoutrements. Made of durable buffalo hide, they could easily be packed on mules or horses by overland emigrants or merchants transporting trade goods. See Lowie, *Indians of the Plains*, 63–67.

to last you to Fort Hall; proceed to the Spanish encampment,[2] twenty miles on the Santa Fe road, and swap your horses for Indian horses, and be not too particular; for the shabbiest Shawnee pony you can pick up will answer your purpose better than the finest horse you can take from the stable.[3] Thus equipped, 25 or more, with a riding horse and pack mule to change every day the trip can be made in 70 or 80 days. Take with you plenty of horse-shoes and nails, a hammer and clincher, and keep your animals shod. If any of your animals give out, leave them, for your time is of more value than all your horses; and be assured that as soon as you arrive in the settlements you will find profitable employment. Go well armed, and never let your guns get out of order; and, to avoid accident, carry them without caps. Take no tents with you, nor any thing of weight that you can dispense with. It will be necessary to keep watch nearly all the way, particularly through the Pawnee country; that is, from the crossing of Big Blue [River] to the crossing of South Platte [River]. The Sioux will not likely molest you in any way;[4] let your watches be divided so as to fall equally on each; but, should any one refuse to bear his part, the best mode of punishment is for some one to fill his place without grumbling. Should

[2]This may have been the small settlement of New Santa Fe (though it did not develop into a town until 1851), which anchored the southern end of a diagonal access that linked the Santa Fe and Oregon trails. It was located on the state line separating Missouri from Kansas. See map provided in Stocking, *Road to Santa Fe*, 28–29, and text 61, 75; and Franzwa, *Oregon Trail Revisited*, 93.

[3]A number of emigrants commented on the wisdom of trading their larger, farm-bred horses for the smaller but more durable Indian ponies, especially those from the extensive herds of the Sioux. Unfortunately, California-bound Benjamin Gatton had expected to trade for Indian ponies during his 1849 trip but found few available because of the large number of miners headed for the gold fields. Similarly, Quincy Adams Brooks had to walk part of the distance because he could not secure replacement animals. See Unruh, *Plains Across*, 162.

[4]During the 1840s, a common perception on the Platte River section of the trail was that the Pawnees might cause some problems for overlanders, but that the Sioux were more interested in trade with passing wagon trains. This perception changed by the end of the 1850s, when the numerically superior Sioux were looked upon as the greater threat, especially following the U.S. Army's bloody 1855 attack on their village on Blue Water Creek. In both cases, the Indians were more interested in taking livestock from nonvigilant caravans than they were in killing white travelers. Pawnees and Sioux alike regarded these purloined horses and oxen as partial payment for the resources—grass, water, wild game—that these travelers were rapidly destroying. See Tate, *Indians and Emigrants*, 126–43, 218–21.

you discover danger from Indians, travel at the top of the speed of your animals, till you get through their territory, when you can stop and recruit [rest] your animals. You should take with you an iron pan, the handle so jointed as to fold up; a kind of knife, fork, and spoon, that all shut in one handle—such knives are common in all hardware stores. In addition to this, you will need a fire-proof iron kettle, to make tea, coffee, boil rice, make soup, &c.; a tin pan, quart cup and a butcher knife, will about complete your kitchen; delay no time to kill game, unless it comes in your way, which will frequently happen along the road from the time you strike the Platte till you reach Fort Hall. At the Kansas crossings you will find a ferry;[5] if the Platte should be high, make a bull-boat, which is made in the following manner: procure two buffalo skins, sew them together water-tight; then get willow poles and make a frame; over which stretch your skins, and your boat is done. Should Green river be high, you will find plenty of dead cotton wood to make a raft: no other water courses will be in your way. Wagons and stock had better cross Snake river on account of grass; those on horse back had better keep down on the south side.

Those who emigrate with families, and consequently, wagons, stock, etc., cannot expect to accomplish the journey in less than four months, under the most favorable circumstances, and, in order that they be prepared in the best possible manner, first buy a light strong wagon, made of the best seasoned materials; for, if the timbers be not well seasoned, your wagon will fall to pieces when you get to the dry, arid plains of the mountains; let the bed of your wagon be made of maple if you can get it, and let the side and end boards be one wide board, without cracks; let them so project the sides and ends at the bottom of the bed as to turn off the water from the bottom.[6] Next, let your wagon sheet be either linen or Osnaburg,[7] well oiled or painted, and

[5]The most important of the Kansas River ferries operating in 1846 was Pappan's Ferry, which had been established four years earlier on the modern site of Topeka. Its story and an 1856 drawing of the operation appears in Benbrook, "Pappan's Ferry," 2–21.

[6]Further discussion of these particular issues about wagon construction and maintenance was voiced in other trail guides and emigrant journals. See Capps, "Wheels in the West," 2–11.

[7]Osnaburg is a tough, unbleached cotton cloth that was developed in Osnabrück, Germany. Its sturdiness made it ideal as an upholstery material, and it was used to manufacture heavy sacks for grain and cement. As Shively indicated, it was also a durable canvas for wagons. See Adams, *Western Words*, 213.

fixed to fasten well down the sides; let the bed be straight; procure wooden boxes of half or three-quarter inch pine boards, of the same convenient height, and let them fit tight in the bed of your wagon. In these boxes place your provisions, clothing, ammunition, and whatever articles you choose to take along; close the boxes by hinges or otherwise, and on them is a comfortable place for women and children to ride through the day, secure from dust or rain, and a place to sleep at night for a small family. Take as much tea, coffee, sugar and spices as you please; but above all take plenty of flour and well cured side bacon[8] to last you through if you can. Let each man and lad be provided with five or six hickory shirts, one or two pair of buckskin pantaloons, a buckskin coat or hunting shirt, two very wide brimmed hats, wide enough to keep the mouth from the sun. For the want of such hat thousands suffer nearly all the way to Oregon, with their lips ulcerated, caused by sunburn. Take enough of coarse shoes or boots to last you through—three or four pair a-piece will be sufficient—moccasins will not protect your feet against the large plains of prickly pear along the road. However much help your wives and daughters have been to you at home, they can do but little for you here—herding stock, through either dew, dust, or rain, breaking brush, swimming rivers, attacking grizzly bears or savage Indians, is all out of their line of business. All they can do, is to cook for camps, etceteras, &c.; nor need they have any wearing apparel, other than their ordinary clothing at home.[9]

Thus equipped, let your team be light oxen from three to five years old,—and if you take horses for servitude along the road, trade for

[8]Shively's advice about taking plenty of bacon was also advocated by other trail guides, but many people ultimately left their overstocks beside the trail and the surplus found no new claimants. As Thomas H. Jefferson warned in his *Accompanyment to the Map of the Emigrant Road from Independence, Mo., to San Francisco, California* (1849), the bacon would spoil and become rancid (p. 4).

[9]Although many overland emigrant families came from eastern backgrounds that stressed the separation of male and female labor tasks, the exigencies of the trail experience sometimes created a greater blurring of duties than was initially anticipated. Far beyond merely performing domestic chores such as cooking, cleaning, and overseeing the children, women sometimes drove wagons, helped with their repair, engaged in trading with Indians, attended ill sojourners, assisted at river crossings, and helped clear the land on which the family ultimately settled. Shively's description of a domesticated helpmate defined women's roles in too limited a way and failed to fully anticipate the shared responsibilities that sometimes accrued on a two-thousand-mile, unpredictable journey. Yet, historian John Mack Faragher argues, most families maintained the strict division of gender roles, and only in time of emergencies did the blurring occur. See Faragher, *Women and Men on the Overland Trail*, 66–87.

Indian horses in the Shawnee nation before you start over the plains; mules will serve you well, if you can get them.—Proceed on your way to the Spanish encampment, as before directed, and here your journey across the plains must commence. You should be ready to take up your march as early as the first of April; and if there is no grass, carry enough of feed for your animals to last you to the crossing of the Kanzas [River], which is 102 miles from Independence; here you will find the grass quite high. See before you start that you have forgotten nothing; and if you have much money, buy some Indian trade, such as small beads of different colors, cotton handkerchiefs, cheap red ribands, mocasin awls, &c:[10]

All equipped, move on in companies of not less than twenty, nor more than fifty wagons together. You will leave this early, and travel in haste until you reach the Platte, for the reason that the district of country along the Kanzas has many creeks putting into it, which are swollen to very great depth, by the hardest rains I have ever seen. Should you take the advice above, you will have passed over the districts of those tumbling floods before they commence. I will instance that the emigration of '43 arrived at a small stream, not more than a foot deep; they struck camp without crossing; it raised in the night, and they were there seventeen days before they could get across.[11]

[10]Indians located in trading villages along the trail bargained for livestock, weapons, gunpowder, food, clothing, and other important items, but overlanders who followed Shively's advice about carrying small items for exchange found themselves in an especially good bartering position because beads, ribbons, handkerchiefs, small strips of cloth, and sewing needles were relatively scarce on the frontier. James M. Maxey's 1845 letter advised future travelers to "take Blue Calico and Beeds [*sic*] in little narrow Red Blue and Green Ribbon" because these were widely prized for personal adornment. Two years later, while camped on the Deschutes River, Elizabeth Dixon Smith Geer recorded in her diary about the magical power of calico and muslin shirts because Columbia River tribes valued them so highly and would trade practically anything for them. See "James M. Maxey to James Frazier Reed, November 10, 1845," in Morgan, *Overland in 1846*, 475; and Geer, "Diary," 169.

[11]Typically, the rivers of northeastern Kansas and southeastern Nebraska posed few crossing problems during most of the year, but they could become raging torrents during April and May, just when most emigrants were crossing through this area. Even if high water was not encountered at the accustomed crossings, mud was often ever-present during the rainy season, and wagons and livestock became mired for days. Pierson Barton Reading, who was traveling in the same 1843 group as John Shively, reported that the weather was cooperative during this initial phase of the journey, but the rivers were running at nearly full bank and with a rapid current. On the Kansas River, they had to construct boats to cross. See Reading, "Journal of Pierson Barton Reading," 149–50. Edward Henry Lenox, traveling in the same massive wagon train, described the near-drowning of William Vaughn on the rampaging Kansas River, followed by bouts with constant rain, mud, and delays at the smaller river crossings. See Lenox, *Overland to Oregon*, 21–25.

Keep your guns in good order, but never have caps on them unless you are going to shoot; when you come in from your hunt, be sure to take your cap off before you put your gun in the wagon. There are many graves along the road, occasioned by the accidental discharge of guns being put away with caps on; flint locks are always dangerous, and should never be taken along.[12]—Forty miles from Independence, take the right hand road, which is the long road to Oregon—there is wood and water plenty,—so you can camp where you please. When you arrive at the crossings of the Kanzas, if it be past fording, there is a ferry there; or, if you choose, caulk and pitch some of your wagon beds, made as before described, and you have a ferry of your own. When you get across, it will be necessary to set a watch at night—and this watch should be kept up nearly the whole way—for where there are no Indians, a guard is necessary to keep the stock out of camp. You will find your cattle, horses and mules will often take fright at night, and run into camp with great fury; this is no particular sign of Indians, and is an occurrence you will often witness. Form a circle or square with your wagons at night, by running the tongue of each hinder wagon between the hind wheel and bed of the wagon before, alternately; chain them together, and you have a secure breastwork against attack by Indians, as well as a secure place to cook, sleep, &c.

Your road to the Platte passes along the north side of the Kanzas, some distance from the river, crossing many of its tributaries; 202 miles from the crossings of Kanzas—wood and water any where—you will come to the river Platte. There the whole face of nature begins to change; the earth in many places is crested with salt—the few springs you meet with are impregnated with mixed minerals—the pools are many of them poisonous—and the emigrants should be careful, and use only the water of the river; for I know of but two good springs from to the head of Blue [River] to the north spring branches of Sweet Water [Sweetwater River]; one is at Scott's bluff on North Platte—the other the well known Willow Springs, between the crossings of North Platte and Sweet Water. You will have several camps to make along

[12]Firearm accidents were frequent causes of death and injury on the trails because many people tended to keep their weapons loaded at all times. Two excellent discussions of this problem even among experienced soldiers and frontiersmen is found in Potter, "'He . . . Regretted Having to Die That Way,'" 175–86; and Potter, "Firearms on the Overland Trails," 2–12.

this river, without wood; but there is plenty of buffalo dung, which is a good substitute for wood. 184 miles will bring you to the forks; you keep up the South Fork 75 miles to the crossings—(plenty of buffalo and antelope)—if it is past fording, off with some of your best wagon beds, and in less than two hours you will have a very good ferry boat. When you are across the river, fill your kegs with water—for there is none fit to drink 'till you reach the North fork, a distance of 20 miles, 143 miles up North Platte to Fort Larima,[13] up a valley similar to the South fork, (thousands of buffalo.) You are now through the Pawnee country, and must look out for the Sioux; and when you get to Larima, make as little delay as possible, for fear the Indians molest you.

You are now 640 miles from Independence, and it is discouraging to tell you that you have not yet travelled one-third of the long road to Oregon. Be off from Larima 12 miles to a spring at the foot of the Black Hills; about 4 days will take you through these dreary hills, and you again come to North Platte. Keep up the stream to the red butes,[14] cross and fill your kegs,—for it is 20 miles to any water fit to drink,—fill your kegs again at the Willow Springs. 20 miles will bring you to the Independence rock on Sweet Water [Sweetwater River]—830; here, a little to your right, is a great basin of Salaratus [saleratus],[15] white as snow; fill your bags with it—it is very good for use, and quite scarce in Oregon—up Sweet Water one hundred and two miles, where you leave it. Your next camp, seventeen miles, will

[13]Fort Laramie had been established in 1834 by William Sublette and Robert Campbell as a fur-trading post, and it had remained an important landmark and occasional supply center for the earliest wagon trains. By the time Shively was preparing his guide for publication, the United States Army was in the midst of negotiations to purchase Fort Laramie and to assume a more significant role in protecting the Oregon and California trails. See McChristian, *Fort Laramie*, 26–49.

[14]The Black Hills he refers to are directly west of Fort Laramie and are not to be confused with South Dakota's Black Hills. The Red Buttes represented a key fording place on the North Platte River at Bessemer Bend, near present-day Casper, Wyoming. See Haines, *Historic Sites along the Oregon Trail*, 188–89.

[15]Saleratus is a chalklike substance composed of potassium or sodium bicarbonate. It was used to make bread rise in the leavening process. Supplies of saleratus could be procured from some of the natural soda springs along the Sweetwater River. Shively refers to a large supply of it occurring naturally at Saleratus (Piaya) Lake, near Independence Rock. See Williams, *Wagon Wheel Kitchens*, 9–10.

be at a spring[16] in the mountain pass, which runs towards the Pacific; fifteen miles brings you to Little Sandy. The road here turns down south, and the traveller must lose at least 100 miles by keeping it to Bridger's fort; here, on Sandy, let your animals rest a few days. Get on your horse and ride back on the road, far enough to get a view of the country westward. You will see a blue mountain in the distance, straight on your course; that mountain is on Bear river, near your track; take a pocket compass and a small party, and see if you can get through with the wagons. I was one of the company that made the road to Bridger's, and opposed it all I could. There is no use in going that way; they have no provisions, nor anything else that you want.[17] Should you fail to find a route for wagons to Bear river, keep down Sandy along the wagon road, 65 miles, to Green river; cross it, as before instructed; keep down Green river 6 miles, and fill your kegs, and cross over to Ham's fork, 16 miles; up Ham and Black's fork, 38 miles, to Bridger; you are now 1059 miles from Independence; fill your kegs; it is 12 miles to Muddy, but the water is salt.

18 miles, another camp on Muddy.

16 miles, another camp on Muddy.

12 miles, a good spring at the foot of the mountain, 5 miles from Bear river.

5 miles brings you to Bear river; keep down Bear river 94 miles to the Soda Springs, (1221 miles,) where you must stop a day or two and enjoy the luxury of those exhilarating Springs. There are in the vicinity a great many of these springs; the best of all of them you will

[16] He refers to Pacific Springs, which was as frequently noted in overland journals as was the nearby South Pass. This is where migrants passed to the west side of the Continental Divide and started to see rivers that flowed westward toward the Pacific Ocean. Its fine spring and abundant grass made it appear like an oasis in an otherwise bleak environment. Unfortunately, livestock sometimes wandered into the boggy marsh and became stuck. See Haines, *Historic Sites along the Oregon Trail*, 236–37.

[17] Shively strongly suggests not following the Oregon Trail southward to Jim Bridger's fur-trading post because it offered little in the way of supplies to emigrant parties. He seems to be suggesting a more direct route across the Sublette Cutoff, which offered a shorter approach to the more substantial trading post of Fort Hall. By 1859, another alternate "shortcut" between Burnt Ranch and Fort Hall was laid out by Frederick W. Lander, an engineer in the Department of the Interior. See Lavender, *Westward Vision*, 377–78, 391; and Harstad, "The Lander Trail," 14–28.

find at the foot of the mountain, one mile and a half from the camping ground on the river; it is situated one hundred yards from a lone cedar tree at the foot of the mountain. It is cool, resuscitating, and exceedingly delicious.

Leave the Soda Springs early in the morning, and when you go down the river about 4 miles, fill you kegs, as you cannot get to the water here, you leave the river. Six miles below, opposite the great Sheep mountain [Sheep Rock], you leave Bear river, from which it is 12 miles to a little branch of good water, but no wood; 6 miles farther to Portniff [Portneuf] creek, one of the tributaries of Snake river, from which it is 48 miles to Fort Hall (1278 miles.) Here you will have an opportunity of buying provisions, swapping cattle for horses, and will receive many acts of kindness from Captain Grant,[18] the superintendent of the Fort. Here you must hire an Indian to pilot you at the crossings of Snake river, it being dangerous if not perfectly understood.[19]

Fort Hall is situated in a large fertile valley on Snake river; you will not travel far, however, 'till the gloom of desolation will spread around you, grass very scarce, water and wood plenty. 160 miles below Fort Hall, you will come to the Salmon Falls, where you will find a great many Indians fishing; you can buy the fish very cheap, but you need not lay in any supply, as you will have opportunities of trading for them the balance of your journey.[20] Two days below, you come to the crossing where you must follow the instruction of your Indian guide; when you are across Snake river, all you will gain is good grass for

[18]Richard Grant was in charge of the Hudson's Bay Company's Snake River fur-trading operations and was headquartered at Fort Hall at the time of Shively's 1843 visit. See Thrapp, *Encyclopedia of Frontier Biography*, 580–81.

[19]The hiring of Indian guides (pilots) along various stretches of the Snake River was a necessity for some wagon trains. These guides were especially helpful at locating the best crossings and aiding the movement of wagons and livestock across the river, as well as locating the best camp sites. By the 1850s, commercial ferries were established at key crossings on the Snake River—especially at Salmon Falls, Three Island Crossing, and Fort Boise. See Haines, *Historic Sites along the Oregon Trail*, 326–29, 339–42.

[20]Salmon Falls was indeed a welcome spot for both Indians and overlanders because various tribes harvested salmon there and, amid the great surplus, were happy to barter for livestock and trade goods. Ralph Geer's party, traveling in 1847, so successfully fished for salmon at that spot that they threw away two-thirds of the catch because it was far more than they could use. See Geer, "Occasional Address for the Year 1847," 36.

your animals—there not being a sufficient quantity for a large band of stock on the south side, from the crossings of Snake river.

It is 70 miles to Bosie river, where you will again get fine salmon,—(45 miles crossing Bosie river to Fort Bosie,[21] 1574 miles)—on Snake river. Here you recross Snake river by ferry. All across, your first camp 12 miles to the Mallair [Malheur] river. Here I wish to remark that, when I left the settlement, a well known mountain man, [Moses] Black Harris, in company with Dr. [Elijah] White, was about to start to look out a road across the Cascade mountain[s], by keeping up the Mallair and crossing over a depression in the mountain to the head waters of the Santyam [Santiam River], the eastern branch of Wilhamet [Willamette River]. If they have succeeded, they have shortened the road for the emigrant at least 300 miles.[22] It would land him just where he wants to be, for the land north of the mouth of the Santyam is nearly all taken up. Another important benefit to be derived is, that there would be no Indians along this way to molest the emigrant; but if the road has not been opened, we must take the old track. And here let me put the emigrant on his guard—for, from this camp to the Dallis [The Dalles], a distance of 320 miles, you will be surrounded with swarms of the most mischievous Indians that ever disgraced the human form. They are now hostile, and you must have your guns in good plight, and travel in large companies; keep them from your camps, one and all. Here for the first time, on the long road, you must set a rigid guard over your camp and stock. 130 miles brings you to the fertile valley of the Grand Round [Grande Ronde]; water, wood, and an abundance of grass all the way. Here you may meet with some friendly Indians of the Skyuse tribe [Cayuse]—but watch them close.

---

[21]The Hudson's Bay Company established Fort Boise in 1834, on the east bank of the Snake River, just below the juncture with the Boise River. Flooding forced changes in location over time, but throughout its history as a British fur-trading post, it was a welcoming oasis to Americans, and its manager willingly sold them supplies when these were available. It closed as a commercial enterprise by 1853, but the U.S. Army constructed a like-named post in 1863, approximately forty-six miles to the east. See Franzwa, *Maps of the Oregon Trail*, 214–21.

[22]This became known as Meek's Cutoff, in honor of fur trader and guide Stephen H. L. Meek, who had previously visited this area of Oregon. Unfortunately, in leading a large wagon train through this little-known region in 1845, Meek became lost, and many of his charges perished. See Clark and Tiller, *Terrible Trail*.

From the Grand Round, it is 70 miles to Dr. [Marcus] Whitman's Mission, over the blue mountain [Blue Mountains], which is not bad. This is a very fertile country, and the Indians raise a quantity of corn, wheat, peas, and the finest potatoes you have ever seen. They have thousands of horses, which are always very fat, they are a treacherous Indian, and retain an unbroken hatred for the white man.[23] From Dr. Whitman's to Walawala [Fort Walla Walla] is 25 miles—here you strike the Columbia, and many would do well to go the balance of the journey by water, were it not for the Indians [to avoid difficult wagon travel on the south bank of the Columbia River]. I would advise all to keep down the river by land to the Dallis [Dalles] mission,[24] 120 miles; here you can repose yourself and families in comparative security. Here you take your wagons to pieces, and take all by water except your stock, which is driven across the Cascade mountain.

Fifty miles below the Dallis is the Cascade falls, on the Columbia; you here make a portage, and find a schooner ready to take you to the falls of Wilhamet. Fort Vancouver is 40 miles below the Cascades. It is a pleasant sight, after months of toil through the wilderness, to see the ships in the harbor, the carts, drays and hammers, and a general stir of business throughout the vicinity of the place. Should any of you be in need of provision or clothing, you can here obtain them. The chief factors of this place, Dr. John McLaughlin [McLoughlin] and James Douglass [Douglas], are universally beloved, and well deserve

[23]Shively overstates the degree of enmity harbored by the tribes of the Columbia River Valley toward overlanders during the 1840s. Many emigrants found them to be friendly and cooperative in their bartering of fish and vegetables for manufactured goods. There were, however, numerous reports of theft by members of these tribes, which the Indians regarded as justifiable compensation for their loss of natural resources. The martyrdom of Marcus and Narcissa Whitman in 1847 hardened public feelings against the Columbia River tribes, and especially the Cayuse, some of whom rose up against the Waiilatpu Mission. See Tate, *Indians and Emigrants*, 65–72. Shively's negative comments about the Columbia River tribes were a result of his own misfortunes in dealing with them during his trips through their territories in 1843 and 1845. See Shively, "Memoirs," 21–23, 26–29.

[24]The Dalles Mission (Methodist mission) was established in 1838 by Daniel Lee and sold to Marcus Whitman in 1847. At the time of Shively's visit in 1843, it consisted of two houses, a school, a stable, a barn and cleared fields for crops. The missionaries assisted emigrants as much as possible and helped care for the survivors of the 1845 ordeal on Meek's Cutoff. Various eyewitness descriptions of the mission at different times are provided in Haines, *Historic Sites along the Oregon Trail*, 381–83.

the gratitude of all nations for their hospitable kindness to all whomsoever come under their notice regardless of birth or country.[25]

From Vancouver to the Wilhamet falls[26] is 30 miles; here is a town of considerable size, (500 inhabitants;) it is very expensive living here. Be off to the country, and take a fresh bag of flour and your family with you, and find a location to suit you—then go to work; a little labor will seed you a fine field of wheat, and this same land that you locate, in a few years will make you rich beyond doubt.

The country is not settled south of the Santyam. The farther you go south, the better the country is. There have been many projects for settling the rich valleys of the Unquair and Clamet,[27] but none have been put into execution. This is unquestionably the most desirable part of the territory. With a soil scarcely surpassed, and a climate much milder than the Columbia, it offers but one barrier to the happiest abode of man; this barrier is the Indians who live on these rivers. It is thought that if a settlement would locate there, that could raise 100 well armed men with a small fort, would meet with success; such a settlement would be of great benefit to all the settlers in Oregon, as well as California; for, at present, none can pass without the loss of their stock and probable death to themselves.

But I did not set out to give a history of the country, nor its resources. The only design is, that you be fitted out in a proper manner, and have your pilot [guidebook] in your pocket. I have carefully warned the emigrant to fill his keg with water at all those places where it is requisite; and though there are many unforseen difficulties to beset

25 The Hudson's Bay Company's headquarters post, Fort Vancouver, provided an impressive complex of buildings for overlanders of the 1840s, who had seen no such "civilized life" since leaving the Missouri River and reaching the Whitman Mission. John McLoughlin, chief factor of the post, was helpful to many American emigrants who passed through the area before they began their turn southward along the Willamette River Valley. His able assistant, James Douglas, supervised the post during McLoughlin's absences and also proved popular among Americans. Detailed profiles of both men appear in Sampson, *John McLoughlin's Business Correspondence*, xxx–xlii, 128–30.

26 Willamette Falls became Oregon City, a primary destination for many overlanders. It was laid out and named Oregon City by John McLoughlin. See McArthur and McArthur, *Oregon Geographic Names*, 559, 793.

27 These locations refer to the Umpqua and Klamath rivers of present-day southwestern and south-central Oregon.

you, be of good cheer—you will find a country in Oregon that will fill your desires, and repay you for all your toil. Lieut. [Charles] Wilkes[28] has given the only impartial account of the Oregon country that I have seen. I should recommend it to your perusal.

Route to California

The emigrant to California travels the same route to Oregon, from Independence to the river Casua [Cassia River]. 60 miles below Fort Hall, keep up the Casua three days, where cross over a southwest course three days to Goose creek—up Goose creek three days; thence a southwest course six days (distressing bad road,) to Mary's river [Humboldt River]—down Mary's river 250 miles to its sink (a small lake.) [Humboldt Sink].

Along this river keep your guns in order, and sleep on your trail ropes, for the arrows of death are pointed at you from every Gulch, and without the strictest care you will lose your animals, if not your lives. This is the most sterile desert on the Continent of America, for a distance of 350 miles; not a tree nor shrub, except the hated sage and gresewood, can be seen. The water is all strongly tainted with mixed minerals, and hundreds of lakes in winter are now dry, and form a crest [crust] at bottom as white as snow. The water, before evaporated, is like lye—the white pearlash at bottom is of the same nature, and is used in California for making soap. Here you will see hundreds of Indians destitute of a particle of clothing, living on snails, crickets, worms, and grass, (where there are any.) They are the last link in the chain of human beings. They occupy the country from Mary's river to Snake river. They dig holes in the ground to shelter them from the storms of winter, and must lie in a partial torpid state 'till spring, when they leave their burrow, and wander over the wide plains of desolation,

[28]In 1841, Lieutenant Charles Wilkes of the United States Navy conducted an important exploration of the Columbia and Snake rivers, as well as the Puget Sound area. He sent a smaller party under Lieutenant George F. Emmons down the Willamette River and eventually into Mexican California. Wilkes's *Narrative of the United States Exploring Expedition* (1845) became a booster for American settlement of Oregon country during the 1840s and 1850s. See Stanton, *Great United States Exploring Expedition*, 247–66.

without the means of killing the few antelope that are thinly dispersed over their unparalleled barren country.

But to proceed, I left you at the sink of Mary's river,—take a due west course 40 miles to the foot of the Cascade mountain.[29] This mountain is a smasher, being 2000 feet higher than the Rocky Mountains; you cannot expect to cross it without difficulty, and if you are as late as November, you will be much troubled with snow; and, as there is no trail which you will be able to follow, keep your course west as well as you can. When you cross over the division of the great mountain you will be on one of the tributaries of the Sacrimento [Sacramento River]; follow it down to its mouth, and you will turn out your animals at Captain [John] Sutter's Fort in California, and rest from the toil of your long journey. From the eastern foot of the Cascade mountain to the Fort, it is 110 miles.

The reader need not be disheartened by reading a description of the expansive desolation along the road; for in California, as in Oregon, the country along the sea is very fertile, and the plains produce an abundance of oats and clover spontaneously. Cattle and horses are so easily raised here, that they are only prized for their hides—consequently, they are diminishing. But we hope that when a few more of our citizens get settled there, they will put a stop to killing stock merely for their hides. Seek a good location for your farm, and stick to it. The Spaniards may molest you—but be firm, and soon the destiny of California will be governed by yourselves.

Distance from Independence to Astoria

From Independence to the Crossings of Kanzas	102 miles.
Crossing of Blue	83
Platte River	119
Crossings of South Platte	163
To North Fork	20
To Fort Larima	153
[Total miles]	640

[29]Shively is speaking of the high peaks of the Sierra Nevadas that must be ascended before reaching the pleasant valleys of California. The term Cascade Mountain(s) was sometimes used in the nineteenth century to refer to the Sierra Nevadas as an extension of the Cascade Range of Washington and Oregon. See Gudde, *California Place Names*, 56.

From Larima to cross'g of North fork of the Platte	140
To Independence Rock on Sweet Water	50
[Total miles]	830
Fort Bridger	229
Bear River	68
Soda Springs	94
To Fort Hall	57
[Total miles]	1278
Salmon Falls	160
Crossings of Snake river	22
To Crossings of Bosie river	69
Fort Bosie	45
Dr. Whitman's Mission	190
Fort Walawala	25
Dallis Mission	120
Cascade Falls, on the Columbia	50
Fort Vancouver	41
Astoria	90
[Total miles]	2117

In preparation by the author a concise description of the Oregon and California Countries, climate, soil, natural productions, together with a map of the same.

Artist William Henry Jackson painted this undated view of *Alcove Springs* near the Big Blue River in northeastern Kansas. Its welcoming cold waters were used by many overlanders, but in some arid years, no reliable source of water could be found at this spot. Jackson's painting paid homage to the Donner party, who refreshed themselves at Alcove Springs. Unfortunately, Sarah Keyes, a blind and deaf seventy-year-old member of the caravan, died from tuberculosis on May 29, 1846, and was buried slightly west of the idyllic setting. *Courtesy of Scotts Bluff National Monument.*

St. Joseph was one of Missouri's most important jumping-off towns from which to begin the westward journey. This engraving of St. Joseph, circa 1851, offers an idealized impression of the commercially vibrant community. During the 1840s, it represented the last "civilized settlement" that some overlanders would see until they reached the Willamette Valley of Oregon. Riverboats brought large cargoes from St. Louis to St. Joseph, and there the supplies were easily sold to eager travelers. *Courtesy of the State Historical Society of Missouri.*

In this undated painting entitled *Old Fort Kearny*, William Henry Jackson recalled the importance of this welcoming landmark on the Oregon and California trails. The post was established in 1848 near the south bank of the Platte River in present-day central Nebraska to replace an earlier military installation built on the Missouri River at present-day Nebraska City. Fort Kearny was a converging point for many overlanders who departed various Missouri River jumping-off towns in Missouri and Iowa. *Courtesy of Scotts Bluff National Monument.*

Many overlanders remarked about their joy at undertaking bison hunts during the Great Plains portion of their trip. Some were content to kill only enough animals for food, but many other emigrants killed purely for sport and left the carcasses scattered about. Over the years, this became a primary cause of worsening relations between whites and American Indians. The wasteful slaughter extended to other animals, as did the destruction of scarce timber, grazing lands, and water supplies. Frederick Piercy titled this drawing *Scott's Bluffs* in his 1855 book. *From Frederick Piercy,* Route from Liverpool to Great Salt Lake Valley *(1855).*

This undated painting, *Crossing the South Platte*, was painted some years after noted artist and photographer William Henry Jackson made his first trip along the Oregon Trail as a bullwhacker. Yet the scene accurately captured a reality encountered by many overlanders. The presence of Indians trading with the caravans and helping move livestock across the shallow river represented the mutual benefits that accrued for both populations. *Courtesy of Scotts Bluff National Monument.*

One of William Henry Jackson's most famous paintings, *Approaching Chimney Rock*, offers a fairly accurate view of the landscape. His attention to detail and the representation of a semicircled wagon train are also realistic. As the approaching wagons take their positions to complete the circle, the emigrants use the formation to confine the movement of their livestock, not necessarily to protect against anticipated Indian attacks. *Courtesy of Scotts Bluff National Monument.*

When British traveler Frederick Piercy visited Fort Laramie in 1853, it was the most instantly recognizable human landmark on the Oregon, California, and Mormon trails. Originally called Fort William when it was established as a fur trade post in 1834, it was sold to the U.S. government as a military installation in 1849. The original walled structure appears beneath the flag, while additional military-use buildings were constructed to the west of the enclosure. There, overlanders could secure some supplies, as well as send and receive mail. *From Frederick Piercy,* Route from Liverpool to Great Salt Lake Valley *(1855).*

Artist and trail veteran William Henry Jackson painted this view of *Independence Rock* in 1936. The oval-shaped granite monolith, measuring approximately 1,900 feet long, 700 feet wide, and 128 feet high at its greatest extent, was a much-anticipated and instantly recognized landmark. Overland caravans hoped to reach this point on the Sweetwater River as close to July 4 as possible to affirm that they were on schedule with their trip. Thousands of emigrants carved or painted their names on to the rock formation, and many of these inscriptions remain today. *Courtesy of Scotts Bluff National Monument.*

Fort Bridger, established in 1843 as a fur-trading post on the Black Fork of the Green River (today's southwestern Wyoming) by James Bridger and Louis Vásquez, was visited by many travelers using the Oregon, California, and Mormon trails. This 1849 drawing by James F. Wilkins shows the primitive nature of the commercial establishment, which was burned by the Mormons during the 1857–1858 Mormon War. The U.S. Army reestablished Fort Bridger as a supply depot, and except for two years, it remained in service until November 1890. *Courtesy of the Wisconsin Historical Society, Madison, Wisconsin, James Wilkins Collection.*

While working as a teamster in 1866, William Henry Jackson made another of his several trips into the west. This time, however, he resigned from the freighting outfit and headed to Salt Lake City, where he spent approximately two unhappy months working as an agricultural laborer. Some seventy years later, he painted this scene, entitled *The Salt Lake Valley.* It celebrated one of the most important events in Mormon history—the 1847 arrival of Brigham Young and the Pioneer Band at Emigration Canyon. From there they could look down into the valley that would become their Zion in the Wilderness. *Courtesy of Scotts Bluff National Monument.*

In this undated painting entitled *Three Island Crossing*, William Henry Jackson captured the beauty associated with this landmark in south-central Idaho. Westbound emigrants usually crossed here to the north bank of the Snake River, which provided a better trail into Fort Boise. Those who avoided the dangerous crossing found the south bank trail to be rough and dry. Three Island Crossing is located two miles southwest of present-day Glenn's Ferry, Idaho. *Courtesy of Scotts Bluff National Monument.*

In 1836, Marcus and Narcissa Whitman established this mission at Waiilatpu, near present-day Walla Walla, Washington. Most overlanders who traveled the Oregon Trail between 1840 and 1844 passed through the Whitman Mission, and many commented that it sported the first frame buildings they had seen since leaving the Missouri River. After 1844, however, a shorter route developed slightly to the south, and fewer travelers diverted their route to the mission. Local Cayuse Indians, angered by a measles epidemic, attacked the mission on November 29, 1847, killing thirteen staff members, including the Whitmans. Artist William Henry Jackson painted this view of Whitman Mission in 1940. *Courtesy of Scotts Bluff National Monument.*

In 1841, John Bidwell (1819–1900) set out from Missouri with a wagon train consisting of sixty-nine people bound for California. Approximately half of those split off at Fort Hall and headed for the Willamette Valley of Oregon. Bidwell and his followers experienced considerable privation crossing the Nevada desert and the Sierra Nevadas, but, minus their wagons, they eventually reached California. Bidwell participated in the Bear Flag Revolt of 1846, made a major gold discovery on the Feather River, and engaged in California's tumultuous politics for many years. *Courtesy of California State University, Chico, Merriam Library, Special Collections.*

Johann August Sutter (1803–1880) emigrated from Switzerland to the United States in 1834, briefly engaged in the Santa Fe trade, and moved to Oregon in 1838. Arriving by ship in San Francisco during mid-1839, he convinced local Mexican officials that he could erect a fort to protect northern California from illegal adventurers. His large land grant near present-day Sacramento grew over the next years, and he aided some of the earliest American emigrants. Gold was discovered on his baronial estate on January 24, 1848, setting off an international rush that ruined Sutter's estate and bankrupted him. *Courtesy of the Library of Congress.*

Lansford W. Hastings (c. 1818–c. 1868) participated in an Oregon-bound wagon train in 1843, and three years later published *The Emigrants' Guide to Oregon and California*, one of the earliest guidebooks assembled for broad public sales. In 1846, he accompanied a party east from California to the Fort Bridger area, where he tried to convince Oregon-bound settlers to redirect their journey to California via the Hastings Cutoff across the Utah-Nevada desert lands. This ill-conceived route contributed to the 1846 Donner party disaster and to the worsening reputation of Hastings.

John Charles Frémont (1813–1890) was commissioned a second lieutenant in the elite U.S. Topographical Engineers in 1838, and within four years he led a reconnaissance to South Pass. His firsthand experience, plus advice from mountain men such as Kit Carson, helped Frémont popularize the main route to Oregon. Frémont's subsequent publications were widely pirated by other writers, who included his descriptive information in their guidebooks and newspaper articles. He made five explorations into the West—including the Great Basin and California—but was plagued by overplaying his hand politically and financially during the rest of his life. *Courtesy of the Library of Congress.*

Brigham Young, as he appeared during the 1850s. Young held official positions that strongly shaped Indian and emigrant relations. Appointed as governor of the Utah Territory in 1851, he simultaneously held the post of Indian superintendent for the territory (1851–1858). Despite widespread American prejudices directed against Mormons, many overlanders relied on Mormon aid during the transcontinental trip, and Salt Lake City became an important wintering and outfitting center for some of the groups. *Courtesy of Utah State Historical Society.*

1844

Willard H. Rees, Letter to Mother from Oregon

This letter captures the pathos and grim reality that faced so many Americans who left their eastern homes in the 1840s and struck out for Oregon or California. Many sensed that they would be seeing family and friends for the last time in their lives. These departing migrants also knew that they would never return home and that, in most cases, their eastern brethren would not join them at some future date. This feeling of disorientation and loss permeated their thoughts even as they simultaneously contemplated a better life for themselves in the new land.

Willard Hall Rees was twenty-four years old in 1844, when he left his home in Riley, Ohio, and, as is evident in the opening lines of this letter, he anguished over not being able to communicate with his mother from distant Oregon. He had written several letters since his journey had commenced, and during the two-year interval, he apparently had not heard from any family members. Such was the nature of mail delivery to and from the Pacific Coast during the first decade of American migration. Rees's repeated attempts to send letters by ship and overland freight wagons had apparently failed. He wondered if any of the reassuring epistles had reached their destination so that his mother would not have to worry about him. And if some of these letters had reached her, perhaps the problem was that her written responses had not traveled west because of the chaotic postal system that existed in the territories. Today's generation, with access to so many different forms of rapid communication, cannot fully appreciate Rees's dilemma, but many can understand the depth of his homesickness.

Willard H. Rees departed Independence, Missouri, with the Cornelius Gilliam wagon train. Despite his young age, he was appointed adjutant, or clerk, of the overland expedition, with the rank of sergeant-major. He maintained a detailed daily record of the "official" and "unofficial" events along the trail, but that important document has not survived for present-day inspection. He loaned the diary to Charles Saxton in 1845, as the latter made a trip to the states, but it was never returned and eventually disappeared from family records.

Rees's later composed recollections did not fare much better, since most of the paper sheets on which they were written were devoured by mice while in storage. Only eight pages have survived in the archives at the Bancroft Library, University of California, Berkeley. This meager record provides only sketchy information and discrepancies when compared with richer information provided by other members of the same train. Likewise, none of the letters to his mother have ever turned up as part of the public record. Rees's September 18, 1879, letter to Hubert Howe Bancroft and another to John Minto dated October 23, 1874, do exist within the collections of the Bancroft Library, but they shed little new light on the standard story.

Although they were both young men and neither had substantial assets, John Minto and Willard Rees had independently decided to make their futures in the West as they left their respective Pennsylvania and Ohio homes. Their lives intersected in St. Louis, and from there they made their way to the jumping-off town of St. Joseph, Missouri. Both hired themselves out to Robert Wilson Morrison in return for wagon passage and provisions to Oregon. The young men grew close to the Morrison family, and they assumed major responsibilities in the trip west. Morrison even entrusted Rees with a large sum of money to purchase necessary supplies at St. Joseph, despite knowing very little about the young man at that point. Rees and Minto proved honorable in all their endeavors, and they were major players in the successes of the Morrison family as its members crossed the western landscape.

While camped at Fort Leavenworth, Kansas, Rees dutifully recorded the names of 108 members of the Gilliam party. Included in the list were a minister, lawyer, millwright, tailor, cooper, ship carpenter, tailoress, wheelwright, weaver, gunsmith, wagonmaker, and merchant, plus two cabinet makers, two shoemakers, three millers, and five carpenters. Not only did this represent a good cross-section of American trades, it also meant that this particular wagon train was relatively self-sufficient in terms of the necessary skills to answer daily needs. Most notable, however, was the preponderance of farmers, who made up a total of eighty-one members of this group.

As the impressive caravan crossed from St. Joseph, Missouri, into northeastern Kansas in late May, it encountered almost daily rains and had to halt for extended periods to let the small rivers crest and recede. The days were also cold, and Rees later recalled that thick ice still existed along some stretches of the Missouri River where they had made their crossing.

Once the Morrison company reached the Great Plains in central Nebraska, "camp fever" broke out among some members. Rees and twelve-year-old Martha Ann Morrison (the future wife of John Minto) were overcome with severe attacks but survived. Among the unfortunates were Henry and Naomi Sager, who were buried along the trail, leaving their children to be cared for by William and Sarah Shaw.

The risks and privations that confronted these emigrants required strong leadership among the disparate groups of people. Like so many wagon trains to follow in subsequent years, this one operated best in small companies that were commanded by popularly elected men. Cornelius Gilliam certainly lacked the qualities to retain the confidence of so many followers, and his position as "general" was terminated by the people early in their sojourn. Members who left written records of these events blamed Gilliam for many of their early problems, but Rees was slightly more generous in his appraisal, which was written thirty-five years later. Rees described Gilliam as "an obstinate, impetuous, uncultivated man," but possessing "some kind sympathetic traits of character, a strong will united with a powerful robust frame and sound constitution. He was better fitted to execute than to command" (Rumer, *Wagon Trains of '44*, 122). Rees also recalled a dimension of trail life that was essentially under the rule of martial law, even though it sounds overly harsh by today's standards. This occurred when Clark Eads was arrested for shooting at another man. By a jury of peers, the unrepentant young man was sentenced to be staked out in the midday sun from 11:00 A.M. to sunset. During the punishment period, the sun disappeared amid clouds, which produced a torrent of rain for much of the day, making his life even more miserable.

Willard Hall Rees remains an important person in Pacific Northwest history because of his many accomplishments after he settled there. He first contracted with French Canadian settlers at French Prairie (Marion County) to build the church at St. Louis. He subsequently purchased a 640-acre homestead from a settler for $975 and, on January 21, 1847, married Amanda M. Hall. Together they eventually had thirteen children.

After serving in the Oregon Provisional Legislature, Rees joined Peter H. Burnett and other Oregon pioneers of the Willamette Valley who went to the California gold fields. Upon his return to Oregon, following discouragement in California, he joined with two partners to build the first grist mill near present Aurora, Oregon. As an enthusiastic supporter of Oregon City's Pioneer Lyceum and Literary Club, he helped collect reminiscences from early pioneers, and from years of hard work came the lengthy manuscript that was eventually destroyed by mice while it was stored in a trunk. Its destruction became one of the great sorrows of his life, because he realized that the meticulous work could not be duplicated. Near the end of the century, Rees helped form the Oregon Pioneer Association, and as its first secretary, he continued to solicit testimonials from other elderly settlers.

Persons wishing to know more about the important Gilliam wagon train of 1844 should begin with a close reading of Thomas A. Rumer, *The Wagon Trains of '44* (1990). Among the best eyewitness accounts are John Minto's two later-written articles: "Reminiscences of Honorable John Minto, Pioneer of 1844" (1901), and "Robert Wilson Morrison" (1894). These sources should be supplemented with the later recollections of two of Cornelius Gilliam's children: Washington Smith Gilliam, "Reminiscences of Washington Smith Gilliam" (1904), and Martha Elizabeth Gilliam, "Reminiscences of Mrs. Frank Collins, Nee Martha Elizabeth Gilliam" (1916). Further information on Gilliam's earlier outrageous actions against Mormons in Missouri is found in Stephen C. Le Sueur, *The 1838 Mormon War in Missouri* (1987), 92, 118, 128–29, 133, 147–48, 258.

One of the Sager children who watched her parents die along the trail and was later captured by Cayuse Indians in the wake of the 1847 attack on the Whitman Mission also left her memoirs, which were published in 1905 and reprinted as Catherine Sager Pringle, *Across the Plains in 1844* (1989). Two additional eyewitness accounts written by adults of the wagon train are Edward Evans Parrish, *The Oregon Trail Diary of Rev. Edward Evans Parrish in 1844* (1994), and Samuel Black Crockett, "To Dear Friend," February 16, 1845, Typescript 1500, Oregon Historical Society Library, Portland. Very helpful for discerning the key events of Rees's later life is Fred Lockley, "Oregon Emigrants of 1844" (1927), which quotes liberally from what has survived of Rees's original manuscript. Descriptions of Rees's work as secretary of the Oregon Pioneer Association is presented in Willard H. Rees, "Constitution and Quotations from the Journal and Register" (1915).

WILLARD H. REES TO MOTHER,
OREGON CITY, MARCH 20, 1846,
HOLOGRAPH LETTER,
NATIONAL FRONTIER TRAILS MUSEUM,
INDEPENDENCE, MISSOURI.

Oregon City 20th March 1846

Dear Mother while addressing you at this time, I am fearful that you will not receive my letter in consequence of our having no other means of conveyance other than by private travelers. Which cannot be relied upon with that degree of confidence & safety as where we have the privelige of Public posts[1]—I wrote several letters addressed to different

[1]As Rees states, letters that were sent east in the 1840s had to travel overland or by ships at sea. In the former case, hopeful writers simply entrusted their personal correspondence to east-bound freighters, returning fur trade caravans, or small groups of travelers headed for the state of Missouri, where established postmasters could forward the letters through normal channels. At best, this was an undependable system that relied on good luck and honorable men to make it work. The postal system would greatly improve during the 1850s, in the wake of increased demands of the California gold rush, but even then many letters were long delayed or not delivered at all. See Hafen, *The Overland Mail*, 53–70; and Winther, *Via Western Express and Stagecoach*, 28–59.

parts of the *U.S.A.* by D Whites[2] party who left this country in Aug. last for the States over land, And have just been informed from an authentic source that the party consisting of 4 or 5 individuals were captured & put to death by the Soux Indians[3] consequently the papers & letters intrusted to their care were all lost some of which, were of Vital importance to Oregon. I have also written several letters which hav been sent by sea on board of American Merchantmen but as yet have not received an answer to any.[4] Which places me in rather an awkward position not knowing whether you have Rec'd any of my letters or not. For in former letters I have went into a jeneral Description of the Country so far as my knowledge of it extended. Which for fear of repitition at the preasant—I shall Defer I am hapy to say that I am in good health, and that this blessing is afforded to all by the mild and celubrious climate of Oregon. Many persons within my knoweledge would have long since fell Victims to Disease had they not by migrating hither found relief in the fresh and balmy atmosphere of this most Excelent Clime The only objection that I have to the country is that there is to much rain falls in the winter season. However they are warm and not injurious to stock The grass is just as good here in January as in July & our farmers sow wheat from Oct until June & Raise from

[2]This probably refers to Elijah White who, with his wife and two children, had sailed to Oregon in 1837 to serve in the Methodist mission established in the Willamette Valley by Jason and Daniel Lee. He served the mission for approximately four years but experienced a falling out with his superiors and returned to New York. White made the overland trip in 1842 to assume duties as the first federal subagent of Indian affairs in Oregon. Although he helped suppress some of the illicit liquor trade among the tribes and arbitrated some important land disputes between Indians and whites, public pressure mounted to remove him from office. He returned to the East in 1845 to argue his case, and this is when Rees probably entrusted him with the letters. A compilation of White's writings was edited by Miss A. J. Allen and published as *Ten Years in Oregon: Travels and Adventures of Dr. Elijah White and Lady* (1848). See Thrapp, *Encyclopedia of Frontier Biography*, 1549–50; and Rumer, *Wagon Trains of '44*, 38–40.

[3]This statement is illustrative of how easily rumors circulated about Indian attacks and other major calamities on the trail. During the return trip, Elijah White's party was not captured and put to death by Sioux or any other Indians. White returned to Oregon in 1861 as a "special Indian agent" under authorization from President Abraham Lincoln. He later established a medical practice in San Francisco and died there in 1879. See Thrapp, *Encyclopedia of Frontier Biography*, 1549–50.

[4]Although correspondence entrusted to ships' captains sailing between the Oregon and California coast to eastern ports might have seemed more reliably delivered than mail that moved informally along the trails, this was not always the case. For a discussion of the special problems of ocean-going mail delivery during the 1840s and 1850s, see Hafen, *The Overland Mail*, 37–49.

40 to 60 bushells pr acre and all sorts of small grain in proportion. We have had no snow in the vally this winter but occsionly a light frost The Emigration of last fall all got in Safely & in good season with the Exception of one Company. Their pilot attempted to bring them into the Vally by a new & as they suposed a nearer rout but unfortunately failed and lost them in the Middle Region of Oregon This Company Suffered severely for the want of Ptrovisions [provisions] and in many Instancies for water[5] Our Legislator[s] have passed a bill making provisions for the viewing and location of a new road into the vally When completed will be of great advantage to Emigrants & to the country[6] Claims that are Improved are selling from $500 to $3000 in Oregon currency which consist of Stock wheat lumber & Salmond [salmon] or all kinds of produce that will bear transportation the principale part of the business of the country is done by barter, our merchants take all kinds of produce in Exchange for goods & our people all live well & accumulate property faster here than in any part of the world I have ever bin in. I bougt a farm a few days sinc for which I paid $1000 It is situated in the Willamett [Willamette] Vally 15 miles above the Citty[7] I am not married yet but have come to the conclusion of doing as Cane [Cain] did when he went into the

[5]Rees refers here to the 1845 disaster associated with mountain man Stephen H. L. Meek trying to popularize a shortcut across central Oregon, which approached The Dalles on the Columbia River from the south. Lack of water, game, and forage turned the promised enterprise into a nightmare for all who followed Meek into the little-explored area. Even Meek became lost in the unfamiliar environs, and perhaps as many as fifty people died during the transit or shortly thereafter. See two full-length secondary accounts for complete details: Clark and Tiller, *Terrible Trail*; and Wojcik, *Brazen Overlanders*.

[6]The provisional government of Oregon appropriated funds for surveying and improving several possible routes through Oregon to the Willamette Valley. Even the much maligned cut off was considered to be a possible route for improvement, based on Meek's personal petition of 1846. It was further explored by Elijah Elliott's party in 1853, by Captain H. D. Wallen's military expedition from The Dalles to Salt Lake, and by Major Enoch Steen's exploration of 1860. Over time, the general route became a useful wagon road, and today it partly parallels highways 97 and 197 from Bend, Oregon, to The Dalles. See Clark and Tiller, *Terrible Trail*, plate 33, and p. 151.

[7]Oregon City (Clackamas County) was planned by John McLoughlin in 1842, on land that he had claimed as early as 1829 when he was chief trader for the Hudson's Bay Company at nearby Fort Vancouver. The Methodist Mission was established there in 1840, when the community was popularly known as Willamette or Willamette Falls. Centered amid the farms first pioneered by American settlers in the 1840s, it grew into a progressive agricultural and trade center. See McArthur and McArthur, *Oregon Geographic Names*, 559.

land of Nod[8] We have our printing office & six churches now in the Vally and the country is improving beyond all calculation. I send my respects to all the family I am in hopes you will wright every oportunity Invellope your letters Directed to "the PM [postmaster] at Indipendence [Independence] Mo & they will be brought throug by the Emigrants or other wise by way of the Sandwish Islands [Hawaiian Islands]. I shall continue to wrigt every oportunity as I feell it a duty incumbent upon me & one that will enver be forgoten or Neglected by me so long as that being by whome I was created shall be pleased to number me among the living of this unjust and unfriendly World. Mother I just now bid you adieu one & all but must first again try to impress upon your mind the anxiety I feel in hearing from you once more it being two years since I have Read a letter There were some persons came over in the last Emigration from Oxford & also some from Hamilton[9] but I could get no Information from home I will say once more that I am pleased with this country and in case the American government custains [sustains] her claim as far as the 48 Degree *N* Latitude which will secure to the [?] Puget Sound, I expect to spend the remainder of my days in Oregon[10] I do not wish to advise any person to come to this country but were I in the states with out much property I should most certainly come to Oregon

W. H. Rees

E. L. Rees & Family

Envelope addressed to: Mrs. Elizabeth S. Rees
Riley, Butler Co
Ohio

[8]This biblical reference (Genesis 4:16) refers to Cain (son of Adam and Eve), who, after killing his brother Abel, went into the Land of Nod (east of Eden), took a wife, and together they bore a son, Enoch, who started a new line of patriarchs.

[9]Oxford and Hamilton are neighboring communities to Rees's hometown of Riley—all in the southwest corner of Ohio.

[10]President James K. Polk negotiated an even more favorable boundary with the British authorities in 1846. He pushed for forty-nine degrees, thus entitling the United States to the entirety of the state of Washington and the panhandle of Idaho. See Merk, *The Oregon Question*, 338–39, 367–69.

Richard Grant, Five Letters, 1844–1847

King Charles II chartered the Hudson's Bay Company (HBC) as early as 1670, and with each new advance across the Canadian wilderness, this British enterprise created a greater economic and political power for itself. It outlasted its French, Dutch, Spanish, and Russian competitors, and eventually extended its authority across 1.4 million square miles of North America, more than one-third of present-day Canada. In 1821, it absorbed its strongest western competitor, another British firm, known as the North West Company, which had been organized in 1784.

By the time American fur trappers and traders began to push into the northern plains and the Pacific Northwest in the 1820s and 1830s, they encountered this well-entrenched financial behemoth. With its wide-ranging Indian trader relationships and its seemingly inexhaustible supply of capital and political influence, it appeared to be invincible. Upon seeing the initials "HBC" stamped on shipping boxes of goods and packs of furs, Americans half seriously suggested that the company initials actually stood for "Here Before Christ."

Many of the prominent Americans who visited Oregon prior to 1840 voiced a decidedly hostile attitude toward this British firm. Boston schoolteacher Hall J. Kelley had originally written favorable comments about the Hudson's Bay Company in his *General Circular to All Who Wish to Emigrate to the Oregon Territory* (1830). Yet, following his lone visit to the Pacific Northwest two years later, he wrote disparagingly about this foreign entity, which existed merely "to cheat and kill Indians, and get gain." Kelley especially directed his vitriol against John McLoughlin, the company's presiding officer at Fort Vancouver. Indeed, McLoughlin had coolly received this booster of America's claim to Oregon precisely because he did not wish to see an American population rush into the Willamette River Valley or into the inland fur-bearing areas.

When legendary American explorer and trapper Jedediah Smith tried to open negotiations in 1828 to share hunting rights in the Snake River country, he was rebuffed by representatives of the Hudson's Bay Company. The following year, Joshua Pilcher offered to lead a combined party of British and American trappers into Blackfoot country, but HBC's executive Sir George Simpson politely refused permission on the grounds that it would set a precedent for trespass across vaguely defined international borders. Although both the United States and Britain were operating under the cordial terms of the 1819 Joint Occupation Agreement in the Pacific Northwest, HBC representatives were trying to protect their interior trapping zones and Indian alliances.

British ambivalence about American presence in Oregon country was also evident in the actions taken by Pierre Pambrun, the company's chief trader at Fort Walla Walla. When Captain Benjamin Bonneville visited the fur-trading post in 1834, Pambrun was courteous and helpful in every way. In other circumstances the two men might have been friends, but Pambrun made it clear that he and other representatives of the Hudson's Bay Company would not tolerate American trappers or diplomats who tried to unduly influence the Indian tribes.

As it turned out, however, Britain would face a different type of "invasion" during the 1840s, not one directed by American trappers and traders, but one composed of settlers. The migration began with a handful of missionaries, and then accelerated after the 1841 Bidwell-Bartleson wagon train lured people to the Willamette River Valley. Each successful year brought larger numbers of overlanders until, by 1846, the demographic profile had reversed itself. Hudson's Bay Company representatives reported fewer than 750 British subjects widely scattered across the immense northwestern landscape. In contrast to those limited numbers, the Americans had settled approximately five thousand people south of the Columbia River.

These population disparities gradually forced a change in British policies. Hudson's Bay Company representatives continued impeding American trapping and fur-trading operations in modern-day Idaho and Washington state, but they remained supportive of the American wagon trains that turned south of the Columbia River into the present-day state of Oregon. By 1840, ranking HBC officers such as John McLoughlin, Richard Grant, and George Simpson came to realize that significant profits could be made in selling supplies and livestock to American overlanders crossing the Snake River and Columbia River country. At about the same time, these men recognized that the area below the Columbia River was virtually trapped out, and thus the

American settlers of the Willamette River Valley were no longer challenging company profits in that district.

During the 1840s, HBC trading posts at forts Hall, Boise, Walla Walla, and Vancouver became welcome oases for Americans who traversed the Oregon Trail. Some groused about allegedly high prices paid for goods, but the majority expressed positive opinions about the company leaders. Some even boldly claimed that without the help of HBC, they would not have completed their trips.

The inevitable diplomatic confrontation between Britain and the United States finally came to a slow boil in 1846, and President James K. Polk's baseless demand for all the land below the southern border of Russian Alaska ("Fifty-Four Forty or Fight") pushed the two nations closer to war. Advice from the Hudson's Bay Company to the British Parliament helped produce a compromise between the two nations. The company had already begun its retrenchment from south of the forty-ninth parallel in January 1845 when it shifted most of its supplies and fur trade operations to Fort Victoria on Vancouver Island. Its leaders informed Parliament that economic opportunities south of forty-nine degrees were too limited to warrant a war with the United States. On June 15, 1846, the compromise treaty was ratified in the United States Senate by a vote of 41 to 14, and the present-day international boundary was established.

The following five letters written by Fort Hall's chief trader Richard Grant between March 1844 and December 1847 provide a personalized glimpse at the problems and prospects that HBC faced during this critical era. Born in Montréal in 1794, to a family well established in the fur trade, Grant represented what historian Merle Wells has called "an aristocrat in the wilderness." He entered the fur business soon after the conclusion of the War of 1812, first as a clerk with the North West Company, and then with the Hudson's Bay Company when the two enterprises merged in 1821. Over the following two decades, his duties carried him to a number of important assignments across the western half of Canada. Then, in 1841, Chief Factor John McLoughlin at Fort Vancouver assigned him to the Snake River country. In this capacity, he took control of operations at Fort Hall in the summer of 1842 and remained in that important position until 1853.

Grant was among the first of the Hudson's Bay Company men to recognize the profitability of selling supplies to American travelers on the Oregon Trail. He pointed out to his superiors that this new economic enterprise could more than offset the inevitable decline of the area's fur trade. Yet, at other times, he seemed greatly disturbed that so many Americans were moving into the region south of the Columbia River. For that reason, he advised some of the Americans to turn southwest from Fort Hall, and to occupy Mexican California rather than the joint-use area of Oregon. In 1846, he also endorsed the Applegate Trail, whereby travelers could approach the Willamette Valley from the south rather than along the Columbia River route.

Poor health began to dictate a different set of realities to Grant by the beginning of the new decade. His superior George Simpson suggested that he take a less demanding company assignment in the Peace River district, but Grant preferred to remain near Fort Hall. He retired in 1853, moved four miles up the trail, and settled his family at the abandoned American military post known as Cantonment Loring. There he remained until 1856, while his son-in-law William Sinclair managed company affairs at Fort Hall. The Hudson's Bay Company closed Fort Hall in the summer of 1856, and Grant moved his personal Indian trade and livestock business into western Montana. There he could be nearer his Flathead tribal relatives. He died while on the trail near Walla Walla on June 21, 1862. Like John McLoughlin, who had elected to settle in Portland at the end of his HBC career, both men had become American citizens by choice, and both men were fondly remembered by the people of their adoptive country. Richard Grant lies buried in the Mountain View Cemetery in Walla Walla, Washington.

Given the Hudson's Bay Company's longevity and importance, there is little wonder that it has received considerable attention among popularizers and scholars alike. Among the best standard works are John S. Galbraith, *The Hudson's Bay Company as an Imperial Factor, 1821–1869* (1957); Edith I. Burley, *Servants of the Honourable Company: Work, Discipline, and Conflict in the Hudson's Bay Company, 1770–1870* (1997); John Phillip Reid, *Contested Empire: Peter Skene Ogden and the Snake River Expeditions* (2002); and the multivolume set of correspondence entitled

The Letters of John McLoughlin from Fort Vancouver to the Governor and Committee (1944). Excellent for understanding divergent American opinions about HBC is William R. Swagerty, "'The Leviathan of the North': American Perceptions of the Hudson's Bay Company, 1816–1846" (2003). The best overview of Grant's life remains Merle Wells, "Richard Grant" in LeRoy R. Hafen, ed. *The Mountain Men and the Fur Trade of the Far West*, vol. 9 (1972).

The footnotes for the following five letters are numbered consecutively, rather than resuming the count with each new letter.

RICHARD GRANT TO SIR GEORGE SIMPSON,
MARCH 15, 1844, D.5/10, FOLIOS 425–28,
HUDSON'S BAY COMPANY ARCHIVES,
ARCHIVES OF MANITOBA, WINNIPEG.

private Fort Vancouver 15 March, 1844

Dear Sir

On the 27th November last while still in the Snake Country, I had the honor to receive your much respected and friendly letter of the 30th June from Red River Settlemt, and in return I shall to the best of my slender ability endeavor to answer your request regarding the transactions in the Snake Country and other matters.

The cause of my not addressing you [in] Spring [18]43 was not altogether from an apprehension on my mind that your bones were likely to remain in the wilds of Siberia,[1] but chiefly from having been employed in accompanying the Boats up and down to [Fort] Walla Walla very shortly after my arrival here up to and after the departure of the Express, which circumstance also deprives me of the pleasure of addressing a number of my other friends.

---

[1]Red River Settlement, the residence of Hudson's Bay Company governor-in-chief Sir George Simpson, was at Winnipeg, Canada. Grant's Siberian reference was to George Simpson's 1841–1842 trip around the world, which took him across the full extent of Russian Alaska and Siberia. The adventure was captured in Simpson's book *A Narrative of a Journey Around the World, 1841–42* (1847). See W. Stewart Wallace, ed., *The Macmillan Dictionary of Canadian Biography*, 4th edition, 772.

With regard to the increase of Snake Country Returns Outfit [18]42 there can be no doubt that having distributed a number of traps among the natives, and being rather more liberal in paying for their hunts, encouraged them to exert themselves, from the 1st January [18]41 to 1st January [18]42 the beaver and otter skins received from Indians as far as I could find were large & small beavers 186, Otters 41 and from 1st January 42 to same date 43 the numbers were 410 Beavers and 63 Otters, showing at Fort Hall alone an increase of 224 Beavers & 22 Otters.[2]

The men who I had sent out to procure dried provisions were fortunate in falling in with a party of Crow Indians, who had beaver, but would only trade them for horses, and our people not having any surplus number of those Animals could not get the Skins from those Indians, but they having traded them, with the Nez Percez [Nez Percé], Flat Head [Flathead], and Bonark [Bannock] Indians, our people who were encamped with them, afterwards retraded several skins for goods.

Another circumstance which also added to the returns of [18]42 was that a party of Trappers were equiped and sent by James Bridger to the Queaterra Country where beaver is reported to be very numerous, those people made great hunts, their leading man called Smith generally known by the appellation of Peg Leg Smith[3] from his having a wooden leg / on his return with the party from the Queaterra Country, from some misunderstanding or other on account of wages with Bridger in beaver, came to me and traded what he had. Since that time he had been Employed on our side and is a severe thorn in the side of Bridger and the other traders, our opponents. He is employed by me as a runner or Trader among such [places] as I believe we are

[2]After several years of declining fur trade with the tribes of today's Idaho and surrounding areas, the Hudson's Bay Company experienced something of a temporary economic bubble in 1841–1842, as increased numbers of pelts were extracted from the area. Grant attributed this rise to indirect trade with the Crow Nation and an expanded company effort to deliver more traps to the Indians. See Merle Wells, "Richard Grant," 174–75.

[3]The precise location of the Queaterra Country is debated, but the incident that Grant alludes to was an important one. Thomas "Peg Leg" Smith was well known among mountain men living between the Rocky Mountains and California. However, he had earned a nefarious reputation for his theft of several thousand head of horses from California. He allegedly cooperated with the Ute leader Walkara to sell these and other purloined herds to merchants in New Mexico. The ease with which Smith deserted Jim Bridger and sold his services to the Hudson's Bay Company is easy to understand in light of his shady reputation. See Lamar, *New Encyclopedia of the American West*, 496, 1151, 1174–75; and Larson, "Walkara, Ute Chief," 343–44.

forbidden to go to, the number of beaver brought to Fort Hall by Smith in about twelve months is 460 besides a few Otters.

These causes and the few remaining freemen trappers on our side having been pretty fortunate in both their trapping and petty trading with Indians out of our way, I believe to have been the principal causes, which swelled the Returns of [18]42.

My nearest American neighbors are Vasquez[4] and Bridger traders established on Blacks Fork, a branch of the Green or Colorado River, their establishment was in 1842 on Green River but in [18]43 fearing the Shyans [Cheyennes] and Sewes [Sioux] Indians, removed to Blacks fork a couple days riding from Green River.[5] They like ourselves have done but very little this year, and in all likelihood they will do far less the next.

Proposals in 1842 were made to James Bridger who was then alone and not in partnership with Vasquez, and as he returned no answer I concluded he did not wish to accept them. They are now equiped by Chauteau [Chouteau] of SLouis. He himself Bridger with a party of freemen trappers & Engaged servants,[6] in all between 30 or 40 men left in Spring 43 to go and make a hunt on the Blackfeet Lands in the upper parts of Missouri [Upper Missouri River], what the result will be I cannot tell, but when in September by two of our men who were

[4]Louis Vásquez received his first license to trade with the Pawnees as early as 1823, but during the 1830s, he moved his operations to the Rocky Mountains. In 1843, he partnered with Jim Bridger, and they operated out of Fort Bridger, making money in both the fur trade and the overland trade. See Hafen, "Louis Vásquez," 321–38.

[5]Jim Bridger established his namesake trading post prior to July 1842 on Black's Fork of the Green River, and it became a common meeting ground for trappers and overland travelers alike. Perhaps as early as 1844, Bridger abandoned the first site and relocated on bottomland that is now encompassed by Wyoming's Fort Bridger State Park. Oregon Trail emigrant Heinrich Lienhard described the structures in 1846: "Fort Bridger consisted of two block houses surrounded by palisades 10 feet high. It could hardly be defended for long against a determined attack." See Haines, *Historic Sites along the Oregon Trail*, 269–73; and Lienhard, *From St. Louis to Sutter's Fort*, 96.

[6]The Chouteaus, among the founding families of St. Louis, had been active in the western fur trade since the 1770s. Much of the financial advance of the family was directed by Auguste Pierre Chouteau (1786–1838), who first pushed up the Missouri River with Indian trade goods, then to the Central Rockies and to Santa Fe. Jean Pierre Chouteau, Auguste's half-brother, expanded family operations until he went into semiretirement in 1820. By the time of Richard Grant's 1844 letter, Pierre Chouteau, Jr., son of Jean Pierre, had expanded the business to ultimately include purchase of forts Union, Laramie, Clark, and Benton. Grant's reference to "freemen trappers" refers to men who traded pelts to various companies but had no formal contracts to do so. "Engaged servants" referred to men who worked exclusively for one company and were under contract. See Lamar, *New Encyclopedia of the American West*, 211–12.

out with the Bonnark [Bannock] & Snake Indians procuring dried provisions, Bridgers party had among them all not above thirty Skins, and no Goods to carry on trade. This partner Vasquez who remained in charge of their establishment on Blacks Fork was seen by Peg Leg Smith in Decr last, and the latter informed me at Fort Hall previous to my departing in January, that he Vasquez had little or no goods, And at the utmost one hundred pounds weight of Beaver. This added to 500 pounds More which they sent down to St Louis, is about all they have made this year.

Another petty trader by the name of Miles Goodyear[7] who use to do business with us, and who had since left us to Equip himself at Towse [Taos, New Mexico], wherefrom he smuggles as much Liquor as he pleases. I am informed [he] got for his share in the neighbourhood of Uintee and the Youtah [Utah] Country about three packs.

A Man by the name of OFallan [William O. Fallon][8] with goods from the States and Liquor from Towse [Taos] also gathered two or three hundred Skins for his share. The trappers of the mountains will do any thing and go any where for Liquor, and those who have it get the preference and the Skins. Although those petty traders are but triffling, I assure you they do a great deal of harm and are the cause of a good many beaver skins not coming our way.

The HBCompany [Hudson's Bay Company] nevertheless get a share of what is going and would get more had those triffling peddlers no Liquor.

If I can judge from what little I have seen the Indians in the Snake Country are inclined to be indolent in working beaver or other furs,

---

[7]Mountain man Miles Goodyear (1817–1849) had accompanied Marcus Whitman to Fort Hall in 1836. By 1842, he was living near Fort Bridger, and he served as a guide for William Drummond Stewart to the Green River during the following year. He was a cofounder of Fort Buenaventura in 1846, at present-day Ogden, Utah, and sold it to the Mormons a year later. Goodyear died from fever in California during the early stages of the gold rush. See Campbell, "Miles Morris Goodyear," 179–88.

[8]William O. Fallon—often mistakenly referred to as O'Fallon, as in his namesake O'Fallon's Bluff in Lincoln County, Nebraska—was trapping furs in the Rockies by 1826. He accompanied Elijah White's 1842 wagon train from Missouri to Fort Laramie, and three years later was in Mexican California. Fallon participated in the Bear Flag Revolt and served in John C. Frémont's California Battalion during the Mexican War. He played a major role in the Fourth Relief Party's efforts to rescue the Donner party and was killed by Indians in 1848, while returning from Fort Hall to California. See Thrapp, *Encyclopedia of Frontier Biography*, 480.

I must however do them justice to say that their country has been overrun and ruined by freeman Trappers and themselves seldom or ever much Encouraged to hunt beaver or supplied with the necessary implements for doing so.

The set called diggers or chochoukos[9] are misserable objects nearly altogether naked and starving the greater part of the year, different Kinds of roots with crickets and nuts are the principal part of their food for several Months of the year.

I beg that you will not be offended or think me presumption in me when I say that but very few beavers are now to [be found?] in what is termed or realy is the Snake [River] Country. And without a party is formed strong enough to go to a distance few can be expected. Only part of the Queaterra Country has been hunted by Peg Leg Smith and party and only a short time in 1841/2 the result of which was twenty four packs of good Beaver were brought back for [Jim] Bridger.

Without a trial is now made by our own people before our opponents try it again, I fear there will be but little done. I have since last year been trying my utmost in the Snake Country to raise a party without the companys supplying some Engaged Servants [contracted trappers] and a leader understanding the leading and other requisites required for the safety of property, camp and Trappers, no party will be got up. The freemen [free trappers] themselves cannot agree or remain together any length of time.

If from 35 to 40 Good Staunch men, freemen and Servants say half of each with a leader as above mentioned, could be raised to hunt the Queaterra Country thoroughly I have not the least doubt but the result might prove profitable to who ever undertakes it, hardships and privations of different Sorts will no doubt have to be undergone, but without trust [?] and perseverance nothing can be ascertained.

I have mentioned this to the Gentlemen here but nothing has yet been decided further than there is no men to spare.

Now that there is but few beavers to be obtained in the immediate neighbourhood of Fort Hall or Boisé, something handsome I think might be made by having on hand at both the Posts a good stock

[9]Grant uses a demeaning reference to the Paiutes and other tribes of the Great Basin that was common to fur trappers and overland travelers alike.

of flour, rice, coffee and sugar. besides what is generally supplied to freemen, to be sold to the Emigrants passing those posts on their way from the United States to Calefornia and Columbia.

The last summer when but a small quantity of the above mentioned articles were on hand in the Snake Country, Sundries, including nine head of cattle, sales to the Emigrants and other passants amounting to 1350 dollars besides 5 Beavers and several kind of horn Cattle & horses exchanged for others not in quite such good condition at the rate of two for one.

Another cause against adding to the Snakes Returns is that the men sent from [Fort] Vancouver to assist in taking in the Snake [River] outfit are ordered to be back at [Fort] Walla Walla by 10th September, the season or near about when the Nez Percez and other Indians are returning from the Plains after their Buffalo Hunts, and who generally have in exchange for Horses procured from the Crow and Blackfeet Indians Several Beaver Skins. Therefore by not having at that time sufficient hands, we are unable to send to meet those Indians on Salmon River and other parts, at the time of their return. And those skins are taken down, more or less of them, I am inclined to suppose find their way to the Wallamette [Willamette River Valley] and very likely into the hands of the Americans, who no doubt keep them untill the American vessels visit the country.

Summer 1842 [when] I had kept the men until a later period, I was found fault with for so doing. The result of my having done so added 160 Beavers to the Returns that year.

This last year according to Instructions I sent them back to be at [Fort] Walla Walla at the appointed time therefore could not have their services at the time they were required.

By the enclosed note [?] your will perceive that the Nez Percez Indians had again the last summer a good few beavers in hand. And sorry I am to say that for want of men at that season I was unable to send to try what could be done in the neighbourhood of Salmon River, I am aware that all could not have been traded, nevertheless I am pretty certain that several skins might have been obtained for articles they required while on their route back & to their own Lands.

With regard to Dr. [Elijah] White I can safely say for my own self that I never recognized either his authority or greatness, nor will I, with any of them untill ordered so to do by yourself, or the Gentlemen of the House in London.[10]

As you have under private cover requested that I should communicate with you fully, I do under the same protection take the liberty to state things, just as I consider them to be.

Not with a view of finding fault with those who are placed over me but for your own satisfaction.

The Returns [18]43 I am Sorry to say are nothing near so good as those of [18]42, and though not profitable it is satisfactory to hear that our opponents have done less, The few freemen on our side were unfortunate in their hunt and the Indians having been more or less at war during last summer brought in very few beavers. But I believe the true fact is as I have already stated there are few or no beaver left in the Snake Country and its near neighbourhood.

No less than 130 & odd Waggons with nearly one thousand souls, besides several hundred head of horned Cattle, Horses, Mules &c. passed Fort Hall last Summer, on their way to Columbia, Calefornia & Flat Head Mission. You will however be better informed about these people and their movements through the correspondence of more able hands than myself.

3rd April [18]44 Since writing the above I was ordered on the voyage where I am still, and in the hurry of starting it appears I have omitted to take along with this letter the note regarding the beaver in the hands of the Nez Percez Indians last Summer and which I intended to Enclose. it however merely stated that nearly 5 or 6 hundred beavers were in their possession, if the number should have turned out to be

[10]Elijah White (1805–1879) sailed from Boston to Oregon via Cape Horn in 1837, to help reinforce Methodist missionary activities in the Willamette Valley. His wife and two children accompanied him there, but after four years of service, he resigned in a disagreement with the superintendent. He returned overland to Washington, D.C., and secured the government position as the first Indian agent for Oregon country. With his writings and lecture series, he helped recruit people for the 1842 Oregon emigration season. He eventually lost his post and moved to San Francisco, where he began a new medical practice. See Thrapp, *Encyclopedia of Frontier Biography*, 1549–50; and White, *Ten Years in Oregon*.

even only half that, it was worth looking after, and as I have already stated for want of men at that season I could not find.

Should any thing further word your attention occur between this time and the starting of the Fall Express, I will in my power give you all the information I can.

Wishing you a safe and pleasant passage to and from the Indian Country

I remain and
have the honor to be
Dear Sir
Your Most Obedt
& Humb. Servt
R Grant

To
Sir George Simpson

"Extract from my letter 25 August 1845.
Addressed to John McLoughlin Esq or the
Gentleman in charge of Fort Vancouver,"
enclosed in Richard Grant to Sir George Simpson,
January 2, 1846, D.5/16, folio 26,
Hudson's Bay Company Archives,
Archives of Manitoba, Winnipeg.

Extract from my letter of 25 August 1845. Addressed To John McLoughlin Esqr. or the Gentleman in charge of Fort Vancouver.

Dear Sir

In the event of the report being true that the American Government, are determined on taking immediate possession of this country, or of war being declared between Great Britain and the United State, please advise in such a case, how, we here are to act; because rest assured that without orders from the Company or the Gentleman superintending the Hudsons Bay Co. affairs in the Columbia [River Valley] I give up nothing before I am overpowered by force. American documents will have no effect on me, therefore for fear of committing myself, or murdering [?] others, Let me know by letter how I am to act. If they do not come too soon, or unawares, I shall take care that the Returns are not in their way[11]

The answer to this I also enclose to your address.

I with great respect
have the honor
to be Dear Sir
Your Very Obed. Serv.
Richard Grant

UNDATED AND UNADDRESSED LETTER EXCERPT FROM JOHN MCLOUGHLIN AND PETER SKENE OGDEN, ENCLOSED IN RICHARD GRANT TO SIR GEORGE SIMPSON, JANUARY 2, 1846, D.5/16, FOLIOS 27–27D, HUDSON'S BAY COMPANY ARCHIVES, ARCHIVES OF MANITOBA, WINNIPEG.

John McLoughlin/Peter Skene Ogden to Richard Grant[12] [McLoughlin's handwriting]

As to the rumors of war we are sorry to say the same accounts reached us from other quarters and Captain [John] Gordon of Her

[11]This brief dispatch addresses two realities that commonly faced international businesses such as the Hudson's Bay Company during the nineteenth century. First, they had no ability to communicate speedily with their governments about what to do during a time of international crisis. Second, they often had no ready access to military power to defend their interests when threatened by a significant force. In the face of President James K. Polk's saber rattling over the Oregon question, and being greatly outnumbered by American settlers in the disputed region, Richard Grant informed his superiors George Simpson and John McLoughlin that he needed to know their orders immediately. He was in no position to defend Fort Hall or the Snake River country from a concentrated American effort to seize either.

[12]Ironically, on the same day that Grant was seeking specific instructions on what to do if Americans threatened a takeover of Fort Hall, John McLoughlin sent this direction to not resist the seizure if the American forces were superior in numbers. As a canny businessman, McLoughlin also ordered that Grant make a written record of all property housed at the trading post. Thus, when a final settlement could be drafted between Britain and the United States, the Hudson's Bay Company could be properly compensated for its losses.

Majesty's Ship of War the America who came to Puget Sound to see how affairs were in this quarter writes us that he is instructed by the Commander in Chief [Sir George Francis Seymour] in the Pacific to inform British Subjects that England will maintain her rights to Oregon happen what may. But as to the part of your Outfit at [Fort] Walla Walla it seems as much risk of being taken there if war unfortunately takes place as at your Fort and therefore all we can say is to go in the usual way. If a public American force from the States came to attack you—of course they would be too strong for you to resist. The plan would recommend if you are Certain they are a Government force is to have the Gates open and hoist no flag and let them come in. You are a civilian and have nothing to do with war but you ought to have a correct account of everything in the fort in case of surprise so as to be able to swear to what was taken if they did so.

Signed
/s/ Jn McLoughlin
/s/ Peter Skene Ogden

RICHARD GRANT TO GEORGE SIMPSON, JANUARY 2, 1846, D.5/16 FOLIOS 23–25, HUDSON'S BAY COMPANY ARCHIVES, ARCHIVES OF MANITOBA, WINNIPEG.

Private Fort Hall, Snake Country
2nd January 1846
Sir George Simpson

Dear Sir

Your favor of the 19th June [1845] from Red River Settlement [Winnipeg], I had not the pleasure to receive it untill the 18th of december last, and in answer allow me to say that in reference to the precipitate retreat of the Queaterra hunting party which at the time of my writing I was not aware of was not found on examination as was reported to be, though it may have had some effect on the party, or some attached to it. They were really attacked by a party or band of hundreds of

Indians, who I am told are very numerous and hostile, not armed with fire arms, but with clubs and Bows & Arrows, but the principle cause of their Return was dissension among the freemen Trappers who are determined to agree with none they were the strongest party, to say the truth and without exaggeration they are a set of the most Sorry, unprincipled, rouges [rogues] that ever walked the face of the globe, and without Force neither [Narcisse] Raymond or any other man is able to make them fulfil any agreement they may enter into.[13] Raymond on finding out that they wished to divide and that a number of them wanted to decoy him into the neighborhood of the Calefornia Settlements, and there leave him to retrace back his steps with but very few men, considered it the most plan to return with the whole party [Jim] Bridger's party and another party equiped from the Arcansas [Arkansas] via Gouse were served in a similar rascally manner, and lost lives on their return, bringing little or nothing. Our people brought back including Trade between 140 or 50 beaver skins, what was killed by the hunters 18 in number is only an average of 6 skins per man in fact some of them were that Lazy that they never as much put a trap in the water what can be expected from such characters, no man can believe what they are without being with them for some time. we have however lost but little besides a very small number of horses that had to be left owing to their lameness & poverty, the debt given to the Freemen at that time were not heavy and I have some expectations of recovering some of them, the Goods which were but few, and in charge of Raymond, were nearly all returned. The country is reported to be rich in Beaver but without force and men to be depended on little or nothing will be done. as for provisions, they merely want a stock to take them into the country where the Beaver is found and there the party can Trade with the natives, wheat, Beans, Pumkins, and melons [of] any quantity. On my return to Fort Hall the Trappers who are all freemen had already left to try their luck in different parts of the country at no great distance, where they well knew no beaver would

[13]Narcisse Raymond led a small party of Hudson's Bay Company men to California in 1842, for trapping and trading purposes. Upon trying to collect company debts owed by some American free trappers, he and his party were threatened. Three years later, he was leader of an HBC trapping operation in the Snake River country. See McLoughlin, *Letters of John McLoughlin*, 6:82 and 7:183.

be found but, there they and their families would live on Antelopes Meat, until the time the Emigrants would make their appearance and with whom they could traffic, horses, Leather, or beaver if they had any all with a view of wronging us of what they are debtor here.

Although the Queaterra expedition did not turn out as I had reason to anticipate, and that I am opposed not only by the traders settled in the country but I may say more or less by all the Emigrants that come to it, I am happy to say that the Snake Country, though condemned by old and experienced traders upwards of thirteen or fourteen years ago, will this year turn out very near 1600 Beaver besides other furs amounting to nearly £3^{000} besides a few hundred dollars picked up among the Emigrants passing here on their way to Oregon and Calefornia. So far I have kept good friends or rather on good terms with them all but I assure you they are a rough and uncouth set, it requires all my Yankeeship and Knowing them and their ways of days past. The Indians in this part of the Country being at war with one tribe against the other prevented me the last summer from visiting the Youtaw [Ute] Indians from whom I always collected a few beavers, and now that there is all the appearance of war between Great Britain and the United States, if it does take place little or nothing will be done. There is no want of people besides those belonging to the Amer. Army who are ready and only wanting that hostilities between the two Governments would take place, to have an excuse to come here & help themselves. I have sounded the Bonack [Bannock] Indians who are brave and numerous, though no great beaver hunters, merely to see how they were inclined in case of anything taking place [and] their answer was "we hate the Americans and they Kill our trader they must do the same to us," but my instructions from below—I send you a copy of [them]—you will see that I have but little encouragement either to secure the property, or fight if I felt inclined, but I am bound to obey. I hope that hereafter people will not throw up to my face that I have given up my post like an old woman.[14]

[14]Grant repeated this concern to his superiors in much of his correspondence of late 1845 and early 1846. He wanted them to know that he could not defend Fort Hall against an American military advance, nor an orchestrated assault by American trappers and overlanders. He certainly did not want to be charged later with cowardice or to be made a scapegoat for the failings of other company officials.

With reference to my children I am sorry they could not get passage, the more so from my means being as I have already stated to you in Spring being so very limited. On that account alone if no other I was inclined to hope you would favor me, and not allow an old Servant to go down to the grave altogether a beggar.

I had written to Mr. [James] Keith[15] that in the event of the company's not granting my request either free or by paying for a passage for my two Eldest Sons[16] and that Mr. [Francois] Payette[17] was returning by the way of the States to get them to come along with him. Here or rather in the Columbia if not employed by the Company, they might do something for themselves as farmers or otherwise, which would curtail my expenses. With regard to their irregularities of habits I was given to understand that the one William who is no more was inclined to have his own way and did not attend to his duty as I wished him, but as to the [line illegible] then I am happy to find nothing against them in my letters from Relations and Acquaintances, and you are aware that we all more or less have enemies, and the more so when we are in favor. As to their Education I dare say it is difficult, but dear Sir where are the well educated men in this country who were educated in Canada, what do they know. I believe the greater number have picked it up in the service under Masters who were educated elsewhere. Was I otherwise situated than I am, I should never after the first time have troubled you on a subject so painful to me. You are the principal one who can assist me if you please, and if you decline granting me your aid and protection, I must make up my mind to expend every farthing of my earnings to

[15]James Keith was superintendent for the Hudson's Bay Company at Lachine, Canada. See McLoughlin, *Letters of John McLoughlin*, 6:xxv.

[16]Richard Grant's correspondence of 1846 also frequently mentioned his concern about the education and future of his two sons—Richard and John Francis—whom he was grooming for employment with the Hudson's Bay Company. Evidence of this concern and Richard's problems in financing the boys' travels and education is found in McLoughlin, *Letters of John McLoughlin*, 6:xxiv-xxvii. John Francis Grant's important memoir, devoted to the events between 1847 and 1867, was published as *Very Close to Trouble: The Johnny Grant Memoir.*

[17]Francois Payette had been involved in the western fur trade as early as 1811, worked for the North West Company until its absorption by the Hudson's Bay Company in 1821, and frequently was second-in-command for company brigades operating in the Snake River country. He was stationed at Fort Boise during the troubles with the United States. See Holmes, "Francois Payette," 325–52.

save my three children, two Sons and a Daughter, besides a Sister from becoming vagrants the moment the Almighty thinks proper to call from this world my aged Mother and if it should be myself then they are left destitute in a strange land without money or friends.

Grant my request I beg, send them all three, and if ever in my power to serve you I will not be ungrateful. Messrs [John] McLoughin & [Peter Skene] Ogden have left it to my option either to go out this winter or remain at Fort Hall, I am very glad of it so I may be at hand if the Americans may come on us earlier than customery. The year [18]45 they were here one month sooner than the year previous, not less than 456 waggons besides several packing parties passed here on their way to Columbia & Calefornia with thousands of cattle. The Indians who trade here have done better on their hunting than I have ever known them to do and Peg Leg Smith remains staunch to our side he [has] a few [line illegible] with one hundred & fifty prime beaver skins. I always keep in mind to keep on the safe side as far as getting him in debt, there is always a small balance left in his favor, by that way he cannot well play pla me a slipery trick.

By the arrival of a Mr. [Lansford W.] Hastings[18] and party in November on their way to Calefornia I was informed that several thousands of Mormons[19] were making great preparations in the States to steer their course [this] ensuing summer to the Promised Land which they say is Calefornia. If so it will be a poor place for Catholics and our venerable Doctor [McLoughlin] had better not go to set himself down for Life. Rest assured dear Sir that nothing on my part

[18]In his famous guidebook of 1845, Lansford Hastings described Fort Hall in detail. He also acknowledged the help of Richard Grant, but reserved most of his cordial comments for John McLoughlin at Fort Vancouver. His flattering description about the Pacific Northwest operations of the Hudson's Bay Company is found in Hastings, *Emigrants' Guide to Oregon and California*, 48–52.

[19]Throughout 1846 and early 1847, many people conjectured that the Mormon faithful who had been driven out of Nauvoo, Illinois, would ultimately make their way to Oregon or California. Brigham Young and other members of the Quorum of Twelve Apostles remained wary of these destinations, which were already attracting so many Gentiles from the States. They sensed that the new Zion in the Wilderness needed to be in a more isolated spot so that the faithful could establish their religious community without undue pressure and harassment from outsiders. See Billington, *Far Western Frontier*, 195–200.

shall be willfully omitted to make the Snake Returns as large [and?] as valuable as times and the Country will permit.

In hope that this may reach [you] in safety, and find you enjoying perfect good health and happiness, I will beg leave to conclude and remain

Dear Sir
With great respect
I have the honor to be
Your Most Obed[t]
& Humble Serv[t]
Richard Grant

Richard Grant to Sir George Simpson, December 31, 1847, D.5/20, folios 712–15, Hudson's Bay Company Archives, Archives of Manitoba, Winnipeg.

Fort Hall 31st December 1847
Sir George Simpson
& & &
Dear Sir,

Your friendly and much valued letter of 12th July 47 from Lachine, I had the pleasure to receive by the arrival of my sons on the 3rd August the perusal of which was pleasing to find both my Sister and Daughter were married. This information was however too gratifying and welcome to be of long duration. A very few moments later my sons gave me to understand that my Daughter was no more, She having died shortly after they had left her. That dear Sir with other family troubles on my mind, you must be aware could not be otherwise than painful. Still, what is to happen cannot be avoided, it appears to be the will of our Maker to Overwhelm me more than some others with the troubles and anxieties of the world. I must therefore bear up my lot with patience.—Richard my eldest Son in whom I had entrusted the charge of bringing up my Daughter if not married and my Son John a smart Boy—like too many of his Countrymen considers I suppose that his Father holding a commission in the Service of the Honble Hudsons Bay Company. It could not be otherwise than he must be a Man of Fortune, on the strength of which the Son must take to himself a wife previous to leaving Canada, this being the case, the necessaries or rather nuisances such as a large Waggon &c was considered required be that as it may. The thoughtless young man contracted debts to the amount of 211 Dollars more, borrowed partly from his Lordship Bishop Blanchette [Blanchet],[20] and a young merchant of Saint Louis, by the name of Poirier [?]. Those good people called on me for payment. The young man is of age and married contrary to my wishes and advise, and had he managed matters as he was ordered & instructed, both Brothers could have reached here without adding one farthing of expense, but save some out of what was allowed them for their Journey. If these Gentlemen particularly the Holy Man are paid by me, it will go against my grain, altho I respect Priests, I love them little.

Regarding my sisters marriage I am sincerely happy it has taken place. And it is now my particular wish and request that no money on my account be either paid, given, or lent her. She has played sufficient on my limited means.

In reference to my inheritance [F.] Burns of Three Rivers[21] has [been] sent the power of attorney, which I have drawn up and signed in [the] presence of Witnesses, there being no Magistrates in this part of the World. And I take it you will not take it amiss at my appointing Mr. [W. Duncan] Finlayson to act as my Attorney. My son, aware of your advice from Canada lead me to suppose I was doing proper. With regard to my deceased Mother's Lawful debt, it would be my humble oppinion be nothing but just that they should be paid off previous to the Estate

[20]Refers to Catholic missionary Augustin Magloire Alexander Blanchet, who in 1846 was appointed the first bishop of Walla Walla. His account of the 1847 Oregon Trail journey and his initial years of church service there are contained in Blanchet, *Journal of a Catholic Bishop*.

[21]A letter from F. Burns at Three Rivers to Richard Grant (August 16, 1844) indicates that the two had made a previous connection when the latter agreed to hire as a trapper Urbain Heroux, a profligate son of another Hudson's Bay Company employee. See McLoughlin, *Letters of John McLoughlin*, 6:xl.

being divided up [?] among the surviving heirs of which there are now but three, including my brother William who as I have already heretofore stated, has not been heard of [since about 1810]. My Brother Frances I have been made to understand by my Sister, had made over his share to her. But if the heirs were only entitled to the inheritance after the death of the Mother how could my Brother Frances dispose of his, He who died previous to our Mother. The yearly amount allowed by me to my Mother during her Life and after for the support and schooling of my Children I certainly considered to have been sufficient had Matters been managed with economy, and good Management, on the part of my Sister, but instead of that the children were badly clothed, half of the time not attending School and still the Bills for Schooling, Doctors attention, Bakers Bills &c &c Still appear to be unpaid, It is hardly fair that I should be made accountable for all particularly Bakers bills when the content of them were consumed by the whole family in common. Still what regards my Children Individually I have no objection to pay Although what I allowed if Justice had been done me would have cleared off all such demands as are now brought against me. Sisters and Priests [?] have taught me a lesson never to be forgotten. Though fully aware that yourself and W. Duncan Fenlayson have thousands to attend to without being encumbered with my private family affairs which to either of you is but trouble and labor. The Kindness of both in offering your Services leads me to expect you will excuse the liberty I have too often taken and may yet take in craving your able Assistance, Your remark [that] it is not probable the parties will pay the Share of my Brother William owing to no proof of his death having been tendered. All the light I can throw on and which in some measure might lead to ascertaining the fact is what I shall now—with your permission relate—William would be now a man of about 60 years old. The last I heard concerning him was in 1812 or [18]13, during the last American war between Great Britain and the United States. A young man then, by the name of John Ryan, who was about that time belonging to our Regiment of the 2nd Batt[n] of Select & Embodied Militia and acting as the Quarter Master. He related to me for a fact that in the year of 1809 or [18]10 Himself with two other young men by name, one Larkin the other Ocallighan and my brother William being at New York and out of employ had all four Engaged themselves on board of a British Letter of Mark, said to be bound to the West Indies, my Brother in the capacity of Captain's clerk the other three as common men before the mast—Sometime after the vessels leaving New York but previous to her being out of sight of Land, they were made acquainted [that] they had been deceived and the fact that the vessel was bound direct to England where neither of them were willing to go—during the darkness of the night, while my Brother as clerk was sleeping in one of the State Rooms, wherefor fear of giving the alarm and frustrating their escape they then let down a light boat and made for Land leaving my Brother on board as already stated. The name of the vessel I do not recollect but the same John Ryan was from St. John's on River Chambly where he married a Miss Waywood, and some years ago resided in Quebec carrying on business of Immstate [?] not in the Bakery Line and If still living most likely there. He I believe is a few years my Senior, should this lead to the discovery of my long absent Brother or be the means of settling our family matters to your Satisfaction and good Judgement I should be satisfied and obliged. In regards to my claim on [the] Government I did according to your instructions, contained in your Letters of the 26th and 27th June 1846 from Red River Settlement Execute the Power of Attorney and Afidavit signed and swore to in the presence of Chief Factor James Douglas[22] and transmitted the same under cover to your address, by the Hudsons Bay Company Express which left Fort Vancouver Spring 1847, since which time expect by the Return of my Son, I have not had the pleasure of hearing from you. If you have honored me with a letter by the return of the Express in Autumn, I have not yet had the gratification of receiving it, and as the Board of Management have considered it expedient and proper, to order me to remain In [?] Land, I cannot in all likelihood receive it until some time in June

[22]Sir James Douglas (1803–1877) joined the Hudson's Bay Company in 1821, after having served in the North West Company during the previous two years. In 1843, he founded Victoria, the first company post on Vancouver Island, where he directed all activities as chief factor. He was appointed governor of Vancouver Island in 1851, and seven years later was appointed governor of the new colony of British Columbia. See Sampson, *John McLoughlin's Business Correspondence*, 128–30.

1848. On the same subject of my claim Mr. Duncan Finalyson wrote me by my Son from Lachine 23 March last informing me his Claim for me obtained from the Crown Lands Commission, I expect [?] the amount of one hundred Pounds, for which, not yet having received the Power of Attorney already stated, Hon Mr Finlayson had to become Security and He having forwarded to me another Power of Attorney to sign in the presence of Witnesses, I have done so and now have sent it back to his address.

I sincerely hope your voyage to and from England has been attended with prosperity and your health is good. In this Wild Mountainous Country great changes are daily taking place, between here and the Great Salt Lake a distance of about two hundred miles, we now see several Mormon Farmers settled down to begin farming and grazing operations. At the Great Salt Lake is already a population of principally I may say all Mormons exceeding 3000 Souls, the work they have done there since their arrival in July last, is hardly to be credited without seeing. They have already built up for their present residences about 600 Adouby [adobe] or sunburnt brick houses, besides three or four mills under way, with a wall enclosing the place about a 1¼ miles square. From what I have seen and the dealings I have had with a number of those people I have found them the reverse of what they are generally represented particularly by the Folks of the western States. They appear to me to be what I found them, a moral good set of people polite [?] in their demands and ready to pay for what they get.

I visited the city on business in the begining of this Month, and was introduced to the leading members politely received and brought back about 600 Dollars for supplies that I sent back after my return. Their community being desirous of transacting their business matters with British Merchants in preference to doing it with Americans.[23] The

[23]Brigham Young and other Mormon leaders invited Richard Grant to Salt Lake City because of their acute shortage of supplies. He arrived at Salt Lake City in November 1848, his pack horses "laden with skins, groceries and other goods." Working together, Hudson's Bay Company representatives and Mormon leaders attempted to direct three other pack trains to Salt Lake City, but the severe winter turned back each of these expeditions. Grant was correct to see the profits that could be made with the Mormons in the foreseeable future because of their reluctance to trade exclusively with Americans. See Arrington, *Great Basin Kingdom*, 58.

leading men applied to me to know whether or not the HBCompany would be willing to undertake to supply the settlement with sundry articles which they now and hereafter may require. Not being authorized to decide, I requested them to address the Board of Management on the subject, a council was assembled for the purpose and me invited to attend I did so. They concluded to make application and addressed the Board to that effect. Considering it might be satisfactory to yourself and friends to see the Platt of the City, the work they have already done, their present population and what more is expected [during the] ensuing Summer. I suggested they would also state such things on their Letter and also send down a copy of the Platt a plan as by them called, they appeared well pleased at my request particularly as I gave them to understand the same would be forwarded to Yourself from Vancouver, and to that effect I have myself addressed the Board. Two of their Elders Leading Characters Mess[rs] [Parley] Pratt and [John] Taylor the latter an English man both visited England last year to make application to the British Government regarding the Settling of Vancouver Island.

So far as they gave me to understand (rather in a private manner) their Mission met with encouragement from such as were spoken to on the Subject, and it is supposed Settlers will come out. They appear to place great confidence in the British Government and if they are to be believed they are much more attached to that side than any other and very likely might be of use in case of being required hereafter.

Beaver being now valueless and other valuable furs rather limited in this quarter, we would require to turn our views to something else, and as the old adage says, Make hay while the Sun Shines. A well assorted shop here or rather in the neighborhood of Salt Lake City, and a number of stout Pack Horses constantly Kept on hand here, for the purpose of selling and bartering with the Emigrants whose animals are generally tired out when [having come] this far, and for other commodities to be sold again to advantage would in my opinion gather up a good few Dollars in the year. If we have not here the means of assisting and in some measures satisfying the Emigrants to and from the United States to Oregon and California it may expose the HBC to the hatred and censure of the Public in the States, and prove injurious to us in the end. So far I am happy to say that generally speaking I believe I have given Satisfaction to the Passants[?]. Between Selling and bartering of horses Waggons, &c for other things afterward sold again I have managed to pick up nearly two Thousand dollars it is truly but a small amount still it is better than none and if there is a loss in Beaver I am certain there is none in this kind of commerce. The Returns in Beaver this year is not much which I suppose will be considered as well since they are valueless—of Foxes and Lynxs the numbers are greater than other years.

Peg Leg Smith has not been heard of since the beginning of September, what he is doing I cannot say. [Jim] Bridger and [Louis] Vasquez have again succeeded in getting an Outfit from the States, but as we are not doing much I am inclined to think they are doing less. They are not liked by the Emigrants particularly the Mormons on whom I believe they wished to impose.

The name of the HBCo and their Trade carried on along the Communication of the Emigration generally speaking is more respected and depended on than with the Traders belonging to the States.

The Members of the Board of Vancouver by their letter to me apprehend danger from my Mormon Neighbours. Rest assured there is none for us British Subjects, I consider myself and Property under my charge safer among them than among the Oregonets, therefore be not anxious about the property or myself on that score.

On the 11th July the first of the Emigrants from the States made their appearance here, from that day up to the 2nd September which brought the last for the Year. 901 Waggons besides several Packing parties passed on their way to Oregon or California to this number may be added about 600 more Waggons arrived at the Great Salt Lake.

Having now given you I believe all the information I am in possession of I will beg leave to offer my best wishes for your health and will remain

I have the honor to be
Dear Sir
Your very humble Obed^{t} Servt
Richard Grant Sr.

1845

Lucy Jane Hall Bennett, "Reminiscences of a Trip Across the Plains"

The streets of Independence, Missouri, bustled with activity during the last weeks of April 1845, as several hundred people prepared their wagons, livestock, and provisions to embark on the great overland migration to Oregon. Instead of composing one vast wagon train, as is often implied by writers, the emigrants actually organized themselves into a series of companies that intersected and separated at different times along the trail. One company, composed of people from Illinois, Arkansas, and Missouri, subsequently chose Lawrence Hall as their captain. Born in 1800 in Louisville, Kentucky and married to Lucy Davidson White of Virginia on September 19, 1822, Lawrence Hall had grown up amid frontier conditions, but Oregon, with its favorable land policies, now beckoned him for a new start. Together with their nine children, including thirteen-year-old Lucy Jane, they awaited the start of a great adventure that nearly killed them all.

First to leave Independence was the forty-wagon company under Captain Samuel Hancock. Soon to follow was the Stephens-Palmer-Barlow company, which departed on May 6. Several other groups headed toward various Missouri River crossings before Lawrence Hall led his thirty wagons toward the crossing at St. Joseph, Missouri. Other groups leaving that point would, without any prior planning, meet up with the Independence companies at various points in northeastern Kansas and south-central Nebraska, and their experiences would become interwoven all the way to Fort Boise. The St. Joseph migrants initially were known as the Tetherow Train in honor of their main leader, Solomon Tetherow, who oversaw sixty-six wagons. Over time and for various reasons, smaller groups under captains H. M. Knighton, Nicholas Ownbey, Wayman St. Clair, and H. D. Martin broke away from the Tetherow Train and traveled separately from the larger party.

As far as is known, teenager Lucy Jane did not keep a diary during the trip, and her only published account is this brief reminiscence recorded perhaps five decades after the actual events. It is unfortunate that her remarks are limited, since her family experienced a lifetime of remarkable encounters within the six-month journey. Predictably, she focused her remarks on the most dangerous events that occurred along the trail, notably the horrors associated with the crossing of central Oregon along the newly pioneered Meek's Cutoff. The deadly journey was ultimately spoken about by the public in the same hushed tones as the Donner party tragedy, which occurred in the Sierra Nevadas of California during the following year.

The decision to take this new cutoff rested on the promises of experienced mountain man Stephen H. L. Meek, who affirmed that the route would save time, present fewer geographic barriers, and avoid potential Indian problems. Instead of advancing up the main Oregon Trail along the Snake River toward the Blue Mountains, and eventually reaching the Columbia River, they would approach their Willamette Valley destination from the south.

By the time Lawrence Hall reached South Pass in central Wyoming, he was leading a sixteen-wagon caravan of 38 men, 9 women and 33 children, as well as 226 oxen and 14 horses and mules. Progress had been slow up to that point, and trail hardships had undermined morale, so Hall eagerly listened to Meek's alternative, which would supposedly reduce travel time by three or four weeks. At Fort Boise, the decision was made. While many of the overlanders stuck to the original plan of following the conventional Oregon Trail, Hall and other captains would follow Meek into an unfamiliar land that no trail guidebook had yet described. Although Meek had trapped for furs in the Malheur River district as early as 1834, and had returned to the region during the following year, his recollections of the area were imprecise and impressionistic. He was unable to remember details about specific landmarks, and even worse, he was unable to relay the information with any precision to the various companies that traveled separately from each other. Just as Lucy Jane remembered decades later, they were lost, and not even Meek knew the best way out of the dilemma.

Upon reaching the Malheur hot springs, the followers of Lawrence Hall, John Stewart, Nicholas Ownbey, James M. Nary, John Waymire, and James B. Riggs decided to veer west along what became known as the Trapper's Trail, where they temporarily found good water and adequate forage along the north bank of the Malheur River. From there, they followed a circuitous route that ran from Castle Rock to Harney Lake and to Wagontire Mountain. Turning north, they eventually reached the area just to the east of the Crooked and Deschutes rivers. From there, they followed a northward course toward The Dalles on the Columbia River. Prior to their reaching the destination, Meek had gone ahead to secure food and other supplies at the Methodist Mission at The Dalles. With the help of Moses "Black" Harris and two Indians, provisions were delivered from Fort Vancouver to each of the beleaguered companies, which by now were facing starvation. Before the ordeal was over, approximately twenty-five people had died while on the journey, and another twenty-five would die soon after their arrival at The Dalles. Fortunately for the Halls, no immediate family members succumbed to disease or the elements. All became permanent residents of Oregon. Lawrence died on February 11, 1867, in Portland, having served in a militia company during the Cayuse War and having been elected to the legislature of the provisional government. He outlived his wife, Lucy Davidson White Hall, who died on December 11, 1865, at the same location.

Daughter Lucy Jane married William Hardin Bennett on February 22, 1849, both having arrived in the same 1845 migration. Bennett, originally from Kentucky, served nine years as sheriff of the Oregon district, which comprised Washington, Multnomah, and Clackamas counties. Between 1862 and 1882, the family operated a general store and livery stable in Portland. Due to Lucy Jane's poor health, they subsequently moved to Spokane, Washington, where they remained until her husband's death on September 3, 1886. Unfortunately, Lucy Jane Bennett has long been misidentified in standard historical sources as Lucy Jane Burnett, a matter confirmed in her death certificate of December 24, 1925, and in other documents. She was buried in Portland's River View Cemetery.

Two excellent sources, both based on a precise reading of all available primary material that has survived the 1845 migration, must be consulted by anyone who wishes to know more about these trail events on a day-to-day basis. They are Donna M. Wojcik, *The Brazen Overlanders of 1845* (1976), and Keith Clark and Lowell Tiller, *Terrible Trail: The Meek Cutoff, 1845* (1966). Although the above-mentioned books quote extensively from original diaries and journals of the trip, researchers will also be well served by reading two eyewitness accounts that are readily available: W. A. Goulder, *Reminiscences: Incidents in the Life of a Pioneer in Oregon and Idaho* (1909), and Samuel Hancock, *The Narrative of Samuel Hancock*, (1927). Two other observers who traveled in the procession across the Great Plains but did not participate in the Meek's Cutoff disaster were Stephen Staats, in "The Occasional Address" (1877), and William Barlow, in "Reminiscences of 70 Years" (1912). Although less accessible for inspection, two additional archival items merit attention for the Meek's Cutoff story: Alfred Baldwin, "Recollections," typescript at the Bancroft Library, University of California, Berkeley; and Samuel Parker "Diary," manuscript at Oregon Historical Society, Portland. Two pages of very useful biographical information on Lucy Jane and William Hardin Bennett's domicile in the Pacific Northwest appear in Joseph Gaston, *Portland, Oregon: Its History and Builders* (1911), 607–608.

LUCY JANE HALL BURNETT [BENNETT],
"REMINISCENCES OF A TRIP ACROSS THE PLAINS IN '45,"
IN *SOUVENIR OF WESTERN WOMEN*,
EDITED BY MARY OSBORN DOUTHIT, 27–28.
PORTLAND, ORE.: ANDERSON AND DUNWAY, 1905.

My father, Lawrence Hall, was elected captain of our train, and we started on our way with thirty wagons and about fifty men.[1]

[1]Thomas Adams, who had made a previous trip to Fort Laramie and had some indirect knowledge of the Oregon Trail as far west as Fort Vancouver, offered to lead several hundred overlanders to the Willamette Valley for a $500 fee. Experienced mountain man Stephen H. L. Meek sought the same employment for $250 and presented references from well-known veterans of the Rocky Mountain fur trade, such as Thomas Fitzpatrick, Robert Campbell and William

A wedding occurred in our company. The bride's cake was made with turtle eggs found in the creek. The event was celebrated by a dance on the grass under the stars.[2]

Near Ft. Boise the Indians made an attempt to attack our train and stampede the stock, but failed through the prompt action of my father, who ordered the teams unhitched and the wagons formed in a circle with the tongues of each run under the wagon just forward, making a strong barricade. The oxen were put inside, each driver standing by his own team. The women and children were also inside by the wagons. All the available men were outside standing with their guns drawn. The captain walked out alone toward the Indians with his gun in one hand and a white flag in the other. He motioned the Indians not to come any nearer or his men would fire upon them. The Indians turned and ran away as fast as their horses could go. They had fine horses. The men were nude and painted.[3]

Sublette. Furthermore, he indicated his willingness to settle for a mere $30 at the inception of the trip, the balance to be paid when they reached their destination. A deal was struck, and in the best democratic fashion, members of each company elected their officers while encamped near present-day Topeka, Kansas. "Captain" Lawrence Hall would preside over thirty wagons and their owners as they headed into unfamiliar lands. See Wojcik, *Brazen Overlanders*, 18–23.

[2]This wedding on May 18, 1845, between Stephen Meek and eighteen-year-old Elizabeth Schoonover, occurred after only a three-day courtship. Music, dancing, practical jokes directed at the bride and groom, and the turtle egg cake put the entire camp in a festive mood, but by the next morning, they were back on the trail as if nothing special had happened during the evening. See Wojcik, *Brazen Overlanders*, 30–32.

[3]As they approached Fort Boise, the different wagon companies encountered Indians eager for trade. These were most likely Shoshones or Bannocks who, during the previous four years, had established an expanding barter system along this stretch of the Oregon Trail. Although many emigrants expressed fear of possible pilfering by some residents of the Indian camps, few expressed any real concern about possible violence. Richard Watson Helm, a teenage member of Lawrence Hall's party, later recalled the specific event that nearly led to bloodshed among the two groups. An old cow belonging to one of the overlanders wandered into the camp with two arrows protruding from its side. At its approach, several Indians stampeded some of the emigrants' horses, and the men went in pursuit of the raiders. The armed men confronted the leader of the Indian encampment, and he dutifully located and returned the stolen horses, along with one extra. Lucy Jane Hall's recollections do not conform to Richard Helm's version of the story, which he related in 1924. A second event that occurred three or four days after the first incident also did not sound like Lucy Jane's description. In this case, another horse was stolen, and three young men rode out to recover it. When they overtook an Indian, the boy named Smith wanted to kill him, but cooler heads prevailed. Since there was no evidence that the man was guilty of any crime and because his execution would probably result in subsequent Indian problems, they released him. See "Richard Watson Helm, Pioneer of 1845," in Lockley, *Conversations with Pioneer Men*, 136–38; and Andrew J. Chambers, "A Brief Account of a Trip Across the Plains," *Washington Standard*, May 15, 1908, 27.

Our most serious troubles began when we took the Stephen Meek cut-off. He represented that this route was much shorter than the other, and that there was no danger from the Indians, as this way did not lead through the Snake River Indians' territory. By vote it was decided to follow Mr. Meek. A contract was signed to pay him for his services, and he agreed to pilot the company safely through in thirty days, or, as was written in his own words, give his head for a football. All were to take turns hauling his goods. He and his wife [Elizabeth] were on horseback.[4]

One day, after three weeks' travel on our new route, our guide suddenly and excitedly exclaimed, "My God, we are lost." Alarmed, but not dismayed, we moved on till night. There was neither grass nor water to be found. All night the men sat by the dim camp fires listening for reports from those who had gone in search of water. If any was found a signal of three shots was to be fired in quick succession; if not three shots at intervals. At sunrise no sound had been heard. The train was soon moving on through sage brush and across dry creek beds which mocked our thirst. So we journeyed till noon, when hark! a shot, but not the three in quick succession, but at intervals; like a death knell they sounded. The men stood in groups talking over the situation, the mothers, pale and haggard, sat in the wagons with their little ones around them. With a determination that knows not defeat the party moved on. About night in quick succession shots were heard, which proclaimed that water had been found. All pushed forward with renewed energy. When in sight of the water the thirsty oxen broke in to a run and rushed into the water and drank until they had to be driven out.[5]

[4]Stephen Meek apparently agreed to help pilot the various companies along his "cutoff" for the fee of one dollar per wagon, plus provisions for himself and his wife. He departed Malheur hot springs on August 24 with the main column, followed by Nicholas Ownbey, who directed about fifty-three wagons. Meek's alleged statement that he would get them safely through to The Dalles within thirty days or "give his head for a football" indicated metaphorically that he would stake his life on the promise. See Wojcik, *Brazen Overlanders*, 247.

[5]It is impossible to discern the exact locations that Lucy Jane Hall was describing in this paragraph. Most likely, it was along the line of march between Harney Lake and the Crooked River, where they encountered the driest conditions and suffered the most. John Martin later recalled that some of the families were short of food and were forced to put salt on grass as their source of sustenance. The Crooked and Deschutes rivers provided more reliable sources of water from there on, but food shortages still posed a serious threat, as did "mountain fever," which had broken out among some members of the wagon train. See Clark and Tiller, *Terrible Trail*, 66–79; and Hancock, *Narrative of Samuel Hancock*, 28–31.

"We are saved, we are saved! Thank God!" cried Stephen Meek, "for now I know the way." He could locate the trail to The Dalles from this stream. Men, women and children were laughing and crying in turn.

The teams were in such a bad condition that we had to lay by here three weeks. Many [people] were sick and some died and were laid to rest in this camp. Mr. Meek would certainly have given his head for a football, had not he and his wife made their timely escape.[6] When we reached the Deschutes [River] the Indians there made us understand that a man and woman had crossed the river a short time before. The man swam the river, leading his horse, and an Indian swam over with the woman on his back. Other Indians tied her clothes on their heads and swam across. We did not hear of the Meeks for more than a year after this.

We were lost in the mountains six weeks. The way was rough beyond description. The women and children walked most of the way.[7]

On reaching The Dalles Meek told the missionaries there that a party of emigrants were in the mountains.[8] A white man [Moses "Black" Harris] and two Indians were at once sent in search of our company. When found we people were on the verge of starvation. But for the provisions brought by the scouts many, if not all, would have perished, as it took a week more to reach The Dalles when guided by these men.

---

[6]Richard Watson Helm later recalled that his father, Reverend William Helm, was among the small group of men who saved Stephen Meek from hanging at that desperate moment. Meek apparently wanted to remain with his charges and guide them northward to safety, but Helm and others convinced Meek that he could no longer reason with some of the enraged overlanders. See "Richard Watson Helm, Pioneer of 1845," in Lockley, *Conversations with Pioneer Men*, 138.

[7]Somewhat surprisingly, Lucy Jane Hall did not mention one of the most ironic turns in the 1845 story of the Meek Cutoff. Amid all the suffering, some of the emigrants thought that they had found gold along the trail. This generated the legend of the "lost" Blue Bucket Gold, which was pursued by prospectors well into the twentieth century. What these mining novices found is unclear, but no one ever found the exact spot again. The legend is well told in Clark and Tiller, *Terrible Trail*, 107–21. It is also widely discussed in eyewitness accounts provided throughout Lockley, *Conversations with Pioneer Men*.

[8]Despite the prevailing notion that the Methodist missionaries showed little initial interest in rescuing the beleaguered wagon train, the Helm family found that Reverend Alvin F. Waller was very helpful in alleviating some of the suffering. Waller encouraged the Helms to share his housing and work at the mission over the winter, which family members happily did. See "Richard Watson Helm, Pioneer of 1845," in Lockley, *Conversations with Pioneer Men*, 138. Also complimentary to Waller was Samuel Hancock in *Narrative of Samuel Hancock*, 32–36.

1846

Lilburn Boggs, "Route to the Pacific"

Lilburn W. Boggs is probably better known in Missouri history than in California history, but he had important roots in both, as he did in two important western trails—first in the southwestern commerce of Santa Fe, New Mexico, and later in the limitless financial possibilities offered by California. Boggs was born in Kentucky in 1792 and made his way to frontier Missouri to serve as a deputy trader under George Sibley at Fort Osage and New Harmony. These important business connections opened doors to broader opportunities in the Santa Fe trade by the late 1820s. Prominent friends likewise helped promote his political career, first as lieutenant governor of Missouri and, from 1836 to 1840, as governor of the state.

This period also witnessed the growing influence of Mormon settlement in the present-day Kansas City area. Like many of his colleagues and other Gentile members of the broader population, Boggs was decidedly anti-Mormon, and he directly contributed to the hysteria that developed in Jackson County. His words and actions provoked mob violence on several occasions, and he refused to give any credence to Mormon complaints. On October 27, 1838, he issued a virtual declaration of war against all Missouri Mormons on the falsified assertion that they had mobilized their forces with the intention of burning the community of Richmond, Missouri. He further called for extermination of the Mormons if they did not hastily leave the state. Gentile atrocities in the Battle of Crooked River and the Massacre at Haun's Mill ensured that most Mormons had to flee the area and seek their Zion in the Wilderness at another place. Most of the faithful would follow the prophet Joseph Smith to form a new settlement at Nauvoo,

Illinois, which less than eight years later would itself become a victim of social prejudice and violence.

Lilburn Boggs escaped an assassination attempt in 1841, but he continued an active role in politics and in the Rocky Mountain fur trade. In 1846, he helped lead an overland party to California, an experience he drew from to write the following letter, which was submitted to the *St. Louis Weekly Reveille*. Upon arrival in these Mexican lands, he participated in the events that assured American acquisition of California through the Bear Flag Revolt. He settled in Napa Valley and served as alcalde north of Sacramento until statehood brought about a new government structure. Boggs died on March 14, 1860.

Unlike most of the trail diaries and letters that were written by overlanders during the 1840s and 1850s, Lilburn Boggs intended this article as a promotional item to encourage massive emigration from Missouri to California. By design, it offers little information on human events. Rather, it provides a practical guide about what items to take on the transcontinental trip, how to manage livestock and sources of water and grass at specific locations, how far to travel in different environments, how to follow precise lines of march, and how to establish oneself upon reaching California. Though not as extensive as the trail guides that became available for purchase in the late 1840s, this letter offers sage advice to people contemplating the overland journey. As a historical document, it invites close inspection and comparison with some of the standard trail guides of the era: Lansford W. Hastings, *The Emigrants' Guide to Oregon and California* (1845); William Clayton, *The Latter-day Saints' Emigrants' Guide* (1848); Joseph E. Ware, *The Emigrants' Guide to California* (1849); and Hosea B. Horn, *Horn's Overland Guide* (1852). Also useful in determining what was necessary to pack and in what quantities is Albert Edward Belanger, "'Equipping Ourselves in Every Possible Way': Contents of Wagons on the 1851 Oregon Trail" (2006). The itinerary of Boggs's 1846 trip to California is detailed in David A. White, ed., *News of the Plains and Rockies, 1803–1865*, vol. 2 (1996), 367–87. Biographical information on Boggs is found in Dan L. Thrapp, *Encyclopedia of Frontier Biography* (1988), 132; Louise Barry, *The Beginning of the West* (1972), 584, 836; and Leonard J. Arrington and Davis Bitton, *The Mormon Experience* (1979), 44, 49–59.

Lilburn W. Boggs.
Official Governor Portrait at Missouri State Capitol.

Lilburn W. Boggs, "Route to the Pacific,"
St. Louis Weekly Reveille, May 22, 1848.
Typescript, Oregon-California Papers, 1804–1876,
Missouri Historical Society Library and Archives,
St. Louis.

The information conveyed in the following letter from ex-Gov. Boggs, formerly of this state, is of great use to emigrants bound to the Pacific; it was written a year since, from Sonoma, north of the Bay of San Francisco:

Prepare good strong two or four horse wagons; crooked or frame [wagon] beds; obtain good stout oxen, say from five to seven or eight years old; large strong active oxen are best—and have at least two extra yoke of oxen to each wagon, at the start. Do not have your wagons too heavy; have good double covers. A tent with necessary tent poles, and iron pins to fasten it down. Provide—say fifty pounds of bacon (middlings) to the person, and about two hundred pounds of breadstuff to each person, large and small; this two hundred pounds will include flour, hard bread or crackers, and corn meal. Common corn meal will keep all the way. A sack of coffee to each family, and a due proportion of sugar-dried fruit, beans, a good supply of hogs lard, and plenty of soap; the last article is important. Rosin and tallow make the best article for greasing your wagon wheels, and a good jack-screw is highly necessary—no man ought to start without one. Bring a number of good milch cows. American cows are very valuable here, and it is the finest country in the world for butter. Bring a large cedar churn, with iron hoops, and plenty of milk vessels. You will need salt, say a bushel to each family will be enough. See that your axletrees are made of good timber, and that your slides and coupleing pole are well ironed—have an extra king bolt to each wagon, and extra tongue bolts and linch pins if you choose, and one set of plough irons—diamond plough and a fro. A small supply of medicine is highly necessary, such as are used in fevers, diarrhea, sprains, etc. Provide plenty of good warm clothing and bedding, feather beds can be bought very easily, and are very useful when you get here; cookery vessels, such as a family needs in the States, are the best to bring, though not too many of them. A good ten gallon cast iron kettle or pot to make soap in after you get here, and to boil clothes in on the road, and good wash tubs, a good Dutch oven and lid to bake bread; sheet iron camp kettles are but of little use—a good five gallon water keg to each wagon, iron hooped and painted—painted or tin buckets for water. Start with good supply of shoes or coarse boots, and any goods you bring for clothing, let them be woollen; cotton goods can be had here, and woollen are more necessary. Start as early as possible, say from the 20th of April to the 1st of May from the boundary line of Missouri.[1] From ten to twenty wagons are enough, and from among that number you can always

[1]Boggs's advice to begin the trip early—between April 20 and May 1—was based on common sense. The jumping-off towns along the Missouri River had the most outfitting supplies and livestock for sale at that time; the grass for grazing livestock along the trail was at its best quality; and getting ahead of the vast majority of emigrants avoided the excessive destruction of trail resources as the hotter months progressed. On the negative side, however, April and May constituted the "rainy season" in eastern Kansas and Nebraska, a time when frequent rain and cold weather made travel very difficult for days on end.

select the one to take charge of the company.[2] Never camp two nights, if you can avoid it, on the same ground, travel on a regular gate from fifteen to twenty miles a day—you need no pilot;[3] the road is large and plain; you can always find water, grass and fuel, anywhere you may think best to camp.[4] Start about six or seven o'clock in the morning, and travel until three or four in the afternoon—stopping at noon a little while to water your cattle and take a check yourselves. Never turn out your teams at noon. It would be prudent for the first part of your journey to correll [corral] your cattle at night, but after you get some two or three hundred miles from the settlements it is unnecessary a guard should be placed around them at night.[5] You should reach Fort Larimer [Fort Laramie] about the 15th or 16th of June, and from there to the South side of the mountains and from there to the Black Hills [of eastern Wyoming] and up Sweet Water [Sweetwater River]. When you get to the Little Sandy,[6] which is about twenty miles from the South Pass; you should then take the right hand road, leaving the Fort Bridger road to your left, and it is ten miles to Big Sandy, there buy one day or more if your teams need it, there is good water and grass there. From Big Sandy to Green River it is forty miles, no water

---

[2]Unlike the usual Hollywood version of large wagon trains moving in precise order across the plains, conventional wisdom of the nineteenth century agreed with Boggs's advice to limit each train to no more than twenty wagons. This allowed for greater flexibility of decision making, more social cohesion among members of a train, and, in most cases, greater speed. Small companies could always temporarily link up with larger caravans if danger threatened, but they could also detach themselves from larger groups anytime they cared to.

[3]Boggs's comment that a pilot, or guide, was unnecessary for a caravan of wagons was generally true in the Great Plains area of travel. The Platte and Sweetwater rivers were virtual highways throughout the first half of the trip. Overlanders bound for Oregon could likewise follow the courses of the Snake and Columbia rivers for much of their remaining trip. Those bound for California, however, were often better served by an experienced guide leading them across such hostile and relatively unmarked landscape of the Great Basin and the Sierra Nevadas. A speed of fifteen to twenty miles a day on the relatively flat areas of the Plains was certainly possible, but in the mountainous areas of Idaho, Oregon, and California, the pace could be limited to only a few miles a day along the steepest grades.

[4]The affirmation of easy accessibility to good water, grass, and fuel seems to be Boggs's greatest exaggeration, although in the earliest stages of the trip, it was generally true.

[5]Boggs's advice not to worry about guarding livestock after the first two hundred to three hundred miles of the journey is curious. It also contradicts some of the advice he gave in later portions of the article about "Indian thieves" along the Humboldt River.

[6]The Little Sandy Crossing, first reliable water west of Pacific Springs, is near present-day Farson, Wyoming. See Haines, *Historic Sites along the Oregon Trail*, 244–45.

or grass; you should start from Big Sandy in the evening, say two hour before sun set, and travel the first twenty miles, then correll your cattle, and start at day-light next morning and you will reach Green river by noon, where there is a good ford; cross and camp there a day or two in fine grass, and then proceed on.[7] You will intersect the Fort Bridger road again in Bear River valley, before you reach Soda Springs, and by avoiding Fort Bridger, you save near one hundred miles in distance, and have equally as good a road. You should spend a day at the Soda Springs; you then proceed on to Fort Hall, on to California by the Portnuaff [Portneuf River], Cassus [Cassia], Goosecreek, Hot Spring Valley, on to Mary's [Humboldt] River; thence down Mary's River to the Sink [Humboldt Sink]. The road down Mary's River is generally good, grass and water plenty, but very dusty—from the Sink to Turkey Creek it is forty-five miles, no grass between, through there is water at the Boiling Springs, twenty miles from the Sink. When you arrive at the Sink of Mary's River, tie up your oxen, or chain them to the wagon wheel that night, and turn them out next morning and lay there all day; then start at night and go to the Boiling-Springs and next day you can get to Turkey [Truckee] River where you will find plenty, water and grass. You should be careful of the Indians all the way down Mary's River, and especially at the Sink and Boiling Springs.

The main difficulty of the whole route is from Turkey [Truckee] River into the settlements in California. You travel up Turkey about sixty or seventy-five miles, crossing it about twenty-seven times before you leave it, and the fords are rapid and rocky—you will be compelled to proceed very slow. After you leave Turkey you will soon get into the California mountains. When you come to the cabins at the Lake, you take the left hand. From these cabins to the road; after you surmount the summit, then your troubles begin.[8] You will have a number of

---

[7]Boggs was correct to warn people to possibly take an extra day at Big Sandy Crossing in preparation for the difficult forty-five-mile crossing of the Little Colorado Desert before abundant water and grass would be struck at the Green River. See Ware's similar warnings in *Emigrants' Guide to California*, 25.

[8]A useful article and map of the various cutoff trails across the Sierra Nevadas westward from the vicinity of Lake Tahoe is Tortorich and Carman, "Big Tree Carson Valley Wagon Road," 90–107. Also useful is the map on page 343 of Unruh, *Plains Across*; and Tortorich, "Opening of the Carson River Route," 20–24.

prodigious steep and rocky mountains to go down, with occasional intervals of good between. From the summit to the first settlements (Johnson's) in California,[9] is about one hundred miles, and it will take you at least twelve or fifteen days to travel it with wagons, although on horseback it can be traveled in three days. After you reach Johnson's, which is the first house, you are then safe; stop two or three days to recruit [rest] your cattle. Here you can get plenty of fresh beef, and other provisions if you need them. From Johnson's to Nichols' it is fifteen miles; at Nichols' the road forks, the left hand goes to Sutter's Fort, and the right to the Sacramento [River] at the mouth of the Feather River. Those of the emigrants who wish to come north of the [San Francisco] Bay, should take the right hand road, and cross the Sacramento [River] at the mouth of the Feather River, ten miles from Nicholas', and then proceed on by Gordon's, Wolfscabs and Barker's, to Nappa Valley: at the crossing of Nappa the right hand goes to Yount's mills[10] and the left hand to Sonoma—nine miles to Yount's, and twelve to Sonoma.

Your first object should be, after you get into the settlements, to procure as soon as possible houses or other shelter as the rainy season will soon set in after your arrival. Those who wish to go south of the [San Francisco] Bay, should take the left hand road at Nicholas' and go on by Sutter's Fort; there you can either go down the Sacramento by water, to Yerba Buena [San Francisco] or Santa Clara, or you can go by land, and get directions at Sutter's.

I must again remind you to be on your guard all the way down St. Mary's [Humboldt] River, and keep a bright look out for the Indians; they will follow you and kill your cattle, by shooting arrows into them. Have no communication with the Indians on the river, they are not to be trusted.

---

[9]Johnson's Ranch, owned by William Johnson, a resident of Boston who came to California in 1840, was acquired from part of an earlier Mexican land grant. By 1846, it was well known as the first settlement reached by overlanders who crossed the Sierra Nevadas via the Truckee River Route. See Steed and Steed, "Rediscovery of Johnson's Ranch," 18–32.

[10]This was named for George C. Yount, who arrived in California from North Carolina in 1831, via the Rocky Mountain fur trade, and five years later received a land grant from Mexican authorities. This Napa County settlement grew and became known as Yountville. See Gudde, *California Place Names*, 371.

If you should be late in the season when you reach the sink of Mary's River, or Turkey River, hurry on as fast as possible to get out of the mountains before the snow overtakes you, or otherwise you might all perish.[11]

[11]These words of warning about the need to hurry along certainly would have resonated among many Americans in 1848. They had read tragic stories about the Donner party, which had become marooned in the Sierra Nevadas only two years earlier.

J. M. Harrison, "Recollections"

Just as J. M. Harrison was in the midst of preparing the following "Recollections" for possible release by Harper and Brothers, he was already working on two important publications about the Pacific Slope. Unlike his "Recollections," these two publications were not autobiographical, but spoke to a new generation that had settled in the Far West during the thirty years that followed his 1846 transcontinental trek, or were contemplating relocation there. The larger of these projects, *Harrison's Guide and Resources of the Pacific Slope, Embracing Washington Territory, Giving a Minute Description of Its Lands and Facilities for Settlement, Land Laws, Climate, Resources, etc.*, was finally published in 1876, by C. A. Murdock and Company in San Francisco. Today, it remains a somewhat rare publication, but its depth of detail about the Pacific Northwest makes it an important reference source.

Production of the second publication actually interrupted completion of the larger project because Harrison sensed a more immediate source of income from this smaller venture. The result of his efforts was a fifty-page booklet entitled *Book of Information, and Settlers' Guide for the Pacific Slope, Including the States of California, Oregon and Nevada, and the Territories of Washington and Idaho* (1875), from the same San Francisco printer. In the introductory pages, the author stated that many people had requested just such a practical guide about the topography, soil, climate, and employment possibilities in the Pacific Northwest. Because he had lived in the region for twenty-eight years, had farmed in several locales, and had traveled extensively throughout the communities, he felt well qualified to write authoritatively about the favorable conditions originally trumpeted by the boosterism literature that had abounded in the 1840s and 1850s.

First, Harrison made it clear that his purpose was not to promote any particular state or territory over any other, but to be frank in his discussion of the pros and cons of each region. Second, unlike the earlier period of boosterism pamphlets, such as Lansford W. Hastings's *The Emigrants' Guide to Oregon and California* (1845) and Joseph E. Ware's *The Emigrants' Guide to California* (1849), this new publication did not concern itself with the overland trails or practical advice on how to prepare for a wagon trip across the Great Plains and western mountains. By the mid-1870s, many people still traveled in convoys of wagons, but railroads extending to the Pacific Coast and improved wagon roads maintained by the federal government and private companies offered alternatives to the primitive trails that had existed for the previous generation. Thus, Harrison's advice was directed more at the issue of how newly arriving settlers could best adapt to the unfamiliar environment and make a living through various enterprises.

In retrospect, Harrison's comments seem reasonably accurate for the times, especially in his agricultural assessments of the most fertile districts. And for areas of California that seemed prone to drought, he speculated that coordinated irrigation efforts could even make some of the arid lands arable. Although most of his detailed analysis concerned agricultural topics, he did include helpful information about livestock raising, climatic conditions, water quality, and proven commercial ventures. Interestingly enough, he made no mention of the California mining industry, which had sparked such rapid growth in that state. In contrast to the seeming omission, he defined Nevada as an expansive desert, blessed by only one economic oasis—the silver towns of the Comstock Lode. Likewise, his overly brief assessment of Idaho Territory reduced it to an underdeveloped gold and silver mining economy, with agriculture serving only the small local market of miners. He did, however, predict the establishment of a future range cattle industry that could use future railroads to deliver beef to the larger urban areas of the Pacific Northwest.

Harrison's most detailed and encouraging descriptions of economic potential were found in his discussion of the well-settled bays and rivers of Oregon, which was the state he knew most intimately. He even offered a five-page practical guide about how to build a log cabin and how to use fire to safely clear forest land for agricultural purposes. His specific instructions on stock raising, hog production, and dairy farming offered tangible help to persons who wished to diversify their efforts beyond agricultural pursuits.

Two concluding sections within *Book of Information, and Settlers' Guide* offered a positive impression about weather, annual rainfall amounts, and wages within some of the representative communities stretching from San Diego, California, to Vancouver, Washington Territory. Typical of the proud declaration was Harrison's observation that "Western Oregon and Washington Territory have a more equable climate than New York City; being milder in spring, and 11 degrees cooler in summer, with about equal temperatures in the fall, and being eleven degrees warmer during the winter months, although New York is more than five degrees of latitude further south" (p. 47). Also listed in similar celebratory style was his claim of high wages for skilled and semiskilled persons who settled on the Pacific Slope. He contended that $30 a month was the customary wage for farm laborers except during harvest times, when pay ranged from $1.50 to $2.00 per day. Skilled carpenters earned on average $2.50 per day as well as board. Puget Sound ship builders could earn $60 to $70 per month plus board, and mine workers allegedly earned $3.00 to $4.00 per day. No one can determine today how many copies of this booklet sold, but it was as Harrison advertised it—"a practical guide for settlers."

Information on Harrison's later personal and professional life is sparse, but the one area that is repeatedly mentioned in other sources is his commitment to public education. He was one of the charter members in the 1857 creation of Jefferson Institute, a primary school for younger students. An advertisement appearing in the *Oregon Statesman,* March 22, 1859, indicated that eighty-nine students were enrolled in the progressive school. Harrison also contributed five hundred dollars to the formation of an institution of higher learning, which soon became known as Willamette University at Salem. He was elected a trustee of the university in 1859.

Persons wishing to compare Harrison's remembrances of the overland trip with two intersecting members of this wagon train should consult Joel Palmer, *Journal of Travels Over the Rocky Mountains, to the Mouth of the Columbia River* (1847); and Anson Sterling Cone, "Reminiscences" (1903). The July 17, 1846, issue of the St. Louis *Missouri Republican* discusses Harrison's and Edward Trimble's ambush by Pawnees and the death of the latter. Further details are related in the July 20, 1846, issue of the St. Louis *Weekly Reveille.* Information on Harrison's later association with Oregon educational institutions appears in Gustavus Hines, *Oregon and Its Institutions* (1868).

"Recollections of J. M. Harrison, 1846."
Typescript, MSS 1508, Kay Threlkeld transcription.
Oregon Historical Society, Portland.
Original manuscript was written at Wooster, Ohio.

On the morning of the 1st of April 1846 in the little village of Birmingham Iowa,[1] might have been seen an unusual bustle and stir, for that small place. Friends and relatives, came in from the surrounding country, to witness our departure for the far off Oregon.

My father had been making preparations for some time previous, for the journey westward to the Pacific. Having new wagons constructed and our whole outfit of the best possible material; two wagons were heavily laden with provisions for the journey, and another for the use of the family, camp equipment, etc.[2]

The reader may ask what induced people at that early day to emigrate through a wilderness of over two thousand miles to those far off regions.

So early as 1842 there was considerable talk in the western states, in regard to Oregon. Glowing accounts were given in regard to its mild and healthy climate, and an idea prevailed that a liberal grant of land would be made to all those emigrating to that section of the Country.[3]

This, together with the fondness of adventure so characteristic of the American people; there was not wanting, those that were willing to cast their fortunes in those far off regions. So, early in the day teams were brought into requisition and everything being in readiness friends were bid adieu, some accompanied us however for some distance. Our route lay through the South part of Iowa and the North west part of

[1]Birmingham, named for Birmingham, England, was and still is a small farming community in the southeastern corner of Iowa (Van Buren County). See Dilts, *From Ackley to Zwingle*, 47.

[2]Harrison's father carefully designed each wagon to serve a different function on the trail. His high degree of planning and access to capital was not typical among most overland pioneers.

[3]The Oregon Donation Land Law of 1850 finally provided the liberal land grant that Harrison spoke about. It provided for 320 acres to every male settler over eighteen years of age who was already an American citizen or agreed to become one before December 1, 1851, and who had occupied the land during four consecutive years. The legislation likewise allowed married women to claim a like amount of land in their own names. Subsequent legislation extended the expiration date of the act to 1855 and awarded claims of 160 acres. See Johansen and Gates, *Empire of the Columbia*, 290–91.

Missouri, crossing the head waters of the Charitan [Chariton][4] and Grand Rivers, at that time a sparsely settled region.

The inhabitants were such as we generally find on the outskirts of civilization, they generally cultivated but little ground, their chief occupation being the hunting of game and wild honey. The children would generally mount the fence on our coming in sight, to get a good view of us, and on our nearer approach would break and run like wild deers.

The roads in this section were exceedingly bad, we often had to construct temporary bridges over small streams, which retarded our progress very much.

On our arriving in the vicinity of Savannah and St Joseph[5] the country improved very perceptibly. We saw large farms and everything betokened thrift and plenty. Here we were detained several days waiting for more company, not deeming it safe to proceed, with less than forty or fifty wagons. Crossed the Missouri River on the 25th of May and on the 26th organized a Company elected a Captain, Sargeant of guard and also passed by-laws for the government of the Company.

This was all very well, but the living up to it and complying with the rules and regulations, was quite another thing, as the sequel will show.[6]

After crossing the Missouri River, we were fairly in Indian Country.[7]

---

[4]The town of Chariton is in Lucas County in south-central Iowa, near the Chariton River. The area had attracted French Canadian traders in the late 1700s, and farther to the south in present-day Chariton County, Missouri, a small trading post operated among the Indians. See Dilts, *From Ackley to Zwingle*, 58.

[5]Savannah, just to the north of St. Joseph, Missouri, welcomed the travelers into a populated area that had grown up in the fur trade era, had enticed reliable farm families, and by 1846 was a logical jumping-off point for people heading west. The improved facilities for ferrying wagons across the Missouri River at St. Joseph increased Savannah's importance with each new year. See Mattes, *Great Platte River Road*, 112–17.

[6]As small companies merged to form larger ones for mutual protection and assistance, it was necessary to elect leaders and devise codes of conduct for all members of the wagon train. Some codes were formal and lengthy, even to the point of trying to anticipate all possible contentious problems. Others merely established ground rules about rotating wagon positions along the trail, managing livestock, maintaining the pace of march, sharing duties at river crossings, assuring the confidence of fellow travelers, and the like. See Billington, *Far Western Frontier*, 99–102

[7]Upon crossing to the west bank of the Missouri River at St. Joseph in 1846, overlanders certainly experienced the sensation of entering Indian Country. Prior to the bestowing of official territorial status in the 1854 Kansas-Nebraska Act, all this land was legally and figuratively Indian land, and whites had no right to occupy any of it without permission from the federal government. Information on the 1834 Indian Trade and Intercourse Act that established Indian rights in this vast territory, and reasons for its ultimate failure, are discussed in Unrau, *Rise and Fall of Indian Country*, xi, 74–79.

We were without the pale of civilization. The space of two thousand miles of plains, sands and deserts, inhabited by numerous tribes of Savages, lay between us and our final goal. Hence the apparent necessity for us to unite for our common good and safety. On calling the roll we were found to be sixty five (men) strong exclusive of women and children. Our company was named "The Iowa Company". We had in all forty one wagons and about five hundred head of stock.

On the 27th everything being in readiness we took up our line of march in regular order, the rule being for the wagon that was ahead the day before, to fall into the rear each morning.

On being strung out on the high rolling prairies we made quite an imposing appearance.

All were in high spirits, our teams were in excellent condition, and everything seemed to augur well.

But, alas, who knows what a day may bring forth, little thought was there, that there was amongst us those who must stare starvation in the face, leaving their bones to bleach on the wayside, and others to be left Fatherless, and in widowhood; by the hand of the wily savage.

The roads were in good condition and we got along finely, indeed it was a beautiful sight to see the long string of white covered wagons moving slowly and magestically over high rolling prairies, covered with verdure of the deepest hue. Little girls might be seen tripping along gathering flowers, and occasionally might be seen a deer or antelope grazing with wonder at our little Caravan. Indeed here was nature in all its grandeur and loveliness.[8] Nothing of note occurred until our arrival at Little Blue River. We found it quite swollen and experienced considerable difficulty in fording it. We had to raise our wagon beds, one wagon was turned over in the stream, with a woman and two children in it, and came very nearly drowning before they could be

---

[8]Harrison painted a familiar image shared by many emigrants who passed through present-day northeastern Kansas into south-central Nebraska. These were the halcyon days of travel, when water and forage were usually plentiful, the trail was unencumbered by steep grades, supplies were ample, ferries aided travel on the larger rivers, and the whole trip was a new and exciting experience. These initial weeks of relatively easy passage were a blessing because they allowed trail novices a chance to adjust to their wagons, teams of oxen, and fellow companions. See Mattes, *Great Platte River Road*, 136–48.

rescued. Several men plunged into the stream and with great difficulty, and at the hazard of their lives, righted the wagon, but not before the inmates were badly strangled; the cover being firmly secured to the box, the inmates could not be relieved until the wagon was righted.[9] The Company laid over here one day, to give the families an opportunity to do their washing.

Some of the men went out hunting. Near the camp was a pond of water where some ducks were. A man by the name of Clymer, in shooting a duck, the ball after passing through the duck glanced upward and struck B. Stark, our Captain, in the shoulder. Mr. Stark was on the opposite side of the pond and out of sight of Mr. Clymer. Upon examination the wound did not prove to be serious, the ball being easily extracted. From here our route lay pretty direct to the Platte River which we struck near where Fort Kearney now stands. We were now getting well into the Buffalo Country; numbers of which we saw at a distance and so eager were the men to kill Buffalo, it was with great difficulty we could keep enough men to attend to the teams and loose stock. Our course here lay up the Platte on the south side over a level plateau. There was something peculier about the atmosphere in this section. It was with the greatest difficulty that the men could keep awake during the day. The ox teams would go to sleep in walking along with their teams, and on horseback you would soon find yourself bibbing. What little timber or brush there was along the river, was nearly all on islands that could not be got at. So we had to use ~~nearly~~ all Buffalo chips, as a substitute for fuel; it answered very well especially if we could obtain some brush to mix with it.

On striking camp our wagons were formed in the shape of a half moon, with the tongue of each (after the first) run between the wheel and bed on the near or left side of the next; forming a corrall where we

[9]Normally, the Big Blue River and Little Blue River crossings posed few problems for overlanders who transited them, but this party's chaotic experience on the Little Blue demonstrated how conditions varied from week to week and year to year. Sudden heavy rains, swelling of rivers, strengthening of the current, and even an inappropriate spot chosen for a crossing could turn this seemingly benign process into a tumultuous and dangerous event. See Marshall, "River Crossings," 14–24.

could guard our stock at night, and it could also be used for a breastwork in case of an attack. Our camp fires and tents were arranged on the outside of the wagons. At night our stock was driven into the corrall formed by the wagons, and a guard placed around ht open space. Although we seemed to be getting along very well, we had some discontented spirits in our midst, that were continually finding fault, nothing could be done to suit them. Matters of this nature became worse every day, and it soon became evident, that we were going to have a split in the Company. There are many men that will do very well while they stay at home, but let them start out on a long journey of this kind, where they may have to put up with many annoyances, vexations, and inconviences, and they soon show their true natures; or in other words it will turn them inside out.

We had seen no Indians, nor the sign of any after leaving Blue River. But it afterward became evident that the skulking Savage was on our trail, only waiting for opportunity to pounce upon us, many because they saw no Indians, though there was no danger. On our arriving about opposite the forks of the platte, we found some water and camped, the more discontented portion of the Company moving off a short distance, to themselves. This threw the guard into confusion, so there was no regular guard that night. During the night there was a considerable shower of rain, and in the after part of the night the cattle took a stampede; they would run from the camp for several miles and stop, and then take a fresh start and run direct for the camp, at times we were in great danger of bcing run over by them. At a distance their running sounded like distant thunder; and on their approach the earth seemed to tremble under their tread.

Several of the men mounted horses and pursued them but they seemed to be unmanageable. At dawn of day, all the men that could be spared from camp went out to look upon the stock; which was brought in about breakfast time, all that could be found. Upon making count found there was about sixty five head missing. As soon as breakfast was over, a number went out again, to look up those still missing; myself and Mr. [Edward] Trimble started out together, not expecting to go far from camp, we took no firearms. We had gone but a short distance when we found fresh cattle tracks and tracked them to where they took the road, east, toward the states.

We followed on for several miles, when, I remarked to Mr. Trimble that we had better go back and get our guns. He replied it would not do to turn back now, that if we did we would not get our cattle. Being only a lad at the time, I gave way to his judgement. We began to urge our horses on, and the further we went, the faster we rode, and did not overtake our stock till near sundown.

Although we had seen no Indians, we had indubitable proof that the Indians had had our cattle, as several of them had marks of arrows shot into them, to make them run. Mr. Trimble remarked that we had better travel till dark, and then stop and let our horses graze an hour or two, and then by traveling at night, reach camp early next morning. The sun had gone down when Mr. Trimble, on looking ahead said, "Yonder is some of our boys coming now." Upon looking ahead I said "I believe there is." Just after making the above remarks we descended into a low piece of ground something like a Swale, some of the cattle gave a snuff and ran out of the road, on the side I was on. As I rode out to drive them back, the Indians rose up from the grass all around us, in the form of a circle, one rose up by my horse and grabbed the bridle. I made an effort to brake loose, but in an instant about half a dozen more were around me. After getting me off the horse they commenced tearing off my clothes; to this we demurred and a lively scuffle ensued, the result of which was, we were not able to sustain the demurrer. In the meantime they commenced shooting arrows at Mr. Trimble, he made several attempts to break through their lines but was unsuccessful. At last an Indian just behind him, dropped on one knee and shot him in the back; he fell instantly, his horse was so frightened, they could barely get hold of it by closing in on it. They had barely secured Trimble's horse, when an Indian stationed on an elevated piece of ground gave a whoop, at which they all ran and left me. I could not imagine what caused them to leave me so suddenly but commenced arranging my somewhat scanty wardrobe, and started toward our camp. On gaining higher ground saw two of our men approaching. It was now getting dusk so that objects could not be seen any great distance. The Indian stationed, on the lookout, had discovered the whites approaching, and gave the alarm, they were the same we had seen just before the Indians surrounded us, but on the Indians rising up around us, I supposed the objects we had seen ahead was Indians also. Upon approaching our men, they were somewhat surprised to meet me on foot and in that condition. Upon informing them what had occurred; they did not deem it prudent to attempt to obtain Trimble's body, as the Indians on discovering their small number, would probably attack them also. The Indians in all probability were lurking in the vicinity, watching our movements. They informed me that Captain [Joel] Palmer with a company of horsemen from Oregon, on their way to the states was camped about eight miles distant. So I mounted on behind one of the men, and they urged their horses on at a lively pace for Palmer's camp.[10]

On reaching Palmer's camp one of his men, and one of ours volunteered to go on that night, to inform our company of what had occurred. Next morning by the break of day Captain Palmer's Company were up and saddled, when we all started to obtain Trimble's body. Upon reaching the scene of the action of the previous day, we found two puddles of blood, some arrows, our whips, also some buttons off my clothes, but could discover nothing of Trimble's body. The Indians had probably returned and scalped him and then taken his body with them to have a war dance around it.[11]

---

[10]Joel Palmer provided his own detailed description of the killing of Edward Trimble and the escape of J. M. Harrison, in which he concluded that had the two men been carrying guns, they would not have been molested. Palmer further observed that Trimble left behind a wife and four children who decided to return to Missouri in the company of Palmer's east-bound party. Four other families of the Harrison wagon train also joined them in heading for the settlements, because they had only five yoke of cattle among them to pull four wagons. See Palmer, *Journal of Travels Over the Rocky Mountains*, 122–23, 181. A slightly different version is provided by a member of the Harrison wagon train. See Cone, "Reminiscences," 251–59, who identified the attackers as Pawnees. The incident was also reported in "News from Oregon," *Missouri Republican*, July 17, 1846; and "From Oregon-California Emigrants," *St. Louis Weekly Reveille*, July 20, 1846.

[11]This scenario of Pawnees or other Plains tribes dancing around the body of Edward Trimble is based more on imagination than reality, and it better suits nineteenth-century novels or twentieth-century movies. The Pawnees and neighboring tribes had strong taboos about such formalized practices, though they did frequently desecrate the bodies of fallen enemies. See Echo-Hawk and Echo-Hawk, "Repatriation, Reburial and Religious Rights," 68–71.

Our contemplated work will be entitled. Twenty three years in the Pacific and Territories[12]

Beginning with a brief account of the journey overland in '46.

Yours Respectfully,

J. M. Harrison

Harper & Bros.
New York

After spending a half day, in unsuccessful search for Trimble's body we started on our return, Captain [Joel] Palmer's Company volunteering to escort us back, for which they deserved and had our thanks. We saw no Indians during the day but saw their signals a number of times on the opposite side of the river. Late in the afternoon we saw a big cloud of dust ahead, the Company halted and carefully examined their firearms; Captain Palmer detailed some of the men to take charge of the pack animals, he himself going ahead to try and make out whether it was friends or foe that were approaching us.

He soon after signaled us to come on, when it turned out to be some of our men coming to meet us. We were now in a fair mood to chastise the red man if we could have found him, but circumstances forbid our attempting to follow him. Emigrants with their families cannot well divide their force to follow Indians; and this the Indians knew full well. After traveling all night we arrived at our camp early in the morning after an absence of two days and nights, one family decided on returning to the states not having enough cattle left to continue the journey, Captain Palmer agreeing to escort them as far as there was any danger.

Mr. Trimble left an interesting family consisting of his wife and four children, to mourn his untimely death. In fact it was felt to be a great loss to the whole company.

[12]At this point, Harrison inexplicably stopped the narrative of Trimble's death and wrote about his publication intentions for the 1875 recollections to an unnamed editor at Harper and Brothers Publishing Company. He then resumed details of the Trimble murder and how it affected the lives of other members of the wagon train.

At this early day ox teams alone were used in crossing the plains with wagons, as it was generally thought that horses could not stand it to work and subsist on grass alone; though of late years it has been quite common for both horse and mule teams to cross the plains. Some on being short on oxen put cows in their place they made a very good substitute.

We traveled up the south fork of the platte about twenty miles to where we crossed it, we found it very deep fording but by raising our wagon beds we succeeded; the bottom being quicksand which made it more dangerous, but luckily all got over in safety.[13]

We soon left the south fork and struck the north fork of the platte at the mouth of Ash Hollow, from here our course lay up the north fork of the platte on the south side, to the Black Hills.[14] Shortly after leaving Ash Hollow we came in sight of Chimney Rock, I never learned its height but it was in plain view of us some three or four days travel. Some fifty or sixty feet of its top has since fallen down. Just below Scotts Bluff we met a company of men on horse back from California. Our company stopped to learn the news from that section of the country, one of their men tarried some time conversing with our company. On starting, his Spanish spurs made considerable noise at which a dog ran out from under a team, barking. One of the oxen bowled and in an instant all but two or three of the teams were going at full speed over the plains in every direction; the women and children screaming, the teamsters whoaing at their teams together with the rattling of the wagons, made a terrible noise and confusion, Most of the teamsters had gathered around the returned Californian to hear the news, when the teams stampeded.[15] One wagon bed with a woman and three children in it was thrown off the running gear and left sitting in the road and

---

[13]The wagon train departed from the South Platte River at the Lower California Crossing, made its way past California Hill, and moved northwestward toward a welcome stop at Ash Hollow.

[14]They followed the North Platte River across the Nebraska panhandle, heading for Fort Laramie and the Black Hills of eastern Wyoming.

[15]This wagon train certainly had its troubles with stampedes of livestock, including the one described here, which was caused by a barking dog. Anson Sterling Cone described the same stampede and attributed it to barking dogs pursuing a jack rabbit under a wagon. The terrible effects of such a sudden calamity were clearly evident in the words of both observers. See Cone, "Reminiscences," 253.

every spoke taken clean out of one wheel, one man and child were run over by a team, and strange to say were not seriously hurt.

A Mrs. E.—was standing by their team at the time when it started to run when with courage so peculiar to western women, she siezed, with one hand the horn of old Duke the near wheel ox, and with a stick in the other hand striking Darb the off ox in the face; they went flying through the air for a time, but by perserverence and the help of old Duke and Darb holding back the lead cattle had to give it up and stop, some of the teams ran until they had to stop from sheer exhaustion. After gathering up our teams with the exception of one wagon wheel being smashed up and the teams rather the worse for their run, we had sustained no serious damage.

For some time after this we had to use great care and watchfulness to keep our teams from stampedeing, at the least unusual noise they were ready to stampede; they had not forgotten their fright by the Indians at the forks of the platte.

Large herds of Buffalo were daily seen and antelope in great numbers, the latter were generally very shy, the hunter would slip out toward them after approaching as near as he thinks it practicle. He lay flat down out of view and put a red piece of cloth or red handkerchief on the end of his ramrod and waves it about gently which attracts their attention, they soon began to walk up toward it to get a better view, after it approaches near enough the hunter fired and generally killed his game. Along the platte we passed numerous villages of prairie dogs, on our passing they would stand on their hind feet and at the mouth of their burrows barking at us, on shooting one of them they generally fell back in their hole, so that we would seldom get one. We arrived at Ft. Laramie on the third day of July and camped about one mile from the fort, on the fourth we were visited by a large war party of Sioux (they were on their way to fight the Pawnees) they came up to our camp under full speed singing and whooping, presenting a hideous appearance. The chief made a speech to us in which he stated they had never shed the white mans blood and professed great friendship for the whites. There was an Indian trader along with us at the time who acted as interpreter. Our company prepared a dinner for them, preparing a large quantity of coffee well sweetened, (an Indian has a great liking for sweet things) with bread, meat etc., after which the pipe was passed around and they all seemed to be in the best of humor, we also gave them a considerable quantity of powder and ball; they promised to kill Pawnee with it, the Pawnees having killed one of our men.[16]

In traveling up the north fork of the platte we saw immense numbers of Buffalo, at times the country was black with them as far as the eye could reach, in one instance we had to stop the train to let them pass for fear of being run over by them, they were traveling north, the teamsters would crack their whips at them, and fire guns and on they went neither turning to the right nor the left. After leaving the Platte the Buffalo became scarce, the last we saw on the Sweetwater; we would occasionally see a Buffalo pate with horns attached, as far as Fort Hall on Snake River, at which place old mountaineers told us they were quite plentiful some fifteen or twenty years before.[17] Crossed the north fork of the platte near where we struck the Black Hills, we found the road quite rough and bad through here. Struck Sweetwater near Independence Rock, this rock where the road passed near by it, was covered with the names of travelers who had passed by it. Not far from the rock was a lake of alkaline substance [Piaya Lake]

[16]Hosting a dinner for visiting Sioux men near Fort Laramie was a common event among overland travelers, but their bestowing of liberal amounts of ammunition on this alleged war party was not such a common occurrence. Harrison indicated that his friends were motivated by the Sioux promise to kill many Pawnee enemies with the powder and musket balls, thus avenging Edward Trimble's death at the hands of Pawnees. Many other travelers, however, expressed concern about trading weapons and ammunition to western tribes that might then turn these against later-arriving emigrants. See Tate, *Indians and Emigrants*, 57–58.

[17]This is an interesting observation about the surprisingly small number of bison encountered along the Sweetwater River in western Wyoming and as far west as Fort Hall. These reduced herds sharply contrasted with the large numbers of bison encountered along the Platte River in Nebraska and eastern Wyoming. The contrasting pattern partly rested on the fact that vast herds were always migrating to the ever-changing sources of water and food. Some years they were abundant in an area, and the following year they had seemingly disappeared. Yet, even with this reality taken into consideration, Harrison's comment suggests a more sinister process under way as early as 1846. The bison hide trade was expanding as the supply of smaller animal pelts had radically decreased in the 1830s and early 1840s, and hunters turned increasingly toward marketing hides. Thus the destruction of bison was well under way even before the more widely studied era of the 1860s and 1870s. See Gard, *Great Buffalo Hunt*, 48–58.

resembling saleratus very much. The emigrants gathered considerable quantities and used it as a substitute for saleratus. A short distance from Independence Rock was the Devils Gate where the Sweetwater had worn its way through the Sweetwater mountains, we walked down into the passage of the river, and looking overhead it looked like we might jump from one wall to the other, it was so narrow at the top. A party of us climbed up the mountain and had a magnificent view of the surrounding country; these mountains are nearly all rock, we saw signs of the mountain sheep in rocky craggy places, where it was with the greatest difficulty we could ascend. Some of our party killed a Big Horn or Mountain sheep here; they have extremely large and heavy horns shaped very much like that of our domestic sheep. It is said on jumping off a precipice, they strike on their horns. Our company by this time got divided up into small parties, though generally not any great distance apart. While traveling up Sweetwater a war party of Arapahoe Indians about five hundred in number came across a party of six wagons and made some attempts to rob it. Some of the young braves reaching over from their ponies and cutting through the wagon cover pulling out whatever they could lay their hands on. The chief rushed up calling out to and striking them on their backs with the flat of his sword, they soon desisted, the whites thinking it best not to shoot unless there was not an other alternative. The Sweetwater is the warground of the Snake, Crow, Blackfoot, and Sioux Indians; there many sanguinary conflicts have taken place between them.

We had now been on the way nearly two months, from the Missouri River, and met two small parties, one from Oregon, the other from California, which was all the whites we had yet seen, with the exception of a few at Fort Laramie. Everything that would give us any word or news from other companies, was examined carefully, we would often find a piece of paper on which some one had written stating where they had passed and any incident of interest. The most common way was to write with a pencil on a Buffalo skull and stick it up near the roadside. We were now getting in full view of the Wind River mountains and Fremonts peak all covered with snow, which was a grand sight for most of us, to see snow in July and August.

On leaving Sweetwater and going over to the southe pass of the Rocky Mountains so gradual was the ascent and descent we could hardly perceive when we were on the summit.

Near the summit we passed Pacific Spring[s] first water flowing to the pacific, thence to Big Sandy and Green River, found the later stream very rapid and dangerous to ford, but all got across without any serious mishap. Our most direct route from here would have been by the way of Green woods cutoff[18] but there being on it a long stretch without water we decided to go the more circuitous route by the way of Ft. Bridger on account of there being more grass and plenty of water by that route.

Our teams were now beginning to fail and we found it necessary to favor them as much as possible the roads being very heavy in places often traveling for miles through deep sand and long stretches without water, the nights were quite cool and the days uncomfortably warm. In the evening after supper was over a violin or other musicle instrument was brought forth to pass away the time as there was only one or two young ladies in the company, the boys would often have what they termed a stag dance.

We found Ft. Bridger a small stockade used as a rendervous for trappers and for Indian trade, we here saw a small band of domesticate mountain goats and sheep. From here to the Bear River valley the road for the most of the way passed through a rough mountainous country. After entering Bear River valley the road was comparatively level to Soda Springs. The most remarkable of these springs was one called the Steamboat Spring. It made a hissing noise very similar to the escape pipe of a steamboat. Some of them had the form of a cone or crater on a small scale probably formed by a sediment from the water. Some of these cones were vacated being entirely dry, the ground in

[18]Although this bypass from the main trail was pioneered by mountain man and fur trader Caleb Greenwood, it was better known as Sublette Cutoff. As indicated by Harrison, this route saved seventy-five miles of travel, but it necessitated a difficult crossing of fifty miles that contained no water or wood and very little grass for the livestock. Travelers were advised to start moving at sundown, travel throughout the night, and reach the welcoming waters of the Green River on the following day. A mixture of historical and present-day maps through this difficult terrain is presented in Franzwa, *Maps of the Oregon Trail*, 160–73.

the vicinity of these springs on passing over it sounded like it might be hollow underneath, many of the company professed to relish the water but I could not drink it. The Indians and trappers were in the habit of collecting in this vicinity when the emigrants were passing to trade with them, one of our company bought a very good pony for which he paid one cotton shirt, fifteen loads of powder and ball, and a small butcher knife, costing in all about two dollars in the states, these were the Snakes or Shawnees[19] were quite friendly and anxious to trade. The second day after leaving Soda Springs we arrived at Fort Hall on Snake River. This was a Hudson Bay Co, Fort and carried on a considerable fur trade with the surrounding Indian tribes. Shortly after leaving Fort Hall we came to where the California road turned off a number of our company took this road the most of them we believe intending to turn off on the Applegate route to the Willamette valley, but by some means most of them kept on for California[20] a number of whom perished from starvation in the Siera Nevada mountains near what is known as Donner Lake.

The most of our company kept on the old emigrant road crossing Snake River near Salmon Falls and thence to the Boise River striking it a few miles above where Boise City now stands. The Snake River country here for about two hundred and fifty miles is a sandy desert country its chief productions being sage brush and rattle snakes. The river is generally difficult of access being shut in on either side with high bluffs of basaltic rock.

Some ten miles above Clarks ferry on Snake River are Falls said to exceed the falls of Niagra in point of height but a far less volume of water. In a number of places we saw considerable bodies of water rushing out of these bluffs in places equal to a small river. Upon reaching

[19]Harrison means Shoshones, not Shawnees, who were an eastern tribe.

[20]Harrison mentioned the confluence of three different routes that could be taken at Raft River Crossing. Travelers could continue the main route westward on the Snake River toward the Columbia River, as the Harrison party did, or turn south down the Raft River, pick up the Humboldt River, and continue to California. The Applegate Trail offered a different route to the Willamette Valley of Oregon by departing from the Humboldt River in north-central Nevada and approaching Oregon's Willamette Valley from the south. See Haines, *Historic Sites along the Oregon Trail*, 314–16; and Applegate, "Notes and Reminiscences," 2–23 (especially map on p. 3).

higher land from ten to thirty miles from the river it is less barren there being considerable bunch grass and some scattering juniper, hare, sage hens and antelope are occasionally seen. The margin of the small streams running from the mountains are skirted with willow also cotton wood in places and occasionally meadow land is found where wild hay is cut for the Oregon over land Stage Company now connecting with the Central Pacific Railroad at Kelton.

The road here was extremely wearisome for both man and beast the suns rays reflecting from the rock and sand made the heat very oppressive but the nights were comfortably cool. Some thirty miles from Clarks ferry and about one and a half miles from Clover Creek station are some hot springs they are about three fourths of a mile from the stage road in this vicinity we saw considerable evidence of volcanic action, we noticed in one place where the earth had been hove up at an angle of about thirty degrees with a large fissure in it of considerable length. About four miles east of Rattle Snake Station is another hot spring, there are probably many such in this section of country. On entering Boise River valley we saw many Indians they had numerous fine horses. A favorite pastime with them seemed to be in chasing hare on horseback. A number of them would mount their horses armed with their bow and quiver the hare being numerous there was no trouble in starting one. After jumping one up they would all pursue it, one Indian leading out a little in advance of the others. The hare on being closely pursued would soon dodge behind sagebrush and track on another course when some of the Indians a little behind would take their turn in pursuit. The Hare, dodge which way he might found himself hotly pursued and in a short time would begin to fag, when an Indian would string his bow sending an arrow through its body.

Our route lay down the Boise River to its junction with Snake River where we crossed over to the south side of the latter stream near old Fort Boise.[21] Our teams being very much fagged we travelled by easy

[21]Harrison refers to the site of the original Fort Boise, built in 1834 by Thomas McKay, of the Hudson's Bay Company, on the east bank of the Snake River, below the mouth of the Boise River. A flood destroyed much of the adobe structure in 1853, and the Hudson's Bay Company abandoned operations in the area two years later. See Ruth, *Great Day in the West*, 56–57.

stages along this stream there being plenty of grass with wood and water convienent. Some twenty miles below Boise City and about opposite Middletown on the south side of the river is the site of the Ward massacre[22] in the summer of 1854, where all but two lads (who were left for dead but afterwards came to and made their escape) some forty persons in all men and women and children were massacred by the hand of the ruthless savages. It appears they had been annoyed by the Indians for some time when while they were moving the Indians being considerably reinforced made a final charge, the men being few in number were soon killed or mortally wounded the woman in endeavering to soothe their dying husbands and brothers were ruthlessly taken away and subjected to the most brutal outrages such as savage demons alone could perpetrate. The savages after satiateing their beastly desires relieved the suffering agonies of their victims by dispatching them with the tomahawk and scalping knife. Two of the boys, the eldest about fifteen years old made their escape, neither one knowing of the escape of the other after wandering some time they were found by some soldiers from Fort Boise. The soldiers together with a number of emigrants that were encamped near Fort Boise went in company to the scene of the massacre and succeeded in capturing a portion of the Indians engaged in the slaughter some of whom they killed in capturing the others, those captured were taken to the scene of the massacre, rude gallows were soon erected and the offenders hung. Their bodys left hanging as a warning to all others in the vicinity. These gallows stood until about a year ago when they fell down. The bodies of the whites were all gathered up and put in one grave near by. The body of one young woman was found in the bushes a considerable distance from the rest, the woman bore evidence of torture that would make your heart sick.

On visiting this grave in October last it brought very vividly before our minds many incidents of by gone days how we ourselves came near

[22]This grisly event occurred on August 20, 1854, about twenty-four miles east of Fort Boise. Shoshone warriors killed nineteen or twenty emigrants of the Alexander Ward wagon train. Two sons of Ward escaped, and one was later rescued. This set off retaliation against the local Indians—guilty and innocent alike—and created more tensions along the trail than had previously existed. See Unruh, *Plains Across*, 189–90.

meeting with a similar fate. Here lie the mortal remains of those who no doubt left their homes with bright visions of the future they had passed through many trials on the way, worried and fatigued traveling through the burning sands of Snake River and no doubt believed they were about through the worst part of their journey when they met with their horrible fate. Other massacres have taken place one near Salmon Falls another in the vicinity of the hot-springs on the south side of Snake River[23] together with many individual lives at different times. It would require volumes to describe the many encounters and conflicts of the early pioneers with the Indians in the Boise and Owyhee country but these are things of the past the red man has had to yield to the superior powers of the pale face.

Paulina[24] (a noted Indian chief of the Shawnee [Shoshone] tribe) the scourge of the mountains has gone to the spirit land, he contended till the last remnent of his followers quailed at the fall of their mighty chief and sued for peace.[25]

Note: Whether this article written for Harper and Brothers was ever finished and published, I do not know, but I do know that J. M. Harrison, my

[23]The bloody event that occurred fifty miles west of Salmon Falls probably refers to the 1860 Utter–Van Ornum Massacre, when forty-four persons traveling in an eight-wagon train were attacked by Shoshones. Eighteen emigrants were killed, and four children were abducted. The second event is less certain, but it may have been the 1862 bloodshed at Massacre Rocks, below the American Falls of the Snake River. Within a two-day period, at least a dozen overlanders were killed and fifteen wounded by Shoshone and Bannock warriors. See David H. Shannon, *The Utter Disaster on the Oregon Trail*, 33–140; and Jane A. Gould, *The Oregon and California Trail Diary of Jane Gould in 1862*, 58–67.

[24]This refers to the Paiute leader Paunina (sometimes called Paulina), who in the mid-1860s led skirmishes against the militia forces of the First Oregon Infantry, as well as against Klamath and Modoc villages whose men served as Indian scouts for the militia units. The small combats occurred along the California-Oregon border. Paunina was killed by settlers in April 1867. See Michno and Michno, *Forgotten Fights*, 209, 240–41, 244, 264.

[25]As Merrill Mattes stated, "This narrative fizzles out some twenty miles below the future site of Boise City" (Mattes, *Platte River Road Narratives*, p. 80). No reason was provided by J. M. Harrison about why he ended his recollections at that point, but apparently he never completed the manuscript. The following two paragraphs, written by his granddaughter Carlotta Lang Quinn, indicate that Harrison copyrighted the manuscript in 1875, the same year that he published the first of his two descriptive books on California and the Pacific Northwest. These two items were published in a small number by C. A. Murdock and Company of San Francisco and are difficult to acquire today except on microfilm.

Grandfather wrote and published two books one called Harrison's Guide and Resources of the Pacific Slope, Embracing Washington Territory, Giving a Minute Description of Its Lands and Facilities for Settlement, Land Laws, Climate, Resources, etc. Published by C. A. Murdock & Co. printers, 532 Clay St. San Francisco, 1876.

Also A Book of Information, and Settlers Guide for the Pacific Slope, Including the States of California, Oregon, Nevada, and the Territories of Washington and Idaho, with a Description of and the Peculiarities of Each. Describing Minutely All the More Important Bodies of the Public Lands on the Pacific Slope, Facilities for Settlement, Markets, Health, etc. Published by C. A. Murdock & Co. Book and Job Printers, San Francisco. 1875.

(Entered according to Act of Congress in the year 1875, by J. M. Harrison, in the office of the Librarian of Congress, at Washington. All rights reserved.)

Carlotta Lang Quinn

Henry King, Letter to His Parents

John C. Frémont, a celebrated officer in the army's elite Corps of Topographical Engineers, gained fame as the "Pathfinder of the West" partly because of his 1842 reconnaissance to South Pass, which popularized the main route to Oregon, and an 1843–1844 expedition into Oregon and Mexican California. Although he found no undiscovered pathways, his writings popularized the Far West among Americans and helped spur later mass migrations to Oregon and California.

Frémont's third western expedition created the greatest international controversy in the impetuous officer's military career. As war clouds gathered along the disputed Rio Grande border between Mexico and the United States, he set out on a mission that had both official and covert instructions at variance with each other. By terms of his written orders, Frémont was to explore the Arkansas and Red rivers through the vast Great Plains region. Unofficial directions from his politically powerful father-in-law, Thomas Hart Benton, and other secretive instructions from President James K. Polk may have suggested that he cross the Rocky Mountains into the Mexican territories and await a possible uprising by Americans who were living there. Sixty well-armed sharpshooters from the United States Army accompanied him. After a confrontation between his soldiers and a larger force of Mexicans under General José Castro at Gavilán Peak, near Salinas, California, Frémont turned north on March 9, 1846, and camped at Klamath Lake near the Oregon-California border. The timely arrival of Lieutenant Archibald Gillespie with new instructions from Washington, D.C., compelled Frémont to break his promise to Castro and redirect his "army" to the lower Sacramento Valley. There, his force aided the Bear Flag Revolt, led by American dissidents who raised the banner of revolution against Mexican authority in California. With the aid of Frémont's men and U.S. naval contingents off shore, the Bear Flag movement achieved early success just as war between the United States and Mexico erupted in South Texas. President Polk's and Senator Benton's contingency plans to position Frémont in troubled California just at the right time paid handsomely in America's national ambitions to claim the Pacific Coast.

Henry King was a member of Frémont's 1845–1846 expedition, and his letter, dated March 30, 1846, from the camp on Deer Creek, was penned before Frémont met with Lieutenant Gillespie to decide the fate of Mexican rule in California. In the wake of subsequent martial events, the letter was published in the *Congressional Globe*, along with other reports about the expedition and Frémont's central role in the conquest of California. It is interesting that this letter was dated too early to contain any hints about the later controversies that would plague Frémont's life, but it remains an important document. King's concluding words proved prophetic: "I think it very likely that we will return yet, and go down through California; peacefully if we can, forcibly if we must."

Henry King's association with John C. Frémont did not end with the expedition of 1845–46, for he volunteered for a fourth expedition in 1848–49. During that winter, Frémont launched a private reconnaissance financed by Senator Benton and St. Louis businessmen interested in establishing a transcontinental railroad through Colorado. This fourth western venture proved to be a disaster because the San Juan Mountains were impassable during the winter months. After losing eleven members of the thirty-three-man party, Frémont finally found refuge among the mountain men and traders in Taos, New Mexico. Not so fortunate was King, who died from exposure and hunger while leading one of the three groups. By several accounts, other members of King's party survived by resorting to the cannibalism of his body.

Published accounts about Frémont and his western explorations are abundant as both primary and secondary sources. Among the earliest interpretations was Allan Nevins, *Frémont: Pathmarker of the West* (1939). This perspective has been refined in Andrew Rolle, *John Charles Frémont: Character as Destiny* (1991), and Tom Chaffin, *Pathfinder: John Charles Frémont and the Course of American Empire* (2002). Two essential sources for understanding the disaster associated with the fourth expedition and details of Henry King's role in it are LeRoy R. Hafen and Ann W. Hafen, eds., *Frémont's Fourth Expedition: A Documentary Account of the Disaster of 1848–1849* (1960), and John C. Frémont, *The Expeditions of John Charles Frémont*, vol. 3, *Travels from 1848 to 1854* (1984).

Henry King to Dear Parents, March 30, 1846,
in "Appendix: Copy of Henry King's Letter from California,"
Congressional Globe, vol. 16 and appendix (29:2): 137–38.
Postmarked Independence, Missouri, September 5.

Camp on Deer Creek
Upper California, March 30, 1846.

Dear Parents: I embrace this opportunity to write you a few lines. I know not whether this will reach you, so I will write but briefly, as I shall probably reach home at least a month or so later than this will probably reach you, and can then tell you of my trip; and then I shall be apt to postpone it until the long winter nights, as I shall have some very tough yarns to tell, but true, nevertheless. I shall merely, then, state now that I have enjoyed excellent health, notwithstanding a good deal of hardship. After leaving Bent's Fort we traveled at a pretty swift rate, and very soon the animals began to give out, (I rode down three horses from Westport to nearly the lower point of the Cordilleras ridge of mountains.) Our usual rate of traveling is about three miles an hour, our horses being kept in a pretty fast walk. We fared very well in the way of provisions, having plenty of game, as far as the Great Salt Lake, if I except being without sugar and coffee for some three weeks, and also flour. I soon fell into the habit of making a hearty meal of meat alone, which will probably surprise you; nevertheless I always thought of the hot rolls and coffee at home.[1]

At the Great Salt Lake the captain, with five hunters and myself, started on an exploring expedition, taking our cylinder boat along—the

[1]At Bent's Fort, John C. Frémont dispatched some of his party under Lieutenant James W. Abert eastward with guide Thomas Fitzpatrick to explore the country along the Canadian River and return to the settlements. Soon thereafter, Frémont enlisted the scouting services of Kit Carson and Richard Owens to lead his sixty-man expedition beyond the Rocky Mountains. By September 5, 1845, they were just west of today's Denver, Colorado, and they pressed on toward the Colorado and White rivers, where the captain hired another experienced mountain man and guide, Joseph Reddeford Walker, who had crossed the intended line of march through the Great Basin in 1833. They reached Utah Lake on October 10 and spent three days exploring the valley that now encompasses the communities of Provo and Orem, Utah. As indicated by Henry King, this leg of the journey proved to be relatively easy. See Goetzmann, *Army Exploration*, 116–26.

lake is probably one hundred and fifty miles long and fifty broad, with several large islands. We forded over a portion of the lake, from the information gathered from an Indian, traveling about two miles on a solid salt crust, with three to five inches of water on the top. The salt crust was the best imitation of ice that I ever saw. We had to travel through the brine about two miles to the island, and to our great surprise we found a large band of antelope. How they got there is a mystery. We also found two springs of fresh water on one side of the island.[2]

The next day, having rigged our boat, we embarked on the deep with the intention of sailing about ten miles to a large island. A gale sprung up shortly after we left the shore. I was at the helm, and also had hold of the sail, or rather the rope. We soon found the boat perfectly at the mercy of the wind, being flat-bottomed. Luckily, on a point of the island which we started from jutted out into the lake, and by shortening the sail brought the boat within thirty yards of the point, when two of the men jumped out (on a bar that ran out) into the water up to their armpits and hauled the boat ashore, and we had to give it up. We were three days upon the island taking the height of the mountains and bearings to the various islands, and to the ridge of mountains on either side of the lake. We then went to camp again, and started on our journey again two days afterward. In about two weeks afterward the captain with seventeen men started out to explore the (so called) Great Desert,[3] and the balance of the party, of which I was one, came down Mary's river[4] [Humboldt] and so across the country until we struck the Cordilleras, and running those down to

[2]Frémont was fascinated by the Great Salt Lake, and he spent two weeks exploring its southeastern shoreline and recording observations about plant and animal life. The water's depth in that region was unusually low, and Frémont, Carson, and several other men took the advice of a local Indian that they should cross the shallow brine water until they would reach a large island, where they would find plentiful game. The explorers discovered abundant grass, fresh water, and antelope on the dry land, which Frémont named Antelope Island—an identity it still retains today. See Frémont, *Expeditions of John Charles Frémont*, 2:17–20.

[3]The "Great Desert" that King referred to is the Great Salt Lake Desert. Within the party, only Joseph Reddeford Walker had any previous experience with this hostile landscape, and that had occurred thirteen years earlier when he had been lost.

[4]King correctly referred to this as Mary's River, the standard place name used since Hudson's Bay Company's Peter Skene Ogden had first assigned the name during his explorations of the 1820s. Frémont gave it the name Humboldt River for the celebrated German geographer Alexander von Humboldt, and the latter designation remains today. See Carlson, *Nevada Place Names*, 138–39.

the point halted to wait for the captain. The captain met us once on the route at a place called Trout Lake after about twenty days' travel, but started the next morning again, and crossing the mountains above us struck on the Sacramento river, and down the valley of that river to the settlements. On our trip from Salt Lake to Trout Lake (foot of the Sierra Nevada) we were on short allowance even of meat, our only subsistence; and when we reached the Trout Lake we had only two small cattle left, and very poor and weak. Those, then, had to last our party from Trout Lake to the point of the mountains. A party of thirty men, we soon used up our cattle and had to resort to our old horses and mules, which were very poor and weak, so much so that all except our mess (and two out of ours, the cook and one packer) were afoot twenty days before we came to game; and after resting twenty days in the mountains (Sierra Nevada) were again twenty-eight days afoot, frequently without anything to eat and often without water.[5]

While we laid by in the mountains we were once four days without eating anything; and at another time three days. My hip bones became so sharp that I could not sleep for several nights. We ate on the trip some twenty-five horses and mules, many of them with miserable sore backs, and scarcely able to get along without anything on them. We had a great treat on Christmas day; having then been two days without anything we killed a mule and had one hearty meal; and I can tell you there was rejoicing that night. We laid by at the point of the mountains by the captain's orders, waiting for him to come to us with provisions; he expected to get there from the settlements before we did; but after crossing the mountains and coming down the Sacramento to the settlements, and getting cattle and flour, he attempted to take a short cut acros [across] to head us off on the other side, but got into the snow and lost everything, animals and all, and

[5]Frémont took fifteen members of the expedition across the Sierra Nevadas at what is known today as Donner Pass. Snow had not yet begun in the pass, and the men moved through it and continued on to Walker Lake without major problems. King's larger party, under the leadership of Joseph Reddeford Walker and Theodore Talbot, somewhat delayed their mountain crossing, and by the time they reached the summit of Walker's Pass, they encountered two and a half feet of snow. King's letter captures their suffering and notes how lucky they were to reach the western valleys of California. See Chaffin, *Pathfinder*, 205–19.

had to go back again on foot. We did not know what had happened, and after waiting twenty days we rounded the point and got into the valley, and were making our way up to the Sacramento settlements to see what had befallen him, when we met two of his men going to him from Captain Suter's [John Sutter] fort. The captain then was near a town called Puebla, so we tacked about and traveled southwest, crossing the coast mountain to the Puebla. We then started on our route down the settlements, intending to travel all over California; but when we got within sight of Monterey, (thirty miles distant,) we were met by a couple of Spanish [Mexican] officers with a proclamation of the Governor's, (Castro.) ordering us out of California, and applying a great deal of abusive language to our party; he threatened us that in case we did not go he would come with two hundred soldiers and drive us out. The captain sent him word to come on. He came out next day with sixty soldiers, and made a junction with another detachment of one hundred and forty men. We waited quietly three days (on the mountain,) but he only fired his cannon at twelve miles distance. We waited for Castro three days; he would not commence the offensive, and we were getting short of provisions and had to retreat.[6] We are now camped at the head nearly of Sacramento valley, on our way to Oregon. I think it very likely that we will return yet, and go down through California; peaceably if we can, forcibly if we must.

[6]King was describing the standoff created when Frémont built defenses along the summit of Gavilán Peak and was subsequently surrounded by superior numbers of Mexican forces. Cooler heads prevailed, and Frémont agreed to withdraw his troops to Oregon and not return to California. Of course, he broke that promise upon receipt of the messages carried by Lieutenant Archibald Gillespie. See Frémont, *Expedition of John Charles Frémont*, 2:xxvi, 123n.

Amanda Esrey Rhoads.
Courtesy of Rootsweb, Ancestry.com.

Amanda Esrey Rhoads, Letter to Her Parents

In 1846, the extensive Mormon family of patriarch Thomas Foster Rhoads (1794–1869) prepared to migrate west from their farmsteads in Missouri because of increasing pressure from Gentile neighbors. Rhoads, who had been ordained a church elder in December 1837, adhered to the leadership of Brigham Young and the Quorum of Twelve Apostles, but he did not travel with Young's much larger group, which assembled on the banks of the Missouri River in the vicinity of present-day Omaha, Nebraska, and Council Bluffs, Iowa. Within the party was Amanda Esrey Rhoads, wife of Thomas's son Daniel. Her letter, mailed at Fort Laramie, reflected some of the problems that her relatives had encountered with their livestock and Indians during the first half of their journey. It also demonstrated how easily wagon companies joined together and then separated, depending on the needs of each party. They quite possibly were one of the Mormon groups that historian Francis Parkman described in his *The California and Oregon Trail*

(1849), since he reached Fort Laramie on the same day that Amanda wrote to her parents, but he did not mention the Rhoads party by name.

Thomas Rhoads and his relatives apparently remained in the vicinity of Fort Laramie for a week or two awaiting the appearance of the fourteen families of Mississippi Saints under the leadership of John Brown as well as Brigham Young's larger migration from Council Bluffs. Neither group intercepted the early arriving Rhoads party. The Mississippi Saints reached Fort Laramie a few weeks later and turned south to winter at the small settlement at Pueblo, Colorado. Young, sensing the lateness of the season and realizing that he could not cross the plains and mountains during the winter, elected to keep his followers on the Missouri River until he led the Pioneer Band westward in the spring of 1847.

The exact route of the Rhoads group is disputed after they left South Pass in south-central Wyoming. Some members apparently followed the Sublette Cutoff almost due west to Fort Hall. The main contingent, still led by Thomas Rhoads, probably turned southwest toward Fort Bridger and from there to the valley of the Great Salt Lake. The two groups reached California in early October and rendezvoused at Sutter's Fort. Two of the sons, Daniel and John, subsequently joined the so-called First Relief Party of thirteen men who tried unsuccessfully to rescue the Donner party from the snowy death grip of the High Sierra's winter. John also joined the Fourth Relief Party, but the seven men had to turn back at Bear Valley due to the rapidly melting snows.

Thomas Rhoads received a land grant southeast of Sutter's Fort and befriended military members of the discharged Mormon Battalion, as well as the *Brooklyn* Saints, who had arrived in San Francisco by ship. Rhoads was one of the men carefully chosen in 1848 to deliver approximately twenty-five thousand dollars in gold collected from Mormon tithing to Brigham Young at Salt Lake City. While the majority of the Rhoads family remained in California, Thomas lived most of the rest of his life in Salt Lake City, where he held important church positions. He died in February 1869 at Minersville, in southern Utah. Several nearby place names in the Wolf Creek Pass area honor him as an early settler.

Daniel and Amanda Rhoads experienced a long and fruitful life in California. Daniel worked briefly for John Sutter and several other ranchers in the vicinity of Sutter's Fort. He was an active participant in the early phases of the gold rush along the American River, and was one of the initial prospectors involved in the Mormon Island discoveries. In 1850, Daniel and Amanda headed east to visit family and friends in Missouri. They returned to California during the following year and began a stock-raising business near the community of Old Gilroy. By 1860, the family had relocated to new grazing lands near the future town of Lemoore, California. Within five years, they turned to farming, and at about the same time Daniel became the founding president of the Bank of Hanford and vice president of the Bank of Lemoore. During the concluding months of the Civil War, he served in the California Eighth Infantry Regiment. They eventually moved to San Francisco to better address Daniel's health problems. He died at that location in 1896, and Amanda died in 1906. Several weeks later, their only surviving son, John, died in Hanford, California.

The standard source on Thomas Rhoads and the other family members who crossed the plains and mountains in 1846 is J. Kenneth Davis, "Thomas Rhoads, Forgotten Mormon Pioneer of 1846" (1983). Considerable information is also related in Dale Morgan, ed., *Overland in 1846* (1963), especially on Daniel and John's roles in searching for the Donner party survivors. Also important as a complement to Amanda's letter reprinted here is the letter drafted by her husband after their arrival in California. Particularly noteworthy is his description of their rough passage of the Sierra Nevadas via the Truckee River, which they had to cross twenty-seven times in making their way through the high country. He also related that Amanda gave birth to a son on November 4, even though she never mentioned in her correspondence that she was pregnant. See Daniel Rhoads, "Letter" (1965).

The most complete account of Daniel and Amanda's later lives is found at http://freepages.genealogy.rootsweb.ancestry.com/~newman/donnacrowtalk.htm (accessed October 15, 2013). This site features the full text of a talk given by Donna Crow in 2002 at a Rhoads family gathering and includes genealogical data for the children of Daniel and Amanda. Most important, it quotes liberally from family letters that were written between the 1850s and 1890s. These letters were published by Stephen P. Emanuels, *The Rhodes-Esrey Letters* (1992). Also impressive in its genealogical detail is the text of a speech given by Ellen Rosa at the 2002 dedication of the Rhoads Family Cemetery. It is available online at http://freepages.genealogy.rootsweb.ancestry.com/~newman/ellenrosaspeech.htm (accessed October 15, 2013).

AMANDA ESREY RHOADS TO DEAR PARENTS,
FORT LARAMIE, JUNE 15, 1846.
PHOTOCOPY, BANC MSS 71/38 C,
RHOADS FAMILY PAPERS, 1846–1856,
BANCROFT LIBRARY, UNIVERSITY OF CALIFORNIA, BERKELEY.
COPY COURTESY OF BERNIE L. RHOADES.

Following is a transcript I made of the June 15th 1846 letter from Thomas Rhoads' daughter-in-law Amanda Esrey Rhoads to her father Jesse Esrey in Ray Co. MO from Fort Laramie WY. One third of the way to Sacramento from Ray Co. The Donner party was one of the groups they passed. Six months later Amanda's husband Daniel Rhoads was one of 7 who back-tracked and became the first Donner Rescue Party, and part of California History.—Bernie Rhoades

Note: Kay Threlkeld obtained a microfilm copy of the original letter from the Bancroft Library and slightly corrected Bernie's transcription, April 2006.

June 15th 1846

Dear Parents, i take my pen in hand to inform you that we are all now in good health and hope that these few lines may find you all enjoying the same blessing. a few days after we struck the plat [Platte] river the bigest part of our company was sick about 2 or 3 days. i my self had a severe spell of the toothache after suffering 3 or 4 day i found a cure disolve assifidity in liquor[,] wet cotton[,] apply it to the tooth will ease the pain in less than 8 hours. we crossed the mo [Missouri] river [at St. Joseph, Missouri] the 6 and 7 of may [1846]. we then passed on 3 days campt on wolf river. the iowa Socks [Sacs] indians stole several of our cattle one of our big oxen. [Father Thomas] Rhoads and Daniel [her husband] went to the indian agency [Great Nemaha Agency] and the agent replaced other cattle. we traveled one hundred miles in a company of 16 waggons. then we left them and traveled 100 and 50 miles our ten waggons through the pawney [Pawnee] nation we passed 5 or 6 Companies on for oregon, we over took a california company and joined them and we are all to gether yet 30 waggons we traveled one week up the waters of the caw [Kaw] for the blew river, one days travel from their to the plat river [reached Platte River on May 26]. we keep the plat 100 and 35 miles their it forked one day and a half up the south fork and we crossed it 2 day travel to the north fork. we are a following the river yet and will to the head it was one mile wide where we forded it, a quick sandy bottom, it was verry bad crossing Some places the water was half way the ~~yoke~~ waggon beds and some places on sand it isent [isn't] aney wander why your rivers is is [so] high at times when there is so much water comes down the plat [Platte River]. the main big plat is from 2 to 3 miles wide we came to the pawney [Pawnee] at the plat we met hundreds of them for several days the night of the 26 the indians encampt 2 sides of us the next morning our horses took a fright at the indians and their pack horses and run away. our men followed about 40 miles the indians saw them and went in before the men run the horses and took them they killed 2 or 3 poneys running them when they caught the horses they then turned on the men and attempted to rob or murder them there was 4 men Rhoads, Jon [?] Rhoa[ds,] John Rhoads. Patterson[,] mr white-man there was a bout one hundred indians run them a verry narrow race they got so close that they got a holt of there horses bridals they run a bout 3 miles in that condition then our men run them a bout 8 miles the indians by that time raised 80 more they run them so close that th[e]y to save there lives was obliged to cross the river there was 2 or 3 ilands in the river by way of islands it was about 3 miles wide by the time the men was a cross the indians was a taking the river the men went up the river about 12 and come in sight of the oregon company and they crossed back and staid all night there the next day they came on and the indians gave them as close a race as before but they got to the Company safe they lost 11 head of horses. Rhoads lost 3 Patterson 2 John Rhoads 2 thomas 1 the ballance from the Company they have stole most all the horses from all the companies it is useless for any person to start with more than 2 horses on this Journey aney person on this road with 3 or 4 waggons should have 5 or 6 yoak of oxen more than their teems there is a great many cattle has sore feet by traveling threw the sand we have traveled through a great deal of sand better roads nature couldent form than we have had altho we had rain the month of may through the last day of may we had snow Daniels arm is so tha he can begin to use his ax to chop we all stand the Journey very well it is quite a pleasan[t] trip so far we met emigrants the 12 of june within 600 miles of missouri that went last spring and returning for their families there is some of them saw they is traveled the Country of oregon and California through they say oregon is the best country it is two hot a climent in california they say in california every thing is cheap as in the states the other country every thing is dear they stopt about 20 minnets told the company to write letters and i wrote a few lines of something i dont know what it was and gave it to them we are at fort larimous [Fort Laramie] which is 700 miles

Included is the envelope dated
"Jul 11" [1846]
St Joseph Mo, [from] Amanda Rhoads"

and addressed to
"Ray county Mo.
Richmond Mo
To Jess [Jesse] Esrey"

1847

Augustin M. A. Blanchet, Letter to Msgr. Peter R. Kenrick

Augustin Magloire Alexander Blanchet was born on August 22, 1797, in Quebec, Canada, to a devoutly Catholic family, and he was ordained a priest on June 3, 1821. Following years of pastoral assignments in Quebec and on the Cape Breton Islands, he was called to duty by his brother, François Norbert Blanchet, the first archbishop of Oregon City, Oregon. Upon appointment by the Vatican, Augustin assumed the position of bishop of Walla Walla on July 28, 1846. His account of the overland journey to Oregon and the initial years of service there was recorded in a detailed journal covering the time span from March 23, 1847, to January 23, 1851. The original journal, written in French, eventually made its way to the Seattle (Washington) Archdiocesan Archives, where it was subsequently translated, edited, and published by Edward J. Kowrach as *Journal of a Catholic Bishop on the Oregon Trail* (1978). Six additional letters from Augustin Blanchet were also discovered by Raphael N. Hamilton and published as "The Journey of the Bishop of Walla Walla" (1927). These sources provide innumerable details that help place the following letter within a broader context and reveal more about Blanchet's story of the martyrdom of missionaries Marcus and Narcissa Whitman. This previously unpublished letter, addressed to Monsignor Peter R. Kenrick, first archbishop of St. Louis, is typical of the correspondence that Blanchet submitted to his church superiors over the years. The source is particularly valuable for its discussion of the rigors of overland travel, Blanchet's negative view of common law marriages between fur traders and Indian women, his troubles with Protestant missionaries who resented Catholics making inroads into the Pacific Northwest, and his friendly association with representatives of the Hudson's Bay Company. Merrill Mattes's *Platte River Road Narratives* awarded Blanchet's *Journal* four stars of excellence, but the journal does not include the letter that is edited here.

Further information on Blanchet's party and the 1847 overland crossing is found in Louise Barry, *The Beginning of the West* (1972), 680; and Hamilton, ed., "The Journey of the First Bishop of Walla Walla" (1927). James Bordeaux and his trading operations in the Nebraska panhandle and eastern Wyoming are discussed in Merrill J. Mattes, *The Great Platte River Road* (1969), and by his daughter in Susan Bordeaux Bettelyoun and Josephine Waggoner, *With My Own Eyes: A Lakota Woman Tells Her Peoples' History* (1988). Likewise, William R. Sampson's *John McLoughlin's Business Correspondence, 1847–48* (1973), offers details about the Hudson's Bay Company employees who are mentioned in Blanchet's letter. Other prominent Catholics referred to in the letter are described in the endnote section to Blanchet's *Journal of a Catholic Bishop on the Oregon Trail*; in Pierre-Jean De Smet, *Western Missions and Missionaries* (1863); and in F. X. Blanchet, *Ten Years on the Pacific Coast* (1982). Coverage of the early Protestant missions is found in Clifford M. Drury, *The Diaries and Letters of Henry H. Spalding and Asa Bowen Smith Relating to the Nez Percé, 1838–1842* (1958); and Drury, *Marcus and Narcissa Whitman and the Opening of Old Oregon* (1973).

[Augustin Magloire Alexander] Blanchet to Kenderick [Msgr. Peter R. Kenrick] March 30, 1848, General Archives of the Society of Jesus, Rome, Italy. Copies at Jesuit Oregon Province Archives, Special Collections, Gonzaga University, Spokane, Washington.

You already know that I left Westport [Missouri] on the eighth of May [1847] to go to the prairies. But since I realized that I could not go further without an experienced guide for this sort of journey I had

Augustin Magloire Alexander Blanchet.
Courtesy of the Archdiocese of Seattle.

to go back to Kansas to get one.[1] Therefore, I could only leave the Methodist mission which is three or four miles away from Westport on the twelfth. The wagons were heavy; to not wear out the beasts, we advanced slowly. We had no troubles from the day we left, except we broke an axle of a wagon. It was the day before Pentecost. On this same holy date we were ready to continue our journey. We arrived at Fort Laramie on the twenty-fifth of June [1847] without having encountered any savages since we crossed the Kansas River. We rested for three days and then we left the fort where I had been welcomed very politely by Mssr. Bourdeau [James Bordeaux] and Mssr. Montalon [Eugene Montalant].[2] There we also baptized several children. But how can

[1]Blanchet left Westport, Missouri, accompanied by several priests who were inexperienced with the country, management of livestock, and the driving of wagons. Their guide, William Wiggins, proved irresponsible, and Blanchet had to hire a new guide, Joseph Huneau, to see them safely through to the Hudson's Bay Company post at Fort Hall. See Blanchet, *Journal of a Catholic Bishop*, 37–39; and Barry, *Beginning of the West*, 679–80.

[2]James Bordeaux, employee of the American Fur Company, was in charge of Fort Laramie at the time of Blanchet's 1847 visit. Among the eight children baptized that day was Antoine, the infant son of Bordeaux by the Indian woman Marie (Huntkalutawin, or Red Cormorant Woman). Eugene Montalant was a clerk at Fort Laramie and his son, Paul, was also baptized at that time. See Blanchet, *Journal of a Catholic Bishop*, 50, 124n; and Bettelyoun and Waggoner, *With My Own Eyes*, 34–48.

one not be deeply hurt when thinking about the fact that all of them, or at least most of the whites, who lived there have concubines who they do not want to marry because they would not want to bring them back to St. Louis. This thought made me wail several times during my trip. We arrived on the seventh of August at Fort Hall after having passed Fort Bridger. We all felt a little ill during the journey. As for me I was quite glad to be in this place at last because I was not able to go on further. The scorching heat we had to endure, the dust we continuously swallowed, and all the worries on my mind had reduced me to a state of great weakness. As I was aware that I would find no other accommodations than the Hudson's Bay Company was willing to grant me, I decided to take the initiative and to prepare a small lodging for the arrival of my party. I took the road with the wagons Mr.Grant [Richard Grant][3] sent to Walla Walla and he rented me the horses we needed. I was accompanied by Rev. P. [Pascal] Ricard and Mr. Rousseau [Louis Pierre Godefroy Rousseau].[4] We sometimes had to travel thirty miles without stopping. The first days were unpleasant but I felt better later on. We walked twenty [?] days traveling twenty-five and even some days thirty-two miles per day, and we arrived on the 5 of September at Fort Walla Walla. . . . Considering that we traveled on horseback at a speed of four miles per hour, it made 510 miles from Fort Hall to Fort Walla Walla, which made a total of 1705 miles. I was warmly welcomed by Mr.Bean [William B. McBean],[5] a

[3]Richard Grant was the chief factor for the Hudson's Bay Company operations at Fort Hall, a man knowledgeable about the terrain and Indian tribes of western Montana and Idaho, who was very helpful to the Blanchet party. See Thrapp, *Encyclopedia of Frontier Biography*, 580–81.

[4]Rev. Pascal Ricard, O.M.I., represented the Oblate order in Oregon and accompanied the Blanchet party as it departed St. Louis in April 1847. Ricard and his followers worked closely with the Yakamas until the Yakima War of 1855 undermined these missionary efforts. In 1848, he also established a church in Olympia, Washington, before failing health forced his return to France, where he died in 1862. Louis Pierre Godefroy Rousseau was a deacon when he volunteered to go to Oregon with Blanchet and was ordained a priest in 1848. He served two years as secretary to Blanchet at The Dalles and ministered to Indians. Bad health forced his return to Canada in 1851, and he died while undertaking the journey. See Blanchet, *Journal of a Catholic Bishop*, 36, 117n, 120n.

[5]William B. McBean, an ardent Catholic, was the chief trader for the Hudson's Bay Company at Fort Walla Walla trading post. He became a somewhat controversial character in the wake of the 1847 Whitman Massacre but apparently was innocent of allegations about his tardiness in rescuing the survivors. He retired in 1855 and died in 1872 in the Walla Walla Valley. See Blanchet, *Journal of a Catholic Bishop*, 129n.

representative of the Hudson's Bay Company, in Walla Walla where I dwelt until the end of November. The devil could not have been happy at the arrival of all these missionaries with me, so he did not take long to try to hamper the good deeds of the missionaries. Dr. [Marcus] Whitman could not feel indifferent to our plight and he was not. Indeed as early as the first discussion we had he disclosed to me how troubled and powerless he had been feeling; and he assured me that he would help me with all his strength. He expressed his fanaticism in telling me he would not sell me provisions, however, he added that if he ever saw me in distress (in starvation) then he would come and rescue me. A few days later, he threatened to oppose me; indeed, he transported me near to the Umatilla River to inspire fear in us of the savages and the American people who pass by. On this occasion he told us that our lives were in danger. Rev. Spaulding [Henry H. Spalding][6] accompanied him on this mission. He also wanted to hire *Piopa Movemox* [Peo Peo Mox Mox, or Yellow Serpent], chief of the Walla Wallas, to go with him to the neighboring nations to discourage them from listening to us; but he did not succeed. Several times he tried to appeal to Tawatoé, [Tauitau, or Young Chief], the first chief of the Cayuse, which he accused of having applied pressure to appoint a bishop!! and who had been asking for a missionary for years, but God did not permit him to achieve his goal. You will understand, Monsignor, that I felt pity for him, but I did not resent his opposition. . . . In every possible occasion I felt a duty to defend him against the savages who spoke ill about him. I was determined to accomplish our Master's principle, "Do good unto those who treat you badly. . . ." All

[6]As representatives of the American Board of Foreign Missions, Marcus and Narcissa Whitman traveled with fellow missionaries Henry and Eliza Spalding in 1836 to Oregon country. The Whitmans established their mission at Waiilatpu, near present-day Walla Walla, Washington, and the Spaldings settled at Lapwai, near present-day Lewiston, Idaho. Despite inadequate help from their eastern board, they made progress among the neighboring tribes, and their letters that were printed in the east encouraged the earliest influx of American settlers to Oregon. By 1843, Waiilatpu Mission was an important landmark on the Oregon Trail. The Whitmans died amid the Cayuse uprising of 1847, which is mentioned in Blanchet's letter. The Spaldings abandoned Lapwai a month later and settled in the Willamette Valley, where Eliza died in 1851. Henry Spalding remarried two years later and, in 1871, returned to the Nez Percé tribe as a representative of the Presbyterian Board of Foreign Missions. He died in 1873 after achieving some success among the Nez Percés. See Thrapp, *Encyclopedia of Frontier Biography*, 1342–43, 1558–60.

my missionaries knew their duty fairly well and did not stray from this evangelical way. In a meeting with the Cayuse I asked if they wanted the Black Robes, that I did not ask for, that they should send the doctor; that he should stay where he was; and that it would not prevent me from establishing a Catholic mission as long as it was their will. On the twenty-seventh of November I went to Tawatoé's camp. . . . The doctor and Mr. Spalding arrived here too on the same day. The doctor paid me a visit on the following day, which was a Sunday, and I invited him to dinner, but he refused because he did not want to stay too late. He had twenty-five miles to travel to Waëlat pou [Waiilatpu Mission] where he dwelt. On Monday Mr. Spalding had supper with us, and he told us the doctor had left, worried, but he was jolly all the time he spent with us. By this time the doctor, his spouse, and several Americans had already been slaughtered . . . Mr. Brouillet [Abbé Jean Baptiste Abraham Brouillet],[7] Vicar General, having been to Waëlat pou on the following day, to baptize children and to visit the sick, only heard the news when he arrived. On Wednesday, he buried the victims and left quickly to return to Umatilla to tell us about the disaster of the 29. A few miles from Waëlat pou he met Rev. Spalding. . . . Mr. Brouillet told Rev. Spalding about the whole affair and gave him all his few provisions and told him to flee for his life. I will only describe the substance. The Oregon Spectator has already published several articles and you will no doubt see these articles published in your newspapers. The Hudson's Bay Company also sent to Canada everything that Mr. [Peter Skene] Ogden[8] has received, therefore I will skip the details. It

[7]Rev. Jean Baptiste Abraham Brouillet accompanied the Blanchet party from Montréal to Oregon and opened St. Anne's Mission among the Cayuse Indians on the Umatilla River, approximately twenty-five miles from Whitman's Waiilatpu Mission. He was one of the first outsiders to reach the scene of the Whitman Massacre, and he wrote one of the first extensive reports on these events. See Edward Kowrach's essay in Blanchet, *Journal of a Catholic Bishop*, 143–47, 149–69.

[8]Peter Skene Ogden was a former employee of the Northwest Fur Company, but upon its business merger in 1821, he went to work for the Hudson's Bay Company as manager of the Spokane House District. Between 1824 and 1830, he oversaw six trapping expeditions throughout the Northern Rockies and the Great Basin. His decisive action in rescuing prisoners of the Whitman Massacre made him popular with many Americans. He elected to remain in Oregon after its acquisition from Britain, and he was buried in Oregon City upon his death in 1854. See Sampson, *John McLoughlin's Business Correspondence*, 144–45.

is enough to tell you that this tragical scene moved the inhabitants of the Willamette Valley to raise a mob of three to four hundred men to avenge the murders and here we are in the middle of the war whose end we cannot foresee. It is important to note that all the Cayuse were not involved in the murders of November 29, and that afterwards, the chiefs seemed to regret it sincerely, since they sent Governor [George] Abernathy a note in which they described the motives of the murderers and their desire to avoid a war with the Americans, and they preferred to send their great men to discuss peace. I went down there in January with the captives who had been held in Waiilatpu, who Mr. Ogden of the Hudson's Bay Company saved from the hands of the savages, trading for presents. All my missionaries being unable to do anything in this state of affairs chose to leave their posts and to come and join me. I cannot tell at present when we will be able to return up the Columbia [River] and dwell again among the savages. Another inconvenience. . . . I have just heard about the existence of law in the Union meant to prevent any white man to dwell among the savages without the authorization of the executive power. It is said that this law may be implemented in our small area. And since the executive power here is more or less opposed to Catholicism, I do fear we will face opposition. That is why I decided to address the Secretary of State in Washington.

1848

William Porter, Letter to His Family

Brothers William and Stephen Porter, of Pike County, Illinois, participated in what was popularly known as the St. Joseph Emigration during the summer of 1848. The *St. Joseph Gazette* reported on May 5 that the Missouri jumping-off town had hummed with excitement for several weeks as migrants assembled and outfitted themselves for the trail drive to Oregon and California. The newspaper article estimated that 210 wagons had already crossed the Missouri River at that spot, and that forty or fifty other wagons were waiting for ferries to convey them to the west bank of the river. The lead group, which had begun the trip in late April, was already traversing northeastern Kansas, guided toward Oregon by fur trader William O. Fallon. Another company was piloted by experienced mountain man James Clyman, who would lead his charges to California.

William and Stephen Porter's small group of perhaps only four wagons crossed the Missouri River on May 2, alongside one of several large companies, and by May 5 they were camped on Peter's Creek, approximately six miles west of St. Joseph. Quite likely, it was here that Porter's family integrated their wagons with the larger company of Bolivar Walker and William Bristow, who in turn were joined by the wagons under the leadership of John Purvine. Accompanying William Porter was his wife, Sarah, and their four small children. On the following day, all were camped near the Great Nemaha Indian Subagency. They reached Pacific Springs on July 8, and their final destination of Oregon City on October 1.

The Porters remained with the Virgil Pringle family at Salem, Oregon, throughout the winter, and ultimately settled on an Oregon Donation Act claim southeast of the present-day town of Aumsville, Oregon (originally called Hoggum). William's wife, Sarah, died soon after their arrival in the Willamette Valley and was the first person to be buried in the Aumsville Cemetery. In October 1849, Porter married his first wife's sister Martha ("Patsy"), with whom he had three additional children. He built a log cabin, farmed the land, and occasionally helped build roads in the region.

William Porter served as chief clerk of the first territorial legislative assembly at Oregon City in 1849 and was subsequently elected as a representative in the state legislature. He profited in his financial ventures and, by 1855, was able to construct a frame building that opened as the first school in the area, with William as the teacher. The school served as a church on Sundays and took the title of Mill Creek Church of Christ. The building was closed in 1868, and the church moved into Aumsville to serve a larger congregation. In 1963, Maude Porter Boone donated five acres from her grandfather's original donation claim on Mill Creek to create the Porter-Boone Park for the enjoyment of all the town's residents.

William Porter's only surviving letter from the Oregon Trail venture is reprinted and edited here as a good example of a didactic for instructing other people on how best to manage trail life. Clearly the letter was intended not for an untargeted eastern audience, but for the author's immediate relatives and fellow townspeople, whom he was encouraging to join him in the Willamette River Valley. The exact location from which this June 24, 1848, letter was written is vague, but other evidence indicates that they were on the North Platte River Crossing at present-day Casper, Wyoming, most likely at the Mormon Ferry.

The contents of this letter are similar to those written by other overlanders to eastern relatives and friends whom they also wished to entice to Oregon. William Porter offered practical advice about wagon repair, types of livestock to employ, liberal supplies of rope to tie down wagons in windstorms, the best tent equipment, and how to avoid the worst effects of a stampede. Also useful were his remarks

William Porter.
Courtesy of Karlene Burton Santibanez.

about dividing the necessary labor among all members of the wagon train so that everyone knew his assigned duties and performed them at the proper time. The letter's concluding words—"In hopes of seeing you again"—were more than a pleasantry intended for the relatives. The phrase represented a buoyant sentiment for eventual reunification of the family in the Willamette Valley. Unfortunately, the appeal had a disastrous outcome. Sixty-eight-year-old David Porter (father of William and Stephen Porter) did depart for Oregon during the following spring with his son-in-law, Samuel G. Sitton. David Porter died on July 17, 1849, while camped near Soda Springs, and Sitton returned to Pike County, Illinois. William's mother, Nancy Culton Porter, remained in Pike County until her death on January 8, 1867. William's long and eventful life ended on March 30, 1899, nine years after his brother Stephen died.

Although no other correspondence from brothers William and Stephen Porter has been discovered regarding the overland trip, William's original diary of these events has survived. The 4 × 6–inch book, with a leather cover, is owned by great-grandson Kenneth Porter of Stayton, Oregon. A typescript copy can be viewed at www.oregonpioneers.com/porter.htm (accessed October 15, 2013). Although most entries merely list daily travel distances, landmarks, and the condition of available grasses at the various campsites, the diary offers an entry for every single day from April 7, 1848, when they left Pike County, Illinois, until October 8, when they reached the Pringle house at Salem, Oregon.

To understand further details of how the initial train of four wagons eventually joined with other companies in northeastern Kansas, it is important to examine Louise Barry's *The Beginning of the West* (1972), 745–48. Departing St. Joseph approximately one week prior to Porter's wagon train was the party containing husband and wife George and Keturah Belknap, who also were headed to Oregon. A comparison of their experiences can be drawn from the more detailed diary of Keturah Belknap, which was published in Kenneth L. Holmes, ed. *Covered Wagon Women*, vol. 1 (1983). Additional information on the Porter family after their settlement in Oregon appears in Margaret Mulkey, "History of Early Aumsville" (www.aumsville.us/Aumsville

History.htm) (accessed October 15, 2013). Additional information on and photographs of the school and church is found at http://ncbible.org/nwh/OrMarion.html (accessed October 15, 2013). A biographical sketch of William appears in Sarah Hunt Steeves, *Book of Remembrance of Marion County Oregon, Pioneers, 1840–1860* (1927). Essential to understanding the full range of William Porter's family members is an excellent 355-page book by Mary E. Porter, *A Family History: William Porter, Jr. of Rockbridge County, Virginia (1740–1804) and Five Generations of His Descendants* (2001). This includes the full text of William's trail diary, as well as several other family letters written before and after the Oregon Trail venture. Also helpful to understanding the trip and its importance is John Porter, *On the Old Oregon Trail* (2006), which was written by the great-great nephew of William Porter. I wish to thank Karlene Santibanez, Don Porter, and Bev Gilson (all descendants of William Porter) of Aumsville, Oregon, and the above-mentioned John Porter of Newark, California, for their friendship and essential aid in assembling this elusive material.

William Porter to Dear Father, Mother,
Brothers and Sisters, June 24, 1848.
St. Boniface Archives, Sublimity, Oregon.

Note: paragraph breaks have been inserted to make the letter more readable.

Crossing of the North Fork of Platte
June 24, 1848

Dear Father, Mother, Brothers and Sisters,

I wrote a few lines to you a few days ago, but lest they should not reach you, I will write as though I had not written at all. We are all well, and getting on as well as common. Some of our company are a little discouraged on account of fatigues of the journey and the reports in reference to the Indians in Oregon. I have felt a little discouraged, sometimes, about the scarcity of grass, though our cattle look well.

As a general thing, there is no difficulty in finding good camping places till you get to [Fort] Laramie, thence to this place there is but one or two good camps. Grass is not as good this season as it commonly is.

I will make a few suggestions from experience, which you may profit by should you ever travel this road. In reference to wagons, oxen, etc: I would say bring wagons made of the best materials and thoroughly seasoned and then have some black-smith's tongs and harness for setting tires. You can get tires cut and set at Laramie but you will frequently have occasion to set them on the road.[1] The most common way is to nail a thin hoop on the felloe or part of its circumference and heat the tire and put it on. Another way is to take off the tire, raise or open the felloe, take pieces of good firm sole leather, cut round holes in them, split into the hole, and slip it on to the spoke, and two or three pieces, according to circumstances, between the felloes and put on the tire. I have put on several this way, which seem to do well.[2]

Well made, stout active cattle, of the common kind of scrub stock should only be brought and about four yoke, or three at least for each wagon; and be sure to bring none except such as you work in the teams. All in our company who have loose cattle regret having started with them, and some sold their loose cattle at Laramie. Be careful to get an industrious, careful hand to drive your team and one that will not leave his post at any time.

I would advise to bring no horses. Mules for working or riding do well. Get a good Mexican saddle. A common saddle, whether rode or not, will be of little value, even after coming this far.

---

[1]At the time of William Porter's arrival at Fort Laramie in 1848, the fur-trading post was still privately owned and a year away from purchase by the United States Army. Yet the post blacksmith shop was already playing a vital role in helping travelers who had experienced problems with their wagons. Both as a fur-trading post and as a regular military installation, Fort Laramie sometimes rented its forge and blacksmithing equipment to overlanders to make their own repairs. On other occasions, the blacksmith and his assistant performed the necessary repairs for a fee. Civilians could thus shoe livestock, repair and cut down wagons, replace wheels, manufacture simple tools, and overhaul other equipment. In 1847–1848, Mormon travelers also set up portable blacksmith shops near Fort Laramie to serve Mormons and Gentiles alike. See Mattes, *Great Platte River Road*, 514, and Hafen and Young, *Fort Laramie*, 125.

[2]An informative article on overland wagons, complete with five detailed diagrams of the various mechanical components (especially the axles and wheels), appears in Davis, "Where Have All the Wagons Gone?," 16–19.

Bring plenty of good strong rope, five or six hundred feet will not be too much. There is a great deal of windy weather and rains are generally accompanied with high winds.

You should therefore, have your wagon covers of very strong material. Good bed-ticking is good. Let the wagon bows be strong and well turned; and the cover should be fixed as to entirely shelter the hind and front end of the wagons when necessary. The wagon bed should be fixed so rain could not drive in on the floor, either at the sides or ends.

A good tent is very necessary. Common domestic is not fit for a tent. Tent poles should be ironed and the pins should be made of iron or buck horns. A light cook-stove will be found very convenient to set at the mouth of the tent. Have a stake to hold up the pipe.

A small dog or two will be useful till you cross the Missouri river after which they are more than useless. They have caused our company to divide. They have caused Walker [Bolivar Walker] and Bristow's [William Bristow] companies' teams to run away twice, and ours once. It is a remarkable thing that teams, especially on the Platte [River] are apt to become frightened very easily and run off. Walker and Bristow's company had 24 teams to run at once, killing some oxen and crippling others, besides other damage. Our company had 19 teams (all except Purvines' [John Purvine] 5 wagons) to run. Isaac Ball of St. Charles Co, Mo. had his thigh broken. He is doing well. It is a frightening sight to see so many teams running. When you stop for dinner or any cause loose the cattle from the wagon. If there is about to be a general runaway turn your oxen from the road and give them a fair start and stick to the wagon; otherwise you will be liable to be run over and wrecked. The cattle will run about 200 yards and stop.[3]

Our company consists of 24 wagons, belonging to Hooker and Purvine of Scott and Morgan Counties: Tucker [Samuel Tucker],

---

[3]Porter's warning about taking too many extra head of livestock (and avoiding extra horses altogether) was a point made by other overlanders who spent considerable time and effort on the trail driving the surplus animals. His discussion of the likelihood of stampedes further drives home the point, because in such a panicked situation, human lives could be lost in a flash, and livestock could disperse in such a way that days might be consumed in rounding up only a fraction of their numbers. William's diary entry of June 4 indicated that Isaac Ball suffered a broken leg, and a number of oxen were also crippled by a stampede near Ash Hollow.

Holmes [Horatio N. V. Holmes], Lewis and Stephen and William Porter of Pike County, Ill and J. Ball [this may refer to Isaac Ball since J. Ball does not appear in other records] of St. Charles Co., Mo. We organized by selecting John Purvine Captain and William Porter Lieutenant. We divided our company into six messes or divisions, each one takes his turn to lead. We have divided our men into seven guards or watches, three of which come on each night to guard the cattle and wagons. This division operates equally upon all.

We are also into nine divisions to herd the cattle, morning and evenings. Every evening we drive our wagons, half to the right and half to the left forming a carel [corral]. The form of a horse-shoe makes a good carel. At night bring the mules and horses if any into the carel and the cattle near its mouth and guard them.

I thought I would give a particular account of the road to this point but will not have time nor space. Procure Palmers' book[4] and Freemont's [John C. Frémont] map[5] which will be very useful. If you have a man in company who has been the route it will be well; otherwise you ought generally to send some two or three in advance to select camping places. For the first 200 miles you will generally have to camp off the road. Wood is very scarce on Platte till you get near Laramie. Plenty of buffalo chips on Platte till you cross the south fork which are preferable to green cottonwood. When you have an opportunity of getting good wood on Platte better lay in two or three day's supply. At Scotts Bluffs, lay in one days supply of wood after which it is not necessary to haul wood up to this place.

[4]Porter refers to Joel Palmer's *Journal of Travels Over the Rocky Mountains, to the Mouth of the Columbia River*, which had been published in 1847 and was viewed by many people as a reliable guidebook. In addition to providing advice on preparing for the overland trip and imparting information about landmarks and areas of difficulty encountered along the trail, the book lists precise distances between important geographical features. A brief profile of Palmer and the importance of his book in stimulating the Oregon migration is found in Edward J. Kowrach's introduction in Palmer, *Journal of Travels Over the Rocky Mountains*, 9–10.

[5]The John C. Frémont map referred to here is possibly the one published with his widely influential government document, *A Report on an Exploration of the Country Lying Between the Missouri River and the Rocky Mountains, on the Line of the Kansas and Great Platte Rivers* (Senate Document 243, 27th Congress, 3rd session, serial set no. 416). It may, however, have been the equally popular and more expansive map that was published with his *Report of the Exploring Expedition to the Rocky Mountains in the Year 1842, and to Oregon and North California in the Years 1843–44* (1845). A brief overview of the later exploration appears in Watson, "Frémont's Second Expedition," 2–9.

Lay in a few good whip stocks of hickory poles. Let all your nailing about the wagons be with wrought nails.

This is the fourth day we have been here waiting to cross the Platte. A small company of Mormons from Salt Lake are here with a canoe boat to cross the immigrants. They charge $1.50 per wagon. It will be two days yet till we can cross. Yesterday a company of Mormons arrived here with their wagons and teams to assist their friends now on the road to Salt Lake. There is now a company in our camp from Oregon, just arrived. They say grass is very scarce on the route from this on, and it will be very difficult getting there. They came the southern route in consequence of the war with the Indians, some seen to think it very dangerous to go either route. Andrew Rodgers was killed with the Whitmans' family.[6] It is thought the war will be brought to a close this year. You will hear later news before spring.

We have been traveling with [Bolivar] Walker and [William] Bristow's Company for some time, but for convenience will separate here till necessity calls us to join again. If thought best, you may have this letter published, and I hope this may suffice for a letter to all whom I promised to write to, and all interested.

I promised to write a letter for Samuel Tucker today, but the company is in such hast[e] to leave I shall not have time. He says to tell all his relations and friends that he is well, and all the family have been well and are in good spirits considering the circumstances. Mr. [N.] Coffey and wife, together with their family wish to be remembered. Give my regards to all my relations and friends, and tell all who may intend to take this trip to be sure to have a good wagon and team and plenty of provisions.

One thing I forgot to mention in its proper place and which I will consider of importance: make use of rosin and tallow to grease wagons. Black lead will do but is very inconvenient to haul. It will black everything.

In hopes of seeing you again, I am, William Porter.

---

[6]Andrew Rodgers was a lay missionary who left Warren County, Illinois, in 1845 to do work among the Indians of Oregon. He taught school at Marcus and Narcissa Whitman's Waiilatpu Mission, but was killed in the Cayuse uprising of 1847. Circumstantial evidence indicates that Rodgers was a cousin of William Porter. See Saunders, *Whitman Massacre*, 29–31; Thompson, *Shallow Grave at Waiilatpu*, 74–88 and 98–102; and Porter, *A Family History*, 281.

John Borrowman, "The Roughest Road I Ever Saw"

John Borrowman was born in Glasgow, Scotland, May 13, 1816, converted to Mormonism while living in Canada, and served in Company B of the Mormon Battalion during the Mexican War. This special military force of approximately five hundred men accompanied Colonel Stephen Watts Kearny in the conquest of New Mexico and California. Mustered out of service at Los Angeles on July 16, 1847, Borrowman and his friend James Park took passage on a small schooner to San Francisco, where they desperately sought work of any type to make ends meet. Other Mormons, known as the *Brooklyn* Saints, had already arrived in San Francisco by ship, most notably Samuel Brannan, a church elder who would soon break with the hierarchy and set about to enrich himself by selling supplies to gold miners.

The January 24, 1848, discovery of gold at Sutter's Mill on the American River had an immediate effect on Borrowman's life and a more delayed but decisive impact on the future of the nation. He apparently received a letter from his friend Henry Bigler, who had been working on the original saw mill where gold had initially been discovered. Borrowman made a quick trip to the diggings at Mormon Island, approximately twenty miles east of Sutter's Fort, and upon finding encouraging pay dirt, set about on his expected road to riches. Unlike most of the eyewitness descriptions of travel on the Oregon and California trails, Borrowman's account is somewhat unique because he and fellow Mormons traveled from west to east to reach Salt Lake City. There they joined the other Saints, who had traveled from Winter Quarters on the Missouri River to found their new Zion in the Wilderness.

The trail laid out by these eastwardly bound Mormons became known as the Carson River Route, in honor of the legendary frontiersman, trapper, and guide Christopher "Kit" Carson. Carson had entered the region with John C. Frémont in 1844, but neither had actually traversed the new route across the Sierra Nevadas. The group relied instead on preexisting Indian trails and advance scouting parties as they left Pleasant Valley, near present-day Placerville, California, on July 3, 1848. They intentionally avoided the more northerly Truckee River Route, which was still associated with the Donner party tragedy, and they hoped to find a more manageable passage through the mountains. The Carson River Route, however, proved to be tough going, as numerous trees had to be felled and many large boulders had to be pushed aside. On some days, the party, which included seventeen wagons and 150 horses and mules, managed only a few miles of travel. Success was finally measured in crossing the highest point at West Pass and the almost equally lofty Carson Pass before reaching the inviting campsite at what they optimistically named Hope Valley. The final barrier of Carson River Canyon also demanded a difficult transit because of thick growths of trees and mounds of boulders. Yet, on August 4, they reached the relatively flat lands on the east side of the mountains and followed the Carson River across open terrain.

On the way toward the Humboldt River, they met three separate parties headed west, groups that included mountain man James Clyman, twenty-five wagons under Pierre Cornwall, and the forty-eight wagons of Joseph Chiles's cavalcade. All three groups listened to the Mormons' descriptions of the new route, and all three set out for California along the newly pioneered route. Perhaps as many as five hundred to seven hundred people used this trail during 1848, and by 1850, a majority of California-bound miners followed the Carson River Route. By 1855, a southern variant known as the Big Tree Carson Valley Wagon Road offered a slightly different way to traverse the mountains. Five years later, enough improvements had been made along the primary route that it became known as the Amador–Carson Valley Wagon Road. Thus, in seeking to find an alternative to the Truckee River Route, these Mormons had pioneered one of the most important branches of the fabled California Trail. John Borrowman's description of the initial exploring adventure is an important eyewitness account of that heroic endeavor.

Borrowman married Agnes Park in January 1849, and they subsequently had five children, who helped work their irrigated farm just outside of Salt Lake City. The Borrowmans answered the call to a colonization mission in 1853, when they moved approximately eighty miles south to Nephi, Utah, where, in addition to farming, John Borrowman served as prosecuting attorney and later as municipal judge. In

1869, he left his family to fulfill a two-year church mission in Canada before returning to Utah. William Borrowman, father of John, never forgave his son for converting to Mormonism, and thus turned his back on the young man for the rest of his life. This development also cost John his inheritance of the family farm in Ontario, Canada. John Borrowman died in March 1898.

Three of the best eyewitness accounts of Mormon military service during the Mexican War are Daniel Tyler, *A Concise History of the Mormon Battalion in the Mexican War* (1881); Henry W. Bigler, *Bigler's Chronicles of the West* (1962); and "Philip St. George Cooke's Journal of the March of the Mormon Battalion, 1846–47," in Ralph P. Bieber and Averam B. Bender, eds. *Exploring Southwestern Trails, 1846–1854*, vol. 7 of Southwest Historical Series (1938). These sources must be supplemented by a wealth of material by participants, which is published in David L. Bigler and Will Bagley, eds., *Army of Israel* (2000). A modern overview that offers detailed information on service in the Mexican War and in the California gold fields is Norma Baldwin Ricketts, *The Mormon Battalion* (1996). Most valuable of all of the interpretive works is Kenneth Owens, *Gold Rush Saints* (2004), which is the definitive treatment of Mormons in California, including the activities of John Borrowman. Two companion articles place this 1848 Mormon Battalion story into a larger context of pioneering the Carson River Route of the California Trail. See Frank Tortorich, Jr., "The Opening of the Carson River Route" (2000), and Frank Tortorich and James M. Carman, "The Big Tree Carson Valley Wagon Road" (2004). A biographical overview of Borrowman's life appears in Jerry Borrowman, "A Halfpenny and a Pearl," at www.lds.org/liahona/1997/05/a-halfpenny-and-a-pearl (accessed October 15, 2013).

The journal of John Borrowman provides the most complete record of the Ebenezer Brown company in its efforts to cross the Sierra Nevadas by the Carson River Route. According to historians Norma Ricketts and Kenneth Owens, twenty-four veterans were in this group, along with three Mormon Battalion wives and one child, Ebenezer Brown's stepson. Forty-three men, women, and children from the Brooklyn colony also accompanied the veterans, as well as one man who had come to California with the New York Volunteers during the Mexican

War. The Brown company left Pleasant Valley on August 12, nearly six weeks after the Holmes-Thompson train, and yet reached the Great Salt Lake on October 10, less than two weeks after the other party arrived at the same destination via the Truckee River Route.

All the brief biographical profiles of individuals mentioned in the endnotes for John Borrowman's *The Roughest Road I Ever Saw* are constructed from information contained in four books: Norma Baldwin Ricketts, *The Mormon Battalion;* Daniel Tyler, *A Concise History of the Mormon Battalion;* David L. Bigler and Will Bagley, *Army of Israel: Mormon Battalion Narratives;* and Kenneth N. Owens, *Gold Rush Saints.* Many of the Utah locations referenced in Borrowman's manuscript were identified and described in these new endnotes with the help of historian Will Bagley.

JOHN BORROWMAN, "THE ROUGHEST ROAD I EVER SAW," 1848.
TAKEN FROM "JOURNAL FROM DEC. 23, 1846 TO MAR. 1870,"
LDS ARCHIVES, HISTORICAL DEPARTMENT,
CHURCH HISTORY LIBRARY,
CHURCH OF JESUS CHRIST OF LATTER-DAY SAINTS,
SALT LAKE CITY, UTAH.

Wednesday 10th [May 1848]. I went to Origin Morey [Mowry] and requested him to pay me 8 dollars for 4 days work I done for him, the usual wages in this town for labourers, but he refused to pay me more than $1 a day saying that was sailors wages and as I had worked on a launch for him he would not pay any more and finally we agreed to leave it to the decision of two men but he did not appear to hear the decision. This evening Elder [Samuel] Brannan called a meeting and informed us of a gold mine being found by Brother Willis [Ira Willes][1] and gave his advice for all to go and work in it.

Thursday, 11th. This day I bought 3 yds of canvas to make a pack, also 1 yard of silk green for a particular purpose also a blank book and

[1]Sidney and Ira Willes had served in Company B of the Mormon Battalion alongside Borrowman, and they became involved in some of the earliest gold-mining efforts in California. See Willis, "Ira Willis Guide to the Gold Mines," 193–207.

two sail needles at the following prices: canvas 50 cents per yd. Silk $1 book 50 cents needles 1 real for two. This morning Brothers [William] Glover and [George Warren] Sirrine[2] gave in their decision in my favor and Brother Morey agreed to settle with me.

Friday, 12th. Made my pack and prepared to start for the gold mines. This evening Brother Morey came to me and said that he was not satisfied with the decision on our difference as he was not present when it was given in and wished the case to be reconsidered which I consent to but as we could not find Brother Glover it was laid over till another time.

Saturday, 13th. This morning I took passage on board Morey's launch for Sutter's Fort and at 2 P.M. we sailed from San Francisco and came too at Marshs landing distance about 100 miles.

Sunday, 14th. At 8 we were under way. Today we got out of our course and in consequence of this we had to run through a very crooked arm of the Sacramento and was much detained with head-winds.

Monday, 15th. Had baffleing winds and had to run with oars to get along.

Tuesday, 16th. Had fair winds but light and arrived at Sutters about noon. In the afternoon we hired a team to take our baggage to the mountains where the gold mines is.

Wednesday, 17th. Started for the mines and got there about sunset and found Brother Willis weighing the gold that had been dug today and there was one man had 128 dollars.

Thursday, 18th. Wrote a letter to Charles Burr this morning and then went to digging gold and together with Brother [William] Wood[3] dug 17 dollars worth.

Friday, 19th. Worked at washing gold and made 22 dollars but as Brannan & Co. requires thirty per cent my share only came to $8 as Brother Wood and I are in company.

---

[2]William Glover came to California by ship with the *Brooklyn* Saints and initially had a close alliance with Samuel Brannan. In 1884, he granted an important interview to an associate of Hubert Howe Bancroft about the events of 1848. George Warren Sirrine married Emeline Lane soon after the arrival of the *Brooklyn* Saints. See Sirrine, "A Little Sketch."

[3]Charles Burr and William Wood, a native of England, had served in Company C of the Mormon Battalion, and both men subsequently settled in Utah.

Saturday, 20th. Worked at washing gold and made $17.75.

Sunday, 21st. Went out and shot a quail as I had no meat to eat, then returned and went to a meeting for the purpose of arranging our labour in the mines and it was agreed to form companies 5 in a company and to have 5 yards square to work in and I am in Brother [James] Slys company.[4]

Monday, 22nd. Worked and made $13.

Tuesday, 23rd. Assisted in making a raft to cross the river but failed in getting across and went to work in the afternoon and made $5.

Wednesday, 24th. Worked and made about $30.

Thursday, 25th. Worked and made about $30.

Friday, 26th. Worked and made about $30.

Saturday, 27th. Worked and made about $40. This day I bought a watch from Jesse Martin for 2 oz. of gold.

Sunday, 28th. Rested in camp.

Monday, 29th. Worked and made about $50.

Tuesday, 30th. It rained in the forenoon and I went prospecting. This day I have said against paying rent as I consider it an imposition. This afternoon I worked and made $25 of gold.

Wednesday, 31st. Went to hunting a new mine but did not find any. This evening I feel rather unwell in consequence of a cold I received last night.

Thursday, June 1st., 1848. Worked and made $90.

Friday, 2nd. Worked and made $40. This day I bought a belt and sheath for my knife, price $1.25.

Saturday, 3rd. Worked and made $28.

Sunday, 4th. Rested in camp.

Monday, 5th. Worked at digging trying to find the granite on which the gold is generally found but was finally compelled to quit because of the rising of the water.

Tuesday, 6th. Worked and made $32.

---

[4]Borrowman's spirits soared with each new day because he could make far more money in the gold fields than he could as a day laborer in San Francisco, but he also had to share his profits with others. Members of the Mormon Battalion formed five-men companies and assigned plots of "five yards square" to each man at Mormon Island. Later prospectors switched to a system where each miner claimed eighteen feet of river frontage.

Wednesday, 7th. Worked and made $25.

Thursday, 8th. Worked and made $38. This day I bought a mare for $15.

Friday, 9th. Worked and made $21. This evening I bought a bridle for $4.

Saturday, 10th. Rested in camp.

Sunday, 11th. Rested in camp.

Monday, 12th. Worked and made $50.

Tuesday, 13th. Worked and made $21.

Wednesday, 14th. Made arrangements with Brother [Francis Asbury] Hammond to get my fitout at San Francisco and weighed out $200 to him for that purpose. I also paid $40 for a rifle. In the afternoon I worked and made $23.

Tuesday, 15th. Worked and made $40.

Friday, 16th. Worked and made $40.

Saturday, 17th. Worked and made $26.

Sunday, 18th. Rested in camp.

Monday, 19th. Worked and made $28. This day I bought a frying pan for $8 and a sauce pan for $4.37½.

Tuesday, 20th. Worked and made $40.

Wednesday, 21st. Worked and made $30.

Thursday, 22nd. Went in search of a waggon to buy but did not find one to suit me.

Friday, 23rd. Went again to hunt for a waggon and found one to please me but could not settle for it as the owner was not at home.

Saturday, 24th. Worked and made $50.

Sunday, 25th. Felt unwell and rested in camp. This day I bought a chain for $20.

Monday, 26th. Went to try to buy a yoke a oxen but could not find any. In the evening worked a little and made $5.

Tuesday, 27th. Worked and made $26.

Wednesday, 28th. Worked and made $36.

Thursday, 29th. Worked and made $32.

Friday, 30th. Worked and made $8.

Saturday, July 1st. I went out to a dry creek 12 miles to prospect for gold and found it but could not find water convenient to wash it in.

Sunday, 2nd. This day I paid Brother Hammond $127 for a waggon he bought for himself, Brother Wood and myself and for freight and for doing business for me at the bay.

Monday, 3rd. Attended to settling business with Brother Hammond and preparing to start for the camp in the mountains.

Tuesday, 4th. Went up the river to try to buy two yoke of oxen but could not find them, then washed about $6 of gold and returned and bought 2 yoke of oxen with Brothers Hammond and Wood for $170.

Wednesday, 5th. Bought another yoke of oxen for $80. Arranged our affairs and went out 5 miles from the river and camped.

Thursday, 6th. This morning we found that we were out of our way and turned back 3 miles to find it again and traveled about 18 miles and camped for the night.

Friday, 7th. Went about 6 miles and broke the fore bolster of our waggon[5] and here we found that we were out of our way again and both Brother [William] Wood and myself had lost our saddle *macheres*[6] of [f] the waggon and we fixed up the waggon and returned to where we camped the night before and camped for the night.

Saturday, 8th. Started back in search of the trail and went about 6 miles and stopt to hunt it up.

Saturday, 9th. Went about 8 miles and broke our waggon bolster again and stopt to fix it again.

Monday, 10th. Started and went out about 6 miles and upset our waggon and broke my rifle and several other things. Then fitted up again and went a little further and stopt for the night.

Tuesday, 11th. Went about 4 miles and in goin down a hill over a creek we broke our waggon tongue and had to stop to put in another and here Brothers [Julius Augustus Caesar] Austin, [Orlando Fish] Mead and Pool [Peter John Poole] overtook us and Brother Austin helped us fix our waggon.[7]

---

[5]This box bolster connected the wagon bed to the front running gears and affected the turning motion of the wagon's front wheels. See Owens, *Gold Rush Saints*, 4, 148n.

[6]Corruption of Spanish term *mochilas*, which referred to a saddle covering or saddlebag used in Mexican California. See Owens, *Gold Rush Saints*, 148n.

[7]Orlando Fish Mead was a veteran of the Mormon Battalion, and Julius Augustus Caesar Austin and Peter John Poole arrived by ship with the *Brooklyn* Saints.

Wednesday, 12th. Started and went seven miles to the camp in the mountains.

Thursday, 13th. Worked at digging gold and made $30.

Friday, 14th. This day I was unwell and stopt in camp all day.

Saturday, 15th. Rested in camp.

Sunday, 16th. Stopt in and traded with the Indians to the amount of $60.

Monday, 17th. Rested in camp and traded to the amount of 24 dollars with the Indians.

Tuesday, 18th. Stayed in camp and tried to arrange things for starting over the mountains.

Wednesday, 19th. Worked at fixing our waggon.

Thursday, 20th. This day I remained in camp fixing things, and here I will just mention a case of difference that has happened between myself and Brother Hammond. When we were at the lower mines it was agreed that Hammond, Wood and myself should join together and buy a waggon and team to carry our effects over the mountains and that we should pay an equal share each for the same and in the meantime we all had to go to San Francisco to purchase our fitout. Accordingly we prepared to go there and when nearly ready to start I asked Brother Hammond if I could not send by him and let him do my business and probably I could make enough during his absence to pay his part of the waggon and mine too. Accordingly, he accepted the offer and I weighed out $200 to him to trade for me which he did with the exception of $29.75 which he received in coin for me and he paid me ten of it when he returned leaving $18.75. He then informed me that he had bought a waggon and he had run in debt considerably and wanted me to pay for it and the freight of both waggon and goods. I then paid him $100 for his share of the wagon and mine and $47 dollars for the freight and $9.45 I owed him for a piece of cloth he bought for me. He had also bought several articles for both of us, my share of which came to $37. My share of the freight also only came to $28.50. This with some other little things made our affairs a little troublesome to settle and when he came to settle with me he brought me upwards of $30 in his debt. I then made up my account and made him $14 in my debt making a difference of more than $40, and when I tried to show him his mistake he would not listen to me, thinking all the while that I was wrong. I then said I would leave it to a third person to decide between us and he agreed to it and Brother [Daniel] Stark came along at the time and it was left to him and when he had reconed our accounts found I was right but Hammond would not agree to it. I then said to him if he would let it go and say no more about it I would say we were even, but he seemed much displeased and said he would have to recon it over again before he would agree to that. Then he had a crate of oil containing 12 bottles which he agreed to devide among us three, 4 bottles to a man if we would pay him our shares of the cost, which we said we would do. He had also a large stock of sole leather and when Brother [William] Wood and me lost our macheres [*mochilas*] he promised to let us have as much leather as would make new ones, but all these things remained unsettled for till we came here. When he found out his mistake in the account and paid me but would not acknowledge that he had done wrong and refused to let me have the oil or leather but offered it to Wood. He then wanted to buy my share of the waggon and team alledging as an excuse that he had more load than the rest of us but I would not sell it. He then offered to sell his share to me provided I would carry 300 weight which I would not do. He then offered to retain his share of the waggon and team and put 300 weight into it and he would pack the rest of his goods and let Wood and me attend to the team for him and he would give us $20. This offer I accepted but Wood would not. He then spoke very hard of us saying he could not get us to agree to anything. I then told him that he had complained a great deal of me because I gave him only fifty dollars for doing my business at San Francisco which did not take him more than one day and yet he could offer me $10 for what would take me 5 or 6 weeks and then think he had made a great offer. He then gave me a good deal of abuse and told me that he had not told me before but he would tell me now that all that he wanted was to get me out of the company and we had our provisions together and [ate] together. He wanted to have them divided and I might have my own side and he would keep his and this we have done today and thus it is with us at present.[8]

[8]Borrowman had a contentious relationship with Francis Asbury Hammond in this financial deal over ownership of a wagon and team, an issue that Hammond did not record in his own writings. See Hammond, "In Early Days," 517–21.

Friday, 21st. Went a prospecting a little for gold but found very little.

Saturday, 22nd. Stopt in camp preparing to move to another camping ground.

Sunday, 23rd. Yoked up our team and went about 2 miles to another camping place.

Monday, 24th. Cut brush and fixed up a tent and here we intend to stop till we get all the company together. This evening Brother Ic [Isaac] Robins [Robbins] arrived in camp with his family. He is sick of fever.

Tuesday, 25th. This day I have nothing to do but lying about the camp and time passes very heavily. This day Brother [Orlando] Mead borrowed $80 of me to buy a team and left 2 mares as security. I also agreed to take the oxen provided he got a good yoke at the rate he paid for them and let him have the use of them to Salt Lake.

Wednesday, 26th. Staid in camp. This day James Clark and Brother Smith came into camp with a team.

Thursday, 27th. Spent the day in camp. This morning Brother [Julius] Austin and Timothy Hoyt came in for their oxen and I bought a pair of *macheres* from Hoyt for $7.

Friday, 28th. This morning I gave Timothy Hoyt[9] $60 to buy a rifle and $248 and lent him. He left this morning with Brother Austin for the lower mines to bring up the waggons. This morning Hoyt bought Hammond's share in our waggon and team for $115 and carries 200 weight of his goods to the [Salt] Lake so today we have been arranging our affairs.

Saturday, 29th. I bought a horse from [James] Ferguson for $62.1/2.

Sunday, 30th. Did little else than attend to the cattle. This day a party with pack mules started for Salt Lake, I think 15 in number.

Monday, 31st. Rested in camp.[10]

Tuesday, August 1st., 1848. I staid in camp and mended my buckskin pantaloons.

[9]New Yorker Timothy Sabin Hoyt had been a private in Company A of the Mormon Battalion. His brother Henry Pike Hoyt died on September 3, 1847, while crossing the Sierra Nevadas after only a few hours of illness. See Ricketts, *Mormon Battalion*, 22, 174–75.

[10]This entire set of entries provides insight into the preparations that were undertaken in Pleasant Valley before the party set out for Carson Pass.

Wednesday, 2nd. I went and hunted our cattle then went to our old camp in search of gold but found none. Then returned and finished mending my pantaloons. This day [William] Prouse [Prows], [Levi] Fifield and [Orlando] Mead[11] came into camp from the lower mines and Brother Mead returned the $60 he borrowed from me not being able to get a team to buy.

Thursday, 3rd. This day the company bought two beef cattle and killed one of them and divided it amongst us and we cut it up and laid it out to dry.

Friday, 4th. Did little else than attend to some little affairs about the camp. This evening we held a meeting for prayer and business.

Saturday, 5th. This day Daniel [Samuel] Clark, Brother [Montgomery] Button and Brother Foulet [John S. Fowler][12] came into camp with their waggons. This [day] I done nothing but fixed my bridle and some other little things.

Sunday, 6th. I assisted Brother Foulet [Fowler] to make a exile [axle] for his waggon. This day Brother Austin arived in camp we also had a visit from some Gentiles [non-Mormons] on pretence of hunting horses and one of them told us that we had one of his and he would take the best one he could find in the drove but finally went off without any. This evening elder [Samuel] Brannan came into camp and told Miles Wever [Weaver] that Eliza Savage[13] had come up to the lower mines and wanted him to take her to Salt Lake. They then started in company with brother [John R.] Stoddard but in about an hour after one of the

[11]William Prows (sometimes spelled Prouse) had served in Company B of the Mormon Battalion and was one of the early miners at Mormon Island. He settled in Mendocino County, California, and later moved to Arizona. See Owens, *Gold Rush Saints*, 291n.

[12]John S. Fowler had sent his family to California aboard the *Brooklyn,* while he crossed overland with Brigham Young's pioneer group to the Salt Lake Valley. He subsequently traveled to California with Abner Blackburn and the 1847 company from Salt Lake City under James Brown. Montgomery Button and Samuel Clark had been part of the detachment of Mississippi Saints, and ill members of the Mormon Battalion who had wintered at Pueblo, Colorado, during 1846–47 had continued on to Salt Lake and ultimately made their way to California, where Borrowman met them. See Owens, *Gold Rush Saints*, 151n; and *Church History in the Fulness of Times*, 328–29.

[13]Susan Eliza Savage was the subject of much gossip, as suggested here by Borrowman's allegations, that included her scandalous association with Samuel Brannan and Miles Weaver. See Owens, *Gold Rush Saints*, 223n.

brethren came in from Sutters and told us that he had heard Brannan swear by the great Jehova that made him, that he would drink a quart of Miles Weaver's blood. Then Franklin Weaver fearing for his brothers safety got John Reid [Reed][14] and James Ferguson and set off in pursuit of them and overtook them but did not let Brannan know their business only they watched him closely. When they came to the mines they found Eliza out of her reason and anxious to go to the lake [Salt Lake City] and wanted Miles to take her there and seemed to be in great distress and Brannan said that Miles had seduced her and promised to take her to the lake and was going to leave her but this Miles denied and when they asked her she said Miles never made any promise to her and all she sent to him for was because she always loved him and she wished to throw herself on his protection but as Miles had no way prepared to take her he was compelled to leave her. Then she seemed to be in great distress and when Franklin Weaver asked her what was the cause of her trouble she told him she would not tell him now for he would hear it soon enough. From this I believe that Brannan had seduced her and then wanted to turn her off on Miles Weaver.

Monday, 7th. Saddled my horse and started with Brothers Austin and Bore for the lower mines after some things we had left there and when we had rode about 30 miles we met the Weavers and brother [John R.] Stoddard bringing our things with him so we turned back 5 miles and camped for the night.

Tuesday, 8th. Started at sunrise and rode into camp where I rested the rest of the day being weary and sore with riding. This evening we held a meeting and organized ourselves according to the pattern the Lord has given to the saints to travel in, Ebenezer Bown [Brown] first Captn Elijah Thomas 2 and James Park 3rd Captn.[15]

Wednesday, 9th. Prepared to start over the mountains.

Thursday, 10th. This morning we yoked up the cattle preparing to

---

[14]John Reed was a *Brooklyn* Saint, having arrived by ship, but he partnered with members of the Mormon Battalion. James Ferguson, also of the Mormon Battalion, wrote to Brigham Young at about this time, reporting the dissension that had broken out among the *Brooklyn* Saints. See Owens, *Gold Rush Saints*, 127,193.

[15]Borrowman therefore traveled in what became known as the Brown company among the several groups that made their way toward Salt Lake City.

start over the mountains but some of the cattle were found to be missing and the day was spent seeking them. Last night I stood guard for the first time on this journey. This evening the missing cattle are not yet found.

Friday, 11th. This day was spent in hunting cattle and preparing to start on the morrow. They are not yet found.

Saturday, 12th. Started and went about 5 miles when Brother [Isaac] Rob[b]ins[16] waggon tongue broke and we had to stop and put in a new one. This day our road lay up a ridge of the mountains and was hard pulling most of the way but all got up without doubling teams except brother [Julius] Austin whose load was too heavy for his team it being weakened by a loss of one yoke of oxen and he was compelled to throw away his tool chest and many of his tools.

Sunday, 13th. This morning brother Robins [Robbins] threw away his tool chest and a number of his tools. This day we traveled ten miles and most all up hill and one place was so steep we all had to double teams to get up.

Monday, 14th. Rested in camp to let the animals rest and feed to prepare them for hard pulling up the mountains and 4 men were sent on to seek for the next watering place and found it about ten miles ahead. In this place there is a little valley with good grass about 2 miles down the creek where we keep our animals but all the rest of the country there is nothing but dry mountains and deep canyons and very little for the animals to eat. Last night I was on guard.

Tuesday,15th. [August 1848]. Went ten miles to the camping ground our pioneers found yesterday. Our road was up hill most all the way and on two hills we had to double our teams. Two men were sent on again today to seek another camping ground and report one ten miles ahead and worse roads than ever being rocky and steep hills.

Wednesday, 16th. We started and traveled about ten miles over a very hard road one hill was about two miles long and some of the teams had to double most of the way and all of them had to double and some of them treble in one place about 4 rods it being very steep and a flat

[16]Isaac Robbins was one of the *Brooklyn* Saints who had come to California by ship. He was one of two "counsellors" who served under Samuel Brannan. See Owens, *Gold Rush Saints*, 35n.

rock so that the cattle could hardly keep their feet and when we came to the top of the ridge it was so steep on our left that we rol[l]ed a large rock over the precipice and it rol[l]ed down about a mile and then we lost sight of it among the brush.[17] At our present camping ground there is a pleasant run[n]ing stream about a rod wide in some places.

Thursday, 17th. We rested in camp and repaired our waggons.

Friday, 18th. Traveled about 15 miles mostly up hill one place about half a mile was very steep and we had to double our teams to get up. The road was full of brush and rock and very dusty which made it very bad. Brother [Albert] Knap[p] also broke one of the axls of his waggon which detained us till night before we got into camp and as the cattle had nothing to eat all day we concluded to rest in camp tomorrow. This evening we met according to order for prayer.

Saturday, 19th. We rested in camp and repaired our waggons and our pioneers went to the next camping ground distance reconed 12 miles and found the graves of our three pioneers that went out in June to search out the road and never returned. They are supposed to have been murdered and buried by the Indians.

Sunday, 20th. Traveled 10 or 12 miles to tragedy spring so called from our pioneers being killed there. The road was mostly up hill and some places exceeding steep and rocky insomuch that it would make one wonder that loaded waggons could come over it and not get broke. We found this evening by our camp the graves of our pioneers. There was a large pile of stones neatly built over it and on a tree at the head of the graves the following inscription was neatly cut[:] To the memory of Daniel Bruiet [Browett] Ezra Allan [Allen] and Henderson Cox who were supposed to have been murdered and buried by the Indians on the night of the 27 of June 1848.[18] This was done by some of the advance company in honour of three of our brethren who died thus trying to push their way through to the Church.

[17]"Rock rolling" offered dangerous entertainment to participants who excavated and rolled massive boulders down mountain sides to see how much damage they could do to trees, bushes, and landscape. See Owens, *Gold Rush Saints*, 189n. Other accounts appear in Bigler and Bagley, *Army of Israel*, 353–54: and Blackburn, *Frontiersman*, 62.

[18]Further primary information on these three murders and the discovery of the bodies is found in Owens, *Gold Rush Saints*, 170–73; and Ricketts, *Mormon Battalion*, 205–15.

Monday, 21st. Went about 6 miles. The road today was much better being mostly in a valley [Rock Valley]. After we came into camp some of the men went up the mountains and brought down handfuls of snow and I went out with two other men to hunt a little and we had not gone far till we saw two deer and went in pursuit of them but we had nor gone far till several Indians made their appearance and made after us so we put about and returned to the camp and then formd a carol [corral] of our waggons to keep our oxen in for the night.[19]

Tuesday, 22nd. We went about eight miles and camped. 3 men were sent on to seek another camping ground and returned and reported that there was an exceeding bad hill to climb and that we would have to pack our loads over it and take up our waggons empty so this evening the company were busy preparing to pack. The road we came over today was very bad being very crooked and full of large rock with several steep hills.

Wednesday, 23rd. This morning all that had animals to pack packed them and them that had none threw out about half their loads and left them under the care of some of the brethren who stopt back to fix their packs and let others have their animals to pack today. But brother [William] Wood and I thought we could take our whole load over on the waggon so we let brother Austin have our horses to take his things on. About ten o'clock we started and went 5 miles up the mountains [across West Pass] over the roughest road I ever saw to be traveled by waggons.[20] Then we went down about 6 miles of still worse road being so steep in some places that the oxen would slide down and we had to turn so short some times between large rocks that we could hardly get through with our waggons without suffering any damage and camped in a fine valley by a lake. The snow still lies deep in places on the mountains and is so hard that the horses walked over it without sinking and hardly left a track where they went.

[19]Borrowman's description of corralling the wagons at night is more accurate than the usual Hollywood movie, which portrays corralling as the method for driving off incessant Indian attacks. Rather, the encirclement of wagons was done to prevent the straying of livestock and to reduce the chances of them being lost or stolen.

[20]The rocky ascent over West Pass was difficult for wagons heading east from California along the Carson Pass route. A modern photograph of the terrain is shown in Owens, *Gold Rush Saints*, 156.

Thursday, 24th. I rested in camp while those that had goods left back went back and brought them on and 3 went on to see what the road was like another days journey ahead and in the evening all returned to camp safe. The pioneers reported very bad road ahead.

Friday, 25th. [August 1848]. This morning we went some 3 or 4 miles of very bad road [to Carson Pass] being mostly through a wood and among large rocks and so crooked that one would wonder how we got through. Then we came to a very steep hill about half a mile long full of larg[e] rocks and in some places sidling so that it was with a great difficulty that we got down with the two hind wheels of our waggons rough locked and a man standing on one of the wheels to keep it from upsetting and after we had got down in this way we went on 4 or 5 miles further to a fine valley [Hope Valley][21] with a beautiful stream running through it. The road after we got over the mountain was very bad being rocky in some places and very rough and marshy in others.

Saturday, 26th. As some of the brethren who were with us were packing they wished now to go on by themselves and leave us as they could go on much faster than we with waggons so we stopt this day and killed a beef that we had along with us and the women baked sweet buisket and the men roasted the ribs of the ox and we had a general tea party and some time of rejoicing. This was done that since we had to part we might part with good feeling there was also 2 Indians come into camp and shared with us. 2 men went on to look out the road and reported it still terrible but I was on guard this day.

Sunday, 27th. We traveled about 9 miles 6 of which was very good and 3 [down West Carson Canyon] was the worst I ever saw being over larg[e] rocks and downhill so that it wrenched the waggons in a way that one would think that something must breake yet all passed through without injury except one that had one boun[d] brake. We camped tonight by a small river where there is very little feed for the animals.

[21]Hope Valley provided temporary relief for overlanders traveling in either direction. Those, such as Borrowman, who were headed east first crossed the sharp ascent of the Carson Pass "backbone," just to the north of the landmark known as Elephant's Back. They then descended the steep incline known as Devils' Ladder before reaching the good campsite at Hope Valley. On the following day, they faced the problematic terrain of Pass Creek (today called the West Carson River), where they transited a seven-mile canyon. See Owens, *Gold Rush Saints*, 181.

This evening we met a company of emigrants from the States consisting I believe of 19 waggons they told us that we would have 3 miles very bad road and then we would get into the plains and have good roads.[22]

Monday, 28th. The roads we had for 3 miles this morning was as bad if not worse than any we have had being a part of a canyon of the mountains. Part we came through last evening and part this morning. The mountains are very high on both sides and very steep and great rocks have rolled down from the mountains and filled the canyon with broken fragments so that one cannot get through without going over many larg[e] rocks and taking such short turns some times in narrow places between rocks that a wagon cannot get through without great difficulty. There is also a brook about 2 rods wide which we had to cross twice and being full of larg[e] rock was very bad to cross but after we got out of the canyon we had a good road in a fine larg[e] valley. This day we traveled 10 miles.

Tuesday, 29th. Went 12 miles and camped on the salmon trout river [Carson River] called by some pilot river. Here the valley widens out probably as much as from 6 to 10 miles and is called Shoshone valley.

Wednesday, 30th. We sent 15 miles again and camped on the river. This morning brother Wood sought for his mare and colt but could not find them and thought perhaps they were hid in the brush and would come out when the drove was gathered up but when we had traveled some distance the drove being behind overtook us and he saw they were not there so he caught his horse and rode back to camp in search of them but found nothing but one Indian and the tracks of a great many more. From this we believe that the Indians stole them in the night.

Thursday, 31st. Went 8 miles through deep sand and camped on the river. Last night brother Wright being on guard saw an Indian by the camp and hailed him upon which he ran away and Wright fired after him not to kill him but to frighten him but this morning one of the asses of brother [James] Fergusons was missing that also had ben stoled by the Indians. This evening I am on guard again and brother

[22]Borrowman is describing one of several westbound wagon trains that battalion veterans encountered on their way to Salt Lake in 1848. This is the Peter Lassen party, which continued on its planned route to Oregon along the Applegate Trail rather than following the Carson River Route into California. See Tortorich, "Opening of the Carson River Route," 22–23.

Robins [Robbins] has began to drive his own team today for the first since we started as a company from our first camp, he being sick all the way coming over the mountains.

Friday, September 1st, 1848. Went 10 miles the road was very rough and rockey all the way and very bad on the oxens feet. We camped again on the river on the head of cottonwood valley.

Saturday, 2nd. Brown killed an antilope. Went 10 miles and camped on the river at the foot of Cottonwood valley the road was good most of the way.

Sunday, 3rd. We went 15 miles. The road lay down the river and was rather rough although in many places there was good grass. We camped again on the river.

Monday, 4th. This morning we found a cow with an arrow sticking in her side she had been shot by an Indian. At 7 we started and traveled down the river. The valley soon widened out and we left the river on our right. The valley is 8 or 10 miles wide and in one continuous sand bed. We went about 15 miles and came to the river again and camped.

Tuesday, 5th. As we were now leaving pilot [Carson] river for truely and according to the information we had we expected 25 miles without water so we let the cattle feed until near noon then watered them and started and went about 16 miles and camped without water or grass. The road was very bad being deep sand all the way and small rock in some places which made it very bad for the cattles feet. The whole face of the country here has the appearance of having been thrown up by a volcanic irruption and the rocks all appear to have been burnt.

Wednesday, 6th. We started at day light and went about 8 miles to Trucky [Truckee] River and camped to let the cattle feed. The road was much the same today as yesterday being a continuation of the same bed of sand. We cut grass here for the cattle as expect 40 miles without water or grass to Mary's [Humboldt] river so we concluded to take some grass with us.[23]

[23]The Brown party followed the Samuel Thompson company's tracks to reach the Truckee River and the main California Trail at present-day Wadsworth, Nevada. A week later, Joseph Chiles apparently made the first direct crossing of the Forty-Mile Desert from the Humboldt Sink to Carson River, thus popularizing what became one of the most familiar and dreaded sections of the California Trail. See Ricketts, *Mormon Battalion*, 217–18, 222–23.

Thursday, 7th. We traveled 20 miles and camped at the boiling springs the first 8 miles that we traveled was through deep sand and then we went down into a large valley which has the appearance of being flooded annually and as far as we went today there was not a sign of vegetation to be seen except a small kind [of] shrub that is found al[l] through this region of country but I do not know the name of it and this only grew on the higher places and al[l] the rest of the vall[e]y looked as if it had been covered with lime and then with water and then dried again. The road was very good but very dusty and the boiling springs are a great curiosity.[24] There is perhaps 15 or 20 holes in the earth from one to 2 feet wide like so many pots are boiling as fast as fire can make them. There is also one larg[e] pool probably 10 or 12 feet long and about 6 feet wide. This also boils but not so furiously as the rest.

Friday, 8th. We went 20 miles to the sink of Mary's [Humboldt] river. The road was very good being in the same vally that we were in yesterday and all the teams got through well except one ox that had to be left till he recovered from his fatigue. The water and grass here is not good but cattle that is hungry and thirsty relish it very well and the water does very well to make tea of. A thirsty person can drink it also.

Saturday, 9th. This morning brother Foulets [John Fowler] ox came up to camp but he thought he co[u]ld not travel with the teams so he left him. This day we went 20 miles but found no water so we turned out our animals and let them rest and feed awhile. Then we yoked up again and went on 6 miles further where we found water and grass although neither was very good and camped for the night. An Indian came to us and pretended great friendship for us but we were rather jealous [suspicious] of him and he soon left us.

Sunday,10th. [September 1848]. We went 15 miles and camped on Marys river. Here the water runs and is good, grass also is good and plenty. This morning when the drove was gathered up it was discovered that 3 horses belonging to Franklin Weaver were missing and when he went in search of them he found their tracks and the track of an Indian after them so we considered them stolen and gave up the search. The road was very good today.

---

[24]Boiling Springs became the most frequently mentioned landmark along the Forty-Mile Desert during the heyday of the California gold rush.

Monday, 11th. We rested in camp. Here a company of emigrants came to us and camped with us. They informed us that the Indians had shot several of their cattle at the western crossing of Marys river and they had also shot one Indian. This they did by 5 men remaining in ambush near their camp after the company had left and when the Indians came into camp as is their custom they shot one.[25]

Tuesday, 12th. I bought a rifle from one of the emigrants this day and we went 13 miles and camped by the river. The road was good but the dust was over the fillies [felloes] of the wheels and rose in clouds and was almost like to suffocate us at times.

Wednesday, 13th. We traveled 18 miles the road was good but the dust like lime lay to the depth of 6 to 8 inches on it and rose in clouds over us all the way we crossed the river and camped about a mile above the crossing. The grass is not very good here [and] last night the moon was totaly eclipst.

Thursday, 14th. We crossed the river and went 25 miles. The dust was as bad as ever wood and grass was rather inferior at this camp.

Friday, 15th. Went 8 miles and camped in consequence of some of the cattle being nearly broke down with long journies and little food. The grass here is good I am very much troubled with a sore ankle and leg at present. It was caused by being scratched with bushes and poisoned with poison vine.[26]

Saturday, 16th. We went 15 miles this morning we had to climb a very steep bank to cross a point that came close up to the river bottom again the road was good but dusty as ever. There is good grass here. This evening there is a thick black smoke to be seen ahead of us we saw it two days ago but do not know what it means.

Sunday, 17th. We went 15 miles and camped in good grass by the river. We passed the place where we saw the smoke yesterday and saw quite a number of Indians in one group. We counted nine they were coming toward us and as our teams were very much scattered the front halted till the rear came up. The Indians then turned about and left us.

---

[25]On the subject of the murder of the Indian, see Edward Smith, "Journal of Edward Smith. From Missouri to California," California State Library; and May, *A Sketch of a Migrating Family to California in 1848*.

[26]The party had reached the vicinity of today's Rye Patch Reservoir.

Monday, 18th. On gard this morning one Indian came into camp but did not seem to have any other business but to try to get something to eat. We also saw some others at a distance but as we were just leaving camp they did not come up. I suppose they were waiting to see what would be the result of the others visit. This day we traveled 12 miles went through the narrow pass of the mountains crossed the river once and camped by the river on the edge of a large valley good water and grass here this evening. 2 Indians came into camp. I think they had been to a council as they came from the direction of the great fire and were going up the river. They were very large strong good looking men and were naked except for a wolf skin wrapt around them.

Tuesday, 19th. This morning six Indians came into camp. This day traveled 20 miles over a large barren plain. It had much the appearance of the desert of Sonora[27] and camped on the river a good camp and good grass.

Wednesday, 20th. [September 1848] We went 18 miles on the river bottom good water and grass most all the way but the grass is all dry except close to the river.

Thursday, 21st. We traveled about 7 miles and camped at the foot of the mountains a little above where the river bends close up to the mountains. Last night or this morning 2 horses were cut loose and taken off by the Indians. This was done in less than 20 paces of the waggons and yet not seen by the guard Prouse [William C. Prows] Palmer [Zemira Palmer] [James] Park and Robins [Isaac R. Robbins] and when 3 men that drove horses came to our present camp they saw 2 Indians and one of them had a horse but not any of ours.

Friday, 22nd. We went 10 miles and camped in good grass the portion of the valley we traveled in was good soil but very dry. It might be a good farming country if it had rain. This evening a number of Indians came into camp to trade fish.

Saturday, 23rd. We traveled 17 miles and camped in good grass by the river. We went through a narrow pass of the mountains and across

[27] Borrowman's comparison of this Utah desert land with similar areas in the northern Mexican state of Sonora is based on his eyewitness experience, since he and the Mormon Battalion had traveled near northern Mexico during their march to California.

a large plain to our camp. The dust today was very bad this evening and had thunder and lightning and a few drops of rain.

Sunday, 24th. This morning we had a light rain. We crossed the river and left it on our right and traveled 20 miles over hills and through canyons till we struck the river again where there is a number of hot springs in the bed of it.[28]

Monday, 25th. We traveled 10 miles crossed a branch of the river went through a deep canyon and crossed the river twice and camped in a little valley near the head of the canyon.

Tuesday, 26th. We left the canyon and traveled 20 miles up the river bottom and camped on the river in good grass. The Indians now crowd into our camp every evening and morning and yesterday morning they brought a child into camp and made motions to show that his mother was dead and brother Ferguson took him and called him Laman.[29]

Wednesday, 27th. We traveled 15 miles and crossed three points where the river puts round through deep canyons we also crossed the Salene [Saline] branch. This day we had thunder and lightening but the storm went round behind us it snowed on the mountains.

Thursday, 28th. We traveled 18 miles up the river bottom and camped near the river. It is nearly dry and does not run here.

Friday, 29th. We traveled 18 miles and camped near the canyon [Bishop's Canyon] at the head of the Marys [Humboldt] river. We have traveled in sight of this canyon for three days. There is good grass and water here but no food except wormwood and willow neither is there any other on all this river.

Saturday, 30th. We lay in camp to wash and let the animals rest.

Sunday, October 1st. We went ten miles and camped at the springs of Marys river. We passed through the canyon passed by two warm springs and crossed the creek nine times in the canyon.

Monday, 2nd. We went 15 miles and camped near the Sulpher and cold springs. These Springs are a great curiosity in one place the water

---

[28]The train crossed Gravely Ford near today's Beowawe, Nevada, and climbed over Emigrant Pass to emerge above Carleton Canyon.

[29]James Ferguson served as the battalion's sergeant major and went on to live a colorful life as an actor, Nauvoo legion general, and Salt Lake County's first sheriff. See Bagley, *"A Bright, Rising Star,"* 4–13.

is boiling up with great force and runs down boiling hot for some distance raising a steem like a steem mill. There is also cold springs within a few yards of the other and the water is cold enough to make a parsons teethache.

Tuesday, 3rd. We went ten miles and camped by the wells of horse springs. Here some Indians came to us and wanted to trade horses and skins for guns and ammunition.

Wednesday, 4th. We went 16 miles and camped by a spring I call spring branch. Good water but poor grass. This evening we had thunder and lightening and a little rain and it snowed on the mountains.

Thursday, 5th. [October 1848]. We traveled 20 miles crossed the divide between lake river and the waters of Salt Lake and camped on goose creek. The day was very cold. Good water and poor grass at this camp. Last night we let our cattle go loose for the first time on the rout we having had to chain them up at night for fear of the Indians.

Friday, 6th. We traveled 22 [miles] down goose creek, a good road all the way, a good camp, good grass and water.

Saturday, 7th. Went 8 miles left goose creek went over to the cedar branch [Birch Creek] and went up that where the road leaves it and went up the hill and camped and turned the cattle back to the creek to feed.

Sunday, 8th. Traveled 20 miles went over the mountains on the devide between cedar branch [Cassia Creek] and providence creek [Raft River] and camped on providence creek good wood and water but poor grass.

Monday, 9th. Went 10 miles down the creek and camped, good wood water and grass here, we had to fix the road at the crossing of the creek, there is at this place two mountains on the south of the creek I call the two sisters.[30]

Tuesday, 10th. We traveled 14 miles and camped by a branch that comes down from the mountains on the south of the valley. This I call flint stone creek [Clear Creek].

Wednesday, 11th. We went ten miles and camped at prospect spring [Emigrant Spring] where for the first time our eyes beheld the great Salt Lake. Our camp was close up to the mountains on the south side of the valley.

---

[30]This is not Twin Sisters at City of Rocks National Reserve in today's Idaho but Bookend Rocks, two deep-red mountains at the Raft River Narrows.

Thursday, 12th. We traveled 20 miles across a large valley to mud creek [Deep Creek]. We also past 2 beautiful springs [Pilot Spring] about half way this morning. James Ferguson through ill will to me caught my horse out of the drove and tied him to a tree near the camp after I had left and caused me to turn back 8 miles after him and walk all the way to camp this evening as I could not ride him his back being sore and this evening I called him [James Ferguson] before the company for trial and it was decided that he would acknowledge a fault to me and pay me a dollar for the trouble going after the horse.

Friday, 13th. Traveled 30 miles mostly in vallies although we had to cross several ridges in passes of the mountains but the vallies here generally connect themselves by narrow passes of the montains.[31] We camped by a warm spring [Blue Springs] which was both salty and sulpheric.

Saturday, 14th. We went 16 miles and the road was much the same as yesterday. We camped by a spring in a deep hollow.

Sunday, 15th. We went 10 miles and crossed bear river [Malad Creek] and camped near the river.

Monday, 16th. This morning as some of the men were hunting the horses they found out our mistake about bear river as the one we crossed headed only a little way above our camp and another and much larger one headed a few miles further up the valley. We crossed it this morning it was no more than 20 yards wide and about 3 feet deep and run very rapid where we crossed it. We traveled nearly 26 miles through a beautiful valley with a great many springs in it and some of them boiling hot and a large lake of fresh water is in this valley. We camped by a beautiful little stream with a grove of cottonwood by it.

Tuesday, 17th. We went 12 miles [and] passed a large number of springs and brooks. One spring was boiling hot and salt[y] as brine. We camped by some little springs about 2 miles from the salt spring. This evening Calvin More [Moore] came into camp from the citty and informed us that we were near Browns settlement. He also informed us respecting the two rivers we had crossed the first is called sick [Malad] river the other is bear river. It appears they both sink for some distance

[31]The party crossed the Hansel Mountains at this location.

at this time of the year which was the cause of our not knowing bear river when we came to it.

Wednesday, 18th. Traveled 8 miles to Capt. Browns and camped in a little grove near his house.[32]

Thursday, 19th. We went 20 miles to what is called the half way house and camped by a creek in a beautiful part of the valley.

Friday, 20th. [October 1848] We traveled 20 miles to the city of the great salt lake we crossed a point of the great desert plains that surrounds the great salt lake and passed several hot springs one of which is fitted up for a bathing place we also passed hot springs lake 4 miles from the citty.

[32]This is the so-called Brown's Fort, which former Mormon Battalion officer James Brown purchased from Miles Goodyear in 1847. It is at the site of present-day Ogden, Utah.

Bibliography

MANUSCRIPTS AND NEWSPAPERS

Baldwin, Alfred. "Recollections." Manuscript. Bancroft Library, University of California, Berkeley.

Beal, Josiah. "Recollections." Manuscript. Oregon Historical Society, Portland, Oregon.

Blanchet, [Augustin Magloire Alexander], to Kenderick [Msgr. Peter R. Kenrick], March 30, 1848. General Archives of the Society of Jesus, Rome, Italy. Copies at Jesuit Oregon Province Archives, Special Collections, Gonzaga University, Spokane, Washington.

Blevins, Alexander. "Reminiscence of 1843 Emigration." Published as "An Interesting Interview with an Aged Couple Who Were With the First Train which Crossed the Rocky Mountains from the East." *The Valley Review* (Lodi, California), March 29, 1879. Digital copy at www.oregonpioneers.com/Blevins_Interview.htm (accessed October 15, 2013).

Boggs, Lilburn W. "Route to the Pacific." *St. Louis Weekly Reveille*, May 22, 1848. Typescript, Oregon-California Papers, 1804–1876. Missouri Historical Society Library and Archives, St. Louis.

Borrowman, John. "Journal from Dec. 23, 1846 to Mar. 1870." LDS Archives, Historical Department, Church History Library, Church of Jesus Christ of Latter-Day Saints, Salt Lake City, Utah.

Brown, Joseph Henry. "Recollections of 1847 Trip to Oregon." Typescript. Special Collections, Knight Library, University of Oregon. Copy in Oregon-California Trails Manuscripts. Merrill Mattes Library, National Frontier Trails Center, Independence, Missouri.

Chambers, Andrew J. "A Brief Account of a Trip Across the Plains." *Washington Standard*, May 15, 1908, 27.

Cleaver, Benjamin. "Letters from the West—1848–1850." Eight letters to the *Alton* (Illinois) *Telegraph and Democratic Review*.

Coon, James Madison, and Nancy Coon. "The Diary of James Madison Coon and Nancy Iness (Miller) Coon on the Oregon Trail From Mercer County,

Illinois to Clackamas County, Oregon in 1847." Edited by Robert Lewis. Electronic transcription at www.rootsweb.ancestry.com/~orbenton/COONDIAR.htm (accessed October 15, 2013).

Cornwall, Joseph Hardin. "Coming to the Oregon Country of the Cornwall Family." *Oregon Statesman*, July 12, 1941–August 13, 1941.

Cory, Dr. Benjamin. "Journal." Transcript. Society of California Pioneers, San Francisco.

Cox, Thomas. "A Pioneer of 1847—Merchant, Manufacturer and Farmer." Digital copy at http://files.usgwarchives.net/or/statewide/history/wpa/wpa78.txt (accessed October 15, 2013).

Crawford, Peter W. "Recollections." Manuscript. Bancroft Library. University of California, Berkeley.

Crockett, Samuel B., to Dear Friends, February 16, 1845. As Copied from the Original by Alfred B. Loop, July 6, 1931. Typescript MSS 1500. Oregon Historical Society Library, Portland.

Estes, Mary Elizabeth Munkers. "Crossing the Plains in 1846: As Told by Mrs. Mary Elizabeth Munkers Estes While Sitting by Her Fireside Christmas Eve 1916." Digital copy at http://freepages.history.rootsweb.ancestry.com/~cchouk/oregon_trail/crossing/munkers.htm (accessed October 15, 2013).

Ferguson, Henry O. "The Moving of W. W. Ferguson and Family from Owen County Indiana to Iowa Territory in 1844 and to California in 1849." Transcript. Bancroft Library. University of California, Berkeley.

Garrison, Abraham H. "Recollections." MSS 1508. Oregon Historical Society, Portland.

Grant, Richard. "Five Letters at Fort Hall, 1844–1847." Hudson's Bay Company Archives, Winnipeg, Canada.

Harden, Absolom. "Diary." MSS 1508. Oregon Historical Society, Portland.

Harrison, J. M. "Recollections of J. M. Harrison, 1846." Typescript, MSS 1508. Kay Threlkeld transcription. Oregon Historical Society, Portland. Original manuscript was written at Wooster, Ohio.

Hill, Sarah Jane. "Our Trip to Oregon." Handwritten reminiscences. MSS 1508. Oregon Historical Society, Portland.

Hockett, W. A. "Experiences on the Oregon Trail." Typescript and letters. Kansas State Historical Society, Topeka.

Hulin, Lester. "Day Book." Typescript. Lane County Pioneer Historical Society, Eugene, Oregon.

Ide, William B. "From our Oregon Correspondent." *Sangamo Journal* (Springfield, Illinois), June 5, 1845, and September 4, 1845.

Kelsey, Nancy. "Nancy (Roberts) Kelsey's Own Story of Her Life." *Pomo Bulletin* (February 1983). Notes by Roy M. Sylar. Lake County Historical Society, Lakeport, California.

King, Henry, to Dear Parents, March 30, 1846. In "Appendix: Copy of Henry King's Letter from California." *Congressional Globe*, vol. 16, and appendix (29:2): 137–38.

King, Maria, and Stephen King to Dear Mother, Brother, and Sisters, April 1, 1846. MSS 1508. Oregon Historical Society, Portland.

"Late from California." *Telegraph and Democratic Review* (Alton, Illinois), August 22, 1847.

Lee, Anna Green. "Recollections." MSS 1508. Oregon Historical Society, Portland.

Lippincott, Benjamin S., to John L. Stephens, February 6, 1847, and Lippincott to Bub, March 22, 1847. Bancroft Library, University of California, Berkeley.

Looney, Jesse, to James C. Bond, October 27, 1843, Waiilatpu, Oregon Territory. Manuscript letter, MSS 2263. Oregon State Historical Society Library, Portland. Typescript letter, folder 30, T-177. Overland Journeys. Washington State Historical Society, Tacoma.

Lose, John, to Mr. Editor, undated letter, early 1847. Printed in *Defiance* (Ohio) *Democrat*, November 4, 1847.

Mauldin, Henry. "Kelsey Family," *Oakland Tribune*, September 9, 1956, September 16, 1956, September 23, 1956.

Morrison, Martha Ann (Minto). "Female Pioneering in Oregon [1844]." 1878 interview. Typescript, MSS P-A 51. Hubert Howe Bancroft Collection, Bancroft Library. University of California, Berkeley.

"Oregon and California." *New York Tribune*, June 11, 1844, and June 24, 1844.

"Oregon and California." Correspondence of the *Pittsburgh Gazette* from the senior editor, dated Louisville, May 16, 1845. Reprinted in *Ohio Repository*, May 29, 1845.

Parker, Samuel. "Diary." Manuscript. Oregon Historical Society, Portland.

Pettijohn, Isaac. "Diary." Manuscript. Bancroft Library. University of California, Berkeley.

Porter, William, to Dear Father, Mother, Brothers and Sisters, June 24, 1848. St. Boniface Archives, Sublimity, Oregon. Digital copy at www.oregonpioneers.com/porter2.htm (accessed October 15, 2013). Copy made available by Stephenie Flora.

Rayner, James O. "Journal of a Tour to Oregon." Typescript. Oregon Historical Society, Portland.

Reed, James F. "From California, a Letter from James F. Reed," August 14, 1848. *Illinois Journal* (Springfield), July 4, 1849. Transcribed by Kristin Johnson.

Reed, Martha Williams. "Old California Pioneer Passes Away at Fallbrook. Martha Williams Reed, Age 87, Crosses the Plaines by Ox-Team in the Early Gold Excitement of California." *Fallbrook Enterprise* (California), January 12, 1917. Unedited digital copy at www.oregonpioneers.com/williams.htm (accessed October 15, 2013).

Rees, Willard H., to Mother, Oregon City, March 20, 1846. Holograph letter. National Frontier Trails Center, Independence, Missouri.

Rhoads, Amanda Esrey, to Dear Parents, Fort Laramie, June 15, 1846. Photocopy, BANC MSS 71/38c. Rhoads Family Papers, 1846–1856. Bancroft Library, University of California, Berkeley. Copy courtesy of Bernie L. Rhoads.

Ross, John E. "Recollections." Manuscript. University of California, Berkeley.

Shaw, Thomas C. "Reminiscences of 1844." *Oregon Statesman*, May 22 and June 12, 1885. Digital copy at www.oregonpioneers.com/tcshaw.htm (accessed October 15, 2013).

Sirrine, Warren LeRoy. "A Little Sketch of the Life of George Warren Sirrine." Manuscript 1377. LDS Archives, Salt Lake City, Utah.

Smith, Abigail, to Brother and Sister Kirby, Walla Walla, September 18, 1840. Typescript of holograph letter. Transcription by John Mark Lambertson. Merrill J. Mattes Library Collection, National Frontier Trails Center, Independence, Missouri.

Smith, Alvin Thompson. "Diary." Transcript. Oregon Historical Society, Portland.

Smith, Edward. "Journal of Edward Smith. From Missouri to California, April 29, 1848–October 21, 1848." Typescript 68c34, vol. 4. California State Library, Sacramento.

Snook, John S. "To Mr. Editor." *Defiance* (Ohio) *Democrat*, August 19, 1847.

Taylor, James. "Recollections." Manuscript. Oregon Historical Society, Portland.

Thompson, Arthur H. "From the Oregon Emigrants." *Chicago Democrat*, August 27, 1845, October 21, 1845, and December 2, 1845.

Walker, Claiborne Campbell. "Diary." Manuscript. Oregon Historical Society, Portland.

Woodworth, Selim E. "Three Letters from Oregon and California." *New York Home Journal*, June 13, 1846, August 8, 1846, and July 31, 1847.

Young, John Quincy Adams. "Recollections." Typescript. Oregon Historical Society, Portland.

Primary Books

Applegate, Jesse. *A Day with the Cow Column in 1843*. Chicago: Caxton Club, 1934.

Applegate, Jesse A. *Recollections of My Boyhood*. Roseburg, Ore.: Press of Review Publishing, 1914.

Belden, Josiah. *Josiah Belden: 1841 California Overland Pioneer: His Memoir and Early Letters*. Edited by Doyce B. Nunis, Jr. Georgetown, Calif.: Talisman Press, 1962.

Belshaw, Maria Parsons, and George Belshaw. *Crossing the Plains to Oregon in 1853*. Edited by Michael L. Tate. Fairfield, Wash.: Ye Galleon Press, 2000.

Bettelyoun, Susan Bordeaux, and Josephine Waggoner. *With My Own Eyes: A Lakota Woman Tells Her People's History*. Edited by Emily Levine. Lincoln: University of Nebraska Press, 1988.

Bidwell, John. *Echoes of the Past: An Account of the First Emigrant Train to California*. Chico, Calif.: Chico Advertiser, 1900.

———. *A Journey to California, 1841: The First Emigrant Party to California by Wagon Train*. Introduction by Francis P. Farquhar. Berkeley: Friends of the Bancroft Library, 1964.

———. *Life in California Before the Gold Discovery*. Palo Alto, Calif.: Lewis Osborne, 1966.

Bigler, David L., ed. *The Gold Discovery Journal of Azariah Smith*. Salt Lake City: University of Utah Press, 1990.

Bigler, David L., and Will Bagley. *Army of Israel: Mormon Battalion Narratives*. Spokane, Wash.: Arthur H. Clark, 2000.

Bigler, Henry W. *Bigler's Chronicle of the West: The Conquest of California, Discovery of Gold, and Mormon Settlement*. Edited by Erwin G. Gudde. Berkeley: University of California Press, 1962.

Blackburn, Abner. *Frontiersman: Abner Blackburn's Narrative*. Edited by Will Bagley. Salt Lake City: University of Utah Press, 1992.

Blanchet, Augustin Magloire Alexander. *Journal of a Catholic Bishop on the Oregon Trail*. Edited by Edward J. Kowrach. Fairfield, Wash.: Ye Galleon Press, 1978.

Blanchet, Francis Xavier. *Ten Years on the Pacific Coast*. Edited by Edward J. Kowrach. Fairfield, Wash.: Ye Galleon Press, 1982.

Braly, John Hyde. *Memory Pictures, An Autobiography*. Los Angeles: Neuner, 1912.

Breen, Patrick. *Diary of Patrick Breen, One of the Donner Party*. Edited by Frederick J. Teggert. Berkeley, Calif.: Publication of the Academy of Pacific Coast History, 1910.

Bryant, Edwin. *What I Saw in California*. New York: D. Appleton, 1848.

Bullock, Thomas. *The Pioneer Camp of the Saints: The 1846 and 1847 Mormon Trail Journals of Thomas Bullock*. Edited by Will Bagley. Spokane, Wash.: Arthur H. Clark, 1997.

Burnett, Peter H. *Recollections and Opinions of an Old Pioneer*. New York: D. Appleton, 1880.

Chambers, Andrew Jackson. *Recollections: Crossing the Plains in 1845*. Fairfield, Wash.: Ye Galleon Press, 1975.

Chiles, Joseph. *A Visit to California in 1841: As Recorded by Hubert Howe Bancroft*. Berkeley, Calif.: Friends of Bancroft Library, 1970.

Christy, Thomas. *Thomas Christy's Road Across the Plains: A Guide to the Route from Mormon Crossing, Now Omaha, Nebraska, to the City of Sacramento, California*. Edited by Robert H. Becker. Denver: Fred A. Rosenstock Old West Publishing, 1969.

Clayton, William. *An Intimate Chronicle: The Journals of William Clayton*. Edited by George D. Smith. Salt Lake City, Utah: Signature Books, 1991.

———. *The Latter-day Saints' Emigrants' Guide: Being a Table of Distances, Showing All the Springs, Creeks, Rivers, Hills, Mountains, Camping Places, and All the Other Notable Places, from Council Bluffs to the Valley of the Great Salt Lake. . . .* St. Louis: Missouri Republican Steam Press,—Chambers and Knapp, 1848.

Clyman, James. *James Clyman, Frontiersman*. Edited by Charles L. Camp. San Francisco: California Historical Society, 1928.

Colton, Walter. *The Land of Gold; or Three Years in California*. New York: D. W. Evans, 1860.

Cooke, Philip St. George. *The Conquest of New Mexico and California: An Historical and Personal Narrative*. New York: Putnam, 1878.

———. "Philip St. George Cooke's Journal of the March of the Mormon Battalion, 1846–47." Ralph P. Bieber and Averam B. Bender, eds. *Exploring Southwestern Trails, 1846–1854*. Vol. 7 of Southwest Historical Series. Glendale, Calif.: Arthur H. Clark, 1938.

Cornwall, Bruce. *Life Sketch of Pierre Barlow Cornwall, by Bruce Cornwall, His Son*. San Francisco: A. M. Robertson, 1906.

Crawford, Peter W. *The Overland Journey to Oregon in 1847*. North Plains, Ore.: Soap Creek Enterprises, 1997.

Cross, Osborne, and George Gibbs. *The March of the Mounted Riflemen: First United States Military Expedition to Travel the Full Length of the Oregon Trail from Fort Leavenworth to Fort Vancouver May to October 1849*. Edited by Raymond W. Settle. Glendale, Calif.: Arthur H. Clark, 1940.

Dawson, Nicholas "Cheyenne." *Narrative of Nicholas "Cheyenne" Dawson*. Edited by Charles L. Camp. San Francisco: Grabhorn Press, 1933.

De Smet, Pierre-Jean. *Letters and Sketches: With a Narrative of a Year's Residence among the Indian Tribes of the Rocky Mountains*. Philadelphia, Pa.: M. Fithian, 1843; reprinted as vol. 27 in Reuben Gold Thwaites, Early Western Travels, 1748–1846, series. Cleveland, Ohio: Arthur H. Clark, 1906.

———. *Life, Letters and Travels of Father Pierre-Jean De Smet, S. J., 1801–1873*. 4 vols. Edited by Hiram M. Chittenden and Alfred Talbot Richardson. New York: Francis P. Harper, 1905.

———. "Report on His 1840 Western Trip." In *Letters and Sketches: With a Narrative of a Year's Residence Among the Indian Tribes of the Rocky Mountains*, vol. 27, 135–55. In Early Western Travels, 1748–1846, series, edited by Reuben Gold Thwaites. Cleveland, Ohio: Arthur H. Clark, 1906.

———. *Western Missions and Missionaries: A Series of Letters.* New York: James B. Kirker, 1863.

Dickenson, Louella. *Reminiscences of a Trip Across the Plains in 1846 and Early Days in California.* Fairfield, Wash.: Ye Galleon Press, 1977.

Downey, Joseph T. *The Cruise of the Portsmouth: A Sailor's View of the Naval Conquest of California, 1845–1847.* Edited by Howard R. Lamar. New Haven, Conn.: Yale University Press, 1958.

Drury, Clifford M., ed. *The Diaries and Letters of Henry H. Spalding and Asa Bowen Smith Relating to the Nez Percé, 1838-1842.* Glendale, Calif.: Arthur H. Clark, 1958.

———, ed. *The Mountains We Have Crossed: Diaries and Letters of the Oregon Mission, 1838.* Lincoln: University of Nebraska Press, 1999.

———, ed. *Where Wagons Could Go: Narcissa Whitman and Eliza Spalding.* Lincoln: University of Nebraska Press, 1997.

Eaton, James. "My Trip to California." In *The Lassen Trail,* edited by F. D. Calhoon, 35–127. Sacramento, Calif.: Cal-Con Press, 1987.

Eccleston, Robert. *The Mariposa Indian War 1850–1851: Diaries of Robert Eccleston: The California Gold Rush, Yosemite, and the High Sierra.* Salt Lake City: University of Utah Press, 1957.

Edwards, Philip Leget. *Sketch of the Oregon Territory or, Emigrants' Guide.* Liberty, Mo.: Herald Office, 1842.

Emanuels, Stephen P. *The Rhodes-Esrey Letters.* Lemoore, Calif.: Kings River Press, 1992.

Evans, Elwood. "Thomas J. Shadden." Biographical profile in *History of the Pacific Northwest, Oregon and Washington,* vol. 2, 552–53. Portland, Ore.: North Pacific History Company, 1889.

Fagan, David D. *History of Benton County, Oregon Including Its Geology, Topography, Soil and Productions, Together with the Early History of the Pacific Coast.* Portland, Ore.: D. D. Fagan, 1885.

Farnham, Thomas. *Travels in the Great Western Prairies and Rocky Mountains and in the Oregon Territory.* Poughkeepsie, N.Y.: Killey and Lossing, 1841.

Field, Matthew C. *Prairie and Mountain Sketches.* Edited by Kate L. Gregg and John F. McDermott. Norman: University of Oklahoma Press, 1957.

Franklin, William B. *March to South Pass: Lieutenant William B. Franklin's Journal of the Kearny Expedition of 1845.* Edited by Frank N. Schubert. Historical Division, Office of the Chief of Engineers. Washington, D.C.: Government Printing Office, n.d.

Frémont, John C. *The Expeditions of John Charles Frémont.* 4 vols. Edited by Donald Jackson and Mary Lee Spence. Urbana: University of Illinois Press, 1970–1984.

———. *Report of the Exploring Expedition to the Rocky Mountains in the Year 1842, and to Oregon and California in the Years 1843–44*. Washington, D.C.: Gales and Seaton, 1845.

Gardner, Archibald. *The Life of Archibald Gardner: Utah Pioneer of 1847*. Salt Lake City, Utah: Alpine, 1939.

Garrison, Abraham E. *Life and Labor of Rev. A. E. Garrison: Forty Years in Oregon: Seven Months on the Plains*. N.p.: n.p., 1943.

Gaston, Joseph. *The Centennial History of Oregon, 1811–1912*. Vol. 4. Chicago: S. J. Clarke, 1912.

———. *Portland, Oregon: Its History and Builders*. Vol. 2. Chicago: S. J. Clarke Publishing, 1911.

Geer, Theodore T. *Fifty Years in Oregon*. New York: Neale Publishing, 1916.

Gould, Jane A. *The Oregon and California Trail Diary of Jane A. Gould in 1862*. Edited by Bert Webber. Medford, Ore.: Webb Research Group, 2001.

Goulder, W. A. *Reminiscences: Incidents in the Life of a Pioneer in Oregon and Idaho*. Boise, Idaho: Timothy Regan, 1909.

Grant, John Francis. *Very Close to Trouble: The Johnny Grant Memoir*. Edited by Lyndel Meikle. Pullman: Washington State University Press, 1996.

Gray, William H. *William H. Gray: Journal of His Journey East, 1836–1837*. Edited by Donald R. Johnson. Fairfield, Wash.: Ye Galleon Press, 1980.

Green, Ephraim. *A Road from El Dorado: The 1848 Trail Journal of Ephraim Green*. Edited by Will Bagley. Portland, Ore.: Prairie Dog Press, 1991.

Hafen, LeRoy R., and Ann W. Hafen, eds. *Frémont's Fourth Expedition: A Documentary Account of the Disaster of 1848–1849, with Diaries, Letters, and Reports by Participants in the Tragedy*. Glendale, Calif.: Arthur H. Clark, 1960.

Hammer, Jacob. *This Emigrating Company: The 1844 Oregon Trail Journal of Jacob Hammer*. Edited by Thomas A. Rumer. Spokane, Wash.: Arthur H. Clark, 1990.

Hancock, Samuel. *The Narrative of Samuel Hancock*. Introduction by Arthur D. Howden Smith. New York: Robert M. McBride, 1927.

Harlan, Jacob Wright. *California '46 to '88*. San Francisco: Bancroft, 1888.

Harrison, J. M. *Book of Information, and Settlers' Guide for the Pacific Slope, Including the States of California, Oregon and Nevada, and the Territories of Washington and Idaho. . . .* San Francisco: C. A. Murdock, 1875.

———. *Harrison's Guide and Resources of the Pacific Slope, Embracing Washington Territory, Giving a Minute Description of Its Lands and Facilities for Settlement, Land Laws, Climate, Resources, etc.* San Francisco: C. A. Murdock, 1876.

Hastings, Lansford W. *The Emigrants' Guide to Oregon and California*. Cincinnati, Ohio: George Conclin, 1845.

Hecox, Margaret M. *California Caravan: The 1846 Overland Trail Memoir of Margaret M. Hecox*. Edited by Richard Dillon. San Jose, Calif.: Harlan-Young Press, 1966.

Hines, Gustavus. *Oregon and Its Institutions, Comprising a Full History of Willamette University*. New York: Carlton and Porter, 1868.

Hines, H. K. *An Illustrated History of the State of Washington*. Chicago: Lewis Publishing, 1893.

Holmes, Kenneth L., ed. *Covered Wagon Women: Diaries and Letters from the Western Trails, 1840-1903*. 11 vols. Glendale, Calif.: Arthur H. Clark, 1983–1993.

Hopper, Charles. *Charles Hopper and the Pilgrims of the Pacific: An 1841 California Pioneer, His Narrative and Other Documents*. La Grange, Calif.: Southern Mines Press, 1981.

Horn, Hosea B. *Horn's Overland Guide, from the U.S. Subagency, Council Bluffs, on the Missouri River, to the City of Sacramento*. New York: J. H. Colton, 1852.

Houghton, Eliza P. Donner. *The Expedition of the Donner Party and its Tragic Fate*. Chicago: A. C. McClurg, 1911.

Ide, Simeon. *A Biographical Sketch of the Life of William B. Ide*. Claremont, N.H.: n.p., 1880.

Ingersoll, Chester. *Overland to California in 1847*. Edited by Douglas C. McMurtrie. Chicago: Black Cat Press, 1937.

Jacob, Norton. *The Record of Norton Jacob*. Edited by C. Edward Jacob and Ruth S. Jacob. Salt Lake City: Norton Jacob Family Association, 1949.

Johnson, Overton, and William H. Winter. *Route Across the Rocky Mountains, with a Description of Oregon and California*. Lafayette, Ind.: John B. Semans, 1846.

Kemble, Edward Cleveland. *A Kemble Reader: Stories of California, 1846–1848*. Edited by Fred Blackburn Rogers. San Francisco: California Historical Society, 1963.

Korns, J. Roderic, and Dale L. Morgan. *West from Fort Bridger: The Pioneering of the Immigrant Trails across Utah, 1846–1850*. Revised and updated by Will Bagley and Harold Schindler. Logan: Utah State University Press, 1994.

Lang, H. O., ed. *The History of the Willamette Valley: Being a Description of the Valley and Its Resources*. Portland, Ore.: George H. Himes, 1885.

Larkin, Thomas O. *The Larkin Papers: Personal, Business, and Official Correspondence of Thomas Oliver Larkin, Merchant and United States Consul in California*. 10 vols. Edited by George P. Hammond. Berkeley: University of California Press, 1951–1968.

Lee, Daniel, and Joseph Frost. *Ten Years in Oregon*. New York: J. Collord, 1844.

Lenox, Edward Henry. *Overland to Oregon*. Edited by Robert Whitaker. Oakland, Calif.: n.p., 1904.

Lienhard, John Heinrich. *From St. Louis to Sutter's Fort, 1846*. Edited by Erwin G. Gudde and Elisabeth K. Gudde. Norman: University of Oklahoma Press, 1961.

Lockley, Fred. *Conversations with Pioneer Men: The Lockley Files*. Compiled by Mike Helm. Eugene, Ore.: Rainy Day Press, 1996.

———. *Conversations with Pioneer Women*. Compiled by Mike Helm. Eugene, Ore.: Rainy Day Press, 1993.

May, Richard M. *A Sketch of a Migrating Family to California in 1848*. Fairfield, Wash.: Ye Galleon Press, 1991.

McLoughlin, John. *The Letters of John McLoughlin*. Vols. 6 and 7. Edited by E. E. Rich. London: Hudson's Bay Record Society, 1943–1944.

Morgan, Dale L., ed. *Overland in 1846: Diaries and Letters of the California-Oregon Trail*. 2 vols. Georgetown, Calif.: Talisman Press, 1963.

Mossman, Isaac Van Dorsey. *A Pony Expressman's Recollections*. Edited by J. Heine Christ. Portland, Ore.: Champoeg Press, 1955.

Murphy, Virginia Reed. *Across the Plains in the Donner Party (1846–47): A Personal Narrative of the Overland Trip to California*. Olympic Valley, Calif.: Outbooks, 1977.

Newell, Robert. *Memoranda: Travles in the Teritory of Missourie; Travle to the Kayuse War; Together with a Report on the Indians South of the Columbia River*. Edited by Dorothy O. Johansen. Portland, Ore.: Champoeg Press, 1959.

Palmer, Joel. *Journal of Travels Over the Rocky Mountains, to the Mouth of the Columbia River*. Cincinnati, Ohio: J. A. and U. P. James, 1847. Reprinted Fairfield, Wash.: Ye Galleon Press, 1983.

Parkman, Francis. *The Oregon Trail*. New York: Washington Square Press, 1963.

Parrish, Edward Evans. *The Oregon Trail Diary of Rev. Edward Evans Parrish in 1844*. Edited by Bert Webber. Medford, Ore.: Webb Research Group, 1994.

Pelzer, Louis, ed. *Marches of the Dragoons in the Mississippi Valley: An Account of Marches and Activities of the First Regiment United States Dragoons in the Mississippi Valley Between the Years 1833 and 1850*. Iowa City: State Historical Society of Iowa, 1917.

Piercy, Frederick H. *Route from Liverpool to Great Salt Lake Valley*. Edited by Fawn M. Brodie. Cambridge, Mass.: Harvard University Press, 1962.

Point, Nicholas. *Wilderness Kingdom: Indian Life in the Rocky Mountains: 1840–1847*. Translated by Joseph P. Donnelly. New York: Holt, Rinehart and Winston, 1967.

Porter, John. *On the Old Oregon Trail: A Personal Journey*. Denver: Outskirts Press, 2006.

Preuss, Charles. *Exploring with Frémont: The Private Diaries of Charles Preuss, Cartographer for John C. Frémont on His First, Second, and Fourth Expeditions to the Far West*. Edited by Erwin G. Gudde and Elisabeth K. Gudde. Norman: University of Oklahoma Press, 1958.

Pringle, Catherine Sager. *Across the Plains in 1844*. Fairfield, Wash.: Ye Galleon Press, 1989.

Pringle, Octavius M. *Magic River Deschutes: Experience of an Emigrant Boy in 1846*. Fairfield, Wash.: Ye Galleon Press, 1970.

Pritchard, James A. *The Overland Diary of James A. Pritchard from Kentucky to California in 1849*. Edited by Dale L. Morgan. Denver: Fred A. Rosenstock, 1959.

Revere, Joseph Warren. *A Tour of Duty in California*. Oakland, Calif.: Biobooks, 1947.

Root, Riley. *Journal of Travels from St. Joseph's to Oregon with Observations of That Country*. Oakland, Calif.: Biobooks, 1955.

Sage, Rufus B. *Rocky Mountain Life or, Startling Scenes and Perilous Adventures in the Far West, During an Expedition of Three Years*. Boston: Wentworth, 1858.

Sampson, William R., ed. *John McLoughin's Business Correspondence, 1847–48*. Seattle: University of Washington Press, 1973.

Saunders, Mary. *The Whitman Massacre: A True Story By a Survivor of This Terrible Tragedy Which Took Place in Oregon in 1847*. Oakland, Calif.: n.p. 1916. Reprinted Fairfield, Wash.: Ye Galleon Press, 1997.

Shively, John M. *Route and Distances to Oregon and California, with a Description of Watering Places, Crossings, Dangerous Indians, Etc.* Washington, D.C.: William Greer, 1846.

Simpson, George. *Fur Trade and Empire: George Simpson's Journal*. Edited by Frederick Merk. Rev. ed. Cambridge, Mass.: Harvard University Press, 1968.

———. *A Narrative of a Journey Around the World, 1841–42*. London: Henry Colburn, 1847.

Sutter, John, Jr. *The Sutter Family and the Origins of Gold-Rush Sacramento*. Edited by Allan R. Ottley. Introduction Albert L. Hurtado. Norman: University of Oklahoma Press, 2002.

Talbot, Theodore. *The Journals of Theodore Talbot, 1843 and 1849–52; With the Frémont Expedition of 1843 and the First Military Company in Oregon Territory, 1849–52*. Edited by Charles H. Carey. Portland, Ore.: Metropolitan Press, 1931.

Thornton, Jessy Quinn. "Journal." In *Oregon and California in 1848*. Vol. 1. New York: Harper and Brothers, 1849.

Told by the Pioneers: Reminiscences of Pioneer Life in Washington. 2 vols. N.p.: Works Progress Administration, 1937–1938.

Turner, Henry Smith. *The Original Journals of Henry Smith Turner: With Stephen Watts Kearny to New Mexico and California, 1846–1847*. Edited by Dwight L. Clarke. Norman: University of Oklahoma Press, 1966.

Tyler, Daniel. *A Concise History of the Mormon Battalion in the Mexican War, 1846–1847*. N.p.: privately printed, 1881. Reprinted Glorieta, N.Mex.: Rio Grande Press, 1969.

Walker, Mary, and Myra Eells. *On to Oregon: The Diaries of Mary Walker and Myra Eells*. Edited by Clifford M. Drury. Lincoln: University of Nebraska Press, 1998.

Ware, Joseph E. *The Emigrants' Guide to California*. Edited by John Caughey. Princeton, N.J.: Princeton University Press, 1932.

White, Elijah. *Ten Years in Oregon: Travels and Adventures of Doctor E. White and Lady West of the Rocky Mountains*. Compiled by Miss A. J. Allen. Ithaca, N.Y.: Mack, Andrus, 1848.

Wilkins, James F. *Artist on the Overland Trail: The 1849 Diary and Sketches of James F. Wilkins*. Edited by John F. McDermott. San Marino, Calif.: Huntington Library, 1968.

Williams, Joseph. *Narrative of a Tour from the State of Indiana to the Oregon Territory in the Years 1841–2*. Fairfield, Wash.: Ye Galleon Press, 1977.

Wislizenus, Frederick Adolph. *A Journey to the Rocky Mountains in the Year 1839, by F. A. Wislizenus, esq.* St. Louis: Missouri Historical Society, 1912.

Wyeth, Nathaniel J. *The Journals of Captain Nathaniel J. Wyeth's Expedition to the Oregon Country, 1831–1836*. Edited by Don Johnson. Fairfield, Wash.: Ye Galleon Press, 1997.

Young, John R. *Memoirs of John R. Young, Utah Pioneer of 1847*. Salt Lake City, Utah: Deseret News, 1920.

Primary Articles

Adair, Sarah Damron. "Sarah Damron Adair, Pioneer of 1843." *Transactions of the Oregon Pioneer Association* (1900): 65–82.

Adams, T. M. "Report from Palmyra *Courier*," quoted in *St. Louis Missouri Republican*, January 14, 1845. Reprinted in *Publications of the Nebraska State Historical Society* 20 (1922): 129.

Applegate, Jesse. "A Day With the Cow Column." *Oregon Historical Quarterly* 1 (1900): 3–143.

Applegate, Lindsay. "Notes and Reminiscences of Laying Out and Establishing the Old Emigrant Road into Southern Oregon in the Year 1846." Introduction by Ella Mae Young. *Overland Journal* 11 (Spring 1993): 2–23.

Aram, Joseph. "Recollections of a Journey from New York through the Western Wilderness and Over the Rocky Mountains to the Pacific in 1846." Edited by Col. James Tompkins Watson. *Journal of American History* 1 (1907): 617–32.

Arthur, John. "A Brief Account of Experiences of a Pioneer of 1843." *Transactions of the Oregon Pioneer Association* (1887): 96–104.

Barlow, William. "Reminiscences of 70 Years." *Oregon Historical Quarterly* 13 (September 1912): 240–79.

Barlow, William, and Mary S. Barlow. "History of the Barlow Road." *Oregon Historical Quarterly* 3 (March 1902): 71–81.

"Barnet Simpson." In *Conversation with Pioneer Men*, edited by Fred Lockley, 29–36. Eugene, Ore.: Rainy Day Press, 1996.

Bayley, Betsey. "Across the Plains in 1845." In *Covered Wagon Women: Diaries and Letters from the Western Trails, 1840–1890*, vol. 1, edited by Kenneth L. Holmes, 31–38. Glendale, Calif.: Arthur H. Clark, 1983.

Belknap, Keturah. "The Commentaries of Keturah Belknap." In *Covered Wagon Women: Diaries and Letters from the Western Trails, 1840–1890*, vol. 1, edited by Kenneth L. Holmes, 189–229. Glendale, Calif.: Arthur H. Clark, 1983.

Boardman, John. "The Journal of John Boardman: An Overland Journey from Kansas to Oregon in 1843." *Utah Historical Quarterly* 2 (October 1929): 99–121.

Bonney, Benjamin Franklin. "Recollections of Benjamin Franklin Bonney." Edited by Fred Lockley. *Oregon Historical Quarterly* 24 (March 1923): 36–55.

Brown, Tabitha. "A Brimfield Heroine." In *Covered Wagon Women: Diaries and Letters from the Western Trails, 1840–1890*, vol. 1, edited by Kenneth L. Holmes, 47–63. Glendale, Calif.: Arthur H. Clark, 1983.

Buffum, William. "Reminiscences." *Transactions of the Annual Reunion of the Oregon Pioneer Association* (1889): 42–44.

Burnett, Lucy Jane Hall. "Reminiscences of a Trip Across the Plains in '45." In *Souvenir of Western Women*, edited by Mary Osborn Douthit, 27–28. Portland, Ore.: Anderson and Dunway, 1905.

Burnett, Peter H. "Letters." *Oregon Historical Quarterly* 3 (December 1902): 398–426.

———. "Recollections and Opinions of an Old Pioneer." *Oregon Historical Quarterly* 5 (March 1904): 64–99.

Case, William. "Reminiscences of William Case." Edited by H. S. Lyman. *Quarterly of the Oregon Historical Society* (September 1900): 269–95.

Clark, Bennett C. "Diary of a Journey from Missouri to California in 1849." Edited by Ralph P. Bieber. *Missouri Historical Review* 23 (1928): 3–43.

Cone, Anson Sterling. "Reminiscences." Edited by H. S. Lyman. *Oregon Historical Society Quarterly* 4 (September 1903): 251–59.

Coonc, Elizabeth Ann. "Reminiscences of a Pioneer Woman." *Washington Historical Quarterly* 8 (1917): 14–21.

Cornwall, Joseph Hardin. "The Cornwall Trek of 1846: Independence County, Arkansas to the Oregon Country." Compiled by Marion Stark Craig. *Independence County Chronicle* 14 (July 1973): 21–44.

Cosgrove, Hugh. "Reminiscences of Hugh Cosgrove." Edited by H. S. Lyman. *Quarterly of the Oregon Historical Society* (September 1900): 252–69.

Crawford, Medorem. "Journal of Medorem Crawford: An Account of His Trip Across the Plains with the Oregon Pioneers of 1842." In *Sources of the History of Oregon*, vol. 1, edited by F. G. Young. Eugene, Ore.: Star Job Office, 1897.

———. "Report of Captain Medorem Crawford." Edited by Charles W. Martin. *Overland Journal* 2 (Summer 1984): 36–42; (Fall 1984): 27–39.

Crockett, Samuel Black. "Diary of Samuel Black Crockett." In *Building a State: Washington, 1889–1939*, edited by Vernon Carstensen, 594–607. Tacoma: Washington State Historical Society Publications 3, 1940.

Crosby, Jesse W. "History of the Life and Times of Jesse W. Crosby." *Annals of Wyoming* 11 (1939): 145–81.

Donner, Tamsen, and Virginia E. B. Reed. "The Donner Party Letters." In *Covered Wagon Women: Diaries and Letters from the Western Trails, 1840–1890*, vol. 1, edited by Kenneth L. Holmes, 65–82. Glendale, Calif.: Arthur H. Clark, 1983.

Empey, William A. "The Mormon Ferry on the North Platte: The Journal of William A. Empey, May 7–August 4, 1847." Edited by Dale L. Morgan. *Annals of Wyoming* 21, nos. 2 and 3 (1949): 111–23; 124–33.

Evans, James B. "A Missouri Forty-Niner's Trip Across the Plains." *Missouri Historical Review* 43 (October 1948): 38–47.

Farnham, Elijah Bryan. "From Ohio to California in 1849: The Gold Rush Journal of Elijah Bryan Farnham." Edited by Merrill J. Mattes and Esley J. Kirk. *Indiana Magazine of History* 46 (September 1950): 297–318; 46 (December 1950): 403–420.

Fisher, Rachel Joy. "Letters from a Quaker Woman." In *Covered Wagon Women: Diaries and Letters from the Western Trails, 1840–1890*, vol. 1, edited by Kenneth L. Holmes, 97–110. Glendale, Calif.: Arthur H. Clark, 1983.

Gaillard, Maurice. "Early Years at St. Mary's Pottawatomie Mission: From the Diary of Father Maurice Gailland, S. J." Edited by Rev. James M. Burke, S. J. *Kansas Historical Quarterly* 20 (August 1953): 501–29.

Garrison, Abraham Henry. "Reminiscences of Abraham Henry Garrison—Over the Oregon Trail in 1846." Edited by James M. Tompkins. *Overland Journal* 11 (Summer 1993): 10–31.

Geer, Elizabeth Dixon Smith. "Diary of Elizabeth Dixon Smith Geer." *Transactions of the Oregon Pioneer Association* (1907): 153–79.

Geer, Ralph C. "Occasional Address for the Year 1847." *Transactions of the Oregon Pioneer Association* (1879): 32–42.

Gilliam, Elizabeth [Collins]. "Mrs. Elizabeth Collins' Story." In *Polk County Pioneer Sketches*, Daughters of the American Revolution, Sarah Childress Polk, chapter 6.. Dallas, Ore.: Polk County Observer, 1927.

Gilliam, Martha Elizabeth. "Reminiscences of Mrs. Frank Collins, Nee Martha Elizabeth Gilliam." Edited by Fred Lockley. *Oregon Historical Quarterly* 17 (1916): 358–72.

Gilliam, Washington Smith. "Reminiscences of Washington Smith Gilliam." *Transactions of the Oregon Pioneer Association* (1904): 202–220.

Gilmore, S. M. "Letter of November 11, 1843." *Oregon Historical Quarterly* (1903): 280–84.

Hamilton, Raphael N., ed. "The Journey of the First Bishop of Walla Walla." *Illinois Catholic Historical Review* 9 (1927): 208–22.

Hammond, Francis Asbury. "In Early Days: My Introduction to Mormonism." *Juvenile Instructor* (June–September 1894): 517–21.

Harritt, Jesse. "Diary of Jesse Harritt, 1845." *Transactions of the 38th Annual Reunion of the Oregon Pioneer Association* (1910): 206–26.

Hastings, Loren B. "Diary of Loren B. Hastings: A Pioneer of 1847." *Transactions of the Fifty-First Annual Reunion of the Oregon Pioneer Association for 1923*, 12–26. Portland, Ore.: F. W. Baltes, 1926.

Haun, Catherine Margaret. "A Woman's Trip Across the Plains in 1849." In *Women's Diaries of the Westward Journey*, compiled by Lillian Schlissel, 165–85. New York: Schocken, 1982.

Hess, John W. "John W. Hess: With the Mormon Battalion." Edited by Wanda Wood. *Utah Historical Quarterly* 4 (April 1931): 47–55.

Hester, Sallie. "The Diary of a Pioneer Girl." In *Covered Wagon Women: Diaries and Letters from the Western Trails, 1840–1890*, vol. 1, edited by Kenneth L. Holmes, 231–46. Glendale, Calif.: Arthur H. Clark, 1983.

Jones, Nathaniel V. "The Journal of Nathaniel V. Jones with the Mormon Battalion (Extracted)." Edited by Cecil Alter. *Utah Historical Quarterly* (January 1931): 6–23.

Jory, James. "Reminiscences of James Jory." Edited by H. S. Lyman. *Oregon Historical Quarterly* 3 (1902): 271–86.

King, Anna Maria. "A Letter from the Luckiamute Valley." In *Covered Wagon Women: Diaries and Letters from the Western Trails, 1840–1890*, vol. 1, edited by Kenneth L. Holmes, 1:39–45. Glendale, Calif.: Arthur H. Clark, 1983.

Lockley, Fred. "Oregon Emigrants of 1844." *Washington Historical Quarterly* 18 (1927): 93–102.

Lovejoy, Asa Lawrence. "Lovejoy's Pioneer Narrative, 1842–48." Edited by Henry E. Reed. *Oregon Historical Quarterly* 31 (September 1930): 237–60.

Matthieu, Francois Xavier. "Reminiscences of F. X. Matthieu." Edited by Horace Sumner Lyman. *Oregon Historical Quarterly* 1 (March 1900): 73–104.

Miller, James D. "Early Oregon Scenes: A Pioneer Narrative." *Oregon Historical Quarterly* 31 (1930): 55–68.

Minto, John. "Reminiscences of John Minto, Pioneer of 1844." *Quarterly of the Oregon Historical Society* 2 (1901): 119–67.

———. "Robert Wilson Morrison." *Transactions of the Oregon Pioneer Association* (1894): 53–62.

Moores, Charles B. "Memorial Address: Commemorating Life, Character and Services of Francis Xavier Matthieu." *Quarterly of the Oregon Historical Society* 15 (June 1914): 73–80.

Munger, Asahel. "Diary of Asahel Munger and Wife." *Oregon Historical Quarterly* 8 (1907): 387–405.

Nesmith, James W. "Diary of the Emigration of 1843." *Oregon Historical Quarterly* 7 (1906): 329–59.

Newby, William T. "Diary of the Emigration of 1843." Edited by Harry N. W. Winton. *Oregon Historical Quarterly* 40 (1939): 220–42.

Parker, Inez Eugenia Adams. "Early Recollections of Oregon Pioneer Life." *Transactions of the Fifty-sixth Annual Reunion of the Oregon Pioneer Association for 1928* (1933): 17–35.

Penter, Samuel. "Recollections of an Oregon Pioneer of 1843." *Oregon Historical Quarterly* 7 (1906): 56–61.

Pringle, Virgil K. "Diary of Virgil K. Pringle, 1846." *Transactions of the Oregon Pioneer Association* (1920): 281–300.

Radford, Sarah B. Findley. "A Sketch of Pioneer Days." *Transactions of the Oregon Pioneer Association* (1926): 23–29.

Ramsdell, T. M. "Reminiscences of T. M. Ramsdell." *Transactions of the Oregon Pioneer Association* (1896): 108–112.

Reading, Pierson Barton. "Journal of Pierson Barton Reading." Edited by Philip B. Bekeart. *Quarterly of the Society of California Pioneers* 7 (September 1930): 148–98.

Rees, Willard H. "Constitution and Quotations from the Journal and Register." *Oregon Pioneer Association* (1915): 5–14.

Rhoads, Daniel. "Letter." *Quarterly Bulletin of California Pioneers of Santa Clara County*, 5 (March 1965): 4–8.

Schallenberger, Moses. "Overland in 1844." In *The Opening of the California Trail: The Story of the Stevens Party*, edited by George R. Stewart, 46–84. Berkeley: University of California Press, 1953.

Sessions, Patty. "A Pioneer Mormon Diary." In *Covered Wagon Women: Diaries and Letters from the Western Trails, 1840–1890*, vol. 1, edited by Kenneth L. Holmes, 157–87. Glendale, Calif.: Arthur H. Clark, 1983.

Shively, John M. "John M. Shively's Memoir." Edited by Howard M. List and Edith M. List. *Oregon Historical Quarterly* 81 (1980): 4–29, 180–95.

Snyder, Jacob R. "The Diary of Jacob R. Snyder, Written while Crossing the Plains to California in 1845." *Quarterly of the Society of California Pioneers* 8 (December 1931): 224–60.

Spalding, Henry H. "A Letter by Henry H. Spalding from the Rocky Mountains." *Oregon Historical Quarterly* 51 (1950): 127–33.

Spencer, Lucinda Brown. "Mrs. Lucinda Spencer." *Transactions of the Fifteenth Annual Reunion of the Oregon Pioneer Association for 1887* (1887): 74–78.

Staats, Stephen. "The Occasional Address." *Transactions of the Oregon Pioneer Association for 1877* (1878): 45–59.

Stanton, Phoebe. "Two Letters." In *Covered Wagon Women: Diaries and Letters from the Western Trails, 1840–1890*, vol. 1, edited by Kenneth L. Holmes, 83–95. Glendale, Calif.: Arthur H. Clark, 1983.

Sutton, Sarah. "A Travel Diary in 1854." In *Covered Wagon Women: Diaries and Letters from the Western Trails, 1840–1869*, vol. 7, edited by Kenneth L. Holmes, 15–77. Glendale, Calif.: Arthur H. Clark, 1987.

Trubody, William Alexander. "William Alexander Trubody and the Overland Pioneers of 1847." Edited by Charles L. Camp. *California Historical Quarterly* 17 (1937): 122–43.

Tuller, Miriam A. "Crossing the Plains in 1845." *Transactions of the Oregon Pioneer Association* (1895): 87–90.

Variel, Mary A., and William J. Variel. "A Romance of the Plains." *Grizzly Bear* (July 1907): 30–32; (August 1907): 62–64; (September 1907): 74–76; (October 1907): 38–40; (November 1907): 46–48.

Welch, Nancy Dickerson. "Recollections." *Transactions of the Oregon Pioneer Association* (1897): 97–103.

Willis, Ira J. "The Ira J. Willis Guide to the Gold Mines." Edited by Irene D. Paden. *California Historical Society Quarterly* 32 (September 1953): 193–207.

Woodworth, Selim E. "Sailor on Horseback: Selim Woodworth Crosses the Plains, 1846." Edited by Kristin Johnson. *Overland Journal* 26 (Spring 2008): 5–15.

Secondary Books

Acuña, Rodolfo. *Occupied America: A History of Chicanos*. 3rd ed. New York: Harper and Row, 1988.

Adams, Ramon F. *Western Words: A Dictionary of the American West*. Rev. ed. Norman: University of Oklahoma Press, 1968.

Alter, J. Cecil. *Jim Bridger*. Norman: University of Oklahoma Press, 1962.

Anderson, Nels. *Desert Saints: The Mormon Frontier in Utah*. Chicago: University of Chicago Press, 1966.

Arrington, Leonard. *Great Basin Kingdom: Economic History of the Latter-day Saints*. Cambridge, Mass.: Harvard University Press, 1958.

Arrington, Leonard J., and Davis Bitton. *The Mormon Experience: A History of the Latter-day Saints*. New York: Vintage Books, 1979.

Bagley, Will. *"A Bright, Rising Star": A Brief Life and a Letter of James Ferguson, Sergeant Major, Mormon Battalion; Adjutant General, Nauvoo Legion*. Spokane, Wash.: Arthur H. Clark, 2000.

———. *So Rugged and Mountainous: Blazing the Trails to Oregon and California, 1812–1848*. Norman: University of Oklahoma Press, 2010.

Bancroft, Hubert Howe. *The Works of Hubert Howe Bancroft*. Vol. 21. *History of California*, vol. 4. San Francisco: History Company, 1886.

———. *The Works of Hubert Howe Bancroft*. Vol. 30. *History of California*, 2 vols. San Francisco: History Company, 1888.

Barry, Louise. *The Beginning of the West: Annals of the Kansas Gateway to the American West, 1540–1854*. Topeka: Kansas State Historical Society, 1972.

Beck, Warren A., and Ynez D. Haase. *Historical Atlas of California*. Norman: University of Oklahoma Press, 1974.

Beckham, Stephen Dow. *Requiem for a People: The Rogue Indians and the Frontiersmen*. Norman: University of Oklahoma Press, 1971.

Bennett, Richard E. *Mormons at the Missouri, 1846–1852: "And Should We Die. . . ."* Norman: University of Oklahoma Press, 1987.

———. *We'll Find the Place: The Mormon Exodus, 1846–1848*. Norman: University of Oklahoma Press, 2009.

Billington, Ray Allen. *The Far Western Frontier, 1830–1860*. New York: Harper and Row, 1956.

———. *Westward Expansion: A History of the American Frontier*. 5th ed. New York: Macmillan, 1982.

Boorstin, Daniel J. *The Americans: The National Experience*. New York: Vintage Books, 1965.

Bowen, William A. *The Willamette Valley: Migration and Settlement on the Oregon Frontier*. Seattle: University of Washington Press, 1978.

Brebner, J. Bartlet. *Canada: A Modern History*. Ann Arbor: University of Michigan Press, 1970.

Brock, Richard K., ed. *Emigrant Trails West: A Guide to the California Trail*. Reno, Nev.: Trails West, 2000.

Brown, A. Theodore, and Lyle W. Dorsett. *K.C.: A History of Kansas City, Missouri*. Boulder, Colo.: Pruett Publishing, 1978.

Brown, Daniel James. *The Indifferent Stars Above: The Harrowing Saga of a Donner Party Bride*. New York: Harper Perennial, 2009.

Brown, Randy. *Historic Inscriptions on Western Emigrant Trails*. Independence, Mo.: Oregon-California Trails Association, 2004.

Brown, Randy, and Reg Duffin. *Graves and Sites on the Oregon and California Trails*. 2nd ed. Independence, Mo.: Oregon-California Trails Association, 1998.

Burley, Edith I. *Servants of the Honourable Company: Work, Discipline, and Conflict in the Hudson's Bay Company, 1770–1879*. New York: Oxford University Press, 1997.

Burns, Robert Ignatius. *The Jesuits and the Indian Wars of the Northwest*. New Haven, Conn.: Yale University Press, 1966.

Canfield, Gae Whitney. *Sarah Winnemucca of the Northern Paiutes*. Norman: University of Oklahoma Press, 1983.

Careless, J. M. S. *Canada: A Story of Challenge*. New York: St. Martin's Press, 1970.

Carey, Charles H. *General History of Oregon Through Early Statehood*. Portland, Ore.: Binfords and Mort, 1971.

Carlson, Helen S. *Nevada Place Names: A Geographical Dictionary*. Reno: University of Nevada Press, 1974.

Cash, Joseph H., and Gerald W. Wolff. *The Three Affiliated Tribes (Mandan, Arikara, and Hidatsa)*. Phoenix, Ariz.: Indian Tribal Series, 1974.

Chaffin, Tom. *Pathfinder: John Charles Frémont and the Course of American Empire*. New York: Hill and Wang, 2002.

Channing, Steven A. *Kentucky: A Bicentennial History*. New York: W. W. Norton, 1977.

Church History in the Fulness of Times: The History of The Church of Jesus Christ of Latter-day Saints. Salt Lake City, Utah: Church of Jesus Christ of Latter-day Saints, 1993.

Clark, Keith, and Lowell Tiller. *Terrible Trail: The Meek Cutoff, 1845*. Caldwell, Idaho: Caxton, 1966.

Cline, Gloria Griffen. *Peter Skene Ogden and the Hudson's Bay Company*. Norman: University of Oklahoma Press, 1974.

Cole, Jean Murray. *Exile in the Wilderness: The Biography of Chief Factor Archibald McDonald, 1790–1853*. Seattle: University of Washington Press, 1979.

Cook, Sherburne F. *The Conflict Between the California Indian and White Civilization*. Berkeley: University of California Press, 1976.

Dary, David. *The Oregon Trail: An American Saga*. New York: Oxford University Press, 2004.

Daughters of the American Revolution, Sarah Childress Polk. Chapter 6. *Polk County Pioneer Sketches*. Dallas, Ore.: Polk County Observer, 1927.

DeLafosse, Peter H., ed. *Trailing the Pioneers: A Guide to Utah's Emigrant Trails, 1829–1869*. Logan: Utah State University Press and Utah Crossroads, Oregon-California Trails Association, 1994.

DeVoto, Bernard. *The Year of Decision, 1846*. New York: Houghton-Mifflin, 1943.

Dilts, Harold E. *From Ackley to Zwingle: The Origins of Iowa Place Names*. 2nd ed. Ames: Iowa State University Press, 1993.

Douthit, Nathan. *Uncertain Encounters: Indians and Whites at Peace and War in Southern Oregon, 1820s–1860s*. Corvallis: Oregon State University Press, 2002.

Drury, Clifford M. *Marcus and Narcissa Whitman and the Opening of Old Oregon*. 2 vols. Glendale, Calif.: Arthur H. Clark, 1973.

Durham, Michael S. *Desert Between the Mountains: Mormons, Miners, Padres,*

Mountain Men, and the Opening of the Great Basin, 1772–1869. Norman: University of Oklahoma Press, 1999.

Emerson, William. *The Applegate Trail: A Documentary Guide to the Original Southern Emigrant Route to Oregon.* Ashland, Ore.: Ember Enterprises, 1996.

Estergreen, M. Morgan. *Kit Carson: A Portrait in Courage.* Norman: University of Oklahoma Press, 1962.

Evans, Elwood. *History of the Pacific Northwest: Oregon and Washington.* 2 vols. Portland, Ore.: North Pacific History Company, 1889.

Evans, John W. *Powerful Rockey: The Blue Mountains and the Oregon Trail, 1811–1883.* La Grande: Eastern Oregon State College, 1991.

Faragher, John Mack. *Women and Men on the Overland Trail.* New Haven, Conn.: Yale University Press, 1979.

Federal Writers' Project of the Work Projects Administration. *Illinois: A Descriptive and Historical Guide.* Chicago: A. C. McClurg, 1939.

———. *Iowa: A Guide to the Hawkeye State.* New York: Viking Press, 1938.

Fey, Marshall, R. Joe King, and Jack Lepisto. *Emigrant Shadows: A History and Guide to the California Trail.* Edited by Stanley W. Paher. Virginia City, Nev.: Western Trails Research Association, 2002.

Foley, William E. *The Genesis of Missouri: From Wilderness Outpost to Statehood.* Columbia: University of Missouri Press, 1989.

Franzwa, Gregory M. *Maps of the California Trail.* Tucson: Patrice Press, 1999.

———. *Maps of the Oregon Trail.* St. Louis: Patrice Press, 1990.

———. *The Oregon Trail Revisited.* Tucson: Patrice Press, 1997.

Frazer, Robert W. *Forts of the West: Military Forts and Presidios and Posts Commonly Called Forts West of the Mississippi River to 1898.* Norman: University of Oklahoma Press, 1965.

Galbraith, John S. *The Hudson's Bay Company as an Imperial Factor, 1821–1869.* Berkeley: University of California Press, 1957.

Gard, Wayne. *The Great Buffalo Hunt.* New York: Alfred A. Knopf, 1959.

Gaston, Joseph. *Portland Oregon: Its History and Builders.* 3 vols. Chicago: S. J. Clarke Publishing, 1911.

Gillis, Michael J., and Michael F. Magliari. *John Bidwell and California: The Life and Writings of a Pioneer, 1841–1900.* Spokane, Wash.: Arthur H. Clark, 2004.

Goetzmann, William H. *Army Exploration in the American West, 1803–1863.* New Haven, Conn.: Yale University Press, 1959.

Golay, Michael. *The Tide of Empire: America's March to the Pacific.* New York: John Wiley and Sons, 2003.

Gowans, Fred R. *Discovery and Exploration of the Great Fur Trade Road, 1739–1843.* Salt Lake City: Utah Crossroads, Oregon-California Trails Association, 1994.

———. *Rocky Mountain Rendezvous: A History of the Fur Trade Rendezvous, 1825–1840*. Laton, Utah: Peregrine Smith Books, 1985.

Gowans, Fred R., and Eugene E. Campbell. *Fort Bridger, Island in the Wilderness*. Provo, Utah: Brigham Young University Press, 1975.

Graebner, Norman A. *Empire on the Pacific: A Study in American Continental Expansion*. New York: Ronald Press, 1955.

Graydon, Charles K. *Trail of the First Wagons over the Sierra*. St. Louis: Patrice Press, 1986.

Grinnell, George Bird. *The Fighting Cheyennes*. Norman: University of Oklahoma Press, 1956.

Grivas, Theodore. *Military Governments in California, 1846–1850*. Glendale, Calif.: Arthur H. Clark, 1963.

Gudde, Erwin G. *California Gold Camps: A Geographical and Historical Dictionary of Camps, Towns, and Localities Where Gold Was Found and Mined; Wayside Stations and Trading Centers*. Edited by Elisabeth K. Gudde. Berkeley: University of California Press, 1975.

———. *California Place Names: The Origin and Etymology of Current Geographical Names*. Berkeley: University of California Press, 1969.

Hafen, LeRoy R. *Broken Hand: The Life of Thomas Fitzpatrick, Mountain Man, Guide and Indian Agent*. Denver: Old West, 1931.

———. *The Mountain Men and the Fur Trade of the Far West*. 10 vols. Glendale, Calif.: Arthur H. Clark, 1965–1972.

———. *The Overland Mail, 1849–1869: Promoter of Settlement, Precursor of Railroads*. Cleveland, Ohio: Arthur H. Clark, 1926.

Hafen, LeRoy R., and Francis Marion Young. *Fort Laramie and the Pageant of the West, 1834–1890*. Glendale, Calif.: Arthur H. Clark, 1938.

Hagan, William T. *The Sac and Fox Indians*. Norman: University of Oklahoma Press, 1958.

Haines, Aubrey. *Historic Sites along the Oregon Trail*. St. Louis: Patrice Press, 1981.

Haley, James L. *The Buffalo War: The History of the Red River Indian Uprising of 1874*. New York: Doubleday, 1976.

Hansen, Harry, ed. *California: A Guide to the Golden State*. New rev. ed. New York: Hastings House, 1967.

Hardesty, W. S. *Representative Citizens of Paulding County*. Toledo, Ohio: W. S. Hardesty, 1902.

Harlow, Neal. *California Conquered: War and Peace on the Pacific, 1846–1850*. Berkeley: University of California Press, 1982.

Hassrick, Royal B. *The Sioux: Life and Customs of a Warrior Society*. Norman: University of Oklahoma Press, 1964.

Hebard, Grace Raymond. *Washakie*. Cleveland, Ohio: Arthur H. Clark, 1930.

Heizer, Robert F., ed. *The Destruction of California Indians*. Santa Barbara, Calif.: Peregrine Smith, 1974.

Hendrickson, James E. *Joe Lane of Oregon: Machine Politics and the Sectional Crisis, 1849–1861*. New Haven, Conn.: Yale University Press, 1967.

Herr, Pamela. *Jessie Benton Frémont: A Biography*. New York: Franklin Watts, 1987.

Herring, Joseph B. *The Enduring Indians of Kansas: A Century and a Half of Acculturation*. Lawrence: University Press of Kansas, 1990.

Hill, William E. *The Oregon Trail: Yesterday and Today*. Caldwell, Idaho: Caxton, 1994.

Hines, Harvey K. *An Illustrated History of the State of Oregon*. Chicago: Lewis Publishing, 1893.

History of Defiance County, Ohio. Chicago: Warner, Beers, 1883.

History of the Pacific Northwest, Oregon and Washington. Portland, Ore.: North Pacific History, 1889.

Hodgkin, Frank E. *Pen Pictures of Representative Men of Oregon*. Portland: Farmer and Dairymen Publishing, 1882.

Hunt, Herbert, and Floyd C. Kaylor. *Washington, West of the Cascades: Historical and Descriptive*. Vol. 3. Chicago: S. J. Clarke Publishing, 1917.

Hunt, N. Jane. *Brevet's Nebraska Historical Markers and Sites*. Sioux Falls, S.Dak.: Brevet Press, 1974.

Hurtado, Albert L. *Indian Survival on the California Frontier*. New Haven, Conn.: Yale University Press, 1988.

———. *John Sutter: A Life on the North American Frontier*. Norman: University of Oklahoma Press, 2006.

Husband, Michael B. "The Backgrounds and Organization of the Great Oregon Migration of 1843." Master's thesis, University of Nebraska at Omaha, 1966.

Hyde, George E. *The Pawnee Indians*. Norman: University of Oklahoma Press, 1974.

———. *Red Cloud's Folk: A History of the Oglala Sioux Indians*. Norman: University of Oklahoma Press, 1937.

Illinois Sesquicentennial Commission. *Illinois: Guide and Gazetteer*. Chicago: Rand McNally, 1969.

Innis, Harold A. *The Fur Trade in Canada*. Rev. ed. Toronto, ON: University of Toronto Press, 1956.

Isenberg, Andrew C. *The Destruction of the Bison: An Environmental History, 1750–1920*. Cambridge: Cambridge University Press, 2000.

Jackson, John C. *Children of the Fur Trade: Forgotten Métis of the Pacific Northwest*. Missoula, Mont.: Mountain Press, 1996.

Jeffrey, Julie Roy. *Frontier Women: "Civilizing" the West? 1840–1880*. Rev. ed. New York: Hill and Wang, 1998.

Johansen, Dorothy O., and Charles M. Gates. *Empire of the Columbia: A History of the Pacific Northwest*. New York: Harper and Brothers, 1957.

Johnson, Kristin, ed. *"Unfortunate Emigrants": Narratives of the Donner Party*. Logan: Utah State University Press, 1996.

Kelly, Charles, and Dale L. Morgan. *Old Greenwood: The Story of Caleb Greenwood: Trapper, Pathfinder and Early Pioneer*. Georgetown, Calif.: Talisman Press, 1965.

Killoren, John J. *"Come, Blackrobe": De Smet and the Indian Tragedy*. Norman: University of Oklahoma Press, 1994.

Kimball, Stanley B. *Historic Sites and Markers along the Mormon and Other Great Western Trails*. Urbana: University of Illinois Press, 1988.

King, Joseph A. *Winter of Entrapment: A New Look at the Donner Party*. Rev. ed. Lafayette, Calif.: K&K Publications, 1994.

LaLande, Jeff. *First Over the Siskiyous: Peter Skene Ogden's Journey through the Oregon-California Borderlands*. Portland: Oregon Historical Society Press, 1987.

Lamar, Howard, R., ed. *The New Encyclopedia of the American West*. New Haven, Conn.: Yale University Press, 1998.

Lang, Herbert O. *History of the Willamette Valley*. Portland, Ore.: Himes and Lang, 1885.

Lapp, Rudolph M. *Blacks in Gold Rush California*. New Haven, Conn.: Yale University Press, 1977.

Larson, Gustive D. "Walkara, Ute Chief." In *The Mountain Men and the Fur Trade of the Far West*, vol. 2, ed. LeRoy R. Hafen, 339–50. Glendale, Calif.: Arthur H. Clark, 1965.

Lavender, David. *Westward Vision: The Story of the Oregon Trail*. New York: McGraw-Hill, 1963.

Le Sueur, Stephen C. *The 1838 Mormon War in Missouri*. Columbia: University of Missouri Press, 1987.

Lowe, Beverly Elizabeth. *John Minto: Man of Courage 1822–1915*. Salem, Ore.: Kingston Price, 1980.

Lowie, Robert H. *Indians of the Plains*. New York: McGraw-Hill, 1954.

Madsen, Brigham D. *The Northern Shoshoni*. Caldwell, Idaho: Caxton, 2000.

Madsen, Susan Arrington. *I Walked to Zion: True Stories of Young Pioneers on the Mormon Trail*. Salt Lake City, Utah: Deseret, 1994.

Mattes, Merrill J. *The Great Platte River Road: The Covered Wagon Mainline Via Fort Kearny to Fort Laramie*. Publications of the Nebraska State Historical Society, vol. 25. Lincoln: Nebraska State Historical Society, 1969.

———. *Platte River Road Narratives: A Descriptive Bibliography of Travel Over the Great Central Overland Route to Oregon, California, Utah, Colorado, Montana, and Other Western States and Territories, 1812–1866.* Urbana: University of Illinois Press, 1988.

McArthur, Lewis A., and Lewis L. McArthur. *Oregon Geographic Names*. 4th ed., revised and enlarged. Portland: Oregon Historical Society, 1974.

McChristian, Douglas C. *Fort Laramie: Military Bastion of the High Plains.* Norman, Okla.: Arthur H. Clark, 2008.

McGinnis, Anthony. *Counting Coup and Cutting Horses: Intertribal Warfare on the Northern Plains, 1738–1889*. Evergreen, Colo.: Cordillera, 1990.

Meany, Edmond S. *Origin of Washington Geographic Names*. Seattle: University of Washington Press, 1923.

Meldahl, Keith H. *Hard Road West: History and Geology Along the Gold Rush Trail*. Chicago: University of Chicago Press, 2007.

Merk, Frederick. *Manifest Destiny and Mission in American History: A Reinterpretation*. New York: Harvard University Press, 1967.

———. *The Oregon Question: Essays in Anglo-American Diplomacy and Politics.* Cambridge, Mass.: Harvard University Press, 1967.

Michno, Gregory, and Susan J. Michno. *Forgotten Fights: Little-Known Raids and Skirmishes on the Frontier, 1823 to 1890*. Missoula, Mont.: Mountain Press, 2008.

Mills, Randall V. *Stern-Wheelers Up Columbia*. Palo Alto, Calif.: Pacific Books, 1947.

Mintz, Lannon W. *The Trail: A Bibliography of the Travelers on the Overland Trail to California, Oregon, Salt Lake City and Montana during the Years 1841–1864.* Albuquerque: University of New Mexico Press, 1987.

Montgomery, Richard G. *The White-Headed Eagle: John McLoughlin: Builder of an Empire*. New York: Macmillan, 1934.

Moore, John H. *The Cheyenne Nation: A Social and Demographic History*. Lincoln: University of Nebraska Press, 1987.

Morgan, Dale L. *The Humboldt: Highroad of the West*. New York: Farrar and Rinehart, 1943.

———. *Shoshonean Peoples and the Overland Trail: Frontiers of the Utah Superintendency of Indian Affairs, 1849–1869*. Edited by Richard L. Saunders. Ethnohistorical essay by Gregory E. Smoak. Logan: Utah State University Press, 2007.

Mullen, Floyd C. *"The Land of Linn": An Historical Account of Linn County, Oregon*. Albany, Oregon: n.p., 1971.

Mullen, Frank, Jr. *The Donner Party Chronicles: A Day-By-Day Account of a Doomed Wagon Train, 1846–1847*. N.p.: Halcyon Imprint of the Nevada Humanities Council, 1997.

Munkres, Robert L. *Saleratus and Sagebrush: People and Places on the Road West.* Zanesville, Ohio: New Concord Press, 2003.

Munnick, Harriet Duncan. *Catholic Church Records of the Pacific Northwest: St. Paul, Oregon*, Portland, Ore.: Binford and Mort, 1979.

Nadeau, Remi. *Ghost Towns and Mining Camps of California*. Los Angeles: Ward Ritchie Press, 1965.

Naske, Claus-M., and Herman E. Slotnick. *Alaska: A History of the 49th State.* 2nd ed. Norman: University of Oklahoma Press, 1987.

Nevins, Allan. *Frémont: Pathmarker of the West.* New York: Longman's, Green, 1939.

Newell, Olive. *Tail of the Elephant: The Emigrant Experience on the Truckee Route of the California Trail 1844–1852.* Nevada City, Calif.: Nevada County Historical Society, 1997.

Nugent, Walter. *Into the West: The Story of Its People.* New York: Vintage Books, 1999.

Nunis, Doyce B., Jr., ed. *The Bidwell-Bartleson Party: 1841 California Emigrant Adventure.* Santa Cruz, Calif.: Western Tanager Press, 1991.

O'Donnell, Terence. *An Arrow in the Earth: General Joel Palmer and the Indians of Oregon.* Portland: Oregon Historical Society Press, 1991.

Owens, Kenneth. *Gold Rush Saints: California Mormons and the Great Rush for Riches.* Spokane, Wash.: Arthur H. Clark, 2004.

Paden, Irene D. *The Wake of the Prairie Schooner.* Gerald, Mo.: Patrice Press, 1985.

Palmer, Rosemary Gudmundson. *Children's Voices from the Trail: Narratives of the Platte River Road.* Spokane, Wash.: Arthur H. Clark, 2002.

Paul, R. Eli. *Blue Water Creek and the First Sioux War, 1854–1856.* Norman: University of Oklahoma Press, 2004.

Paul, Rodman W. *The California Gold Discovery: Sources, Documents, Accounts and Memoirs Relating to the Discovery of Gold at Sutter's Mill.* Georgetown, Calif.: Talisman Press, 1967.

———. *Mining Frontiers of the Far West, 1848–1880.* New York: Holt, Rinehart and Winston, 1963.

Phillips, George Harwood. *Chiefs and Challengers: Indian Resistance and Cooperation in Southern California.* Berkeley: University of California Press, 1975.

Phillips, Paul Chrisler. *The Fur Trade.* 2 vols. Norman: University of Oklahoma Press, 1961.

Porter, Mary E. *A Family History: William Porter, Jr. of Rockbridge County, Virginia (1740–1804) and Five Generations of His Descendants.* Reprint. N.p.: n.p., 2001.

Portrait and Biographical Record of the Willamette Valley Oregon. Chicago: Chapman Publishing, 1903.

Prescott, Cynthia Culver. *Gender and Generation on the Far Western Frontier.* Tucson: University of Arizona Press, 2007.

Quaife, Milo Milton, ed. *Pictures of Gold Rush California.* New York: Citadel Press, 1967.

Rarick, Ethan. *Desperate Passage: The Donner Party's Perilous Journey West.* New York: Oxford University Press, 2008.

Rawls, James J. *Indians in California: The Changing Image.* Norman: University of Oklahoma Press, 1984.

Rawls, James J., and Walton Bean. *California: An Interpretive History.* New York: McGraw-Hill, 2003.

Reid, John Phillip. *Contested Empire: Peter Skene Ogden and the Snake River Expeditions.* Norman: University of Oklahoma Press, 2002.

Ricketts, Norma Baldwin. *The Mormon Battalion: U.S. Army of the West, 1846–1848.* Logan: Utah State University Press, 1996.

Robbins, Roy M. *Our Landed Heritage: The Public Domain, 1776–1936.* Princeton, N.J.: Princeton University Press, 1942.

Robertson, Frank C. *Fort Hall: Gateway to the Oregon Country.* New York: Hastings House, 1963.

Rogers, Fred Blackburn. *William Brown Ide, Bear Flagger.* San Francisco: John Howell Books, 1962.

Rolle, Andrew. *John Charles Frémont: Character as Destiny.* Norman: University of Oklahoma Press, 1991.

Ronda, James P. *Astoria and Empire.* Lincoln: University of Nebraska Press, 1990.

Rosenus, Alan. *General M. G. Vallejo and the Advent of the Americans: A Biography.* Albuquerque: University of New Mexico Press, 1995.

Roske, Ralph J. *Everyman's Eden: A History of California.* New York: Macmillan, 1968.

Ruby, Robert H., and John A. Brown. *The Cayuse Indians: Imperial Tribesmen of Old Oregon.* Norman: University of Oklahoma, 1972.

———. *The Chinook Indians: Traders of the Lower Columbia River.* Norman: University of Oklahoma Press, 1976.

———. *Indians of the Pacific Northwest: A History.* Norman: University of Oklahoma Press, 1981.

———. *The Spokane Indians: Children of the Sun.* Norman: University of Oklahoma Press, 1970.

Rumer, Thomas A. *The Wagon Trains of '44: A Comparative View of the Individual Caravans in the Emigration of 1844 to Oregon.* Spokane, Wash.: Arthur H. Clark, 1990.

Ruth, Kent. *Great Day in the West: Forts, Posts and Rendezvous Beyond the Mississippi.* Norman: University of Oklahoma Press, 1963.

Samek, Hana. *The Blackfoot Confederacy 1880–1920: A Comparative Study of Canadian and U.S. Indian Policy*. Albuquerque: University of New Mexico Press, 1987.

Schlissel, Lillian. *Women's Diaries of the Westward Journey*. New York: Schocken, 1982.

Schwantes, Carlos A. *The Pacific Northwest: An Interpretive History*. Revised and enlarged. Lincoln: University of Nebraska Press, 1996.

Scott, Harvey Whitefield. *History of Portland, Oregon*. Syracuse, N.Y.: D. Mason, 1890.

Sellers, Charles. *James K. Polk: Continentalist, 1843–46*. Princeton, N.J.: Princeton University Press, 1966.

Shannon, David H. *The Utter Disaster on the Oregon Trail*. Caldwell, Idaho: Snake Country Publishing, 1993.

Simpson, Peter, ed. *City of Dreams: A Guide to Port Townsend*. Port Townsend, Wash.: Bay Press, 1986.

Smith, Cornelius C., Jr. *Fort Huachuca: The Story of a Frontier Post*. Washington, D.C.: Government Printing Office, 1976.

Snyder, Eugene E. *We Claimed This Land: Portland's Pioneer Settlers*. Portland, Ore.: Binford and Mort, 1989.

Soulé, Frank, John H. Gihon, and James Nisbet. *The Annals of San Francisco*. New York: D. Appleton, 1855.

Sowell, A. J. *Early Settlers and Indian Fighters of Southwest Texas*. Austin, Tex.: Ben C. Jones, 1900.

Stamm, Henry E., IV. *People of the Wind River: The Eastern Shoshones, 1825–1890*. Norman: University of Oklahoma Press, 1999.

Stanton, William. *The Great United States Exploring Expedition of 1838–1842*. Berkeley: University of California Press, 1975.

Steeves, Sarah Hunt. *Book of Remembrance of Marion County, Oregon, Pioneers, 1840–1860*. Portland, Ore.: Berncliff Press, 1927.

Stegner, Wallace. *The Gathering of Zion: The Story of the Mormon Trail*. New York: McGraw-Hill, 1964.

Stewart, George R. *The California Trail: An Epic with Many Heroes*. New York: McGraw-Hill, 1962.

———. *Ordeal by Hunger: The Story of the Donner Party*. Boston: Houghton Mifflin, 1960.

Stillson, Richard T. *Spreading the Word: A History of Information in the California Gold Rush*. Lincoln: University of Nebraska Press, 2006.

Stocking, Hobart E. *The Road to Santa Fe*. New York: Hastings House, 1971.

Sunder, John E. *Bill Sublette: Mountain Man*. Norman: University of Oklahoma Press, 1959.

Tate, Michael L. *Indians and Emigrants: Encounters on the Overland Trails*. Norman: University of Oklahoma Press, 2006.

Taylor, Quintard. *In Search of the Racial Frontier: African Americans in the American West, 1528–1990*. New York: W. W. Norton, 1998.

Terrell, John Upton. *Black Robe: The Life of Pierre-Jean De Smet*. Garden City, N.Y.: Echo Books, Doubleday, 1964.

Thompson, Erwin N. *Shallow Grave at Waiilatpu: The Sagers' West*. Portland: Oregon Historical Society Press, 1973.

———. *Whitman Mission National Historic Site*. National Park Service Historical Handbook Series No. 37. Washington, D.C.: Government Printing Office, 1964.

Thrapp, Dan L. *Encyclopedia of Frontier Biography*. 3 vols. Spokane, Wash.: Arthur H. Clark, 1988.

Tortorich, Frank, Jr. *Gold Rush Trail: A Guide to the Carson River Route of the Emigrant Trail*. Pine Grove, Calif.: Wagon Wheel Tours, 1998.

Townley, John M. *The Trail West: A Bibliography-Index to Western American Trails, 1841–1869*. Reno, Nev.: Jamison Station Press, 1988.

Trenholm, Virginia Cole, and Maurine Carley. *The Shoshonis: Sentinels of the Rockies*. Norman: University of Oklahoma Press, 1964.

Unrau, William E. *The Rise and Fall of Indian Country, 1825–1855*. Lawrence: University Press of Kansas, 2007.

Unruh, John D., Jr. *The Plains Across: The Overland Emigrants and the Trans-Mississippi West, 1840–60*. Urbana: University of Illinois Press, 1979.

Utley, Robert M. *The Lance and the Shield: The Life and Times of Sitting Bull*. New York: Henry Holt, 1993.

———. *A Life Wild and Perilous: Mountain Men and the Paths to the Pacific*. New York: Henry Holt, 1997.

Vestal, Stanley. *Joe Meek: The Merry Mountain Man: A Biography*. Caldwell, Idaho: Caxton, 1952.

Victor, Frances Fuller. *The River of the West: The Adventures of Joe Meek*. Edited by Win Blevins. 2 vols. Missoula, Mont.: Mountain Press, 1984.

Wallace, W. Stewart, ed. *The Macmillan Dictionary of Canadian Biography*. 4th edition. Toronto: Macmillan of Canada, 1978.

Walling, A. G. *Illustrated History of Lane County Oregon*. Portland, Ore.: A. G. Walling, 1884.

Webb, Walter Prescott, and H. Bailey Carroll, eds. *The Handbook of Texas*. 2 vols. Austin: Texas State Historical Association, 1952.

Weinberg, Albert K. *Manifest Destiny: A Study of Nationalist Expansion in American History*. Baltimore, Md.: Johns Hopkins Press, 1935.

Welsh, William D. *A Brief Historical Sketch of Port Townsend*. Port Townsend, Wash.: Port Townsend Chamber of Commerce, 1973.

White, David A., ed. *News of the Plains and Rockies, 1803–1865: Original Narratives of Overland Travel and Adventure Selected from the Wagner-Camp and Becker Bibliography of Western Americana.* 8 vols. Spokane, Wash.: Arthur H. Clark, 1996–2001.

Williams, Jacqueline. *Wagon Wheel Kitchens: Food on the Oregon Trail.* Lawrence: University Press of Kansas, 1993.

Wilson, D. Ray. *Fort Kearny on the Platte.* Dundee, Ill.: Crossroads Communications, 1980.

Winther, Oscar Osburn. *The Old Oregon Country: A History of Frontier Trade, Transportation, and Travel.* Stanford, Calif.: Stanford University Press, 1950.

———. *Via Western Express and Stagecoach: California's Transportation Links with the Nation, 1848–1869.* Stanford, Calif.: Stanford University Press, 1945.

Wishart, David J. *The Fur Trade of the American West, 1807–1840: A Geographical Synthesis.* Lincoln: University of Nebraska Press, 1979.

———. *An Unspeakable Sadness: The Dispossession of the Nebraska Indians.* Lincoln: University of Nebraska Press, 1994.

Wojcik, Donna M. *The Brazen Overlanders of 1845.* Portland: n.p., 1976.

Writers' Program of the Work Projects Administration. *Missouri: A Guide to the "Show Me" State.* New York: Duell, Sloan, and Pearce, 1941.

Youngberg, Elsie. *1850 Oregon Territorial Census.* Lebanon, Ore.: End of Trail Researchers, 1970.

Zanjani, Sally. *Sarah Winnemucca.* Lincoln: University of Nebraska Press, 2001.

Secondary Articles

Aldous, Jay A., and Paul S. Nicholes. "What Is Mountain Fever?" *Overland Journal* 15 (Spring 1997): 18–23.

Andrews, Thomas F. "The Ambitions of Lansford W. Hastings: A Study in Western Myth-Making." *Pacific Historical Review* 29 (November 1970): 473–91.

———. "The Controversial Hastings Overland Guide: A Reassessment." *Pacific Historical Review* 37 (February 1968): 21–34.

———. "'Ho! For Oregon and California!' An Annotated Bibliography of Published Advice to the Emigrant, 1841–47." *Princeton University Library Chronicle* 33 (Autumn 1971): 41–64.

Ault, Philip H. "Pioneer Nancy Kelsey: 'Where My Husband Goes, I Go.'" *Californians* 5 (March–April 1992): 32–41.

Bagley, Will. "Lansford Warren Hastings: Scoundrel or Visionary?" *Overland Journal* 12 (Spring 1994): 12–26.

Baresel, Karl, and Dorothy Baresel. "Trails and Fords Above the Junction of the North and South Platte." *Overland Journal* 6, no. 2 (1988): 13–24.

Becher, Ronald. "Oregon Trail Fords of the Wakarusa River." *Overland Journal* 8, no. 1 (1990): 2–10.

———. "Whatever Happened to Fitzhugh's Mill? Rendezvous Point for the Great Migration of 1843." *Overland Journal* 9 (Winter 1991): 2–14.

Beckham, Stephen Dow. "The Barlow Road." *Overland Journal* 2 (Summer 1984): 4–29.

Belanger, Albert Edward. "'Equipping Ourselves in Every Possible Way': Contents of Wagons on the 1851 Oregon Trail." *Overland Journal* 24 (Winter 2006): 143–59.

Benbrook, Jimmie G. "Pappan's Ferry and the Oregon-California Trail." *Overland Journal* 19 (Spring 2001): 2–21.

Benson, William R. "The Stone and Kelsey 'Massacre' on the Shores of Clear Lake in 1849: The Indian Viewpoint." *California Historical Society Quarterly* 11 (September 1932): 266–71.

Blair, Roger. "The Romantic Overland Trails: Intimacy and Social Interactions." *Overland Journal* 24 (Winter 2006): 130–42.

Boag, Peter. "Idaho's Fort Hall as a Western Crossroads." *Overland Journal* 16 (Spring 1998): 20–26.

———. "'The Indians of This Place Are Snakes in the Grass': The Overlander Perspective on Native Americans in Southern Idaho, 1836–1860." *Idaho Yesterdays* 37 (Fall 1993): 16–26.

Burgess, Barbara. "The Vermillion Crossing." *Overland Journal* 9 (Fall 1991): 26–32.

"A California Heroine." *Grizzly Bear* (February 1915): 6.

Camp, Charles L. "Colonel Philip Leget Edwards and His Influence Upon Early Immigration to the Far West." *California Historical Quarterly* 3, no. 1 (1924): 72–83.

———. "William Alexander Trubody and the Overland Pioneers of 1847." *California Historical Society Quarterly* 16 (June 1937): 122–43.

Campbell, Eugene E. "Miles Morris Goodyear." In *The Mountain Men and the Fur Trade of the Far West*, vol. 2, ed. LeRoy R. Hafen, 179–99. Glendale, Calif.: Arthur H. Clark, 1965.

Capps, Michael A. "Wheels in the West: The Overland Wagon." *Overland Journal* 8, no. 4 (1990): 2–11.

Clark, Robert A. "Kenneth L. Holmes and the Development of the Covered Wagon Women Series." *Western Historical Quarterly* (Winter 1997): 547–55.

Davis, J. Kenneth. "Thomas Rhoads, Forgotten Mormon Pioneer of 1846." *Nebraska History* 64 (Spring 1983): 81–95.

Davis, Richard M. "Where Have All the Wagons Gone? Gone, Gone Long Ago, or Very Nearly So." Part 1. *Overland Journal* 15 (Autumn 1997): 16–39.

DeMallie, Raymond. "Touching the Pen: Plains Indian-Treaty Councils in

Ethnohistorical Perspective." In *Ethnicity on the Great Plains*, edited by Frederick C. Luebke, 38–53. Lincoln: University of Nebraska Press, 1980.

Dodd, Charles H. "Over, Around, and Across: The Truckee Trail Through Reno and Sparks, Nevada." *Overland Journal* 22 (Spring 2004): 3–17.

Dodds, Gordon B. "Fort Hall." In *The New Encyclopedia of the American West*, ed. Howard R. Lamar, 384. New Haven: Yale University Press, 1998.

Echo-Hawk, Walter R., and Roger C. Echo-Hawk. "Repatriation, Reburial, and Religious Rights." In *Handbook of American Indian Religious Freedom*, edited by Christopher Versey, 63–80. New York: Crossroad, 1993.

Ellison, William Henry. "San Juan to Cahuenga: The Experiences of Frémont's Battalion." *Pacific Historical Review* 27 (1958): 245–61.

Ewers, John C. "Intertribal Warfare as the Precursor of Indian-White Warfare on the Northern Great Plains." *Western Historical Quarterly* 6 (October 1975): 397–410.

Fey, Marshall. "The Truckee Meadows Trail Reconfirmed." *Overland Journal* 22 (Spring 2004): 18–32.

Firkus, Angela. "Nineteenth-Century Overland Travelers Returning East." *Journal of the West* 46 (Summer 2007): 50–55.

Fountain, Mrs. Eugene. "The Four Kelsey Brothers." *Sonoma County Historical Society Journal* 2 (June 1964): 13; 3 (March 1964): 5–8; (June 1965); 7–8; (September 1965): 8–9.

Gillis, Michael J. "The 1841 Trans-Sierra Route of the Bidwell-Bartleson Party." *Overland Journal* 16 (Winter 1998–1999): 21–29.

Guenther, Todd, Erin Hammer, and Fred Chaney. "The Women Who Carried the Star of Empire Westward: Eliza Spalding and Narcissa Whitman Catalyzed the Great Migration and Launched the American Future." *Overland Journal* 20 (Winter 2002): 130–51.

Hafen, LeRoy R. "Louis Vásquez." In *The Mountain Men and the Fur Trade of the Far West*, vol. 2, ed. LeRoy R. Hafen, 321–38. Glendale, Calif.: Arthur H. Clark, 1965.

Haines, Francis. "Goldilocks on the Oregon Trail." *Idaho Yesterdays* 9 (Winter 1965): 26–30.

Hämäläinen, Pekka. "The First Phase of Destruction: Killing the Southern Plains Buffalo, 1790–1840." *Great Plains Quarterly* 21 (Spring 2001): 101–130.

Hammond, Andy. "Peter Lassen and His Trail." *Overland Journal* 4 (Winter 1986): 33–41.

Harstad, Peter T. "The Lander Trail." *Idaho Yesterdays* 12 (Fall 1968): 14–28.

Holmes, Kenneth L. "Francois Payette." In *The Mountain Men and the Fur Trade of the Far West*, vol. 6, ed. LeRoy R. Hafen, 325–52. Glendale, Calif.: Arthur H. Clark, 1968.

Johnson, Kristin. "Survivor: Sarah Graves Fosdick." *Overland Journal* 26 (Spring 2008): 16–24.

King, Guy Q. "Crossing the Forty-Mile Desert." *Overland Journal* 21 (Winter 2003–2004): 122–37.

Kroll, Helen B. "The Books That Enlightened the Emigrants." *Oregon Historical Quarterly* 45 (June 1944): 105–23.

Laidlaw, Tom. "Fort Vancouver: A Brief History and Account of Its Restoration." *Overland Journal* 22 (Summer 2004): 54–73.

Lewin, Jacqueline, Marilyn S. Taylor, and Bonnie Watkins. "St. Joseph, Missouri: Early Impressions." *Overland Journal* 6, no. 1 (1988): 2–7.

Lupton, David W. "Fort Platte, Wyoming, 1841–1845: Rival of Fort Laramie." *Annals of Wyoming* 49 (Spring 1977): 83–108.

Marshall, Ross. "River Crossings." *Overland Journal* 9 (Fall 1991): 14–24.

Martin, Charles W., and Charles W. Martin, Jr. "The Fourth of July: A Holiday on the Trail." *Overland Journal* 10 (Summer 1992): 2–20.

Mattison, Ray H. "James Kipp." In *The Mountain Men and the Fur Trade of the Far West*, vol. 2, ed. LeRoy R. Hafen, 201–216. Glendale, Calif.: Arthur H. Clark, 1972.

Meldahl, Keith H. "The Forty-Mile Desert and Sierra Nevada: History Meets Geology Along the California Trail." *Overland Journal* 26 (Fall–Winter 2008): 100–117.

Mothershead, Harmon. "River Town Rivalry for the Overland Trade." *Overland Journal* 7, no. 2 (1989): 14–23.

Mullin, Frank Anthony. "Father De Smet and the Pottawattamie Indian Mission." *Iowa Journal of History and Politics* 23 (April 1925): 192–216.

Munkres, Robert L. "The Arrival of Emigrants and Soldiers: Curiosity, Contempt, Confusion and Conflict." In *Red Men and Hat Wearers: Viewpoints in Indian History*, edited by Daniel Tyler, 63–91. Boulder, Colo.: Pruett, 1976.

———. "Crime on the Trails." *Overland Journal* 12, no. 3 (1994): 29–34.

———. "Fort Bridger." *Overland Journal* 8, no. 2 (1990): 25–34.

———. "The Plains Indian Threat on the Oregon Trail Before 1860." *Annals of Wyoming* 40 (October 1968): 193–221.

Murphy, Robert F., and Yolanda Murphy. "Northern Shoshone and Bannock." In *Handbook of North American Indians*, vol. 2, *Great Basin*, edited by Warren D'Azevedo, 284–307. Washington, D.C.: Smithsonian Institution, 1986..

Ostler, Jeffrey. "'They Regard Their Passing as Wakan': Interpreting Western Sioux Explanations for the Bison's Decline." *Western Historical Quarterly* 30 (Winter 1999): 475–97.

Palmer, Rosemary G. "The Sabbath According to Female Diarists on the Trail." *Overland Journal* 22 (Winter 2004–2005): 160–70.

Potter, James E. "Firearms on the Overland Trails." *Overland Journal* 9, no. 1 (1991): 2–12.

———. "'He . . . Regretted Having to Die That Way': Firearm Accidents in the Frontier Army." *Nebraska History* 78 (Winter 1997): 175–86.

Powers, Ramon, and Gene Younger. "Cholera on the Overland Trails, 1832–1869." *Kansas Quarterly* 5 (Spring 1973): 32–49.

Powers, Ramon, and James N. Leiker. "Cholera among the Plains Indians: Perceptions, Causes, Consequences." *Western Historical Quarterly* 29 (Autumn 1998): 317–40.

Rieck, Richard L. "A Geography of Death on the Oregon-California Trail, 1840–1860." *Overland Journal* 9, no. 1 (1991): 13–21.

Riley, Glenda. "The Specter of a Savage: Rumors and Alarmism on the Overland Trail." *Western Historical Quarterly* 15 (October 1984): 427–44.

Rose, James J. "Saga of the Stephens-Townsend-Murphy Party of 1844: First Pioneer Wagons Over the Sierra Nevada." *Nevada County Historical Society Bulletin* 48 (July 1994): 17–26.

Solberg, Winton U. "The Sabbath on the Overland Trail to California." *Overland Journal* 8, no. 4 (1990): 20–27.

Spedden, Rush. "The Donner Trail Across the Salt Lake Valley." *Overland Journal* 26 (Spring 2008): 25–35.

———. "The Fearful Long Drive: The 1846 Hastings Cutoff." *Overland Journal* 12 (Summer 1994): 2–16.

———. "Who Was T. H. Jefferson?" *Overland Journal* 8, no. 3 (1990): 2–8.

Steed, Jack, and Richard Steed. "The Rediscovery of Johnson's Ranch," *Overland Journal* 4 (Winter 1986): 18–32.

Swagerty, William R. "'The Leviathan of the North': American Perceptions of the Hudson's Bay Company, 1816–1846." *Oregon Historical Quarterly* 104 (Winter 2003): 478–518.

Tea, Roy D. "'The Limitless Plain': The Great Salt Lake Desert—The Trail Location and the Trials and Tribulations of the Emigrants While Crossing This Desert on the Hastings Cutoff." *Overland Journal* 23 (Spring–Summer 2005): 20–38; 61–89.

———. "The Tragic Decision of James Hudspeth: The Donner/Reed Party, Hastings Cutoff, and the Weber Canyon Route." *Overland Journal* 28 (Summer 2010): 52–82.

Tea, Roy D., and Peter H. DeLafosse. "The First Wagons Across Utah: The Bidwell-Bartleson Party of 1841." *Overland Journal* 12 (Winter 1994): 19–31.

Tobie, H. E. "From the Missouri to the Columbia, 1841." *Oregon Historical Quarterly* 38 (June 1937): 135–59.

Tompkins, Jim. "The Law of the Land: What the Emigrants Knew That Historians Need to Know About Claiming Land at the End of the Oregon Trail." *Overland Journal* 19 (Fall 2001): 82–112.

Topping, Gary. "Overland Emigration, the California Trail, and the Hastings Cutoff." *Utah Historical Quarterly* 56 (Spring 1988): 109–128.

Tortorich, Frank, Jr. "The Opening of the Carson River Route: An Essay." *Overland Journal* 18 (Spring 2000): 20–24.

Tortorich, Frank, and James M. Carman. "The Big Tree Carson Valley Wagon Road: A Branch of the Carson River Route." *Overland Journal* 22 (Fall 2004): 90–107.

Troxel, Kathryn. "Food of the Overland Emigrants." *Oregon Historical Quarterly* 56 (March 1955): 12–26.

Watson, Jeanne H. "Frémont's Second Expedition." *Overland Journal* 12 (Fall 1994): 2–9.

———. "Women's Travails and Triumphs on the Overland Trails." *Overland Journal* 9 (Winter 1991): 28–36.

Wells, Merle. "Richard Grant." In *The Mountain Men and the Fur Trade of the Far West*, vol. 9, ed. LeRoy R. Hafen, 165–86. Glendale, Calif.: Arthur H. Clark, 1972.

Williams, Carol. "'My First Indian': Interaction Between Women and Indians on the Trail, 1845–1865." *Overland Journal* 4 (Summer 1986): 13–18.

Woody, Clara T. "The Woolsey Expeditions of 1864." *Arizona and the West* 4 (Summer 1962): 157–76.

Index